MILK & HONEY

MILK&HONEY

edited by

Joel R. Beeke

REFORMATION HERITAGE BOOKS
Grand Rapids, Michigan

Milk and Honey
©2010 by Joel R. Beeke

Reformation Heritage Books
2965 Leonard Street, NE
Grand Rapids, MI 49525
616–977–0889 / Fax 616–285–3246
orders@heritagebooks.org
www.heritagebooks.org

Library of Congress Cataloging-in-Publication Data

Milk and honey / edited by Joel R. Beeke.
    p. cm.
  ISBN 978-1-60178-111-6 (hardcover : alk. paper) 1. Bible—Devotional literature. 2. Devotional calendars—Reformed Church. 3. Reformed Church—Prayers and devotions. I. Beeke, Joel R., 1952-
  BS491.5.M56 2010
  242'.2—dc22
                        2010042936

Printed in the United States of America
13 14 15 16 17 18 / 10 9 8 7 6 5 4 3 2

TABLE OF CONTENTS

We are delighted to offer this new daily devotional, *Milk and Honey*, as an interdenominational work with an international flavor. Why another devotional? After reading many of the classic devotionals written by godly men of the past, such as Robert Hawker, J. C. Ryle, Charles Spurgeon, Octavius Winslow, we felt a need to have one written by contemporary authors who stand in the same Reformed, experiential tradition. Rooted in the European Reformation, this tradition was expanded and refined by the English Puritans, the Scottish Covenanters, and the Dutch Further Reformation divines. This heritage is ably represented by men such as John Bunyan, Wilhelmus á Brakel, Robert Murray M'Cheyne, Jonathan Edwards, and Archibald Alexander.

This Reformed tradition strives to be thoroughly biblical in doctrine, life, and worship. At its roots is a preaching and pastoral ministry that is warmly experiential, realistically discriminating, and boldly evangelistic — both in its uncovering law work as well as in its freeness by which Christ and His benefits are offered to saints and sinners. Building on this tradition, this devotional seeks to provide spiritual lessons based on sound exegesis and helpful applications drawn from the Scripture passage under consideration.

The contributors hail from various Reformed denominations in Scotland, England, Canada, and the United States. It is our prayer that the Head of the Church would eventually bring the denominations they serve closer together for the unity and well-being of His church and kingdom. What a witness to the world it would be to see brothers and sisters in the Lord as united ecclesiastically as they already are spiritually.

The contributors have been assigned a variety of Bible books to write on, reflecting the numerous and diverse lessons offered in Scripture. They and we covet the applicatory work of the Holy Spirit, whose gracious operations uncover us to our sin and apply Christ in His person and work.

The title *Milk and Honey* was chosen because it symbolizes our basic need for solid spiritual food and sweet communion with the Triune God through Christ. The devotional offers a variety of styles and lessons based on the passage being explained. Each contributor was given freedom in this regard and we trust that you will enjoy the variety they offer. Some of the contributors have selected portions throughout the Bible book or books assigned. Others have focused on a part of a book or a theme in the book. Some have focused on one particular verse for each meditation, others have focused on several verses, including their context. Some devotions are decidedly experiential, while others are more practical. The aim has been to provide a balanced diet.

We thank each of the contributors for their hard and capable work. We express our gratefulness to Joel Beeke for editing this book as well as his staff at Reformation Heritage Books for seeing it through to publication. We pray that believers will be nourished and that sinners will be awakened and led to receive Christ and all His benefits through reading this book. Then God's name will truly be glorified.

—Connor and Susan Keuning
Hamilton, Ontario

MILK & HONEY

from Genesis

JOEL R. BEEKE

In the beginning God....
—GENESIS 1:1a

It makes good sense to begin a new year with Genesis, the first book of the Bible. The Greek word "genesis" means origin or beginning—an appropriate term because Genesis traces history from the very beginning of time. All great biblical themes begin here. The truths about God, the world, the creation of man in God's image, the Sabbath, marriage, the devices of Satan, man's fall into sin, judgment, election, salvation, justification by faith, Christ and His priesthood, prayer, God's covenant people, and blessing and cursing are all grounded in Genesis. Man's complete ruin in sin and God's perfect remedy in Christ are strikingly presented.

Meditate on this amazing book packed with ancient truth that is still relevant today. Can you think of other major truths that Genesis shows us?

The structure of Genesis clearly shows it is a book of origins. Genesis includes eleven distinct sections, each starting with the word "beginning" or "generations." The opening words of each section are usually something like: "These are the generations" or "The book of the generations." These sections include the history of creation (1:1–2:3), heaven and earth (2:4–4:26), Adam (5:1–6:8), Noah (6:9–9:29), Noah's sons (10:1–11:9), Shem (11:10–26), Terah and Abraham (11:27–25:11), Ishmael (25:12–18), Isaac and his sons (25:19–35:29), Esau (36:1–37:1), and Jacob and Joseph (37:2–50:26).

Genesis takes us through various stages of history to trace God's design of redemption through the line of His chosen people. Chapters 1–11 provide us with a wide-angle view of the history of mankind, while chapters 12–50 offer a more telescopic view of the history of God's chosen people in Abraham and his family.

Without Genesis, the Bible would be seriously impoverished, for Genesis covers at least one-third of human history. Ultimately, it is God's story—His-story. In Genesis we find special revelation in three-dimensional color and profound doctrinal, practical, and experiential truth, all directing us to Jesus Christ, the Savior of sinners.

On New Year's Day, thank God for His Word, and particularly for the book of Genesis.

In the beginning God....
—GENESIS 1:1a

The purpose of the Bible—Genesis in particular—is to reveal God to us. It is to show us His person and nature, insofar as we are able to know Him, and His plans and works, insofar as we are able to understand them. The very first words in the divine canon—"In the beginning God"—set us in the presence of the living God in whom we live, move, and have our being, both physically and spiritually.

The Bible begins with God. His existence is presupposed as a fact to be believed. With a few strokes of his pen, Moses, the author of Genesis, repudiates atheism (for he declares the existence of God), materialism (for he distinguishes between God and His material creation), pantheism (for he presents God as a personal Creator), and polytheism (for he sets God forth as the only God).

The infinite source of true blessedness is set before us in four words: "In the beginning God...." The purpose of Genesis is to reveal God to us as the Creator and Provider, as the Redeemer and Lord of history. Like all of Scripture, Genesis is not so much a history of man as of God's sovereign, gracious redemption of fallen sinners.

Genesis is primarily theocentric (God-centered) and only secondarily anthropocentric (man-centered) and geocentric (earth-centered). "In the beginning God" is the foundational truth of Genesis, the Bible, and all theology. False systems of theology begin with man or this earth and attempt to work up to God, whereas true theology begins with God and works down to man.

Genesis is not primarily a book about biology or geology but theology. That does not mean it is scientifically inaccurate. Rather, the focus of the book of Genesis is on God, which sets the foundation for the God-centeredness of the Bible. Genesis is written and designed so that we as needy sinners might come to know and worship God in Jesus Christ, whom God has sent to us unto our everlasting life (John 17:3).

Is God the center and focus of your life? Do you know Him in Jesus Christ?

In the beginning God….
—GENESIS 1:1a

The Genesis 1 creation account is remarkably God-centered. God is the consistent subject of sentence after sentence: "and God said," "and God saw," "and God called."

All of creation is a revelation of God; it is given so that we might know Him. Creation shows us who God is, what He is like, how He acts, and what is important to Him. Psalm 19:1–2 says, "The heavens declare the glory of God; and the firmament sheweth his handywork. Day unto day uttereth speech, and night unto night showeth knowledge."

Similarly, re-creation, sometimes called new creation, is also God-centered. We are re-created, not just to be born again, but to know God. Paul says in 2 Corinthians 4:6, "For God, who commanded the light to shine out of darkness, hath shined in our hearts, to give the light of the knowledge of the glory of God in the face of Jesus Christ."

God is the great *subject* of creation, as He is of the whole Bible. That means that He alone is the Author of the creation process as Father (Gen. 1:1), as Son (John 1:1–4), and as Spirit (Gen. 1:2). He speaks and the earth, the heavens, and all that is in them, including man, come into being. That is also true in re-creation, is it not? God raises dead sinners to life. We are saved by His sovereign, initiating grace.

God is also the great *object* of creation. Everything that God does—both in Genesis 1 and throughout Scripture—is for His glory. That is true from eternity past to eternity future. God determined to create all things for His own glory in eternity past, and He is the object of glory in eternity future. In Revelation 4:11, the elders in heaven testify to this: "Thou art worthy, O Lord, to receive glory and honour and power: for thou hast created all things, and for thy pleasure they are and were created."

Likewise, you and I cannot truly live until God becomes the supreme subject and object of our lives. Do you meditate upon Him as the supreme subject? Do you think, speak, and act for His glory so that He may be the supreme object of your faith? "Whether therefore ye eat, or drink, or whatsoever ye do, do all to the glory of God" (1 Cor. 10:31).

In the beginning God....
—GENESIS 1:1a

Genesis 1 teaches us several major truths about God. First, it teaches God's *priority over creation* and His independence of it. "In the beginning God" tells us that God existed before the cosmos existed. Jesus confirmed this by speaking of the glory He had with the Father before the world began (John 17:5).

God did not create the world because He needed man or the world. He is completely self-sufficient; He has need of nothing outside of Himself.

Has the Holy Spirit taught you that God does not need you? God doesn't need helpers or defenders. He doesn't even need worshipers. He doesn't need you and me at all.

Second, God is *eternal.* The Psalmist says, "Before the mountains were brought forth, or ever thou hadst formed the earth and the world, even from everlasting to everlasting, thou art God" (Ps. 90:2) and "The heavens are the work of thy hands. They shall perish, but thou shalt endure" (Ps. 102:25b–26a).

Third, God is infinitely *gracious.* He created the universe in all its glory, and man as the crown of it, because He was pleased in His compassionate grace in Christ to share His joy with people like us. Creation is therefore an expression of the grace of God. We are introduced to God's graciousness here because this is what God is like all the way through Scripture.

In the new creation in Christ, God persists in loving His rebel creatures, not because He has any need of us, but because He longs to share His joy, holiness, righteousness, and beauty with us. He is truly a God of grace.

Finally, God is *beautiful and orderly.* Study the beautiful parallels between the first and fourth days of creation, the second and fifth, and the third and sixth. How much more beautiful God's method of creation is than man's evolutionary theory!

In the beginning God....
—GENESIS 1:1a

We often come to Genesis 1 with a kind of inquisitiveness about creation. Instead, shouldn't we come in a spirit of worship, bowing before the glorious majesty of the God who has created the universe and given us life and breath and all things? Then we will recognize that He has revealed Himself so that He might touch our lives.

One practical effect Genesis 1 ought to have on us is to help us recognize the primacy of God over all of life. If God is the subject of creation, that is, if He occupies a place of primacy in the universe, then the simple, logical conclusion is that He must occupy the same place in our lives, both individually and corporately. That, indeed, is how God intends us to live. The Lord Jesus says it this way: "Seek ye first the kingdom of God, and his righteousness" (Matt. 6:33a).

We run into all kinds of trouble when we don't embrace this practical principle of bowing before the primacy of God over all of life. For example, think of the primacy of God in our planning. Too often we first decide what we want to do, then approach God for confirmation, hoping that our desires will be acceptable to Him. But the biblical principle is "In the beginning God." That means before we make any plans, we should recognize the right of God over all of our lives. If we truly believe that God's initiative is the foundation of all of our plans, we will understand that our position is to seek grace to discern His will and good pleasure, then to do it, no matter how much self-denial that requires.

When God becomes primary in our plans, situations often change. Difficulties, even seeming impossibilities, are overcome. Doubts are dissipated; deliverance is received.

Are you seeking to bow to the primacy of God in every sphere of your life? Is your limited time, your limited money, your limited energy devoted to the will of God? Do you really want to live by the principle, "In the beginning God"?

And God said..., And God created..., and God saw that it was good.
　　　　　　　　　　　　　　　　　—GENESIS 1:20–21

Genesis 1 teaches us three additional truths about God. First, God is *perfect wisdom*. His creation followed an astonishing divine plan for an orderly universe and for the amazing phenomenon of human life. Already in the first chapter, the Bible implies that God has a perfect plan for the created order and for man as the crown of His creation.

When you read Genesis 1, doesn't it seem absurd for us to think we know better than God or have more wisdom than He does? We who are foolish cannot judge the all-wise God.

Second, God is *perfect goodness*. Repeatedly, Genesis 1 tells us that when God made something, He "saw that it was good." All that God made was perfectly good because He is perfect goodness. Nothing marred the perfect beauty of God's creation. Everything He does is like that.

Even today, when God's hand is upon our lives, what He does is perfectly good. So we can believe that "all things work together for good to them that love God" (Rom. 8:28a).

The revelation of God's goodness ought to revolutionize our attitude toward everything in life; it ought to change our thinking. It ought, above all, to bring us with open hearts and arms to embrace His will rather than to suspect it, scrutinize it, fear it, or want to change it.

Finally, God is *perfect power*. His strength is unlimited. Did you notice the ease of His work in Genesis 1? It is evident in the refrain: "And God said…and it was so." God's very word is creative; by it He called the heavens into being, He commanded the earth to be formed, and He spoke and set the stars in their places.

A healthy dose of the doctrine of creation is needed in our lives to bring fiber into our spiritual being, to strengthen our souls, and to help us understand that the same God who commanded the light to shine out of darkness also desires to shine in our hearts. God unites perfect wisdom and perfect goodness with perfect power to produce overwhelmingly wonderful glory. That is the character of our God.

How else does God reveal Himself here in Genesis 1? What implications do all these revelations have for your life?

And God said, Let us make man in our image, after our likeness: and let them have dominion.... The LORD God formed man of the dust of the ground, and breathed into his nostrils the breath of life; and man became a living soul.
— GENESIS 1:26a, 2:7

The creation of man in Genesis 1:26 is markedly different compared to everything God has previously done. Until this point, God has simply been issuing commands to create. Now He allows us to overhear the sacred conversation between His own triune persons regarding the creation of man.

The Lord God is doing something very special here. Francis Schaeffer, in *Genesis in Space and Time*, says, "It is as though God put exclamation points here to indicate that there is something special about the creation of man."

The Lord created us in such a wondrous, solemn way for several reasons:

- Because we alone were to bear God's image (Gen. 1:26);
- Because we alone were to be God's deputies, His vice-regents, on earth (Gen. 1:28);
- Because we alone were given immortal souls (Gen. 2:7); and
- Because the Son of God was to appear in our nature (Isa. 7:14).

The creation of mankind has important ramifications for two issues commonly raised today. First, some people wrongly assert that Genesis 1 and 2 represent contradictory accounts of creation. The two accounts are complementary, not contradictory. Genesis 1 deals with man in his cosmic setting, that is, against the whole background of creation; Genesis 2 puts man at the center of creation, showing us that the focus is on man as the pinnacle of God's creative work. Genesis 2 is simply a more detailed, complementary account of God's creation of man, setting before us in an orderly way a progressive focus on man in God's world.

Second, the special creation of mankind stresses that Adam and Eve were real people, not just mythical beings. You and I belong to a different order from everything that God had previously created. The New Testament decisively speaks of Adam and Eve as historical individuals. For example, Romans 5:12 says, "By one man sin entered into the world, and death by sin; and so death passed upon all men, for that all have sinned." Paul here parallels the two Adams: the actual Adam, through whom sin entered the world, and a second Adam, Christ Jesus, through whom salvation came to us. Paul maintains the historicity of both Adam and Jesus.

Let us make man in our image.… So God created man in his own image, in the image of God created he him.

—GENESIS 1:26–27a

God created man specifically different from the rest of His creation in terms of bearing His image and likeness. These unique aspects of man's creation give him great dignity.

What does it mean to be created in the image or likeness of God? That is an important question because, even as fallen creatures, we still bear, in some sense, the image and likeness of God, though every aspect is flawed by sin. The image of God in man includes three important capacities:

First, the image of God in man includes *the capacity for intellect or reason*. God has a mind and is perfectly wise. So when God addresses man, He does so in rational terms. For example, He says, "Come now, and let us reason together" (Isa. 1:18).

We have an intellectual capacity that distinguishes us from the animals. We can reason, remember, and communicate better than all other creatures. We are self-conscious, self-critical, and able to assess ourselves. In all of this, we reflect God.

Second, the image of God in man includes *moral capacity*. The God of Genesis is good and righteous. He says of everything He created, "It is good." His creation was beautiful not only externally but internally; it was essentially morally good. The prohibition to eat of the tree of the knowledge of good and evil was a moral imperative in which God appealed to man's unique moral consciousness.

In comparison, if you have trained it well, your dog may obey you when you command it. The dog's behavior, however, is not its moral choice but because of instinct that results from training. A dog does not have the moral capacity that is an important part of the image of God in man.

Finally, the image of God in man includes the *capacity for spirituality*. God did not commune with any animal in Eden in the sense that He communed with Adam and Eve. He did not call out to any animals, "Where art thou?" There is a unique capacity in us to have communion with Him. Nature does not choose to praise God because it does not have the capacity for spirituality. By grace, we worship God voluntarily and rationally because of our spiritual capacity.

And God said, Let us make man in our image, after our likeness: and let them have dominion.... And God blessed them, and God said unto them, Be fruitful, and multiply, and replenish the earth, and subdue it: and have dominion over the fish of the sea, and over the fowl of the air, and over every living thing that moveth upon the earth.... And the LORD God took the man, and put him into the garden of Eden to dress it and to keep it.
—GENESIS 1:26, 28; 2:15

Truly, we are uniquely made. God has given us dominion, or vice-regency, over all creation. God has created us for this purpose (Gen. 1:26, 28).

Man was created to be a caretaker of God's creation, to exercise dominion over it in subjection and submission to God. We must understand the total picture of creation here. Man does not suddenly appear on the scene and assume dominion over creation. He is under the dominion of God; he therefore exercises dominion he has been given by God.

So there are two levels of dominion: God rules over all, including humanity; and humanity rules over the rest of the created order. God created man to rule over all the resources of the earth to reflect His own wise and perfect rule over man.

This rule includes delegation, for God gives dominion to man. The rule also includes reflection, for God's perfect government is reflected in man's rule over creation. God offered man enormous responsibility when He made him vice-regent over the created order.

Many tasks derive from this role, such as protecting and caring for the environment. We are responsible for managing all the resources in the world. Therefore, selfish spoiling of the environment, including failing to explore the world in which God has set us or ignoring scientific research about dominion over our resources, is contrary to God's will. God commands man to subdue the earth and bring it under his dominion. No biblical believer should be afraid of scientific inquiry that is made in subjection to the Word of God.

Those of us who are called to science should be grateful to God for the privilege of serving in this sphere as you bring both yourself and your vocation into subjection to God. Then, too, all of us, no matter what our line of work is, should bring ourselves and our vocation into subjection to God. How can we do that on a daily basis? Do you prayerfully and conscientiously strive for this?

And God blessed them, and God said unto them, Be fruitful, and mul-
tiply, and replenish the earth, and subdue it: and have dominion over
the fish of the sea, and over the fowl of the air, and over every living
thing that moveth upon the earth.... And the LORD God took the
man, and put him into the garden of Eden to dress it and to keep it.

—GENESIS 1:28, 2:15

We must cultivate a right attitude to God's created order. As Genesis itself suggests, we can do that by observing the following principles:

- We should not deify nature. The creation is separate from the Creator. Unlike pantheists, who believe that God is in nature and that nature and God are therefore one, we believe our God is above nature. So we must never worship "Mother Nature." Nature is not our God.
- We should delight in God's creation. We should not adopt the pagan, Greek idea that the human body and other material things have no value. If God had made our soul but some human being had made our body and the universe, the Greeks would have been right in devaluing all that is physical. But the Bible says God made all that is; therefore, all should be valued. Because it is God's creation, we should bask in its beauty.
- We should show respect for nature and be responsible for it. We should not destroy the world we live in but elevate it to its fullest potential. Do you respect this earth as the Lord's world? Do not damage nature in any way without a compelling cause.
- We should study and explore nature's grandeur. Christianity gives us the basis for scientific research. That mandate is summarized in Psalm 111:2: "The works of the LORD are great, sought out of all them that have pleasure therein." The order of the universe makes scientific inquiry possible. The scientist depends upon this order, which helps him formulate the laws that he aims to describe. Those laws are really just the customs of God.
- We should praise God for nature. Some see no beauty in the created order and do not bow before its majesty and exclaim, "How great Thou art!" Are we absorbed more in the works of men than in the works of God?

We will see more of God in nature once we've seen Him in grace. Grace opens sightless eyes to beauty in creation. Nature therefore becomes the Lord's handmaid to enable true believers, like the writers of many of the creation psalms, to magnify the Lord.

How do you view nature?

So God created man in his own image, in the image of God created he him; male and female created he them.... The LORD God formed man of the dust of the ground, and breathed into his nostrils the breath of life; and man became a living soul.

—GENESIS 1:27; 2:7

The two complementary accounts of the creation of man in Genesis 1:27 and Genesis 2:7 are both necessary for a biblical understanding of who man is. The first account tells us that we were made in the image of God. That is our uniqueness. The second tells us that we were made from the dust of the ground.

Thus, combined in us is the infinite lowliness of being made of the dust of the earth and the infinite dignity of being made in the image of God. We were created of both dust and glory. If we forget or ignore either aspect, we will fail to understand how God made us.

Theologians often point out that man has always been his own greatest problem. His first great cry, "Who am I?" is the search for identity. His second great cry, "Why am I here?" is his search for significance. The biblical answer is that man is both dust and glory.

Dust speaks of lowliness. In Psalm 103:14b we read, "He remembers that we are dust." That should remind us of our lowly origins. God said after man's fall in Eden, "Dust thou art, and unto dust shalt thou return" (Gen. 3:19b). Dust speaks of our frailty and finiteness, and the fact that we are not like God, who is eternal, omniscient, and omnipotent. When Abraham came into the presence of God, he acknowledged his finiteness by saying, "Behold now, I have taken upon me to speak unto the Lord, which am but dust and ashes" (Gen. 18:27).

Dust and glory must be kept in balance. If we forget that we are dust, we will ignore or minimize our finiteness and our absolute dependence upon God, who personally breathed into our nostrils the very breath of life (Gen. 2:7). But if we forget the other truth—that we are made in the glorious image of God—we will be content to live as the animals, and we will miss our eternal destiny. If we believe that we are nothing but dust, we will lose the glory that distinguishes us as the crown of creation.

How can this combination of being dust and glory work itself out experientially and practically in our lives?

And God said, Behold, I have given you....
—GENESIS 1:29a

Another practical effect Genesis 1 ought to have on us is to cause us to recognize the sufficiency of God for our every need and the whole of our lives. This is summarized well in the opening words of verse 29, "And God said, Behold I have given you...."

Since our Creator is unchangeably eternal, gracious, wise, good, and powerful, He is solely sufficient for all of our lives. That is what the saints of God in the Bible learn from this doctrine of creation. In Isaiah 40, the prophet addresses those who are weary, saying: "Hast thou not known? hast thou not heard, that the everlasting God, the LORD, the Creator of the ends of the earth, fainteth not, neither is weary? there is no searching of his understanding. He giveth power to the faint; and to them that have no might he increaseth strength. Even the youths shall faint and be weary, and the young men shall utterly fall: but they that wait upon the LORD shall renew their strength" (Isa. 40:28–31a). Isaiah is speaking of the sufficiency of our giving Creator-God for all of life.

Similarly, Jeremiah says, "Ah Lord GOD! behold, thou hast made the heaven and the earth by thy great power and stretched out arm, and there is nothing too hard for thee" (Jer. 32:17). God's glory revealed in creation is so perfect that Jeremiah comes to God with the kind of confidence that we greatly require today.

If our faith and confidence are not in God and His sufficiency, we are not truly spiritually alive. Our lives are empty if they do not begin with God. Without Him, we miss the purpose of life, miss our true identity as God's image-bearers, and miss the only comfort in life and death of belonging to God in Jesus Christ.

The first four words of Genesis, "In the beginning God," are a stark contrast to the last four: "a coffin in Egypt." You cannot be prepared for death, dear friend, until in all of life you rely in confidence on the God of beginnings, for Christ's sake—the God who is willing to give you everything you need in every area of your life.

The LORD God planted a garden eastward in Eden; and there he put the man whom he had formed.
　　　　　　　　　　　　　　　　　　　　　　　　—GENESIS 2:8

The Garden of Eden is a microcosm of the loving, detailed, wise, and lavish provision of God for man as the crown and glory of creation. The world God prepared for man included:

- *Physical provision.* God gave man food to eat from the trees of the garden (Gen. 2:9), and He has been supplying food ever since. God also supplied man with physical work. He put Adam in the garden "to dress it and to keep it" (v. 15). Work is a pre-fall gift of our Creator. We were created to be industrious. Lack of discipline and laziness are results of our fallen condition.
- *Spiritual provision.* God gave man the Sabbath for his spiritual profit and physical rest. God wove rest and work into the pattern of His creation by His own example (vv. 2–3). The Lord offers the Sabbath as the day in which we meet with Him, learn of Him, enjoy Him, and commune with Him. In this communion, we find our highest work and chief glory. Do you know the Sabbath joy of communing with God?
- *Moral provision.* Having set man in the bounty of Eden, God told him what he must and must not do (vv. 16–17). Without this moral stimulus, man would have remained less than man. This moral requirement of man is often caricatured as only prohibitive, but God did not put man into the garden and say, "Now don't touch," like a parent warns a child going into a department store. Rather, God said: "The entire garden, with all its trees, is for you, except one, so that you might learn obedience to Me as your perfect Creator and Father. You will remain free and happy as long as you live in obedience to My holy commandments, which are good and perfect. My commandments are not a burden to be carried but a blessing to be embraced."
- *Aesthetic provision.* God provided trees "pleasant to the sight" (v. 9). Eden's trees were not just useful; they were beautiful.
- *Social provision.* God met Adam's social needs by providing a helpmeet for him (v. 18). He provided a marital relationship that was complementary (v. 18) and exclusive (v. 24), creating another means by which man could give God glory.

That is lavish provision indeed! Still today, God, in and through Christ, meets all our needs as He sends us into the world to live for Him. But our true freedom and full humanity can be realized only when we live within the boundaries of His good and perfect will. We become developed as God's creation when we live in obedient faith to our Provider and pursue His glory with all that is within us. Are you striving to live to the glory of God alone (*soli Deo gloria*)?

> *And the* LORD *God took the man, and put him into the garden of Eden to dress it and to keep it. And the* LORD *God commanded the man, saying, Of every tree of the garden thou mayest freely eat: but of the tree of the knowledge of good and evil, thou shalt not eat of it: for in the day that thou eatest thereof thou shalt surely die.*
>
> —GENESIS 2:15–17

The Bible is covenant-centered. It consists of the Old Testament, or old covenant, and the New Testament, or new covenant. The word covenant, which is used more than three hundred times in the Bible, comes from the Latin term *con venire*, meaning "coming together." It presupposes that two or more parties come together in an agreement that includes promises, stipulations, privileges, and responsibilities. A covenant is an agreement between parties that binds them to certain acts on each other's behalf.

When the Bible speaks of covenant, it refers mostly to God making a covenant with man. God is a covenant God; He deals with man in a covenantal way. A biblical covenant is an agreement between God and man that stipulates the conditions of our relationship with Him.

The covenant between God and man that is commonly called the covenant of works almost jumps out at us in Genesis 2:15–17, even though the word "covenant" is absent. All the essential parts of a covenant are here:

- The sovereign God and sinless Adam, representing all mankind, are the two parties of the covenant of works (vv. 15–16).
- The condition of the covenant of works is perfect obedience (v. 17).
- God offers a clear test or stipulation. Genesis 2:16 says, "The LORD God commanded the man" not to eat of the forbidden tree.
- In this covenant, God promises life. He will graciously reward obedience by attaching a token of His promise in the tree of life (Gen. 3:24).
- The penalty for violating this covenant is death: physical death of the body, spiritual death of the soul, and eternal death of the soul and body in hell, which is the ultimate punishment for sin (Gen. 2:17).

Such punishment is just because sin is injurious to an infinite God. Sin is an offense to infinite majesty. It is contempt of infinite authority, abuse of infinite mercy, and dishonor to infinite excellence. It is an affront to infinite holiness, a reproach to infinite glory, and an enemy of infinite love.

Has the Holy Spirit convinced you of your lost state before God? Do you identify with Adam in his tragic fall and see yourself as a covenant breaker? Have you then taken refuge in Christ and the covenant of grace?

And the Lord God caused a deep sleep to fall upon Adam, and he slept: and he took one of his ribs, and closed up the flesh instead thereof.

—GENESIS 2:21

Genesis 2:18–24 describes God's creation of the first woman. God caused a deep sleep to fall on Adam. This "deep sleep" must have been something like anesthesia, and the operation that God performed much like medical surgery. God took away one of the man's ribs and filled the empty place with flesh, closing up the wound. From the rib, God then "made"—literally, "built" or "constructed"—woman. God miraculously, meticulously, beautifully formed woman with His own hands, making her every bit as special as the created man.

There is something particularly beautiful, even poetic, about this creation. The woman is made for the man and might therefore be thought of as man's servant. But Genesis says nothing of this. Instead, as Matthew Henry puts it: "The woman was not made out of the man's head to rule over him, nor out of his feet to be trampled upon by him, but out of his side to be equal with him, under his arm to be protected, and near his heart to be beloved."

Then the Lord God presented the bride that His own hands formed to the man. He "brought her unto the man" (v. 22b), literally, "presented or conducted her to the man." The word translated as "brought" also implies the formal, solemn giving of the woman within the bonds of the marriage covenant. God brought her to the man, as the Puritans said, "as his second self, to be a help meet for him."

In bringing the woman to the man, God establishes marriage as the first, most basic human institution. Before governments, churches, schools, or any other social structures exist, God establishes a household based on the mutual respect and love of a husband and wife. All other human institutions derive from that. From the authority of the father comes the patriarchal system of human government, which eventually gives rise to monarchies and democracies. From the responsibility of parents to educate their children come schools, colleges, and universities. From the need to care for the family's health come physicians and hospitals. From the obligation of parents to train their children in the knowledge of God come temples, synagogues, and churches. All human organizations can be traced back to the home, the family, and ultimately to marriage.

Does the way you think about, speak to, and treat your spouse, your children, and your parents show that you have a biblical understanding of the importance and the integrity of marriage and family?

An help meet for him....
—GENESIS 2:18, 20

Genesis 2:18 says, "It is not good that the man should be alone." This "not good" is emphatic. Here, for the first time, we find something lacking in creation. Without female companionship and a partner in reproduction, man cannot fully realize his humanity.

Eve was created as a perfect woman. How striking she must have been! In addition to Eve's physical, mental, and moral excellence, verses 18 and 20 say she was made "for" the man, "an help meet [or suitable] for him."

This concept angers some women and is a cause for concern, if not anxiety, for others. Many think the role of "help meet" is outdated and prejudiced against women. But that concern is based on misunderstanding the term.

First, the word *help* is not a derogatory term. God created us to serve Him and to help our neighbors. It is an honor for a woman to help her husband, for help is a word frequently used in reference to God Himself (Ps. 22:11; 28:7; 46:1; 54:4). If God is not ashamed to be the help of fallen sinners, why should we look askance at Eve being a help to her husband?

Meet comes from the Hebrew word meaning "opposite." Literally, it is "according to the opposite of him," meaning that a woman complements her husband. She is equal to and adequate for man.

Are men and women truly equal? Yes, in that: (1) they are both created in the image of God; (2) they are both placed under the moral command of God and thus are given moral responsibility; (3) they are both guilty of disobeying God's covenant; (4) they are objects of God's gracious redemption in Christ (Gal. 3:28); and (5) as husband and wife they are both called to leave father and mother, and to love each other as one flesh.

In another sense, man and woman were not created equal. Because the woman was created for the man, they were not created equal in authority. God has a different authoritative structure laid out for husbands than He does for wives. That does not mean that one position is better than another.

In the God-given structure of authority, a husband and wife mutually submit to Christ (Eph. 5:21), then, under Christ, to each other to fulfill each other's needs. Already in Paradise, there is glory and humility in both man and woman. The man's glory is that he is the head; his humility is that he is not complete without the woman. The woman's glory is that she gives the man fulfillment; her humility is that she is made of man.

Does your marriage reflect this biblical understanding of the roles of husband and wife? If not, what can you do to realign your marriage?

And the rib, which the LORD God had taken from man, made he a woman, and brought her unto the man.
                                                              —GENESIS 2:22

In Ephesians 5, Paul describes the complementary roles of husband and wife within marriage in Christ. The husband is to love his wife as Christ loves the church: absolutely (He gave Himself, v. 25b), realistically (Christ realized that the church, in herself, needed cleansing, v. 26), purposely (i.e., to make the church holy and blemish-free, v. 27), and sacrificially (i.e., to care for the bride as one cares for his own body, vv. 28–29).

In turn, the wife is to show her husband reverence and submission, as Paul says in verses 22 and 33. Elsewhere, Paul gives four reasons why: because the woman is made from man (1 Cor. 11:3, 8), because the woman is made for man (1 Cor. 11:9), because the man was created first (1 Tim. 2:12–13), and because sin first entered the world by the woman (1 Tim. 2:14). As the man is to show loving headship, so the woman is to show loving submission.

Submission is not degrading, for it is found even within the persons of the Godhead. Theologians speak not only of the essential Trinity, in which all three Persons are coequal, but also of the economic Trinity, in which the Son submits to the Father as Mediator and Servant. Paul indicates the parallel between these submissions when he says, "The head of every man is Christ; and the head of the woman is the man; and the head of Christ is God" (1 Cor. 11:3; see also Eph. 5:22–24.)

Some people respond to such texts by arguing that submission is a result of the curse, now abrogated by Christ's atonement. However, their arguments do not reckon with submission among the divine persons or with the subordinate relationship of wife to husband (Gen. 2) before the fall.

Submission within marriage also has parallels within the church, the family of God. Though women may and should exercise numerous roles of caring in the church, Paul makes clear that the headship principle prevents them from bearing office. Moreover, submission in marriage and in the church is to be voluntary. In short, if a woman cannot be a loving, submissive helper to the man who proposes to her, she should not marry him any more than a man should propose marriage to a woman to whom he will not show loving, self-denying leadership.

Are you fulfilling your God-ordained role? Husbands, are you increasingly striving to treat your wives as Christ treats the church? And wives, are you increasingly striving to treat your husbands as the church treats Christ?

And Adam said, This is now bone of my bones, and flesh of my flesh: she shall be called Woman, because she was taken out of man.

—GENESIS 2:23

When God awakened Adam, he immediately recognized Eve as the perfect fit for the longing that had been awakened in him. He knew, after naming the animals, that none of them could be a help meet for him because none had a soul (Gen. 2:20). At the sight of Eve, Adam broke into a kind of wedding song, celebrating his similarity and union with the woman by naming her.

Adam said, "This is now" (v. 23a)—i.e., "this time," at long last, he had received what he has been longing for. The close association is emphasized in their titles. The Hebrew word for "woman" simply adds the feminine ending "–ah" to the word for "man." Thus, she is called "woman" (*ishah*) because she was taken out of man (*ish*). Parallels for this naming are the lion and lioness or tiger and tigress. By divine revelation, Adam realized the woman was taken out of his body. Naming his wife reinforced his leadership and authority over her but also indicated that he understood her equality with him as his partner.

The divine miracle that Adam witnessed filled him with inexpressible joy, inspiring him to cry out in verse 23: "This is now bone of my bones, and flesh of my flesh: she shall be called Woman, because she was taken out of Man."

Adam and Eve then were united in a perfect marriage. "Marriage is honorable, but this surely was the most honorable marriage that ever was, in which God Himself had all along an immediate hand," writes Matthew Henry.

The Puritan Thomas Adams says, "There is no such fountain of comfort on earth, as marriage." What could you do to rekindle more of the poetic excitement in your marriage that you had at its beginning?

Therefore shall a man leave his father and his mother, and shall cleave
unto his wife: and they shall be one flesh.
—GENESIS 2:24

God now offers a beautiful, sacred blueprint for marriage, which includes
leaving, cleaving, and weaving (cf. Matt. 19:5). Here's what they mean:

- Leaving. Leaving one's father and mother is a tremendous adjustment.
  The closeness of family unity must yield to a new family unit with a new
  head. This new unity takes priority over the parent-child relationship.
  But the leaving is necessary, for without leaving, one cannot cleave to or
  become one flesh with another.
- Cleaving. A newly married couple come together in a union described
  in the original Greek as "cemented together." The bridegroom and bride
  form a new relationship in which they become inseparable. The woman
  becomes part of the man, and vice versa. They cleave to each other.
- Weaving or oneness. The expression "one flesh" in Hebrew indicates
  a complete change of state. The goal of marriage is not just for two to
  become one physically, as important and fulfilling as that may be, but
  to become interwoven or one in every aspect of the relationship: one in
  heart, one in love, one in trust, one in purpose, one in thinking, and, above
  all, one in Christ. A great marriage in Christ produces great intellectual,
  spiritual, emotional, and physical oneness.

The goal of marriage is to first become one with God through Christ,
and then, out of that oneness, to be one with a spouse. How can a sinner who
is separated from God become one with God? Only through the Savior, who
Himself led the way in leaving, cleaving or joining, and becoming one with
His bride, the church. As Paul puts it, "This is a great mystery: but I speak
concerning Christ and the church" (Eph. 5:32).

Christ left His Father willingly to find His bride. On Calvary's cross, He
joined Himself to her, the church. Through profound suffering that included
heart-wrenching separation from His Father, Christ paid the price so that
His bride might become one with Him. His bride was mystically formed out
of Him as the Second Adam, just as Eve was formed out of the first Adam.
As the woman came from Adam's side to symbolize their union, so the
church of God was taken from the wounded, bleeding, dying side of Christ
so she might be joined with her Savior. This is a great mystery indeed!

How does this leaving, cleaving, and oneness play out in your earthly
marriage with your spouse? Do you know spiritual marriage with Christ?

They shall be one flesh.
—GENESIS 2:24b

How great is the dignity of Eve's creation as a woman, of being one with her husband and of sharing that dignity with him! Today, through saving faith, believers also share that dignity in the re-creation of Christ's bride. We are made one with the Bridegroom to share in His dignity and glory, and to share that love with which God loves His Son! Truly, there is no dignity like the dignity of the re-creation of being made the bride of Jesus Christ.

The church's union with Christ provides an unspeakable mystical "fullness" for Christ as Mediator. Christ's mediatorship is empty without the church. Christ is the Head; the church is the body. "And [God] gave him to be the head over all things to the church, which is his body, the fullness of him that filleth all in all" (Eph. 1:22–23). This mystical union one day will be perfected in heaven.

To be born again through the regenerating power of the Holy Spirit is to be personally united with Jesus Christ. It is to be "in Christ." Paul never tires of describing a Christian in this way; throughout his epistles, he uses the phrases "in Christ," "in Christ Jesus," or "in him" at least 164 times. It was his favorite way of describing a Christian.

For example, Paul writes, "If any man be in Christ, he is a new creature," or, as the original has it, "a new creation" (2 Cor. 5:17). In being united with Christ, a person becomes a new creation. Likewise, in Ephesians 1:3, Paul says, "Blessed be the God and Father of our Lord Jesus Christ, who hath blessed us with all spiritual blessings in heavenly places in Christ."

The believer's union with Christ is profoundly intimate. When Paul speaks of union with Christ, he uses a special prefix in Greek to indicate that the tie is indissoluble. Literally, he says in Galatians 2:20, "I am crucified with Christ." In Romans 6:4, Paul speaks of being buried with Christ; in Ephesians 2, of being raised with Christ and of sitting with Him in heavenly places; and in Romans 8, of being glorified together with Christ. Thus the intimacy of the believer's union with Christ is so great that, in a sense, when Christ was crucified, the believer was also crucified; when He died, the believer also died; when He was buried, the believer was also buried; when He was raised from the dead, the believer was also raised; and when He ascended, the believer also ascended.

Who can comprehend this mystical union?

Are you in union with Christ?

Now the serpent was more subtle than any beast of the field which the
LORD God had made.
—GENESIS 3:1a

Genesis 3 is, perhaps, the most pivotal chapter in Scripture. It is the black chapter of sin because of the entrance of sin into the world (v. 6); the red chapter of atonement because of the first proclamation of the coming Messiah (v. 15), typified in the first blood-shedding (v. 21); and the white chapter of hope because it contains the first confession of faith in Adam's naming his wife, Eve (v. 20).

Our understanding of Genesis 3 affects our understanding of the rest of biblical revelation. It profoundly affects our understanding of our lives, our radical depravity, our desperate need for the Savior, and our daily experience in a fallen world.

Many of the questions people have about their Christian experience come from a failure to understand the implications of the fall and what it means to live not in the world as God made it, but in the world as sin spoiled it. Many people try to live as if we are not in a fallen world. Few grasp the gravity and depth of our tragic fall and our dire need for a Savior.

Genesis 3 raises the question of how it was possible for sin to enter a beautiful and perfect world that was governed by a man and woman who lived unashamedly naked before God, each other, and all creation (Gen. 2:25).

The answer is that sin entered the world through Satan in the guise of a serpent (Gen. 3:1–5; Rev. 12:9). Though he was one of the highest and brightest angels prior to his fall, Satan (according to Ezek. 28:11–19 and Isa. 14:12–14) seems to have become so preoccupied with his own beauty and glory that he thought he could instigate a demonic coup and unseat the God of glory and take His place. When God cast Satan out of heaven, Satan's aim was to tempt man, the crown of God's creation, with the very sins that had motivated Satan to fall.

That is as far as we can go in answering the age-old question of where evil came from. Only the sovereign God knows how sin permeated heaven itself in Satan's rebellion. It is more important for us to understand the nature of sin on earth than to understand the origin of sin in heaven.

Are you convinced of the heinous nature of sin? Are you convicted of the anti-God character of sin? Have you learned to hate sin as exceeding sinful with all your heart, mind, and strength?

Yea, hath God said?
—GENESIS 3:1b

How did Satan tempt Eve and Adam to sin, and how does he tempt us today? What is the nature and character of sin?

According to Genesis 3, sin is defiance of and rebellion against the word that God has spoken. Adam and Eve rebelled against the will of God made known to them by God's own mouth. Rebellion against that word was what the serpent aimed to produce in Eve's heart. One reason why Genesis 3 is so practical for us is that Satan's devices, cunning and varied as they are, do not change over time. He comes to us with the same kind of devices that he exerted on Eve in the garden.

In Genesis 3, Satan exercises his dreadful work of temptation in four steps. The first is doubt. Satan casts doubt upon God's Word by raising questions about its validity. He asks Eve, "Yea, hath God said?" (v. 1b). With a touch of cynicism he implies, "Do you really believe God would say this?" At the very beginning of his attack on Eve's mind, heart, and emotions, Satan smuggles in the idea that God's Word is subject to man's judgment.

It is critically important for us to defend ourselves against doubt, for doubting God in any way gives the Devil a foothold in our minds. So often, the intellectual and spiritual battles that we are engaged in focus upon the authority of Holy Scripture. That is because the authority, supremacy, sufficiency, infallibility, and inerrancy of Holy Scripture all are necessary for our spiritual well-being. Satan knows that, even if we are inclined to forget it.

Satan loves to cast doubt on God's Word. Doubting God's Word is the very heart of sin. It is the essence of the mother sin of unbelief. Skepticism about God's Word means not only doubting the inerrancy of Scripture but also doubting that Scripture can be applied to you.

Whenever doubts about God or His Word enter you, take warning. You are on a battlefield, and the antagonist who seeks to destroy you is the Devil. The only way to defeat him is to use the very Word of God he is trying to make you doubt. The New Testament tells you to resist the Devil and promises that he will flee from you. Resist him with the sword of the Spirit, which is the Word of God (Eph. 6:17). That is how Jesus resisted Satan in three major temptations that He encountered in the wilderness. Three times He responded, "It is written." Likewise, we must defy him with the sword of the Word of God.

Neither shall ye touch it, lest ye die.
—GENESIS 3:3b

Having gained a foothold in Eve's mind, Satan now helps her distort God's Word in the second step of temptation. The woman says to the serpent, "We may eat of the fruit of the trees of the garden: but of the fruit of the tree which is in the midst of the garden, God hath said, Ye shall not eat of it, neither shall ye touch it, lest ye die" (Gen. 3:2b–3).

This distortion is evident in three ways:

- Eve disparages her privileges by misquoting the terms of God's provision. God specifically said to Adam, "Of every tree of the garden thou mayest freely eat" (Gen. 2:16). That was lavish provision, indeed, and well satisfied the needs of Adam and Eve.

  But Eve misquotes God by telling Satan, "We may eat from the trees in the garden, but God hath said...." She is not adequately persuaded of the goodness of God, and that is tragic. There is no defense against Satan more effective than a heart that is overwhelmed by a sense of the goodness, mercy, and lavishness of God's grace. By contrast, there is no life more open to Satan's wiles than one marked by a complaining, ungrateful spirit.

  Have you ever noticed how, like Israel in the desert, a murmuring spirit destroys your relationship with God and opens you up to the wiles of the Devil?

- Eve overstates God's restrictions. She says God told Adam and her that they were not to touch the tree, but Genesis 2:16–17 says nothing about touching the forbidden tree. Another favorite device of Satan is to motivate us to minimize God's goodness and maximize His prohibitions. When we do that, we begin to believe that God's ways are impoverishing, His laws restricting, and His commandments grievous and heavy. This, too, is a very dangerous temptation.

- Eve minimizes her obligations by misquoting the divine penalty. She says God told Adam and Eve not to eat of the forbidden tree "lest" they die. In truth, God had said, "Thou shalt surely die," or as the Hebrew has it, "Dying you will surely die." Eve allows only the possibility of death as the result of sin, whereas God had declared the absolute certainty of death as the result of sin.

When Eve quotes God's prohibitions to Satan, she exaggerates them; when she quotes the penalty, she understates it. In every way, she distorts the Word of God. Can you think of ways you tend to do the same?

> *Ye shall not surely die.*
> —GENESIS 3:4b

The next stage of temptation is denying God's Word. Satan says to Eve, "Ye shall not surely die." He uses as strong a negative here as the positive God uses in Genesis 2:17. In this he denies the true nature of man as well as the true nature of God.

Satan says, "Ye shall not surely die: for God doth know that in the day ye eat thereof, then your eyes shall be opened, and ye shall be as gods, knowing good and evil" (Gen. 3:4b–5). He first denies the truth of judgment. "You can sin with impunity," the Devil says. "You will be able to disobey God and nothing will happen. It will be perfectly all right."

Isn't that exactly what we say today when Satan lures us into sin? He first minimizes the penalty of sin, saying, "Everybody is doing it anyway—and they're not being punished." After we have fallen into sin, Satan maximizes the penalty of sin by saying, "Now that you have committed this sin, God can no longer have mercy on you; you are doomed."

Satan is a liar who distorts the nature of God. We must realize that every sin has a penalty. The wages of sin is death. If you serve sin, you will receive the wages of sin. You live in a moral universe. If you sow the seed of sin, you will reap a harvest of judgment. If you sow the wind of unbelief, you will reap the whirlwind of destruction. "It is appointed unto men once to die, but after this the judgment," says Hebrews 9:27. Judgment is always imminent. There is a moment when God sends us the bill, and we have to pay it.

But we also need to know that God offers the penitent sinner the way to come back to Him through Jesus Christ. Even the chief of sinners can be saved (1 Tim. 1:15). Satan is dead wrong both in minimizing the penalty of sin and in minimizing the power of grace. He denies the true nature of God as a sin-hating God who also delights in mercy.

Notice, too, how Satan denies the true nature of man by saying, "Ye shall be as gods, knowing good and evil" (v. 5b). Adam and Eve do not become like God after they sin. God's knowledge of evil is an objective understanding of sin; man simply learns the experimental taste of evil, which is something God never had. In this, Satan is also blinding Adam and Eve to the truth that they already are like God. God has made them in His image. Satan is attempting to dehumanize them, making them less than a man and a woman.

In what ways have you learned that true humanity is discovered only in obedience to God?

And when the woman saw that the tree was good for food, and that it was pleasant to the eyes, and a tree to be desired to make one wise, she took of the fruit thereof, and did eat, and gave also unto her husband with her; and he did eat.

—GENESIS 3:6

The final stage of temptation is open defiance of the Word and will of God. That, of course, is what Satan is aiming for all the time. He persuades Eve to doubt the Word of God, then to distort it, then to deny it, and then, finally, to defy it. The result is that both Eve and Adam sin by eating the forbidden fruit.

We can look back now and trace Satan's process of dislodging man's trust in God and His Word. All along, the sinister aim of the Evil One was not to produce intellectual enlightenment or cultural experience, but to produce moral rebellion against the will of God. The nature of sin is ultimately this: moving from worshiping and serving the Creator to worshiping and serving the creature.

God said to man from the beginning that the whole world was his, but God was its center. But sin told man, "The whole world is mine, and I am the center around which it all revolves."

Sin is the failure to conform to the Word and law of God in our actions, in our attitudes, or in our nature, either by doing what we should not do (sins of commission) or by failing to do what we should do (sins of omission).

Adam and Eve disobeyed God. In that, they were guilty essentially of the sins of pride, unbelief, and rebellion. Those sins are the roots of what we call "original sin." The guilt of original sin is imputed to us through our representative, covenant head, Adam, as Paul tells us in Romans 5. We inherit the pollution of sin from our parents. We are conceived and born in iniquity as children of disobedience and are filled with pride, unbelief, and rebellion.

Sin is dreadful. It mocks God. It is blasphemy and apostasy. It leads us away from God and good. It means not living for His glory and transgressing His boundaries. Every life misses the target for which it was created; every life transgresses God's prohibitions; every life disobeys God's voice. All of us have sinned and come short of the glory of God.

What, then, is our hope? Our only hope is Jesus Christ, who suffered and died in our place (2 Cor. 5:15). When God restores us, we learn to live like Christ, who died for us. Are you increasingly being conformed to Christ, learning more and more to live like Him?

> *And the eyes of them both were opened, and they knew that they were*
> *naked; and they sewed fig leaves together, and made themselves aprons.*
> —GENESIS 3:7

Eating a piece of forbidden fruit was not a small act of disobedience. It was a grievous travesty in the sight of God for several reasons:

- Adam knew God had strictly forbidden eating this fruit upon punishment of death; this was a blatantly premeditated sin, not a sin of ignorance.
- Adam knew that the tree of knowledge of good and evil represented God's authority. He knew that the tree tested his willingness to obey God.
- Adam knew that in eating of this tree, he would be calling God a liar by refusing to believe that the threatened penalty would be death.
- Adam knew that he would sever himself from God if he ate the forbidden fruit, for God was too holy to commune with sinners.
- Adam knew that he was the covenant head of the entire human race, so that if he sinned, all his descendants would be plunged into sin and death.

Do you realize the seriousness of Adam's sin? Have you considered the reality that Adam's sin and all of its pollution has been passed on to you?

Satan tried to minimize Adam and Eve's sin by promising them that it would open their eyes and give them God-like knowledge. In one sense, he was right. They gained knowledge, but not the kind of knowledge they wanted. Their eyes were opened to see what they did not want to see. Genesis 3:7 says, "And the eyes of them both were opened, and they knew that they were naked; and they sewed fig leaves together, and made themselves aprons."

Remarkably, God then pays a special visit to Adam and Eve in the Garden of Eden. God comes calmly, decisively. He does not run but walks. He comes in the cool of the day, which is the most pleasant time. He comes by degrees, calling as He comes. His voice is not terrifying in itself, but it is to Adam and Eve. They are petrified because they are now sinners. Like children who hear their father's voice moments after they have broken a window, they run into the bushes. Their hearts beat wildly; they fear for their lives.

God calls them to Himself. Somehow they know, even as they try to escape, that God is inescapable. They know that running away will bring them only more misery. We, too, know that we cannot escape from God, particularly when we are guilty of disobeying Him. But like Jonah and the prodigal son, we foolishly run from the triune God, who alone can be our loving Father and our true home!

*And the eyes of them both were opened, and they knew that they were
naked; and they sewed fig leaves together, and made themselves aprons.*
—GENESIS 3:7

God comes to Paradise to reveal to Adam and Eve the immediate consequences of their sin. These five consequences still affect us today, since Adam
is our covenant head.

The first consequence of sin is bitter shame. The moment our first parents
fell, they plunged into the darkness of shame. The light of the image of God
in them burned out. Suddenly their physical condition became so important
that shame and self-consciousness seized them. They knew they needed to
be covered. Adam and Eve received what they thought they wanted, but, too
late, they learned it was not what they hoped it would be.

Bitter shame is still the consequence of sin today. You see, when sin
promises to open your eyes to something in some new way, it certainly will,
but you will not like what you see. Sin may promise you a bargain, but that
will prove to be more than you bargained for. When you eat something that
promises to bring you enlightenment, you will find that the light will go
out, and fear and shame will take its place. Your imaginary paradise will not
be enhanced but exchanged for a mirage and an illusion. Your eyes will be
opened to see what you do not want to see.

Sin makes us ashamed of ourselves. When we feel shame, we, like Adam
and Eve, reach for the nearest thing to cover ourselves. We can do that in
a variety of ways. We can look at the outside of things rather than deep
within us. We can focus on corporate sin rather than our own wrongdoing.
We can assume that time will cancel our sin. That's why some people joke
about the sins of their youth. But if those sins have never been washed in
the blood of Christ, how can we fool ourselves by thinking that God will
not remember them?

What kinds of coverings do you use to conceal your sin? Sooner or later,
God will tear away all our fig leaves, and we will have to face the consequences of our sin. God tells us that now so that we may confront the reality
of our sins and turn to His Son while there is yet hope.

And the eyes of them both were opened, and they knew that they were naked; and they sewed fig leaves together, and made themselves aprons.
—GENESIS 3:7

The second consequence of sin is bitter knowledge. Eve thought the fruit of the forbidden tree was "to be desired to make one wise." Literally, she believed it was "desirable for the knowledge it would give." But God did not want Adam and Eve to experiment with that kind of knowledge. In telling Adam and Eve not to eat of the forbidden tree, God told them everything they needed to know about evil. They were not ignorant about evil, just innocent of it. There is a world of difference between being ignorant and innocent.

"Do not eat" was all they needed to know. Why? Because knowing about evil will kill you. Once you pluck the forbidden fruit, you cannot tie it back on the tree; you have to live with it. And once you sink your teeth into that fruit, it becomes a part of you. What may look attractive and promise to be sweet will prove bitter. No one can eat forbidden fruit and escape the bitterness that it leaves in the soul.

God warned Adam and Eve about that bitter knowledge. He did not want to deny them the experience of life, as Satan insinuated, but He warned them so that they might delight only in the experience of life, not death. God knows precisely what the Devil still tries to cover up today—that no matter what sin promises, it cannot enhance our lives or our appreciation of life. Sin takes us precisely in the opposite direction. It dulls our perception of life and deadens our appetite for it. It spoils our ability to appreciate life. It brings hardness, bitterness, and shame into our souls. Sin reduces our sensitivity to the joys of this world that God has given us.

The Devil says, "Take the forbidden fruit and you will truly live." That is a lie, friends. Sin kills, births shame and fear, and leaves a bitter aftertaste. Oh, how many of us long to put forbidden fruit back on the tree! How we wish we never had tasted it!

Think of David writhing on his bed after he was convicted of committing adultery with Bathsheba and of killing her husband. How he thrashed about, discovering that the eyes of his soul were open to sin, visible to God and man. David then cried out to God: "Oh, I know my transgression; my sin is ever before me. I cannot hide from it, I cannot cover it up, I cannot blot it out. It is there; it haunts me!" What he thought would be sweet became bitter; the delight of his eyes became the torment of his soul.

Do you know the bitterness of sinning, having gained the kind of knowledge you did not wish to know?

And the eyes of them both were opened, and they knew that they were naked; and they sewed fig leaves together, and made themselves aprons.... The woman whom thou gavest to be with me, she gave me of the tree, and I did eat.

—GENESIS 3:7, 12

The third consequence of sin is bitter corruption. As Thomas Boston points out, Adam broke each of the Ten Commandments with this first sin:

Commandment #1: He chose new gods. Boston says: "He set up a new trinity: belly, self, and devil. He set all three ahead of the Lord; anything placed before Him is idolatry."

Commandment #2: He set up his own means of worshiping the Lord, rejecting the ordinance that the Lord had plainly appointed.

Commandment #3: He took the name of God in vain by despising His attributes and by profaning God's ordinance, His Word, and His works.

Commandment #4: He cast away the Sabbath state of rest in which the Lord created him and stained with unholiness everything God had given him.

Commandment #5: He refused to honor his Father in heaven, forgot his duty to all posterity, and yielded to the temptation of casting off authority.

Commandment #6: As covenant head, he murdered himself, his wife, and all his posterity. In one sense, he became the greatest murderer who ever lived.

Commandment #7: He committed adultery with the truth and Word of God, then tried to cover his nakedness with flimsy fig leaves.

Commandment #8: He stole what was not his own, against the will of His Owner and Creator.

Commandment #9: He bore false witness against the Lord by testifying that God's Word was not to be believed.

Commandment #10: He was discontent with the happy state in which God had placed him and coveted evil to his own ruination.

Meditate on the interconnectedness of the Ten Commandments. What does that teach us about the essence of law-breaking?

The fourth immediate consequence of sin was bitter alienation. Sin raised a barrier between Adam and Eve, so they tried to hide from each other. Immediately, open, honest communion was destroyed. More tragically, it cut them off from fellowship with God.

Are you experientially acquainted with this tragedy? How does sin affect your marital relationship? Your walk with God?

Dust thou art, and unto dust shalt thou return.
—GENESIS 3:19b

The final immediate consequence of sin was bitter death. "Dying thou shalt die," God had said. This statement particularly referred to spiritual death. The moment Adam and Eve ate the forbidden fruit, their relationship with God was severed. Their souls were immediately separated from Him, which is the most profound and serious result of sin.

The most apparent result of sin is what people see: sadness, agony, and suffering. But the deepest result of sin is the wedge it drives between God and man. Communion with God is what we were created for, what this world is all about, and what God still has in mind when He reforms and reshapes our lives in Christ; when that communion is broken, everything else lies broken at our feet.

Physical death and eternal death are also the wages of sin (Rom. 6:23), but those come later. Physical death comes to all who are not alive at Christ's return (Gen. 3:19b, "Dust thou art, and unto dust shalt thou return"), but eternal death in hell is for all who persist in unbelief until the end of their lives

The heart of alienation from God is spiritual death. By nature, we are born spiritually dead. That's our great problem; we are not just sick but dead to God by nature. We have no heart for God, no love for Him, and no communication with Him. Hatred for God marks us as children of Adam.

When Adam fell, we as his progeny fell lower than the rest of creation; we, the apex of creation, exchanged God's image for our own. In reaping spiritual death, we lost God's image in the narrow sense by replacing knowledge with ignorance, righteousness with unrighteousness, and holiness with perversity. As natural as it was prior to the fall to be righteous and holy, so after the fall it became natural to be unrighteous and unholy.

This alienation is so radical that it has plunged us into a state in which it is no longer possible for us to find our way back to God without His enabling grace. You and I, by nature, are both unwilling to be saved and unable to save ourselves. Paul says in Romans 3:10–12, "There is none righteous, no, not one: there is none that understandeth, there is none that seeketh after God. They are all gone out of the way, they are together become unprofitable; there is none that doeth good, no, not one."

So the immediate consequences of Adam and Eve's disobedience are bitter shame, bitter knowledge, bitter corruption, bitter alienation, and bitter death—all of which will soon lead to bitter expulsion (Gen. 3:22–24).

And I will put enmity between thee and the woman, and between thy seed and her seed; it shall bruise thy head, and thou shalt bruise his heel.

—GENESIS 3:15

God confronts Adam and Eve in the garden. The confrontation is inevitable because of the very nature of God. The God who is light must confront the crown of His creation, which is now darkness.

God is omniscient. Sin doesn't take him by surprise. God is always in control, and He is always love. In His covenant-keeping love, He does not want man to be swallowed up by darkness. He does not want him to run away and hide. In His grace, God longs for a renewed relationship with man. Adam's dreadful "I's" in Genesis 3:10—"I heard...," "I was afraid...," "I hid myself"—cannot thwart God's love. Even as Adam and Eve hide, the voice of God rings out in the garden, "Where art thou?" (3:9).

God's cry is the cry of love. He calls because He wants Adam and Eve to know where He is, even when they don't want Him to know where they are. He calls and confronts His children because He cares enough to love Adam and Eve with His sovereign, electing, omniscient, covenantal love!

Adam, Eve, and the serpent all make futile excuses for sinning. God pronounces sentences on each of them. The woman will experience pain and sorrow in what should have been her greatest fulfillment: bringing forth children and loving her husband (v. 16). The man will be separated from his own environment, so that even the ground will be cursed for his sake. His work will become tedious and difficult (vv. 17–19). The serpent will be forced to eat the dust and eventually will be defeated (vv. 14–15).

In verse 15, God promises to give life in the midst of death. He promises that the seed of Eve will wage war against Satan and his followers. The woman's seed will gain victory through the coming Messiah, who is the Seed. Satan will bruise the heel of Christ and His followers, but Christ will fatally crush Satan's head in Christ's own death (Heb. 2:14).

When Adam realizes this, he gives his wife a new name, "Eve," which means "life" or "the mother of all living." Through the promise of the coming Messiah (v. 15), Adam sees life (v. 20) in the midst of death (v. 19). Is that what the gospel means to you—seeing life in Christ in the midst of the death of your own sin? Thank God for the Seed of the woman, even Immanuel, God with us!

MILKHONEY

from Exodus

GERALD M. BILKES

*But the midwives feared God, and did not as the king of Egypt com-
manded them, but saved the men children alive.*

—EXODUS 1:17 (read Exodus 1)

The world is not the Christian's friend. Whether we recognize it or not, God's Word is clear that there is a real struggle that rages beneath the surface. It is a struggle between the seed of the serpent, Satan, and the seed of the woman (Gen. 3:15), the church of God throughout all ages. Satan's design is nothing less than to destroy the promised seed, as he showed through Herod in the widespread murder of babies around Bethlehem.

Our passage reminds us that this struggle is a real struggle. It is not simply fought in the invisible world of angels or demons; in this passage, mothers and fathers, midwives and children are participants in the struggle. It is playing itself out in birthing rooms and halls of government. It involves real people with names like Shiphrah and Puah, and later Jochebed and Miriam. It produces real toil and real anguish.

And the struggle is ongoing still today. Sin, Satan, and the world unite in assaulting and tempting Christians. According to the book of Revelation, the old serpent still tries to swallow up the church (Rev. 12:16). The apostle John said: "Marvel not if the world hate you" (1 John 3:13). Because they bear the stamp of God's approval in their lives, God's people, like Job, are a serious threat to Satan.

The best weapon in this struggle is true godly fear, as verse 17 indicates. That means saying "no" when God's Word says "no." It means taking the side of the people of God, even if it involves suffering affliction. Shiphrah and Puah were commended not because they plotted a coup or wielded the sword against the enemy, but simply because they obeyed God rather than men.

And remember, the outcome of this struggle between the serpent's seed and the woman's seed is not in doubt. Let the Pharaohs of this world issue their edicts and threaten with their rivers. It won't be long before they will lie at the bottom of the sea, with God's people safe on the distant shore.

And when she could not longer hide him, she took for him an ark of bulrushes, and daubed it with slime and with pitch, and put the child therein; and she laid it in the flags by the river's brink.

—EXODUS 2:3 (read Exodus 2:1–10)

How often does the thing that frightens us the most prove to be the finger of God to work something good? We see this in the Bible time and again. When Abraham was called to sacrifice Isaac, this trial gave him an even surer promise of blessing. Jacob lost Joseph in order in the end to gain the survival of his whole family. Likewise, Jochebed now had to entrust her son to the waters of the Nile so that he could come into Pharaoh's household, and later deliver Israel. The Psalmist describes the Lord's mysterious dealings this way: "Thy way is in the sea, and thy path in the great waters, and thy footsteps are not known" (Ps. 77:19).

It is impossible to imagine the anguish of Jochebed as she placed her three-month-old into a basket of bulrushes. What must have gone through her mind as she quietly journeyed to the Nile and left her son to what had become the watery grave of so many Hebrew children.

Yet, like Abraham, who was told to sacrifice Isaac, she showed great faith. The book of Hebrews tells us that it was faith that moved Moses' parents to hide their child for three months (Heb 11:23). Likewise, it must have been faith that enabled them to hide their son in this basket on the river of death. Faith is indeed the only way to go forward where God's footsteps are hidden. When His path in our lives seems mysterious, He is not asking us to understand every step.

Did Jochebed perhaps remember what God had promised Abraham (Gen. 15:13–14; see Acts 7:17)? Or did she and her husband think of Noah, who prepared an ark for the salvation of his house? Certainly, we know that God used both arks to fulfill His purpose in saving His people. Even Pharaoh's own river and his own daughter will serve the purpose of God.

Jochebed even received her son back for a time. This was something only the Lord could have devised. If we put our case into the hand of the Lord like Jochebed, we will not be put to shame. Sooner or later, and certainly in eternity, God's people will acknowledge and worship God's wisdom. The sooner we learn to do that here, the better off we will be.

*And she bare him a son, and he called his name Gershom: for he said, I
have been a stranger in a strange land.*

—EXODUS 2:22 (read Exodus 2:11–22)

Moses was a believer, and the Bible tells us that it was by faith that he forsook the palace of Pharaoh, taking the reproach of Christ (Heb. 11:24–15). But faith, especially young faith, has so much to learn.

The first lesson God taught Moses was that His clock does not run according to human standards. By his own calculation, the time had come to deliver the people. He was young; he was energetic; he was visionary. He had learned all the wisdom of Egypt and he knew Pharaoh's court. His people were in bitter bondage. But Moses was too early by forty years! God's time had not yet come.

Second, Moses had to learn that his success did not depend on his own abilities. When he took things into his own hands, killing the Egyptian, he was going in his own strength. Moses had to learn the timeless lesson: "Not by might, nor by power, but by my spirit, saith the LORD of hosts" (Zech. 4:6). In his own strength, Moses might kill one Egyptian, but what would he do with the millions of others? Did he think he was the angel of death that could go through the land, smiting all the firstborn so that his people would be freed? Israel needed much more than Moses. Israel needed the Lord.

Moses also learned from the rejection he experienced. One of his own people challenged him, asking who had made him a prince and judge over them. This was the first of the countless rejections he would face from his people. What was the Lord doing? He was preparing him by conforming him to the image of the great Deliverer—Christ—who also was despised and rejected.

And Moses was taught in his years of wandering. As he named his first son, Gershom, he spoke of it: "I have been a stranger in a strange land" (Ex. 2:22). Think of how these forty years of wandering must have helped to prepare him to lead the people of Israel through another forty years of wandering.

These are standard lessons in God's school of affliction. Through all of them, we, like Moses, need to learn: "He must increase, but I must decrease" (John 3:30). If you are in this school today, pray for a submissive heart and a teachable spirit, so that afterwards you can say, "It is good for me that I have been afflicted; that I might learn thy statutes" (Ps. 119:71).

*And the LORD said, I have surely seen the affliction of my people which
are in Egypt, and have heard their cry by reason of their taskmasters;
for I know their sorrows.* —EXODUS 3:7 (read Exodus 2:23–3:10)

Have you ever thought about what this burning bush signified? It was a
miraculous sign that revealed God's presence and power, His holiness and
condescension. The bush symbolized Israel in the furnace of Egypt, terrorized by hard bondage and affliction. And yet, like the bush Moses saw, Israel
was not consumed because God was with His people as He would be in
Jesus Christ. In Christ, the sympathizing High Priest, God now also can
say of His people: "I know their sorrows" (v. 7). From out of this mysterious
sign, God unveiled to Moses His purpose of saving Israel.

You might have thought that Moses would have leaped for joy. The
flames of fire that greeted him from the bush were like the strong rays of the
sun beginning to drive away the night of Israel's bondage. How the people
had sighed and cried for the morning (v. 23)! And now Moses was the first
to witness the magnificent dawning of a new day.

Instead of joy, however, "Moses hid his face; for he was afraid to look
upon God" (Ex. 3:6). The manifestation of the presence of God was so majestic, Moses could do nothing but hide his face. His reaction demonstrated
deep awe at the revelation of God.

Do you today share Moses' response of awe at God's revelation? You will,
if you also have a sense of the holiness of God. How often we read similar
words in Scripture: "Woe is me, for I am undone" (Isa. 6:5); "O LORD, I have
heard thy speech, and was afraid" (Hab. 3:2); "Lord I am not worthy that
thou shouldest come under my roof" (Matt. 8:8); "Depart from me, for I am
a sinful man, O Lord" (Luke 5:8).

We will share this response of awe if we have any sense of the great
distance between God and ourselves. God is in heaven and we are on the
earth. Moreover, there is our sin. When God comes down, He must stoop
down. This is what He was doing for Israel, for He told Moses: "I am come
down..." (Ex. 3:7–8).

You will have this response of awe especially if you know the miracle of
God's grace. God's people are not consumed because God is with them in
and through Jesus Christ. He knows His people's afflictions from the inside
out and has purchased their redemption with His own blood.

"Grant, Lord, that I would know such awe in my soul today."

And Moses said unto God, Who am I?... And God said unto Moses, I AM THAT I AM.
— EXODUS 3:11a, 14a (read Exodus 3:11–22)

Moses' opportunity appeared to be long gone. The man primed to be the deliverer of Abraham's oppressed seed seemed to have wasted his energy and intellect on sheep in the desert. All his good intentions of rescuing his people seemed to have disappeared. From Moses' side, there was no way back to his suffering people. So Moses objected in verse 11, "Who am I, that I should go?" After forty years of tending sheep in the wilderness, his ambitions of saving Israel seem to have completely disappeared.

Notice, the Lord did not reassure Moses by reminding him of his former status, his abilities, or even the lessons he learned in the solitude in the wilderness. Instead, He pointed Moses to Himself: "Certainly I will be with thee" (v. 12). He met Moses' question "Who am I?" with His own infinite "I will be." As Christ taught, only through losing our life do we find it (Matt. 16:25).

Moses' next objection centered on his people (vv. 13–18). They had rejected him the first time he came to them. Why would they accept him now? The Lord again answers this objection by making clear that Moses would not come in his own name, but in the name of the Lord, the "I Am that I Am." This name reveals the glorious, unchanging nature of the one only God. He is what He is, and everything that opposes Him will either bend or break. And so God reassured Moses: "They shall hearken to thy voice" (v. 18).

But what about Pharaoh, who certainly wouldn't listen, and would not let the people go? God silenced this objection as well. He promised that "he will let you go" (v. 20).

There is no objection the Bible does not address and answer. None of us can bring anything against the all-knowing One that He cannot answer. In fact, the Bible teaches us that, like Moses' mouth, our mouths must be stopped (Rom. 3:19). Through bowing under God's Word, we must lose our resistance and come under God's miraculous design of delivering His people. How can you bow under His Word today?

> *And the LORD said unto him, What is that in thine hand? And he said, A rod.*
> —EXODUS 4:2 (read Exodus 4:1–9)

The Lord was kind to fortify Moses' weak faith. We read here how He confirmed His Word with special signs, each one speaking powerfully of what He would do. The first sign involved the rod of Moses, which God instructed him to cast to the ground and then pick it up. This demonstrated how God's Word would frighten and even kill; and yet, that same rod would lead the people out of bondage.

The second sign was equally shocking. God instructed Moses to put his hand against his chest, and it turned completely leprous. When he returned it to his chest again, his hand was restored to health. This sign showed that the Lord has power over man's life and health. With His sovereign hand, He could bring down a plague to destroy life, and he could just as quickly remove the plague and restore life again. This is precisely what he would do in Egypt.

It is worth noticing that Moses' hand became leprous upon contact with his heart. At the deepest level, it is sin in the hearts of men that brings the judgments of God. Evil deeds spring from the heart (see Mark 7:21–23). Yet the second part of the sign proved that though God would bring terrible plagues upon the Egyptians, He would, in the meantime, be restoring Israel. Later on we read that He would heal His redeemed people and let none of Egypt's diseases come upon them (Ex. 15:26).

The third sign was the sign of irreversible judgment. Water, normally a sign of life, would be unalterably turned into blood and would bring death. While the two previous signs had both negative and positive elements, this one would only bring punishment.

What do the signs of God's power do to us? We read them in the Bible, but we also see them displayed around us today. Like Moses' signs, they are messages to confirm faith. Yet they also harden where there is no true faith. The Egyptians saw all these same signs but only hardened their hearts.

"Lord, soften my heart so that I would hear the message of Thy works of power."

*And the people believed: and when they heard that the LORD had vis-
ited the children of Israel, and that he had looked upon their affliction,
then they bowed their heads and worshipped.*
—EXODUS 4:31 (read Exodus 4:18–31)

God has promised to work all things together for good to them that love
Him (Rom. 8:28), but we often wonder how it will all happen. Moses must
have felt the same way as he left the burning bush. So many things still
needed to fall into place. Would He who called indeed be faithful?

First, God worked out everything in Moses' family (v. 18). When he
asked his father-in-law for permission to leave, Jethro simply answered, "Go
in peace." Family bonds gave way to the purpose of God.

Second, God worked out everything in Egypt. You can imagine that
Moses worried about the people in Egypt who wanted to kill him. Yet God
assured Moses: "all the men are dead which sought thy life" (v. 19). He would
no longer be in danger of revenge for his murder of the Egyptian.

Third, God worked things for good by sending his brother Aaron to be a
close work associate for Moses. God often lays a burden in the heart of two
men to accomplish a task. Think of David and Hushai or Paul and Barnabas.
How kind of the Lord to give His people faithful helpers in their work!

Fourth, God also worked by removing the unbelief of the Israelites (vv.
29–31). Earlier, Israel had rejected Moses rather than receiving him. But
now they believed and bowed their heads and worshiped (v. 31). Their hearts
were made submissive to God's purpose. The obstacles were overcome.

Finally, God even worked when He seemed to come against Moses! At
first, it seemed such a surprising twist when God came to meet Moses on
his way back to Egypt. After calling him, would God now kill him? This was
simply a test, as Jacob had at the Jabbok or Balaam on his way to Balak. God
often comes in a way that seems so contrary to what we think. However,
in the end, Moses came out of this encounter with God with an important
lesson. God visibly displayed that He would deliver His people through the
shedding of blood (vv. 24–26). This event also helped shape Moses for his
future work. God indeed worked all things for good—even the things that
seemed so contrary. Truly, "faithful is he that calleth you, who also will do it"
(1 Thess. 5:24).

And Moses returned unto the LORD, and said, Lord, wherefore hast thou so evil entreated this people? why is it that thou hast sent me?
— EXODUS 5:22 (read Exodus 5:1–23)

God's fatherly hand mixes prosperity and adversity in exactly the right proportions in His children's lives. The wonderful confirmations God gave Moses right after calling him made way for the string of adversities he would encounter next. This is a pattern we see more frequently in Scripture: David's victory over Goliath gave way to years of being pursued by Saul; the disciples, though they first found even devils subject to them, soon fled for their lives as their Master was apprehended. Even Paul, after bringing the gospel all over the Mediterranean and winning many new converts, had to suffer long years of imprisonment.

Why do God's ways often seem contradictory? The answer is: He orders all things as they suit the sanctification of His people and His own greater glory.

Imagine if Pharaoh had let the people go at the first word of Moses. The people might have thought that Pharaoh was quite harmless. Later, in the wilderness, they would have had all the more reason to complain and to wish to return to Egypt. God worked in such a way that Pharaoh's wickedness appeared in full color.

Or imagine what the people might have thought about Moses if his first word with Pharaoh had been successful. They may have been tempted to revere him instead of the Almighty. God always works in such a way that He alone gets the glory.

And just as the people needed to look away from Moses, Moses needed to look away from the people. Whatever illusions Moses had about the Israelites through this stretch of disappointments, he would have learned to seek approval from above rather than from people around him.

In our adversities, do we do what Moses did? Moses ended up before the Lord in the secret place. He said, "Lord, wherefore hast thou so evil entreated this people? why is it that thou hast sent me?" (v. 22). It is best to keep our complaints for a secret place before the Lord. Then He can and will answer us, as He did Moses: "I am the LORD" (Ex. 6:3). He teaches us: "My ways are higher than your ways." He is bringing glory to Himself. Is that sufficient for us?

I am the LORD.
— EXODUS 6:2 (read Exodus 6:1–30)

Any question we can ask ultimately has its deepest answer in God. One of our problems is that we often look for answers apart from God. When we think about the fact that God is all-sufficient, the Creator of all things seen and unseen, the One who works out all His purposes to His own glory, we should not be surprised that He is the final answer, the true source of all answers.

Chapter 5, which we just finished, began and ended with questions. In verse 2, Pharaoh had asked a question out of unbelief: "Who is the LORD, that I should obey his voice?" At the end of the chapter, in verse 22, we find the other question, now from Moses: "Lord, wherefore hast thou so evil entreated this people?" and, "why is it that thou hast sent me?" These were questions born out of bewilderment. He was confused because of the seeming contradiction between the promise of God and his own experience.

In chapter 6:1–11, we have God's answer to Moses, and it answers Pharaoh's question as well. It can be summed up in these words: "I am the LORD" (v. 2). It's an answer that centers on God's "I." There are at least fifteen "I's" in these verses. Each one unfolds the being, character, and purpose of the Lord. It is as if the Lord wants Moses and Israel to know: "What I say I am and will do is more certain than anything else in all the world. I am more concerned about My promises than you or anyone else can be. My reputation is at stake. My promise, My oath to Abraham, Isaac, and Jacob, is at stake. I cannot and will not go back on that. I am the LORD. I have established my covenant. I have heard. I have remembered. I will bring you out of bondage. I will redeem you and take you as My people. I am the LORD."

This answer should have stopped all the doubts of Moses, but he still managed to ask, "How shall Pharaoh hear me, who am of uncircumcised lips?" (vv. 12, 30). If only we could be more content to rest in the character and name of the eternal God! Our many questions and doubts would be answered by the one answer to everything.

And the Egyptians shall know that I am the LORD, when I stretch forth mine hand upon Egypt, and bring out the children of Israel from among them.
—EXODUS 7:5 (read Exodus 7:1–25)

Throughout history, many have failed to see God's control over natural events. We do the same today. Yet the Bible teaches that natural disasters are not outside of His control; rather, He is speaking through them.

First, they are tokens of God's power. It is true, the magicians of Egypt were able to imitate a few of the features of the signs. God allowed them to do this so that they would harden themselves even further in their pride. In reality, however, their power was no comparison to that of the Lord. They could never reverse the sign. At most they could occasionally replicate the miracle on a small scale.

Second, natural disasters are warnings to the impenitent. Each plague threatened Pharaoh with further devastation and destruction. Every week that Pharaoh held onto the Israelites put his country at risk of further destruction.

Third, natural disasters tell us to turn away all our confidence from the earth and people in it. Just as the Egyptians worshipped creation, modern man puts his confidence in things he sees and makes. And just as each plague took aim at a god of Egypt, so hurricanes, earthquakes, forest fires, tsunamis, and epidemics challenge the confidence we place in people and things.

Fourth, natural disasters often harden many hearts. With each judgment, Pharaoh's heart became harder rather than softer. How many people today blame God when disaster strikes and lift their fist against Him? Is this not evidence also of a hardening of our hearts?

Finally, natural disasters are footsteps of Christ's return to finally deliver His people. Like birth-pangs ultimately bring about the birth of a baby, so these plagues were used by God to birth Israel as a nation. Out of Egypt He called His son (Hos. 11:1). Creation still groans in travail, anticipating the "manifestation of the sons of God" (Rom. 8:19).

Micah 6:9 tells us to "hear ye [the voice of] the rod" and Christ has called us to discern the signs of the times in Matthew 16:3. Do we have ears to hear in this way?

And when Pharaoh saw that the rain and the hail and the thunders were ceased, he sinned yet more, and hardened his heart, he and his servants.

— EXODUS 9:34 (read Exodus 9:22–35)

God's dealings with Pharaoh have been recorded as a beacon of warning for all generations. The many pages devoted to God's dealings with Pharaoh are filled with warnings, threats, and reprieves. And they record for us the religion of Pharaoh — despite what many might think, Pharaoh was not a man without religion. Yet this religion did not proceed from a heart set free to love God and His attributes. It was the religion of an unbroken spirit.

All of this prompts us to examine whether our religion is true or not. Hearing powerful sermons and seeing powerful displays of God's glory does not set us apart from Pharaoh. Even Pharaoh's own superstitious magicians were forced to acknowledge: "This is the finger of God" (Ex. 8:19).

Neither does asking someone to pray for you set you apart from Pharaoh. Pharaoh did plenty of that (Ex. 8:8). Receiving answered prayers does not set you apart from Pharaoh. Pharaoh received many answers to his prayers that the plagues be reversed (Ex. 8:10). Acknowledging your sin and wickedness does not set you apart from Pharaoh (v. 27). Neither does simply acknowledging the Lord's justice or praying for forgiveness (Ex. 10:17).

It's a sobering fact that being willing to surrender everything except the smallest part of what God demands does not set you apart from Pharaoh either (Ex. 11:24). Pharaoh excels many so-called Christians of our own time who believe they don't need to surrender much of anything.

Don't be deceived: simply because people acknowledge something of God does not mean they truly fear God. When Christ was on earth, the demons acknowledged the deity of Christ (Mark 3:11), just as they also acknowledged the true servants of God (Acts 16:17). James tells us the demons believe and tremble (James 2:19). Paul tells us that one day every knee shall bow and every tongue confess, including the inhabitants in hell, that Christ is Lord.

So what sets a true believer apart? The mercy of God revealed to our souls, bringing about a godly sorrow that leads to repentance not to be repented of. "The sacrifices of God are a broken spirit: a broken and a contrite heart, O God, thou wilt not despise" (Ps. 51:17). Has His mercy been revealed in your heart?

> *But against any of the children of Israel shall not a dog move his tongue,*
> *against man or beast: that ye may know how that the LORD doth put*
> *a difference between the Egyptians and Israel.*
>
> —EXODUS 11:7 (read Exodus 11:1–10)

Scripture tells us about a line of division that runs through the human race: a division that separates God's people from those who are not His people. In our passage we read that "the LORD doth put a difference between the Egyptians and Israel" (v. 7).

It is important to remember that this is a sovereign difference. It is not owing to anything in God's people themselves. Our passage says that the Lord puts a difference there. Paul would say it like this: "Therefore hath he mercy on whom he will have mercy, and whom he will he hardeneth" (Rom. 9:18).

This difference is a gracious difference. It wasn't that God saw something in the people to move Him to deliver them. No, it is solely owing to the Lord's unmerited love for His people. He had made a promise to Abraham, and He would graciously remember His promise and oath. Out of love, He delivered them from bondage, sanctified them, and made them a kingdom of priests, a holy nation, to serve Him. It would be a visible difference, and a dramatic one. Already with the fourth plague, God put a division between His people and the Egyptians (8:23). It was a sign to the Egyptians; God's plagues were not going to come down indiscriminately. In Goshen, and among the people of God, there would be safety. As the plagues progressed, the difference became all the more evident until, in the tenth plague, the difference would be the starkest. What a vast difference! Even the animal kingdom would hush before it. No dog would as much as growl at the Israelites as they leave the land (v. 7).

Finally, what an enduring difference! The consequences would be lasting. It would be a picture of the great gulf that is fixed between those in heaven and those in hell. On the one side of the line, people would lose their firstborn. But on the other side, people would lose, once and for all, their oppression.

Lord, make me experience that difference and understand Paul's wonder when he wrote: "For who maketh thee to differ from another? and what hast thou that thou didst not receive?" (1 Cor. 4:7).

And the people bowed the head and worshipped.
— EXODUS 12:27b (read Exodus 12:1–42)

God usually sends His blessings not singly, but in bunches. Just as His rainbow has many colors, so His grace is manifold. The great privilege of Passover illustrates the variety of blessings all bound up in the blood on the doorposts.

Behind the blood on the doorposts, there was, first of all, safety. The avenging angel would pass by any doors marked with blood. Israel's firstborn were safe as long as they were behind those doors. Egyptian homes that were not marked with blood on the outside soon saw blood on the inside, as the angel of death claimed their firstborn. But there was safety through the blood.

Behind the blood, there was provision. Israel was not cowering in the corners of their houses, relieved just to be alive. Of all things, they were eating and being nourished. The lamb both saved and supported the people. There was provision behind the blood.

Behind the blood, there was also celebration. God called it "a feast." The day would be a day of mourning for Egypt, but a day of solemn rejoicing for Israel. The people who had slaved so long without rest would now enjoy a "holy convocation" without any work at all.

Behind the blood, there were families. God chose doorposts for the blood, not chairs or clothes. God appointed a way of salvation that had whole families in view. The children were not left to dig some hole for safety by themselves. The Lord appointed a lamb for every house, and the father protected his family behind the blood in obedience to the Lord's command.

Behind the blood, there were answers. Clearly, the children would have questioned: "What mean ye by this service?" (v. 26). But, thankfully, behind the blood there were answers. These answers pointed to the Lord, to His grace, and deliverance. "It is the sacrifice of the LORD'S passover, who passed over the houses of the children of Israel in Egypt, when he smote the Egyptians, and delivered our houses" (v. 27). The Egyptians had no time for questions, much less answers. All they could say was: "We be all dead men."

It is not surprising, then, that behind the blood there was worship. "The people bowed the head and worshipped" (v. 27). God's manifold blessings cannot but fill the soul of those who receive them with worship and adoration, as we find it in the Song of Moses and the Lamb: "Great and marvelous are thy works, Lord God Almighty" (Rev. 15:3).

Are you behind the blood of the Lamb? If so, give thanks to the Lord for all His marvelous works then and now.

One law shall be to him that is homeborn, and unto the stranger that sojourneth among you.
—EXODUS 12:49 (read Exodus 12:43–51)

The gospel of God's grace in Jesus Christ is attractive, not to the natural man, but to those whom God ordained unto salvation, from every tribe and tongue. In the Old Testament, we read of Rahab the Canaanite, Ruth the Moabite, Barzillai the Gileadite, Uriah the Hittite, and Naaman the Syrian. After Pentecost, we find Parthians and Medes, strangers of Rome, and Jews and proselytes. God's purpose is to take people from all nations, wash them in the blood of His Son, and fit them for an inheritance that is incorruptible and unfading.

The Passover was a message that sounded this same truth loud and clear. Thus we read of even strangers coming to hide behind the blood. The blood-stained doorposts gave visible expression to the gospel of safety through the shedding of blood. It was the preaching to the world around them that God would save through a Substitute. Each doorpost proclaimed the only way to come through the judgment of God safe and secure.

We don't live in ceremonial times, but do people around us hear the message of the blood? We should long to have people ask us: "How can I find a gracious God? How can I be received into His favor?"

How did these strangers come to shelter beneath the lamb that God provided? It was not by force or military might. It was not through buying converts for money. Neither was it simply whoever was intrigued by Israel's ceremonies and wanted to join in without being marked as the people of God. No, that is not the way (v. 45). Anyone who wishes to reap the benefits of salvation must submit to the way of salvation. He must personally receive the sign of blood, which in those days meant circumcision for every male in the household. In our day, it is through faith in the blood of Christ. That is how strangers come in and foreigners become citizens.

Have we come as strangers of the commonwealth of Israel to take shelter beneath the blood? Christ's cross still preaches to everyone, far and near. Because of His blood, there is room for the stranger. The gospel calls out: "Come; for all things are now ready" (Luke 14:17). Those who come in faith and repentance will join with the people of God, built upon Christ into the household of God and inhabited by Him (Eph. 2:19, 22).

He took not away the pillar of the cloud by day, nor the pillar of fire by night, from before the people.

—EXODUS 13:22 (read Exodus 13:1–22)

Some people reserve their religion for their baptism, their times of penance, or their death bed. How easy it is to observe high and holy days, but little or nothing in between. But God ordained it differently for His people. The gospel is for every day; every day we need to live out of the Substitute, Jesus Christ. So we must remind ourselves frequently throughout the day that life is only through death, and safety through surrender.

God did not ordain His laws and statutes for Israel as ways to maintain eternal life, much less to earn eternal life, but instead to surround the people with the gospel in everyday life. When their first child was born, the people had to remember the gospel of the Firstborn (vv. 1–2). Every spring, even in the land flowing with milk and honey, the people had to remind themselves of the gospel through keeping the ordinance of unleavened bread (vv. 3–10). Every time an animal gave birth for the first time, the people had to remind themselves how God had redeemed them (vv. 11–16).

For that same reason, the people had to carry the bones of Joseph with them (vv. 17–19). As they accompanied them day after day, these bones preached the promise made by God to their fathers. Every time an Israelite saw Joseph's coffin, he or she could remember that God had promised an inheritance, no matter what would happen.

Finally, God gave the people a pillar of cloud and a pillar of fire to remind them of His care and support, His direction and presence throughout each day and night (vv. 20–22). No part of the day, no season of the year or of life, would be without a witness to the gospel.

It's no wonder that God the Teacher instructed the people with signs on their hands and frontlets between their eyes (vv. 9, 16). Let's read the gospel in the sun that rises in the morning and sets at night. Let's see it in the newborn child in our family, or the obituaries that we read. Let's see it in the seasons of life. And above all, let's fill our minds with the Word of God, and make clear to others: the gospel is for every day.

And the LORD said unto Moses, Wherefore criest thou unto me? speak unto the children of Israel, that they go forward.
— EXODUS 14:15 (read Exodus 14:1–22)

People often suppose that the life of faith removes all struggles, questions, and contradictions. Just one look at our chapter proves that this is not so. Israel might be delivered out of slavery, but they are not yet delivered out of struggles.

First, there is a struggle over our condition. Think of Israel, freed from their old master; yet the old tyrant was still at their heels, breathing down their necks. Israel might have Egypt behind them, but they have the Red Sea before them. They may be rid of the whips; yet now there are swords and spears clanging behind them. Similarly, believers can struggle over what their spiritual condition really is. They have been made free from sin (Rom. 6:18); yet they still struggle with their old nature. They wonder: if I am the Lord's child, why do I struggle like I do?

Then there can be such a struggle over our circumstances. Believers can respond in as conflicted a way as Israel at the Red Sea. Not long ago, Israel groaned and longed to be rid of the bondage they felt; but they groaned to be back in their bondage (v. 12). Likewise, believers can feel very conflicted. The man with the demon-possessed son said it well: "Lord, I believe; help thou mine unbelief" (Mark 9:24).

Next, there can be the struggle over the commands of God. On the one hand, we are told to "wait on the Lord"; on the other, "strive to enter in at the strait gate." Likewise, Israel was told to "stand still," and immediately thereafter, "Go forward." So often there seems to be a contradiction in the command of God and the reality we see around us. In front of Israel, the water clearly closed off their path. Yet, precisely there, God commanded them, "Go forward."

How honest and forthright the Bible is about these struggles. Many Psalms also speak about them at length. These things have been recorded for "our learning, that we through patience and comfort of the scriptures might have hope" (Rom. 15:4). Though the life of faith comes with these struggles, faith helps God's children resolve them—and when they can't resolve them, to continue believing, knowing that the resolution lies in the future. No wonder the disciples prayed: "Lord, increase our faith" (Luke 17:5).

The LORD is my strength and song, and he is become my salvation: he is my God, and I will prepare him an habitation; my father's God, and I will exalt him.

—EXODUS 15:2 (read Exodus 15:1–19)

When God had originally called Moses, He taught him the meaning of His Name: "I am that I am." After that, He proved the truth of His Name in the plagues. Egypt would learn that there was none like Him, and Israel would experience the benefit of that. But now, finally, Israel echoes what God had both given and proven. "The LORD is his name" (v. 3). This whole song unfolds that truth: "He is what He is; He is His Name." What a glorious echo this song is! Through the Scriptures, this song has reverberated down the ages and over all the earth. It is Israel's testimony of who God is.

The Lord is the incomparable God. "Who is like unto thee, O LORD, among the gods" (v. 11)? Bring forward any so-called god, and see if there is even any comparison. Baal, Dagon, Mammon, Herod, Caesar—they are nothing. It is not even worthy comparing anything about them to the Lord.

He is the glorious God. The text says that He is "glorious in holiness" (v. 11). His uniqueness and purity are such that there is no one so majestic and filled with splendor. He is "fearful in praises" (v. 11). The only fitting response to God is awe and praise. He is "doing wonders." His actions are entirely in a league of their own—so mysterious, miraculous, and marvelous. He is powerful (vv. 3, 6, 12). He is merciful (v. 13). He is sovereign and He will reign forever (v. 18).

Moreover, Moses sang that He is "my God" (v. 2). He is a personal God, a God who is approachable, a God who is near. He is not a God only of the past—"my father's God" (v. 2)—but also a God for today. Through His deeds of redemption, the Lord has become "my strength and song." He is "my salvation" and "my God" (v. 2).

Finally, He takes His people to live with Him. He guides them to His own "holy habitation" (v. 13), the place, "which thou hast made for thee to dwell in" (v. 17). Someone once said: "The palace doors will close behind a man whom an earthly king pardons. But when God pardons, heaven's doors don't close, but rather open." There is no other God like that. Let this truth draw you to worship this God throughout today.

For I am the LORD that healeth thee.

—EXODUS 15:26b (read Exodus 15:23–27)

Most of us know what an unexpectedly bitter drink does to a person. It makes our bodies shudder, and we quickly spit it out and reach for something to help get rid of the taste. But most of us do not know what it is to go three days without water. Even though the victory of the Red Sea was still fresh in the minds of the Israelites, intense thirst had a way of reshuffling all their feelings and emotions. Three days is a long time without water; when this thirsty nation saw water in the distance, their expectations were heightened and they must have run to slacken their thirst. The first people to reach the water probably went in for a deep gulp, only to come up convulsing and complaining: "Marah, marah." It's as if they were saying, "If anything defines bitter, this is it."

Bitter providences often sadly elicit bitter perspectives. That is what we learn from Israel's experience at Marah. The physical convulsions were not half as strong as the spiritual convulsions that racked these people fresh out of Egypt. The people looked at the water and cried, "Marah." But God could have looked at the people and said, "Marah. These people are bitter."

Are you shuddering over some bitter providence God has given you to drink in your life? Listen to the cure God's Word outlines for us here. It involves, first of all, submitting to God's gracious provision (v. 25). Second, it involves diligent obedience to the voice of the Lord (v. 26). That is how the waters were cured. When Moses obeyed what the Lord showed him, soon sweet waters were lavishing the people's thirst.

Let's listen to God's gracious instructions throughout His Word. Throughout Scripture, He instructs us to look to His Son, who drank the bitter cup of the wrath of God, so that there would be a cup of blessing for all who come to the waters without money, and without price (Isa. 55:1). "If you will diligently hearken to My voice, you will lose your bitterness. Do you remember those diseases the Egyptians suffered because of their rebellion? You won't suffer them. Remember, I am the Healer. I heal through My Word. I can heal your bitterness. You will be healed by hearkening." That is the cure for a bitter spirit.

This is the bread which the LORD hath given you to eat.
—EXODUS 16:15b (read Exodus 16:1–36)

When a mother begins to feed her child solid food, she feeds him in such a way as to teach very important lessons, such as: he can expect food from his mother. He should eat three times a day. If he cries for food in the middle of the night, he will need to wait until the morning. As God fed His child, Israel, in the wilderness, He also taught her many such lessons—lessons that we, too, must learn—with respect to the Word of God and especially with respect to Christ, the true Bread from heaven.

The first lesson manna teaches us is that we lack the resources we need to live physically and spiritually. In Deuteronomy 8:3, we read that God allowed them to become hungry in order to teach them that they need God's Word to live spiritually. Not only did they lack the resources, but their murmuring showed that they didn't deserve God's provisions. They wouldn't toil for the food, so they wouldn't deserve the food.

The second lesson is that heaven has greater blessings to give us than we expect or appreciate. We might think that grain only grows on fields, but God tells us that He can "rain bread from heaven" (v. 4)! Think of that! Food dropped down from heaven. Isn't that what God does in His Word, and in Christ, the true Bread sent down from heaven (John 6:55)?

The third lesson is that heaven's blessings are glorious. The quails at night and the manna in the morning come with a revelation of God's glory (see vv. 7, 13). The people could look out on the horizon and see the radiance of God's splendor as He gloriously provided. When we read God's Word, we should do so with God's glory on our minds and hearts.

The fourth lesson is that God's provisions are always sufficient, suitable, and sanctifying. There is always enough, and these supplies suit our needs perfectly. But God's provisions should also sanctify us, and teach us the Sabbath principle, as they did the people (vv. 27–29), since everything should tend to the worship of God.

The final lesson we learn from the manna is our continued ignorance and dependence. When Israel first saw these little small round entities on the ground, they confessed their ignorance and called it "what is this?" Since manna never lost this name, each time it was mentioned, its meaning confronted the people with their ignorance and need to depend on God's grace.

Jehovah-nissi: For the LORD hath sworn that the LORD will have war with Amalek from generation to generation.
—EXODUS 17:15b–16 (read Exodus 17:8–16)

Israel had no earthly skill in war. These ex-slaves had been used to trowels, not swords. What were an unwieldy mass of men, women, and children on foreign territory to do against a race of skilled desert fighters like Amalek? This picture is not unlike that of a group of believers who, although they are redeemed from sin, are of themselves no match to the skill and experience of Satan, a murderer from the beginning. So how can believers prevail?

First, we need to know and aim at our enemy. So far, Israel has accumulated a record of aiming its attacks at Moses and Aaron or God. However, through the instrumentality of Moses and Aaron, Israel recruits a fighting force and mounts an assault on Amalek. If at this point Israel had begun to murmur or turn on Moses, their bodies would lie strewn throughout the wilderness.

Second, we need to fix our hopes on heaven. Moses raised his hands and the rod of God up to Him who is enthroned in the heavens. This showed that earthly help was vain compared to heavenly help.

Third, we need to realize that a human mediator will not suffice. Though a great man, Moses was a man of the same passions as we. His hands grew heavy, and Aaron and Hur had to supply what was lacking in Moses. Thank God, there is Christ, who can sympathize with the feelings of our own infirmities. Yet He is also higher than the heavens, set down at the right hand of the Father, and interceding for His people under attack (Heb. 7:26).

Fourth, we need to persevere until the enemy is routed. We cannot throw in the towel halfway through or close to the end. Moses and Joshua settled for nothing less than victory.

Fifth, we need to find all we need in the name of the Lord, which the Bible calls a strong tower (Prov. 18:10). What did Moses actually do when he raised up the rod of God to heaven? He was lifting up the name of Jehovah—the God of the Bush, the God of the Red Sea. That was his banner. "Some trust in chariots, and some in horses: but we will remember the name of the LORD our God" (Ps. 20:7). That's how we can and will prevail.

And Moses told his father in law all that the LORD had done unto Pharaoh and to the Egyptians for Israel's sake, and all the travail that had come upon them by the way, and how the LORD delivered them.

—EXODUS 18:8 (read Exodus 18:1–27)

For the Christian church, this life brings not only pain, but also gain. There is not just conflict, but also victory. Not every stranger who appears on the horizon is an adversary. He may be an advantage, like Jethro was. The name "Jethro" means "gain," or "advantage." God's people gained much when Jethro, the priest of Midian, came to visit them in the wilderness of Sinai.

1. Moses gained his wife and children. We are not told why, but apparently Moses had sent them back to Jethro. And now he received them back again. From now on, they would journey together with the people of God. They would partake of the manna together, follow the pillar of cloud and the pillar of fire together. Together they would come under the blood of the covenant. How wonderful it is when a whole family truly serves God! That is real gain.

2. Jethro gained a glorious perspective of God's dealing. Jethro had already heard some reports (v. 1), but now Moses told him all. What a sermon that must have been! Moses exalted the name of the Lord as he told Jethro of all God's wonderful works. What great gain is to be had when people hear and believe the great works of God!

3. The Lord gained a worshiper. Jethro exalted the Lord by blessing Him and confessing Him. He publicly attested to the fact that God is over all and above all. He showed that he understood God's excellency and majesty, and how God looks upon pride (v. 11). Jethro even led Israel in worship as they offered a burnt offering and ate bread with the elders before the Lord.

4. Israel gained a counselor. When Jethro saw how Israel's mediator, Moses, was being overextended, he proved to be a suitable counselor. "Hearken now unto my voice, I will give thee counsel" (v. 19). Jethro's advice helped Moses be a more effective mediator to Israel. He would stand between the people and the Lord, teaching them the will of God and bringing the people's cases to the Lord, which were too much for the other appointed rulers.

5. Midian gained a witness. Jethro was not to stay with the people of Israel. Like Naaman the Syrian, the Ethiopian eunuch, and so many others, God sent Jethro back to his own country to be a witness of the power and grace of God.

Ye have seen what I did unto the Egyptians, and how I bare you on eagles' wings, and brought you unto myself.

—EXODUS 19:4 (read Exodus 19:1–8)

When God's people arrive in Zion at last, it will not be through their own strength. They will not have loosed their bonds on their own and set out as pilgrims and strangers. Their own strength will not have saved them. It will not have been their own ingenuity that will have delivered them from temptations, assaults, and discouragements. It will be free grace alone that makes all the difference.

If it had been up to Israel, they would have stayed in Egypt in their hard service and bondage. But like an eagle who flutters violently around the nest where her young ones have long been comfortable, God had troubled Egypt. He had so jostled Egypt that His people could not but come out of the place that was so severely constricting them.

If it had been up to Israel at the Red Sea, they would have gone back to their taskmasters and begged them to bake bricks once again. But like the eagle who spreads out her strong wings to catch her falling and fledgling young, the Lord came under His complaining children and brought them safely across.

If it had been up to Israel, they would have returned to the fleshpots of Egypt instead of waiting for God's daily provision of bread from heaven. They would have stoned their mediator, Moses, at Rephidim, and thought nothing of the sure death that would have awaited them without him.

If we've begun the journey towards the heavenly Canaan, it is because eagles' wings have jolted us out of our habitats. If we've come anywhere on the road that leads to heaven, it's because God's eagle's wings have carried us along. If we've been kept from falling prey to our mortal enemies, it is because of His wings under us. Should we not join Israel in saying: "If it had not been the Lord that was on our side, our enemies would have swallowed us up quickly"?

Especially when we think of where God is bringing His children, that is, to Himself, we can be sure that it is free grace alone. How can a high and holy God receive such pathetic and murmuring people? Only through the love He has like a mother eagle towards her children.

Give thanks today for the protecting and guiding wings the Father has used in your life.

I am the LORD thy God, which have brought thee out of the land of Egypt, out of the house of bondage.

—EXODUS 20:2 (read Exodus 20:1–17)

When God delivers His people from the service of sin, He brings them into His own service, which is a lovely service. God's people look back on their service of sin with holy hatred. Its master was merciless, its rigors were severe, and its wages were death. That is why their service of the Lord is a service of love for their Redeemer and Lord.

It is a thankful service. We can never repay the Lord for so great a deliverance, bought at such a great price: the price of the blood of the Son of God. How can we not but be thankful?

It is a freeing service. Only in the Lord's service is there true freedom. When rightly understood, every one of God's commandments keeps us from enslaving ourselves to our idols and lusts. A covetous person is a slave to his desires. An idolater is a slave to his idols. A Sabbath-breaker is a slave to his work or pleasures. Only in the Lord's service is there true freedom.

It is an exclusive service (1st commandment). God does not tolerate anything ahead of Him or beside Him. He is Lord over all. God's people have a holy preoccupation with the Lord. No one else deserves their affection and their exclusive attention like the Lord. Anything that tries to compete with Him must be unmasked and avoided.

It is a spiritual service (2nd commandment). It cannot be tied to things touched, tasted, and handled. Moreover, it is a sincere service (3rd commandment). It cannot be approached formally or insincerely. It is a service that affords rest (4th commandment). God entered in His rest and calls His people into that same rest.

It is an all-encompassing service. It honors God-appointed authorities, like father and mother (5th commandment). It honors the life that He created (6th commandment). It is a service that honors the bonds of marriage and forbids everything that destroys them (7th commandment). It respects private property and good stewardship (8th commandment). It is a service that honors the truth (9th commandment). It directs even the smallest desire of the heart and claims that for God's service (10th commandment).

As you walk through your day, consider all the benefits and rewards God has built into these commandments. If you are in the Lord's service, offer thanks for the freedom it has given you!

And if the servant shall plainly say, I love my master, my wife, and my children; I will not go out free.

—EXODUS 21:5 (read Exodus 21:1–11)

In Israel, two regular events would remind them of their redemption from Egypt and the privilege of serving the Lord. The one event would go something like this. "Servant, your day of freedom has come." That is what a master was to say to a Hebrew servant who had served him for six years. "I can't keep you in bondage forever. Just as God redeemed our fathers from the bondage of Egypt, He also wants you to go free. This is a new day for you. Thank you for your service. I can no longer keep you against your will. Today you're free." Down the centuries, this announcement of freedom would ring to remind Israel that God had had respect to the bondage of Israel. The freed Israelites could not turn around and become harsh masters who never gave their servants freedom.

However, there could on occasion also be this event, which also had a spiritual significance: the servant could respond to his master and say, "Master, I do not desire to go out in the world to fend for myself. I love you and I want to stay with you and serve you with my wife and children." Then the master and the servant would go to the judge. The servant would receive a sign, and whoever saw this sign would know: "This is a servant for life. He loves his master and prefers to serve him rather than make it on his own." This would be a reminder that Israel was to love the Lord, their new Master, and seek to serve Him with their families.

The psalmist of Psalm 116 saw the spiritual significance of this second scenario. Like that servant at the gate of the city, he sang: "I love the LORD" (Ps. 116:1). The Lord had delivered him from the sorrows of death and the pains of hell; he knew of no better life than serving the Lord. "O Lord, truly, I am thy servant; I am thy servant and the son of thine handmaid: thou hast loosed my bonds" (Ps. 116:16).

If there was ever reason to love a human master, there is infinitely more reason to love the Lord God. Everyone He has truly freed has in turn desired to serve Him. There is no Master like Him! Are you in His service?

*By little and little I will drive them out from before thee, until thou
be increased, and inherit the land.*

—EXODUS 23:30 (read Exodus 23:20–33)

God's children often can be discouraged that they are not making faster progress in obtaining the promises God has laid out for them in His Word. A lot
of the Christian life seems to be striving, seeking, and losing, with little attain-
ing, finding, and prevailing. They long to see their mortal enemies routed in
one day—or at least one year. They desire to see more love for Christ, more
delight in God's ordinances, more access in prayer, and so on. This is the
lesson the Israelites found when they were taking the land: alongside our
Jerichos, there are the Ais; alongside our victories, there are our defeats.

It is actually comforting that God has promised that He would drive out
the enemies "by little and little" (v. 29). He would do it. If it depended on us,
there would not even be the little. He makes sure that the enemies don't win
little by little, but that His people inherit the promises bit by bit, until they
possess it fully, beyond this life.

How gracious of the Lord to tell His people of the slow progress before-
hand, lest they be discouraged beyond measure. If you know a Christian who
has just begun to tread the long and stony road to Zion, tell him what the
Lord tells His people in verse 29: "I will not drive them out from before
thee in one year." The devil will meet certain destruction, but not necessarily
tomorrow. One day, sin will be gone forever, but not necessarily next year.
Amelek might still continue a few more years before its cup of iniquity has
reached to overflowing.

Let me instead set my sights on the Angel who has gone before me
(v. 20). He is the Pioneer and Captain of my salvation. As surely as He has
entered His inheritance, so certainly will I prevail through Him, albeit "little
by little." Let me look for that "little" that He has given for today. The worst
thing I can do is to compromise with the enemy little by little (v. 32). "Lord,
forgive me for all my little compromises. Let me content myself with Thy
little conquests even as I pray for larger conquests."

The Lord encouraged the people by referring to His hornets (v. 28). They
are stronger than Canaan's hosts. He's unleashing them swarm by swarm to
prepare His people's way. How awful to have to run little by little from God's
hornets until you fall into perdition. How much better it is to come behind
God's hornets and possess His promises—even if it is "little by little."

And it came to pass, when Moses went out unto the tabernacle, that all the people rose up, and stood every man at his tent door, and looked after Moses, until he was gone into the tabernacle.

—EXODUS 33:8 (read Exodus 33:1–23)

What was Moses to do? His heart must have been terribly grieved. On the one hand, he had watched while God had engraved with His own finger the words: "I am the LORD thy God." He had seen how God had come and bound himself to this band of freed slaves. He had heard every commandment, and would have agreed with the psalmist: "Righteous art thou, O LORD, and upright are thy judgments" (Ps. 119:137).

But, on the other hand, he had seen the graven image by which Israel had said back to the Lord: "Thou art not our God. Instead, this calf is our god." How Moses must have been grieved! Again he would have agreed with the psalmist: "Rivers of waters run down mine eyes, because they keep not thy law" (Ps. 119:138).

As a result of their sins, God had threatened to consume this people, despite all He had done for them. But Moses, their mediator, could not abide it. He went to the tabernacle (Ex. 33:8) to intercede for these law-breaking people, like the great Mediator would do in the fullness of time—He would go to the tabernacle not only to pray for transgressors, but to pay for them with His own life's blood. He would say to His Father: "I love Thee and Thy honor, but I also love these law-breaking people. Put their law-breaking upon my account. I will repay. Accept My blood in their place, and let these go their way."

This Old Testament picture of Christ's intercession had an instructive effect on the people.

1. They humbled themselves. They mourned, took off their ornaments, and sought the Lord (Ex. 33:4, 6, 7). They humbled themselves in the sight of the Lord until He would again lift them up.
2. They stood afar off. They watched as their mediator went into the tabernacle on their behalf. They could not follow; they could not even draw near. Not only physically, but spiritually, too, they stood afar off until the matter was settled.
3. They worshiped. Not long ago, they had bowed before the calf; now they bowed under the Lord and His righteous judgment.

How much greater even Christ's perfect intercession is! How can you worship Him today?

And the LORD descended in the cloud, and stood with him there, and proclaimed the name of the LORD.

—EXODUS 34:5 (read Exodus 34:1–9; 29–35)

"God is light and in him there is no darkness at all" (1 John 1:5). In Psalm 80, the psalmist prays: "Thou that dwellest between the cherubim, shine forth" (v. 1). That is certainly what Moses experienced on the mount with the Lord. Thirty-one chapters back, Moses had hid his face. At that time, there in the burning bush, the sun had begun to shine. Now, however, it was like the noon sun.

Here in the secret place, Moses would experience what it means to live in the light of God's countenance. He had asked for the Lord to show him His glory (Ex. 33:18). God told him that he couldn't see His face and live (Ex. 33:20), but we still read that he knew God "face to face" (Deut. 34:10).

The only explanation we are given is that God mercifully kept him from succumbing under the brilliance that the Lord is in the radiance of His splendor. God says, "I will put thee in a clift of the rock, and will cover thee with my hand while I pass by" (Ex. 33:22). Moses experienced what the psalmist desires of the Lord: "in the secret of his tabernacle shall he hide me" (Ps. 27:5).

Truly, God was a Sun and a Shield for Moses (Ps. 84:10). God is of purer eyes than to behold evil and cannot look upon sin (Hab. 1:13). For the sake of Christ and the darkness that He would go through on the cross, God accepted Moses and both shined on him and shielded him at the same time.

By grace, for Christ's sake, Moses was privileged to walk before God's face and not be consumed. Here on Mount Horeb, he was allowed to behold the beauty of the Lord and inquire in His temple. In God's light, he saw light (Ps. 36:9).

Do you see the greater excellence of the New Testament Mediator? He came down, this time from the bosom of the Father. Though His glory was hid from men in general, nevertheless, John and the church confessed it: "We beheld his glory, the glory as of the only begotten of the Father, full of grace and truth" (John 1:14). "Open our eyes, Lord, that in the darkness of our sin we might behold this shining Mediator."

And when the cloud was taken up from over the tabernacle, the children of Israel went onward in all their journeys.

—EXODUS 40:36 (read Exodus 40:34–38)

Moving on in life can be difficult, whether we are in a difficult stage or an easy one. With all the blessings Israel had received, it would have been understandable if, like Peter on the Mount of Transfiguration, Israel had said: "We have built a tabernacle and God is with us. Let us stay here." Yet, as long as they are on this side of eternity, God wants His people to go "onward in all their journeys" (v. 36). The Christian life is marked not by setting up camp, but by pilgrimage.

It is worth pondering that God journeys with His people. He did not simply command them to set off; He didn't just send an angel to lead them. He stooped down to journey with them. He is the immutable God; yet, He stoops down to journey through the wilderness with His people. He fills heaven and earth, and yet He marches with His people in the parched places of this cursed earth.

The Lord not only journeys with His people, His glory leads them. He leads His people like a general leads his troops. We are not left to wonder when and where to go; we have an infallible Guide.

He accompanies them day and night. This General neither sleeps nor slumbers. How many feel alone when darkness falls. Friends who have been with us during the day often leave at night. But this Friend stays close morning, noon, and night. Moreover, He shows Himself no matter how dark things become. Darkness hides even people who are close to us, but the darkness is never too dark for Him. God's presence shines in the dark of night as a pillar of fire. The darkness and the light are both alike to Him.

One day, the journey will reach an end. The pillar of cloud and fire stayed with Israel until they reached the Promised Land. It led them each step until they arrived safely in Zion. There God's presence would enter the rest of the sanctuary. And so it is today: God leads His people. They go onward where saints have trod. They go from strength to strength until at last they arrive safely in Zion, where God will be forever among His people as a Sun and Shield. They will no longer "go onward," but "be home."

Who appeared in glory, and spake of his decease which he should accomplish at Jerusalem.
                                            —LUKE 9:31 (read Luke 9:28–37)

All the themes of Exodus come together in Christ Jesus and the great Exodus that He accomplished in His death and resurrection. The passage for today reveals this to us by using the word "exodus" in verse 31 (in our translation, "decease"). Notice, first, who is with Christ on the Mount of Transfiguration—Moses and Elijah. Christ had appeared to Moses in the burning bush before Moses had led the people out of Egypt. Hundreds of years later, Elijah had visited Mount Horeb, where he would hear the still, small voice of God. Now Moses and Elijah appear with Christ as He is transfigured before His three disciples.

Notice, second, what they talk about. It was Christ's exodus. Scripture does not tell us all that was said, but we know that Christ would be the great Passover Lamb. Christ would be the Mediator, the new Moses, whom we need to heed. He would be the new Israel, God's final Son, whom He called out of Egypt once and for all. He would be the spiritual Manna to feed His people. Christ would be the High Priest, offering and interceding for His people. Christ would be the Cloud to guide His people by day and by night. Christ would be the Mercy-seat, above which God would speak to His people. He would be greater than the tabernacle. He would be their Lawgiver and the Rock to follow His people and slake their thirst. His death and resurrection would be the great fulfillment of the Exodus.

Notice, third, how Peter wished to build three tabernacles. He had to learn, however, that Christ was a High Priest of "a greater and more perfect tabernacle, not made with hands, that is to say, not of this building" (Heb. 9:11). He even had to learn that he would "shortly lay off this my tabernacle," namely, "his body" (2 Pet. 1:13) in order to experience that eternal tabernacle (Rev. 21:3).

Reflect with me as we close our meditations of Exodus: Has Christ brought you out of the slavery of sin? Are you sheltering behind the blood that will keep the avenger of blood from reaching you? Has He brought you through the Red Sea and put your feet on the other side? Is He daily guiding you, supplying your needs, writing His commandments upon the tables of your heart? If so, will He not safely lead you through the wilderness of this world to the heavenly Canaan? "Lord, fulfill this exodus in my life, for Jesus Christ's sake."

MILK & HONEY

from Judges
Ruth
1 & 2 Samuel
1 & 2 Kings
1 & 2 Chronicles

HUGH M. CARTWRIGHT

Then Gideon built an altar there unto the LORD, and called it Jehovah-shalom.

—JUDGES 6:24

"Jehovah" is a glorious name which reveals the self-determined, self-sufficient, sovereign character of the holy God who has covenanted to be the Savior of His people. To have that name proclaimed in connection with "shalom"—peace—in the days of the Judges, when "every man did that which was right in his own eyes" (Judg. 17:6), and in a situation characterized by forgetfulness of God, disobedience, apostasy and divine judgment, was indeed a wonder of grace. Gideon could scarcely believe that it really was the Lord who declared that He was with him (vv. 12, 13) and would use him to save sinful Israel from the Midianites (vv. 14, 16). The connection of peace with the approach of God to sinners amazed his gracious soul.

Whether one translates "the LORD is peace," "sends peace," or "may He give peace," the marvel is that "Jehovah" and "peace" are brought together in a revelation to sinners. A gracious soul, convinced of the infinite breach made between God and men by sin, fears an unfounded peace. But here is peace of which God is the Author—peace which can survive the approach and presence of God. This peace is ordained by God the Father in the everlasting covenant; grounded in the Person and atoning work of the Mediator, God the Son, and brought home to the believer's conscience, heart, and mind by God the Holy Spirit. Only the fact that God is Jehovah, acting "according to his good pleasure which he hath purposed in himself" (Eph. 1:9), can account for this.

The presence and aid of Jehovah-Shalom did not relieve Gideon of the need to engage in battle. "The peace of God, which passeth all understanding, shall keep your hearts and minds through Jesus Christ" (Phil. 4:7). It does not prevent conflict with indwelling sin, providential trials, temptations from the world and from the devil. But it means that strength is given to persevere and overcome.

Gideon's altar expressed his wonder, gratitude, and worship at the revelation of the God of peace. It reflected the truth that only in connection with atoning sacrifice can the God of peace be known. It still stands in the Scripture record, giving permanent testimony to this character in which God revealed Himself and encouraging the faith of embattled believers.

And Gideon said unto God, If thou wilt save Israel by mine hand, as thou hast said, behold, I will put a fleece of wool in the floor; and if the dew be on the fleece only, and it be dry upon all the earth beside, then shall I know that thou wilt save Israel by mine hand, as thou hast said.
—JUDGES 6:36, 37

Gideon's action does not warrant seeking external signs to confirm the word God has spoken and confirmed as His. But, as God does not condemn him, we should consider what there is in his action which is worthy of our imitation. Gideon, who is named among the outstanding examples of faith in Hebrews 11:32, brings his doubts and fears and unbelief to God and asks God to slay them, to give him victory over them, and to help him to trust God's Word as he believes it should be trusted. He is like Mary (Luke 1:34, 45) rather than Zacharias (Luke 1:18, 20). He is not seeking justification for unbelief but strengthening for faith.

We should not deny our questions, doubts, fears, and difficulties or be content with feeble faith. Let us follow Gideon in going to God with our concerns and our desire to be assured that His promise is really for us. While lack of faith most likely contributed to his request, he was taking the side of God against his unbelief when he showed no doubt that God had spoken.

The promise of God was very much before his mind. God had said that He would save Israel by Gideon's hand. Gideon was not so much asking God to prove the truth of what He had said as asking Him to have pity on him in his weakness—his faith was finding it difficult to take in that God would use such a person as he was to do such a great work. It was not a light matter with Gideon that his faith was so little able to contend with unbelief and his sense of insignificance, weakness, and unworthiness. He obviously felt the danger of provoking God to anger with his lack of trust. He comes with reverence and humility, feeling his need of mercy for having to come with such a request. "Lord, I believe; help thou mine unbelief" (Mark 9:24).

"Like as a father pitieth his children, so the Lord pitieth them that fear him" (Ps. 103:13, 14).

And the Lord said unto Gideon, The people that are with thee are too many for me to give the Midianites into their hands, lest Israel vaunt themselves against me, saying, Mine own hand hath saved me.

—JUDGES 7:2

God knows what is in man. Though man has nothing to be proud of, the sinful tendency remains to take glory due to God and to make God's gracious gifts reasons for self-congratulation and independence of God.

God is jealous for His own glory and will not give it to another. All His dealings with Israel were meant to bring them back to Himself, to trust and love and glorify Him as their God. He has provided for the salvation of His people "according to the good pleasure of his will, to the praise of the glory of his grace" (Eph. 1:5, 6). "For his own glory, he hath foreordained whatsoever comes to pass" (*Shorter Catechism*, 7). "Not unto us, O LORD, not unto us, but unto thy name give glory, for thy mercy, and for thy truth's sake" (Ps. 115:1).

God often reduces the strength of His people to an extent which takes away any occasion for self-reliance and makes them so dependent on Him that they give Him all the praise for their deliverance. Israel was given a vivid impression of the enemy's strength. Their numbers were reduced to next to nothing, comparatively. Their weapons were trumpets, pitchers, and lamps. They still had to confront the formidable foe. The combination of felt weakness with all-sufficient divine power made them conscious that the glory of their deliverance belonged only to the Lord.

We are taught this lesson by our conflict with the sin which so easily besets us. We are also taught it by providences which overwhelm us with a sense of personal weakness. This message is also brought home to the church when it is weakened because, as Matthew Henry puts it, "its friends are too many, too mighty and too wise, for God to work deliverance" by. John Newton discovered that, when God met his request for growth in faith, love, and every grace with devastating experiences, He was saying to him: "these inward trials I employ, from self and pride to set thee free."

The Lord's people desire God's glory and will yet be thankful for all those spiritual and providential experiences that make them more dependent upon Him and ready, with faithful Gideon, to worship Him (v. 15).

And Manoah said unto his wife, We shall surely die, because we have seen God. But his wife said unto him, If the Lord were pleased to kill us, he would not have received a burnt offering and a meat offering at our hands, neither would he have showed us all these things, nor would as at this time have told us such things as these.   —JUDGES 13:22, 23

These saints of God, about to be the parents of Samson, lived during the centuries of darkness which engulfed Israel between the death of Joshua and the crowning of Saul. God had just revealed Himself to them in the form of the Angel of the Lord. They had fallen to the ground, overwhelmed by a sense of the divine glory and of their own sinfulness. They had seen something of the unapproachable holiness of the One who came so condescendingly near to them and conversed with them.

As far as it went, Manoah's fear was well grounded. God said to Moses: "There shall no man see me, and live" (Ex. 33:20). The more real God is to us, the more aware we become of our sinfulness and demerit. Isaiah had similar feelings. "Woe is me! for I am undone; because I am a man of unclean lips, and I dwell in the midst of a people of unclean lips: for mine eyes have seen the King, the Lord of Hosts" (Isa. 6:5).

But Manoah's wife's consolation was also well grounded. Heirs together of the grace of life, she was a true help to him. The revelation that caused fear brought comfort. She acknowledged that God might well have been pleased to kill them but took encouragement from the gracious and condescending manner in which God revealed Himself and dealt with them. He had accepted their burnt offering and their meat offering. He had showed them that they were to be the parents of a child through whom He would begin to deliver Israel from their oppressors.

Should not those who have seen by faith the glory of God in the face of Jesus Christ and who are relying upon His atoning sacrifice which God has accepted at their hand be encouraged by His gracious revelation of Himself to them? Should they not believe that His promise is the guarantee that they shall not perish? They are worthy of death and their experience of the fulfillment of the promise may bring them much trouble, but they shall never perish.

And they lifted up their voice, and wept again: and Orpah kissed her mother in law; but Ruth clave unto her.

—RUTH 1:14

Elimelech and Naomi could not have known that when they made the perhaps questionable move to Moab they were instrumentally bringing a Moabitess into the line from which Christ would come. Sovereign grace operating along with an all-controlling providence brought Ruth from darkness to light, from Moab to Israel, and gave her a place in the genealogy of Jesus.

No doubt natural attachment to Naomi was a link in the chain which drew Ruth from her idols to God. But Orpah had the same background, the same relation to Naomi, and the same affection for her. It was not a breakdown of natural affection which took Orpah back to Moab; it was something more than natural affection which took Ruth on to Israel. Earthly attachment to the people of God, however intense, and resolutions accounted for only by human nature and inclination, cannot break the power of the world, the flesh, and the devil. Ruth did not go back in spite of Naomi's gloomy representations and Orpah's defection because she saw beyond the visible and temporal and was drawn by the cords of grace and everlasting love to Naomi's God and people. She wished to have God as her God and His people as her people whatever the earthly circumstances might be. She wished to be of His people all her days and forever—in life, in death, and in eternity.

In His grace, God made Ruth "steadfastly minded" (v. 18) to go with Naomi. Naomi tested her resolve by placing before her aspects of following her which would not appeal to carnal nature, as our Lord Himself did with some who seemed enthusiastic to follow Him (Luke 9:57–62). But the cords of everlasting love were drawing her and constraining her to deny herself and take up her cross and follow. There is no excuse for sinners choosing to continue with the world to which we all belong by nature. But when sinners do break with it, the credit all belongs to God's grace.

The rich young ruler, who seemed so intent on obtaining eternal life, also went away sorrowful. Are you among those who do not bid Christ farewell, however regretfully, but who hear His voice and follow Him?

The LORD recompense thy work, and a full reward be given thee of the LORD God of Israel, under whose wings thou art come to trust.

—RUTH 2:12

Questions arise regarding whether Elimelech was right to take his wife and family to heathen Moab to escape the famine in Judah, the land of promise—and whether he was right to allow his sons to marry Moabite women. That "all things work together for good to them that love God, to them that are the called according to his purpose" (Rom. 8:28) does not legitimize all that they have done or experienced. It does magnify the grace of God who rules and overrules in His holy providence, harnessing all events and experiences to the gathering of His elect to Himself. That it was grace that brought Ruth to faith is clear from the contrast between her and Orpah, who had the same external providences, encouragements, and obstacles.

Ruth became acquainted with the truth concerning the God of salvation. She assented to that truth. She trusted in God, fleeing to Him for safety, making Him her resort and her refuge. This picture of saving faith is illuminating and encouraging. The Psalms often use this figure (17:8; 36:7; 57:1; 61:4; 63:7; 91:4). Sometimes the imagery is taken from the protectiveness of birds towards their young; other times the reference may be to the wings of the cherubim overshadowing the mercy seat in the most holy place and representing the Lord's reception of sinners into His favor and protection through Christ. In either case, it means that everything in God, every attribute of God, justice as well as mercy, contributes to the safety of His people. He is their defense. "Your life is hid with Christ in God" (Col. 3:3).

Boaz saw the evidence of Ruth's faith in what it motivated her to do. She left father and mother and the land of her birth. She came among people previously unknown. She showed much kindness to her mother-in-law. Her faith worked by love (Gal. 5:6). Boaz's desire reflects the Lord's way of dealing with His people: they owe their faith and all its fruits to His grace and yet He views it with pleasure and rewards them abundantly for it.

What great reward believers have even in the assurance that they are "kept by the power of God through faith unto salvation ready to be revealed in the last time" (1 Pet. 1:5)!

And the LORD came, and stood, and called as at other times, Samuel, Samuel. Then Samuel answered, Speak; for thy servant heareth.

—1 SAMUEL 3:10

The calling of young Samuel to be a prophet through whom the Lord would speak to God-forsaking and seemingly God-forsaken Israel was a significant event in the history of redemption. He was to be instrumental in bringing the truth of God, regarding both judgment and mercy, to bear on a people who generally lived in neglect of God's Word—the Five Books of Moses—and in establishing the line of monarchs descended from David from which Christ was to come according to the flesh. How thankful we should be that through Samuel and other prophets and apostles raised up by God we have inspired and infallible Scriptures which are God's Word to us—"a more sure word of prophecy; whereunto ye do well that ye take heed, as unto a light that shineth in a dark place" (1 Pet. 1:19).

On the personal level, we learn from Samuel how we should respond with alacrity to the Word of God and how necessary it is that we should be taught to do so. He had the advantage of a godly education in his earliest years. He was given wise counsel by Eli when he failed to recognize that God was speaking to him. But it was when the Lord not only called but came and stood that Samuel responded as he had been counseled to do. The Word of God carries its own evidence and authority, and the explanations of others can be made helpful to us. But "our full persuasion and assurance of the infallible truth and divine authority thereof, is from the inward work of the Holy Spirit, bearing witness by and with the word in our hearts" (*Westminster Confession*, 1.5).

Samuel's heart towards God was indeed that of a servant. He received the word which God spoke to him and, when charged to do so, though painful to himself and others, he faithfully made it known. How we need to learn, as only God can teach us, to "hear what God the Lord will speak" (Ps. 85:8). We need to hear as David desired to hear when he said: "Teach me, O LORD, the way of thy statutes; and I shall keep it unto the end" (Ps. 119:33).

Then Samuel took a stone, and set it between Mizpeh and Shen, and called the name of it Ebenezer, saying, Hitherto hath the LORD helped us.

—1 SAMUEL 7:12

Many years before, at this very spot, Israel was defeated by the Philistines and the ark of God was taken. For years, the people had lamented the loss of the ark and of the presence of God which it symbolized, but had continued in their sin and idolatry. Now, at Samuel's call, they gathered near the scene of their former defeat to pray and fast in penitence before God. When the Philistines came expecting to repeat their former victory, they were defeated because the Lord helped His people. Just as the Lord's displeasure had brought about His people's earlier defeat, His blessing now gave them success. His help was not the little assistance that made the difference between defeat and victory but the enabling on which victory altogether depended.

Samuel built a memorial of the Lord's help to them. It is good to take notice of particular instances of the Lord's goodness to us and to use these particular instances to remind ourselves of His constant help. "Whoso is wise, and will observe these things, even they shall understand the lovingkindness of the LORD" (Ps. 107:43).

Those who "wisely consider of his doing" (Ps. 64:9) will be kept humbly dependent upon the Lord's gracious help and will be made cautious against anything that would cause Him to hide His face and leave them to themselves. They will be encouraged for the present and future as they consider the unchangeableness and covenant faithfulness of the God whose earlier help they remember. Their testimony may be useful to others whom they can comfort with the same comfort wherewith they themselves are comforted of God (2 Cor. 1:4). Their remembrance of the Lord's help stirs them up to glorify God by their praises and by their dependence upon Him.

"Whatsoever things were written aforetime were written for our learning, that we through patience and comfort of the scriptures might have hope" (Rom. 15:4). While our fundamental encouragement is the testimony of God's Word concerning His readiness to come to the aid of His people, our own Ebenezer raised in testimony to our own experience of His help only confirms what is written. Do you have such memorials in your life?

For the LORD will not forsake his people for his great name's sake: because it hath pleased the LORD to make you his people.
—1 SAMUEL 12:22

Those who were not God's people have been made His people with all the glorious implications of that relationship: "which in time past were not a people, but are now the people of God: which had not obtained mercy, but now have obtained mercy" (1 Pet. 2:10). "Know that the LORD he is God: it is he that hath made us, and not we ourselves" (Ps. 100:2). This is brought about in accordance with God's eternal purpose of grace, through what He has done for them in Christ and what He has done in them by His Spirit. It is accounted for by "his good pleasure which he hath purposed in himself" (Eph. 1:9). The grace which accounts for God having a people and for His choice of them comes by His own free and sovereign will, not by anything in them.

We have given the Lord so many reasons to forsake us if He would deal with us as our sins deserve (vv. 19, 20). To be forsaken of God could only mean destruction. The Lord will chasten His people for their sins (v. 15), but He will not forsake them. He may bring them low, but "the LORD will not cast off his people, neither will he forsake his inheritance" (Ps. 94:14)—"his people which he foreknew" (Rom. 11:2). He finds His reasons in Himself: in the sovereignty and grace and faithfulness He revealed in the work of salvation, especially in the Person and work of His Son who has manifested His name. His honor and glory and reputation are bound up with the preservation of His people. Their security depends on what God is and what He has revealed of Himself. "Because he could sware by no greater, he sware by himself" (Heb. 6:13).

This truth is not intended to encourage presumptuous sin—to sin that grace may abound. It is to encourage repentance and the abandonment of false confidence, to trust in the Lord and in His covenant faithfulness, and that gracious fear of the Lord which promotes concern to live godly and holy lives. "Turn not from following the LORD, and serve the LORD with all your heart; and turn ye not aside" (vv. 20–21). Have these fruits been born in your life?

And Samuel came to Saul: and Saul said unto him, Blessed be thou of the Lord: I have performed the commandment of the LORD. And Samuel said, What meaneth then this bleating of the sheep in mine ears, and the lowing of the oxen which I hear? —1 SAMUEL 15:13–14

Saul was commanded to destroy all the possessions of the heathen Amalekites. Their sheep and oxen were specifically mentioned. The ungodliness of King Saul in response to the ungodly desire of the people to be like the nations around about them was revealed in his response to this commandment of the Lord. He spared the best of the sheep and oxen for his own use and for the people, piously pretending to have destroyed them, and then blamed it on the people rather than himself, and had the audacity to claim that it was so that they could sacrifice them to the Lord.

Faithful Samuel communicated to him the Lord's verdict on him, his character, and his conduct. "Hath the LORD as great delight in burnt offerings and sacrifices, as in obeying the voice of the LORD? Behold, to obey is better than sacrifice, and to hearken than the fat of rams. For rebellion is as the sin of witchcraft, and stubbornness is as iniquity and idolatry. Because thou hast rejected the word of the LORD, he hath also rejected thee from being king" (vv. 22–23).

Saul's obedience was tested by the commandment of the Lord. His sin was exposed in spite of his efforts to cover it by in turn professing obedience, shifting the blame to others, claiming good motivation for his disobedience, and trying to balance it out by drawing attention to what he had done. His eventual protestations of repentance in an attempt to retain his position as king were manifestly false.

The evidences of our sin and hypocrisy may not be so obvious to others as Saul's were to Samuel, but it is said of the God of Samuel that "his eyes behold, his eyelids try, the children of men" (Ps. 11:4). "He knoweth the secrets of the heart" (Ps. 44:21). Our professions of obedience, our sins, our repentance are subject to the scrutiny of God. What need we have of honesty in our dealings with God! "He that covereth his sins shall not prosper: but whoso confesseth and forsaketh them shall have mercy" (Prov. 28:13).

And Samuel came no more to see Saul unto the day of his death: nevertheless Samuel mourned for Saul: and the LORD repented that he had made Saul king over Israel.
—1 SAMUEL 15:35

It ever was God's purpose that Israel should have a king to reflect something of the qualities of the King who was also to be Prophet and Priest to His people. David realized that even he was at best a faint reflection of the promised King: "He that ruleth over men must be just, ruling in the fear of God. And he shall be as the light of the morning, when the sun riseth, even a morning with clouds; as the tender grass springing out of the earth by clear shining after rain.... [M]y house is not so with God" (2 Sam. 23:3–5).

Israel sought a king, not that God might rule them through him, but that they might be like the nations around them. In doing so they rejected God (1 Sam. 8; 12:12, 19). "I gave thee a king in mine anger, and took him away in my wrath" (Hos. 13:11).

Although Saul and Samuel did meet again (e.g., 1 Sam. 19:24), Samuel never again visited him in a formal or friendly capacity. He did not convey to Saul another word or warning from God, whose prophet he was. This was not due to hardness of heart, for Samuel grieved over Saul. It was part of the judgment Saul brought on himself and his people by his and their sin. The Lord was making known that it was not His purpose that the kingship of Israel should be settled in Saul and his descendants. As one has put it, when the Lord is said to repent it does not mean that He has changed His mind but that He has minded a change. Samuel has just said: "And also the Strength of Israel will not lie nor repent: for he is not a man, that he should repent" (v. 29). "I am the LORD, I change not" (Mal. 3:6). "The counsel of the LORD standeth for ever, the thoughts of his heart to all generations" (Ps. 33:11).

The Lord gave them their heart's desire that they might learn from experience to submit to His will and not put their trust in princes but in the Lord. Christ was to come from God, even with regard to the line of human ancestry. So must all our blessedness.

Then said David to the Philistine, Thou comest to me with a sword, and with a spear, and with a shield: but I come to thee in the name of the LORD of hosts, the God of the armies of Israel, whom thou hast defied.

—1 SAMUEL 17:45

David had been anointed as the future king of Israel. The Spirit of the Lord had come upon him to equip him for that office. Zeal for God and His glory and his confidence in the Lord, whose help he had previously experienced, fortified him in his encounter with Goliath, whom he regarded as the embodiment of defiance of God. The battle was not merely between a shepherd lad and a giant, but between the Lord and the idols of the heathen and the satanic power behind their pretended existence. It faintly foreshadowed the accomplishment of David's Son and Lord who triumphed over principalities and powers and destroyed him who had the power of death in order to deliver His people from the dominion of sin and the curse by means of His cross, despised as weak and foolish by the world.

David was courageous and expert in the use of his sling, but he made it very clear that what was at stake was the Lord's reputation. The victory would be achieved by the power of God in a way that would be to His glory, not the glory of David or the armies of Israel. "Ye are of God, little children, and have overcome them: because greater is he that is in you, than he that is in the world.... This is the victory that overcometh the world, even our faith" (1 John 4:4; 5:4).

If by grace we are on the Lord's side, we do not wrestle against flesh and blood but against the devil and the powers of darkness (Eph. 6:11–12). But "if God be for us, who can be against us?" (Rom. 8:31). We need to be concerned as David was for the Lord's glory and cause, and dependent as he was upon the Lord. Then we can face any foe in the strength of the Lord, however feeble we may feel in ourselves. "For though we walk in the flesh, we do not war after the flesh: (for the weapons of our warfare are not carnal, but mighty through God to the pulling down of strongholds)" (2 Cor. 10:3–4).

And David was greatly distressed; for the people spake of stoning him.... But David encouraged himself in the LORD his God.... And David enquired at the Lord....

—1 SAMUEL 30:6, 8

Pursued by Saul, sent away by Achish, spoiled by the Amalekites, and threatened by his own followers, David had every reason, humanly speaking, to be distressed. Being human, and having been subjected to much stress and to depression (e.g., 1 Sam. 27:1), he had reached a breaking point. Troubles would not be troubles to us if we did not feel them as such. But with all his own schemes for self-preservation having failed, David now encourages himself in the Lord his God. For so long his course of action had been determined by fear of Saul and by his own resourcefulness; now that he has no human help, he falls back upon the Lord. Sadly, it is often only when all else fails and we have nowhere else to go are we driven to seek help in God.

David found encouragement in his God and in His covenant faithfulness. He brought considerations to bear upon his situation which outweighed all that discouraged and distressed him. "Ye are of God, little children, and have overcome them: because greater is he that is in you, than he that is in the world" (1 John 4:4). He finds encouragement in the thought that this God is his God; that He is faithful to Himself, to His promises and to His people; and that power belongs to Him. That "he encouraged himself" suggests that David exercised his mind and heart with these truths. The encouragement came from God, by the work of the Divine Encourager or Comforter of His people, but it came through David thinking on these things.

That David's confidence was in the Lord is seen in the fact that he now inquired of the Lord in the appointed way—through the priest—as to what he should do. He renounced his own wisdom and strength. His faith found expression in prayer, in submission to God's will, and in dependence upon Him. Sometimes the Lord has to bring us to the end of ourselves before we will really consult His Word, submit to His will, and cast ourselves on His mercy. "When I am weak, then am I strong" (2 Cor. 12:10). Have you reached the end of yourself? How can you submit to His will today?

*And now, O Lord God, the word that thou hast spoken concerning
thy servant, and concerning his house, establish it for ever, and do as
thou hast said.*
                                                          —2 SAMUEL 7:25

The promise made to David regarding his house and his throne was fulfilled
in Christ, David's Son and Lord. The biblical accounts of the kings of Israel
make it very clear that it could not be fulfilled in anyone else, not even in
David or Solomon.

The Lord's people in all ages have the same interest in this promise as
David had. This verse is part of David's response to the promise. It is a prayer
of faith, which finds foundation and encouragement in the promise spoken
by God—a word which expressed what was in the heart of God (v. 21). It
was characterized by truth (v. 28) and was the word of One who had always
done as He had said (vv. 22–24). David heartily embraced the promise (v. 27)
and this was manifest in the earnest, persistent, and prayerful desire which it
created within him—desire regulated as well as stimulated by the promise.
That he truly embraced the Word of God was demonstrated in his embracing
its precepts as well as its promises, as appears in his frequent description of
himself in this context as God's servant. Prominent in this believing, prayerful response to the promise of God is concern for God's glory (v. 26). David
uses the way in which the Lord's glory is bound up with His performance of
His promises as an argument for Him doing so. What will become of God's
name, reputation, or glory if His promise fails? Fulfilling His promise proves
how great a God He is.

"Do as thou hast said" is the language of holy, humble boldness. David
is using words which God has given to him (Hos. 14:2). He could not have
asked for such things had not God promised them. It would be unbelief
for him not to plead the promise. "I the Lord have spoken it, and I will do
it. Thus saith the Lord God: I will yet for this be inquired of by the house
of Israel, to do it for them" (Ezek. 36:37). When we pray as David did for
things agreeable to God's revealed will, we can present our plea with similar
humble importunity.

And David said unto Nathan, I have sinned against the LORD. And Nathan said unto David, The LORD also hath put away thy sin; thou shalt not die.

—2 SAMUEL 12:13

These words may seem easily uttered, but Psalm 51 and probably Psalm 32 make clear the depth of conviction of sin which lay behind David's confession and the wonders of divine grace which accounted for his forgiveness.

Whatever terrors of conscience he experienced during the months since his notorious fall, he had kept silence (Ps. 32:3–4) and had not acknowledged his sin. But now, through the faithful ministry of the Word of God by Nathan, he was brought to confess his sin against the Lord who had shown such kindness to him. He had "despised the commandment of the LORD, to do evil in his sight" (v. 9) and had specifically broken the sixth, seventh, and tenth commandments. This was not only in contempt of God's law, but also in despite of His grace. This is what really came home to him now and prostrated him before the Lord in confession of sin. He also appeals for mercy—for cleansing from the guilt of sin through the atoning sacrifice provided by God and from the corruption of sin by the work of God's Spirit.

Putting away his sin—the essential character of forgiveness—was accounted for by the lovingkindness of the Lord, the multitude of His tender mercies (Ps. 51:1), and not by any merit in David or in his God-given repentance. It was the Lord against whom he had sinned who put his sin away and it was as the Lord He did it, in the exercise of His sovereign mercy. David had in effect pronounced the sentence of death upon himself, but "where sin abounded, grace did much more abound: that as sin hath reigned unto death, even so might grace reign through righteousness unto eternal life by Jesus Christ our Lord" (Rom. 5:21).

The sentence upon sin was not executed because the sin was atoned for and no longer called upon justice for vengeance. David had to live with the temporal consequences of his sin in himself, his family, and his kingdom. Forgiven sin should not be lightly regarded; David's soul was humble within him as he sang: "As far as the east is from the west, so far hath he removed our transgressions from us" (Ps. 103:12).

Although my house be not so with God; yet he hath made with me an everlasting covenant, ordered in all things and sure: for this is all my salvation, and all my desire, although he make it not to grow.

—2 SAMUEL 23:5

King David's situation was unique. He was typical of his greater Son and Lord, and the promise made concerning his household was fulfilled ultimately in Christ. Though the promise did not find fulfillment in himself, he believed that it would certainly be accomplished.

But these words also give expression to the experience of everyone whose hope is grounded in the gracious covenant made with Christ as the great Head of His Church. They have their regrets that they are neither as holy nor as happy as the covenant warrants them to expect. In character and conduct and in their relationship with God, they often feel so little correspondence between the expectations raised by the promise of God and the reality they see in themselves.

However, with a shameful sense of poverty before God there coexists a dependence upon what God has done and undertaken. The God on whose covenant they rely is their Rock, a God of power and sovereignty and grace. He has engaged in the counsels of eternity, through the mediation of Christ and the applicatory work of the Holy Spirit, to put His people in possession of all that He has promised. Eternal in its origin, His covenant is everlasting in its duration and effects and will make them "perfectly blessed in the full enjoying of God to all eternity" (*Shorter Catechism*, 38). It is well ordered in that each Person of the Godhead has His own function, each aspect of salvation is provided for, and all the circumstances of providence are finely balanced. It is as sure as the word and oath of God the Father, the blood and intercession of God the Son, and the power of God the Holy Spirit can make it. The title deeds of salvation are safe in God's keeping and cannot be destroyed by sin or death or Satan.

Though His people may see so little fruit of the covenant in their own lives, they look to that covenant fulfilled in the Person and work of Christ for all their salvation. The desires that grace has created find satisfaction only there.

Blessed be the LORD, that hath given rest unto his people according to all that he promised: there hath not failed one word of all his good promise, which he promised by the hand of Moses his servant.

—1 KINGS 8:56

As he blesses the people at the dedication of the Temple, Solomon traces the peace and prosperity which were then the possession of Israel to God's promise. The Tabernacle had given way to the Temple. The wanderings in the wilderness and the battle for existence with the enemies around had given way to rest in the place which God had chosen for them. The reality represented by the Temple and the land and the peaceful reign of Solomon is found in Christ and in the spiritual blessings He offers to His people. In Him, all that God has promised is enjoyed by His covenant people, and they can join with Solomon in his ascription of praise to God: "for all the promises of God in him are yea, and in him Amen, unto the glory of God by us" (2 Cor. 1:20).

Solomon's blessing of the people begins with his blessing of God. He recognizes God as the source of their blessedness. He testifies to His faithfulness in performing what He has promised. And he emphasizes just how complete and comprehensive that performance of His Word has been. Abraham's faith in God was such that he was "fully persuaded that, what he had promised, he was able also to perform" (Rom. 4: 21). Moses shared that faith, having nothing to rely upon but the Word of God. When God promised, "My presence shall go with thee, and I will give thee rest" (Ex. 33:14), Moses could speak confidently to Israel of the rest and safety which the Lord would give His people in the Promised Land (Deut. 12:10). Solomon is bearing testimony to how well founded that confidence was as seen in the exact fulfillment of all that God promised.

As the context suggests, God's people are encouraged by this testimony to the Lord's faithfulness and power to hope in Him for His presence and preservation in the future and to plead His promises in believing prayer. "The LORD hath been mindful of us: he will bless us" (Ps. 115:12). How it should motivate us to bless the Lord and respond in such heartfelt obedience to the will of God as will glorify Him on earth!

So he went back with him, and did eat bread
in his house, and drank water.

—1 KINGS 13:19

The man of God from Judah faithfully delivered the message given him by God regarding the idolatrous worship of Jeroboam, king of Israel, at Bethel. God bore testimony to him, preserving him from the wrath of Jeroboam by withering the hand he stretched forth against the prophet, breaking the altar at which the king was burning incense, and hearing his prayer for the restoration of Jeroboam's hand.

He was charged by God to refuse any hospitality—to accomplish his errand and not to return by the way he went. He faithfully complied with his instructions when Jeroboam invited him home for refreshment and a reward. When the old prophet in Bethel went after him to bring him to his house, he refused and made clear his reason: the Lord had forbidden him to accept any such invitations. But when this old prophet claimed that an angel from the Lord had told him to bring him back, he yielded to the temptation. While they sat at the table, the Lord forced the old prophet to speak words condemning the man for his disobedience to the word of the Lord and assuring him that he would die and be buried away from home.

We need not speculate as to the motives or reasons for the old prophet from Bethel tempting the man to disobey the commandment of the Lord. Whatever the source and instrumentality of the temptation, it was obviously intended by the Lord as a test of the man's perseverance in obeying the word of God. The word of God was clear. He knew it was God's word. He faithfully resisted strong temptations to disobey it. The threats and offered friendship of the king and the initial invitation of the prophet from Bethel did not sway him. But when the devil came as an angel of light, he succumbed.

The good man ought not for a moment to have given place to a temptation which contradicted what he very well knew to be the word of God. God's word does not change, and our safety lies in closely adhering to it. "O that my ways were directed to keep thy statutes" (Ps. 119:5). How we need to persevere to the end! How we need to rely on the keeping power of God!

And Elijah came unto all the people, and said, How long halt ye between two opinions? if the LORD be God, follow him; but if Baal, then follow him. And the people answered him not a word. —1 KINGS 18:21

After Ahab married Jezebel, daughter of a heathen king and priest, Baal worship was practiced at the royal court. The forces of the crown were used to exterminate prophets and preachers holding to the true religion. The public religion and morals of Israel rapidly declined. Judgments such as drought and famine failed to produce repentance even though they demonstrated the inability of the supposed nature god to help his devotees. With courage given by God, Elijah summoned the people to Carmel to confront them with God's call to repentance.

Elijah affirms that no one can say that the Lord is God without acknowledging Him as the only living and true God and rejecting every contrary opinion. The name of the Lord contains all that is revealed of God in the Bible. If the Lord is God, then every alternative deity or view of God is false. People should stop trying to limp along holding to the vain idea that somehow they can worship the Lord and serve their own gods (2 Kings 17:33). This is done by those who advocate a "multi-faith" approach to religion. It is also done by those who profess that the Lord is God but practically think and live under the influence of the ungodly and idolatrous spirit of the age. "No man can serve two masters: for either he will hate the one and love the other; or else he will hold to the one and despise the other. Ye cannot serve God and mammon" (Matt. 6:24).

Elijah is not suggesting that there can be any doubt as to whether the Lord or Baal is God, or who should be followed. They must take one way or the other, be one thing or the other. Those who are decidedly of one opinion or the other will manifest that in practice consistent with their belief. He is calling for a wholehearted return to God, manifested in lives conformed to His will and devoted to His glory.

The silent response to his call may have evidenced the penitence of some and the continued indecision of others or their stubborn refusal to acknowledge guilt. What is your response?

> *And he came thither unto a cave, and lodged there; and, behold, the word of the LORD came to him, and he said unto him, What doest thou here, Elijah?*
>
> —1 KINGS 19:9

By any standard, Elijah was a greatly significant figure of church history, exercising a faithful ministry in degenerate times and contending for God's truth amidst apostasy and idolatry—a man whose effectual, fervent prayers availed much. In God's fellowship and strength, he had triumphed over many humanly insurmountable difficulties. But here he is, hiding in a cave, despondent, feeling that he has labored in vain. Unlike Paul, who was buoyed up by the thought of heaven, Elijah was pulled down by the thought of earth. His soul was cast down within him. He wanted to get away from it all. God was still his God; in fact, love for God lay behind his dejection on account of the widespread ungodliness. But he had lost the comfort which comes from realizing the implications of the fact that the Lord is God indeed. "Strong in the Lord, and in the power of his might" (Eph. 6:10), he was frail, feeble and fearful in himself.

No doubt physical fatigue and a reaction to the excitement he had come through contributed to bringing him down mentally and spiritually, which was why God gave him food and sleep. Apart from the rebuke implicit in His question the Lord did not directly criticize him. We cannot throw a stone at him. But he had become so preoccupied with the dark and depressing situation, with his own helplessness in the face of it, and with the failure of the Lord to act as he expected that he lost sight of the fact that everything was still in God's hands and that the situation was not beyond His control.

He had to learn that the Lord was not in the strong wind, nor in the earthquake, nor in the fire. He had to recognize God's presence in the still, small voice. Had he been hoping that the wind or earthquake or fire of such events as took place on Carmel would bring the nation back to God? He had to come to terms with the fact that "My thoughts are not your thoughts, neither are your ways my ways, saith the LORD" (Isa. 55:8).

"Why art thou cast down, O my soul?... Hope thou in God: for I shall yet praise him, who is the health of my countenance, and my God" (Ps. 42:11).

And he took the mantle of Elijah that fell from him, and smote the waters, and said, Where is the LORD God of Elijah? And when he also had smitten the waters, they parted hither and thither: and Elisha went over.
—2 KINGS 2:14

Elijah was translated to heaven and Elisha had to take his place as the principal prophet in that degenerate age. Generations come and go, but the work of God goes on. Elisha found encouragement in Elijah's testimony to, and experience of, God. He was making use of Elijah's testimony to and experience of God's grace and power and faithfulness to encourage his own faith. He did not focus on the greatness of the departed prophet but on the greatness of his God. What he had seen of the Lord God in the life of Elijah made an abiding impression on him. The Lord God of Elijah was his God also.

While Elisha made use of means employed by Elijah, he did not depend on them. Elijah's mantle confirmed that Elijah's office and responsibilities and message were entrusted to him. But he was conscious that the means used so effectively by Elijah would be helpless in his hands unless the Lord made them effective. He knew that doing what Elijah did would not guarantee the same results. His dependence was upon the Lord God of Elijah. "For they got not the land in possession by their own sword, neither did their own arm save them: but thy right hand, and thine arm, and the light of thy countenance, because thou hadst a favour unto them. Thou art my King, O God: command deliverances for Jacob" (Ps. 44:3–4).

We must adhere to the doctrines and practices so greatly blessed in the hands of those who were true to the Lord in past generations, but we must recognize that we are dependent upon God for their blessing. Men like Elijah are our examples. What God did through them is recorded for our benefit. What we should learn from them is complete dependence upon God. As Elisha did, we must cry to Him for help. Thinking of Him as the Lord God of Elijah reminds us that the one living and true God is holy and just, merciful and gracious, omnipotent and omniscient, and that He works when and how it pleases Him. This should be our encouragement when rivers have to be crossed on our way.

And his servants came near, and spake unto him, and said, My father, if the prophet had bid thee do some great thing, wouldest thou not have done it? how much rather then, when he saith to thee, Wash, and be clean?

—2 KINGS 5:13

Naaman was one of the most prominent and powerful men in Syria, a nation God used to chastise Israel. "Many lepers were in Israel in the time of Eliseus the prophet; and none of them was cleansed, saving Naaman the Syrian" (Luke 4:27).

His case illustrated the sovereignty of grace and the intention of the Lord to gather a people from all nations. His conversion to God would have affected relations between Syria and Israel at that time (cf. 2 Kings 8:7–8) and brought a period of respite from attacks upon God's people. On the personal level, his case has significance for sinners estranged from God and subject to the leprosy of sin, as our Lord's words above show.

However great Naaman was, he was a leper. The king of Israel knew that to cure a leper was as humanly impossible as to raise the dead. When Naaman came in search of a cure, he had his own ideas of how it should be effected; he wanted a method suited to his proud notions of himself and his own dignity. Similarly, the unhumbled pride of the human heart makes the sinner unwilling to be saved in the gospel way. "For the Jews require a sign, and the Greeks seek after wisdom: but we preach Christ crucified, unto the Jews a stumbling block, and unto the Greeks foolishness; but unto them which are called, both Jews and Greeks, Christ the power of God, and the wisdom of God" (1 Cor. 1:22–24). "Except ye be converted, and become as little children, ye shall not enter into the kingdom of heaven" (Matt. 18:3). It is part of our fallen condition and our need of salvation that we are not naturally disposed to come to terms with the gospel's way of salvation.

We need a persuading and enabling beyond what any man can bring to bear upon us. Just as the Lord used the little maid to set Naaman off in search of a cure, and used his servants to persuade him to submit to the terms prescribed by the prophet, so the Lord uses His Word to break sinners down and make them willing to be saved by grace.

*And his servant said unto him, Alas, my master! how shall we do?
And he answered, Fear not: for they that be with us are more than they
that be with them.*
— 2 KINGS 6:15–16

Elisha's servant could only see the great Syrian host surrounding Dothan and cutting off all possibility of escape. The Syrian king wished to capture the prophet whom he believed was informing the king of Israel of his plans and frustrating them. It was the young servant's faithful attachment to Elisha which accounted for him being in this predicament. He did not have the spiritual experience and insight of his master, but he had the benefit of having as companion one who could give good counsel and plead with God on his behalf. The Lord graciously condescended to show him the reason behind Elisha's "Fear not." So many exhortations not to fear are baseless, but this had the stamp of divine authority on it and was founded on reality.

Elisha did not minimize the numbers or strength of the enemy, but he drew the attention of the young man to other factors in the situation— factors too easily lost sight of amid the strains and stresses of life, and which need something more than human senses to grasp them. What was against them was real enough, but there was far more for them than against them. If we are for God, as these men were by His grace, then God is for us, and "if God be for us, who can be against us?" (Rom. 8:31). "Ye are of God, little children, and have overcome them: because greater is he that is in you, than he that is in the world" (1 John 4:4).

The encouraging exhortation was reinforced by the vision given to the young man of the host of horses and chariots of fire round about Elisha. He was enabled to see the unseen and to be aware of the protection of God around His people. The Lord's people may not always be preserved from danger as Elisha and his servant were, but no real harm can befall them, for God is their defense. How we need with Paul by faith to "look not at the things which are seen, but at the things which are not seen: for the things which are seen are temporal; but the things which are not seen are eternal" (2 Cor. 4:18).

And Jabez called on the God of Israel, saying, Oh that thou wouldest bless me indeed, and enlarge my coast, and that thine hand might be with me, and that thou wouldest keep me from evil, that it may not grieve me! And God granted him that which he requested.

—1 CHRONICLES 4:10

Jabez's name permanently commemorated the exceptional sorrow his mother experienced in connection with his birth, yet he is identified as more honorable than his brethren, and he alone of the sons of Judah listed here has testimony given to his character and prevailing prayerfulness.

The particular circumstances of his life, sorrowful or joyful, are not recorded, but he was enabled to put his spiritual and temporal concerns into proper perspective and make both the subject matter of his prayers. His all-comprehending desire was for the blessing of the God of covenant mercy and faithfulness, whatever God might be pleased to give or withhold. He desired to truly have God's favor, knowing that only then would all be well.

In praying for the enlarging of his coast, he brought his earthly affairs and projects to the Lord, recognizing his dependence upon Him and making his temporal circumstances subservient to the enjoyment of blessing. He felt his need of the Lord's hand with him and for him, guiding, upholding, strengthening, and protecting him. He renounces self-sufficiency and self-reliance.

In praying that God would keep him from evil that it might not grieve him, he was most likely asking to be kept from experiencing more trouble than he would be given grace to bear. God approves such petitions, promising that He "will not suffer you to be tempted above that ye are able; but will with the temptation also make a way to escape, that ye may be able to bear it" (1 Cor. 10:13). But Jabez indeed fears sinning more than suffering, and in his prayer there was a concern that in all his earthly activities he would be kept from that which would offend God and bring sorrow to himself.

God grants such requests. It may not be in the way expected as Paul found (2 Cor. 12). It may be that trials which cause grief are sent to preserve from sins which cause grief, but sooner or later the tried one will see that in this God was granting the prayer for His blessing and preservation from evil and not denying it.

And thou, Solomon my son, know thou the God of thy father, and serve him with a perfect heart and with a willing mind: for the LORD searcheth all hearts, and understandeth all the imaginations of the thoughts: if thou seek him, he will be found of thee; but if thou forsake him, he will cast thee off for ever.

—1 CHRONICLES 28:9

David was given the assurance that, however his descendants might break God's law and become subject to His displeasure, He would not withdraw His love from him nor break His covenant regarding the perpetuity of his throne—an assurance fulfilled by the coming of David's Son and Lord at the time appointed. This assurance did not make David feel that it was unnecessary to exhort his son and heir to godly living, but rather encouraged him to give Solomon plain and pointed parting counsels. That God will do as He has promised does not relieve those believing the promise of the need to use appointed means.

Solomon is exhorted to acknowledge his father's God as his God and seek personal acquaintance with Him. Knowing about Him is one thing; knowing Him is another. "And this is life eternal, that they might know thee the only true God, and Jesus Christ, whom thou hast sent" (John 17:3). The knowledge of God will promote worship and obedience; Solomon is exhorted to remember that this must be wholehearted and with a mind that delights in God's service. In 1 Chronicles 29:19, we find David pleading with God: "And give unto Solomon my son a perfect heart, to keep thy commandments, thy testimonies, and thy statutes."

Solomon is warned against hypocrisy and urged to seek truth in the inward parts by the reminder that God follows us into the innermost recesses of our souls and perceives our thoughts even before they take conscious form. The exhortation is enforced by a promise and a warning. God will make Himself known in all the riches of His grace to those who seek Him, but those who forsake Him shall be cast off forever. This does not mean that any true servants of God can forsake Him and be cast off eternally by Him, but rather that true servants are preserved in the way of seeking and knowing and serving the Lord from the heart. To enjoy the blessings promised, let us seek grace to heed the exhortations given.

But will God in very deed dwell with men on the earth? Behold heaven and the heaven of heavens cannot contain thee; how much less this house which I have built.

—2 CHRONICLES 6:18

In 2 Chronicles 2:5–6, Solomon says, "And the house which I build is great: for great is our God above all gods. But who is able to build him an house, seeing the heaven and heaven of heavens cannot contain him? who am I then, that I should build him an house, save only to burn sacrifice before him?" In Old Testament times, the Temple was the center of worship and of Israel's experience of God's merciful presence, but the Israelites recognized that it spoke of a reality infinitely greater than itself. It pointed to God whose "greatness is unsearchable" (Ps. 145:3). It represented the wonder spoken of in Isaiah 57:15: "For thus saith the high and lofty One that inhabiteth eternity, whose name is Holy; I dwell in the high and holy place, with him also that is of a contrite and humble spirit, to revive the spirit of the humble, and to revive the heart of the contrite ones" (compare Isaiah 66:1–2). It pointed to what lies at the heart of that wonder: "Behold, a virgin shall be with child, and shall bring forth a son, and they shall call his name Emmanuel, which being interpreted is, God with us" (Matt. 1:23).

Solomon had some awareness of God's infinite greatness. He was aware that the vastness of space did not provide a measure for the greatness of God. Unsearchable greatness characterizes God and all His attributes. "God is a Spirit, infinite, eternal and unchangeable, in his being, wisdom, power, holiness, justice, goodness, and truth" (*Westminster Shorter Catechism, 4*). But this greatness of God before whom he bowed assured Solomon that He would fulfill His covenant engagements and would indeed dwell with men on the earth. God is present everywhere and is present with His people as a God of mercy, accessible to them in Christ. Though not containable in any space, however large, He dwells with men on this little planet. He who once "dwelt among us" in the Person of His Son (John 1:14) so that He was seen with human eyes (1 John 1:1), dwells with His people still by His Word and Spirit. "God is in the midst of her; she shall not be moved" (Ps. 46:5).

For the eyes of the LORD run to and fro throughout the whole earth, to shew himself strong in the behalf of them whose heart is perfect toward him. Herein thou hast done foolishly: therefore from henceforth thou shalt have wars.

—2 CHRONICLES 16:9

The Lord is rebuking King Asa for showing sinful lack of confidence in Him and enlisting the aid of the king of Syria. How often we merit a similar rebuke!

Accommodating His language to our understanding, the Lord asserts His all-inclusive providence. He knows everything. He is no mere observer but puts His purposes into effect in everything that takes place. His interest, care, and supervision of all things are constant. He is active and personally involved, in different ways, in all things.

He has a special care for His own people. While He beholds "all the sons of men...the eye of the Lord is upon them that fear him, upon them that hope in his mercy" (Ps. 33:13–19). Those who have been put right in their relationship and attitude to God can be assured that, in His complete control of all that takes place throughout the earth, the Lord aims at their good. His strength is exerted on their behalf. His knowledge, wisdom, grace, justice, and power secure their true interests. To demonstrate this and ensure that no flesh shall glory in His presence, the Lord may have to make His people feel their own weakness. As Charnock says, He will sometimes disappoint His and their enemies only "when they seem to have got to the goal, with the ball at their foot." "Most gladly therefore will I rather glory in my infirmities, that the power of Christ may rest upon me. Therefore I take pleasure in infirmities, in reproaches, in necessities, in persecutions, in distresses for Christ's sake: for when I am weak, then am I strong" (2 Cor. 12:9–10).

Unbelief is so foolish as well as sinful; it brings on us the Lord's displeasure and much trouble and, as with Asa, leads on to other sins. It dishonors God, weakens us, and makes us succumb to fightings without and fears within. Like Asa, the Lord's people have evidences in the pages of Scripture, the history of the church, and their own experience, of how sufficient God's strength is for those who put their confidence in Him.

"Trust ye in the LORD for ever: for in the LORD JEHOVAH is everlasting strength" (Isa. 26:4).

And Jehoshaphat said unto the king of Israel, Inquire, I pray thee, at the word of the Lord today.
—2 CHRONICLES 18:4

David's kingdom was broken in two. Humanly appointed kings ruled in Israel. The best of the kings of Judah in the God-appointed line of David showed themselves to be weak and sinful. These facts demonstrate that the accomplishing of the purposes of God's grace for His people in Christ was altogether His own doing. Here is good King Jehoshaphat combining with the ungodly and idolatrous Ahab; yet, in spite of the sad lapse of the one and the ungodliness of the other, God brought His purposes to pass.

His piety and the awakening of conscience made Jehoshaphat realize belatedly that enquiry should be made as to the Lord's mind regarding their plans. We cannot send for living prophets as they did, but we have the sure revelation of God's will in the Scriptures and ought to seek His mind there in prayerful dependence upon the Holy Spirit. There we find the principles and precepts to apply in all the decisions which we have to make.

Ahab certainly, and perhaps Jehoshaphat at this time, wanted the word of the Lord to confirm their own ideas and plans. Ahab knew that the word of the Lord spoken by faithful Micaiah condemned him, for which reason he had probably already imprisoned the prophet (v. 25), and he did not want to hear it. How we must beware of rejecting truth when it cuts across our own desires and way of thinking. Jehoshaphat, who had a very different basic attitude to the Word of God from that of Ahab, still joined with him in implementing his plan in spite of what the word of the Lord had said to them, virtually casting His words behind them (Ps. 50:17). They would not hearken to His voice and He left them to walk in their own counsels (Ps. 81:11–12).

Ahab discovered at great cost that despising the word of the Lord does not prevent its accomplishment. Although Jehoshaphat's life was spared, he also found that there was wrath upon him from the Lord because he had helped the ungodly and entered into a cordial relation with those who hated the Lord (2 Chr. 19:2).

May we seek grace to make the Word of the Lord our guide in every matter. "In all thy ways acknowledge him, and he shall direct thy paths" (Prov. 3:6). Is there a decision you are facing today for which you need God's Word and guidance?

But are there not with you, even with you,
sins against the LORD your God?
—2 CHRONICLES 28:10

Because in Ahaz's evil reign they had forsaken the Lord their God, many of the people of Jerusalem and Judah were delivered into the hands of the Syrians. Others were slain or carried captive by Pekah, who ruled the ten tribes known as Israel. Oded, a prophet in Israel, rebuked those who slew some of their brethren and carried others captive for this great rage.

The Lord used Syria and Israel to chasten Judah. Oded is not arguing with the justice of God in His dealings with sinful Judah. He is not encouraging a light-hearted attitude to sin. A holy God who is not angry with the wicked every day is a contradiction in terms. A godly person who is not grieved by personal sin and by sin in the surrounding church and society is also a contradiction in terms. The Lord's people must feel indignation against all that blasphemes and dishonors God's holy name. Trivializing sin is inconsistent with love to God.

What Oded was rebuking was the self-righteous failure of the people to recognize how they themselves had offended against the Lord and the fact that the fierce wrath of the Lord was upon them. It was not God's glory, hatred of sin, or concern for the reformation of Judah which inspired their attack on Judah; they only sought their own advantage and gratification. They enjoyed destroying Judah. They were oblivious to their own sins and God's displeasure with them.

If it is really holy hatred for sin that characterizes us, we will hate it in ourselves more than we hate it in others. We will not apply a more lenient standard to ourselves than to others. We will be saying with the psalmist: "For I acknowledge my transgressions: and my sin is ever before me" (Ps. 51:3). We will be concerned that our sin is against God. We will be more mercifully inclined towards others than towards ourselves. While not condoning sin in others, we will be most hard upon ourselves.

Are there sins against the Lord your God in you? Sin around us does not usually trouble us as it ought, but how we should consider our own sins and need of repentance!

But Hezekiah prayed for them, saying, The good LORD pardon every one that prepareth his heart to seek God, the LORD God of his fathers, though he be not cleansed according to the purification of the sanctuary.
—2 CHRONICLES 30:18–19

As part of the reformation of religion and morals Hezekiah endeavored to bring about, the observance of the Passover was restored. But by the time the Temple was ready, the Passover could not be kept at the stipulated time. The king and his counselors resolved that it was better to observe it at a later date than to postpone it for another year. Many met the summons to repentance and to renewed observance of the divine institution with scorn. However, the Lord gave others a mind to respond obediently to this call. The problem was that they were unable to prepare for the Passover as the ceremonial law prescribed.

Hezekiah's prayer does not imply that what God prescribes can be dispensed with, or that exceptional circumstances justify disregard for His revealed will. It is a fallacy to suggest that whether or not one is obedient to the revealed will of God does not matter "so long as the heart is right." But even under the ceremonial law, the emphasis was on the attitude to God that motivated the observance of what God required. Thus God could dismiss the feasts and offerings of those who diligently performed the outward ceremonies but whose hearts were alienated from Him and whose doings were evil. On the other hand, He could pardon those who bemoaned their inability to conform to His will as He required and they desired, and whose hearts were truly engaged in seeking Him. This heart was given to them by God (vv. 11–12).

The Lord prepares our hearts to seek Him in regeneration, but there is a particular preparedness of heart required when we engage in prayer or worship or the sacraments. The imminence of such an event often reminds of how ill-prepared we are. It calls us to consider the solemn privilege of drawing near to God to examine ourselves, to seek to stir up repentance, faith, love, and reliance upon the Intercessor of whom Hezekiah was just a faint shadow and who secures the acceptance and service of those who come unto God through Him.

And when he was in affliction, he besought the LORD his God, and humbled himself greatly before the God of his fathers, and prayed unto him: and he was intreated of him, and heard his supplication, and brought him again to Jerusalem into his kingdom. Then Manasseh knew that the Lord he was God.
                                    —2 CHRONICLES 33:12–13

Manasseh was easily the most wicked king who had reigned in Jerusalem. Responsible for leading his people into worse ways than the heathen, he filled Jerusalem with the blood of the innocent. His sin was aggravated by his elevated position, by his godly parents, and by the Lord speaking to him through His prophets. Like Saul of Tarsus he was a blasphemer, a persecutor, and injurious—but he obtained mercy. This is not intended to encourage people in sin by the hope that they will obtain mercy, but to encourage repentance by the assurance that even the chief of sinners may obtain mercy and repentance and forgiveness, that God may be feared (Ps. 130:4).

The Lord brought Manasseh into affliction and then sanctified his affliction so that he was brought to heed the Word of God he had despised for so long. God harnessed His providence for accomplishing His gracious purpose, as with the prodigal son. The truth concerning his sin against God was brought home to him to bring him to humbly cast himself upon God's mercy. Though in his sin and pride he had been putting the God of his fathers from him all his days, he now sought access to Him. Humbled by God, he humbled himself in the dust of self-abasement and no doubt prayed from the heart the prayer of David which he may have learned at his mother's knee: "For thy name's sake, O LORD, pardon mine iniquity, for it is great" (Ps. 25:11).

God heard the cry which He had put in Manasseh's heart and revealed Himself to him in His holiness and grace. He restored him to the place where he was able to demonstrate the reality of his repentance—in acknowledging the Lord and endeavoring as best he could to undo the evil he had done. He and his people had to live with many of the consequences of his earlier sinful life, and his wickedness is generally remembered more than his repentance. Yet he is a witness to us that God's grace is sovereign, powerful, and free.

MILK & HONEY

from The Psalms

JERROLD H. LEWIS

Blessed is the man that walketh not in the counsel of the ungodly, nor standeth in the way of sinners, nor sitteth in the seat of the scornful.
—PSALM 1:1

The book of Psalms is the only book of the Bible that begins with a benediction, "Blessed." It can also be translated "truly happy." Happy is the man who does not do three things: The first thing he does not do is "walk in the counsel of the ungodly." That is, his way or walk of life is not in the flesh, but in holiness. Romans 8:7 tells us why it cannot be in the way of this world: "Because the carnal mind is enmity against God: for it is not subject to the law of God, neither indeed can be." The world will always have its own counselors who only bring us to the rocky terrain of self-gratification. The believer must wage war against this temptation, remembering that "[w]hosoever therefore will be a friend of the world is the enemy of God" (James 4:4). We are reminded of Amos 3:3: "Can two walk together, except they be agreed?" Our counsel then must be the delight of the law of God.

Second, he does not "stand in the way of sinners." "To stand" literally means to "continue" or to linger in a certain place. The redeemed soul will invariably stumble into sin, but his first reaction will be to flee back to the path of righteousness. The question we must ask ourselves is, whose company do we feel most comfortable in?

The last thing the blessed man does not do is sit "in the seat of the scornful." This is the final progression of the ungodly. It is the resting place of those who have never been converted, be they ever so religious. One Puritan said about the progression of sin, "First we hide it, then we defend it, and finally we boast of it." Is this not true in this passage? To sit "in the seat of the scornful" means that we have not only walked in the counsel of sinners, not only stood in the folly of sin, but we have taken up the banner of sin itself, instructing others in sin.

If we desire the benediction of this verse, we must, by the power of the Holy Spirit, delight in the Word of God as our daily counsel, and always be mindful of the path of the ungodly. "Lord, make us trees of righteousness."

APRIL 2

Kiss the Son, lest he be angry, and ye perish from the way, when his wrath is kindled but a little.
—PSALM 2:12

This verse is full of doctrinal instruction, covering everything from the incarnation to propitiation, mercy and grace to eternal wrath. It is a command to humble ourselves before Christ in repentance, lest we experience the slightest motion of His eternal wrath. Yet mercy is set before judgment, as is the case in every gospel call.

There is one expression of Christ's which gives us a clearer view of divine vengeance than all the pain of the damned can do. Our blessed Redeemer—in whom was found no guile, in whose face no personal guilt could stare—when suffering in our place and carrying our sorrows here on earth, gave us a window into the torment of eternal wrath when He said, "Father, if it be possible, let this cup pass from me." It is as if He had said, "Couldest Thou be glorified, Thy justice satisfied, and the elect saved, any other way than by My drinking this tremendous cup, O let it be done! Yet not my will, but Thine be done." Now, if the Son of God expressed Himself this way under a sense of eternal wrath, how dreadful, terrible, and unbearable it must be. What rivers of melted brimstone, floods of fire, and utter blackness engulfs the body and soul in hell, where the worm never dies, the fire is never quenched, the gulf never bridged, the bottom never found! The exquisite horrors of hell will be a perpetual discovery of the lost.

Yet today's words shine like a lighthouse beacon on every penitent heart, "Kiss ye the Son." Here is one more opportunity to have the fires of hell quenched by the blood of Christ. Three things will remain a wonder: the compassion of the Father, the condescension of the Son, and the insensibility of the sinner. Oh, may we be wise before instructed in the world of flames.

Now therefore, kings, be wise; be taught,
Ye judges of the earth:
Serve God in fear, and see that ye
Join trembling with your mirth.
Kiss ye the Son, lest in his ire
Ye perish from the way,
If once his wrath begin to burn:
Blessed all that on him stay.
—Scottish Metrical Psalter, 1650, Psalm 2

LORD, how are they increased that trouble me! many are they that rise up against me.
—PSALM 3:1

This psalm is written for our encouragement against any sudden change in the soul's plight in this world, be it for the better or, as is so often the case, for the worse. Let us follow David as a pattern in times of trouble when the winds of persecution beat against the door of the soul. First, like David, let us acknowledge our sins to God and confess to Him how often we rise up against the truth of His Word. In difficult times, we may take refuge in identifying with the Old Testament prophets, the apostles, the early church, Huguenots, and the Puritans who, like King David, were named the children of Belial (1 Sam. 25:17). Let the wicked world brag that they will prevail against us and overcome us, and that God will give us over and be our God no more. Let the world put their trust in Absalom, with his flowing golden locks and his many chariots and horsemen; yet may we say with David, "Thou, O Lord, art my defender, and the lifter up of my head."

Are you in distress today? Are you pursued from every side by inward and outward enemies that desire your downfall? Persuade yourself, as David did, that the Lord is your defender and shield in times of trouble. The word "shield" in verse 3 is the same word used elsewhere in the Psalms as buckler, a cover made of alligator hide which protects on every side. Jehovah alone can compass you about with glory and honor. He alone will bring down the enemy from his high place and exalt the lowly and meek. It is the Lord who will "smite" your "enemies on the cheek bone" and break the teeth of the ungodly. He will, in His own time, hang the Absaloms of our life by the long hairs of their vanity.

And know this, that to identify with David here is to identify with Christ. These are His words in the midst of His own sufferings. Remember that it is the prayer of the saint to pray the words of Paul, "That I may know him, and the power of his resurrection, and the fellowship of his sufferings, being made conformable unto his death" (Phil. 3:10).

APRIL 4

Hear me when I call, O God of my righteousness: thou hast enlarged me when I was in distress; have mercy upon me, and hear my prayer.
—PSALM 4:1

David did not think it enough to ask once, so he doubles his request in the first verse, "Here me when I call..., and hear my prayer." The only prayers that reach the throne of grace are fervent, offered in a kind of grateful violence to heaven. Anyone who offers cold prayers may expect a cold response. How can we expect God to answer a prayer that we ourselves have lifelessly offered and have soon forgotten? Surface prayers, formed on the lips, are not forged on the anvil of the heart. One ancient said of this verse, "Forth from his breast he pounded a mighty cry." This we all must learn to do.

"O God of my righteousness." Not, "God the righteous," or even "God of righteousness," but "O God of my righteousness." David is saying, "O God, who art righteousness Thyself, the root of my righteousness, of my righteous cause, and of my righteous life." Any holiness, piety, or purity in us is alien righteousness, owned by Christ and given in mercy. The humble heart will notice right away that all that he has is in correspondence to the mercy God has shown. It is a reflection of Himself in us, and this is a delight to Him. "For the righteous LORD loveth righteousness; his countenance doth behold the upright" (Ps. 11:7). However, the words of the wicked when he prays are as a wind that stirs up divine displeasure into a flame. How can he appease God who does not at all please Him, who utterly disregards His pure laws and that holiness which is so dear to Him?

"Thou hast enlarged me when I was in distress." Jehovah never tires of rescuing His children. It is also during this time of pain that we are most likely to grow in grace. Can you recall times of pain in your life that brought about growth and grace?

My voice shalt thou hear in the morning, O LORD; in the morning will I direct my prayer unto thee, and will look up.
—PSALM 5:3

The word "morning" in our text means "at dawn" or first light of day. The word "direct" means "to set in a row or "order." Here the emphasis is placed on an early prayer time, as well as an ordered prayer time.

Too much sleep is a mark of laziness, but, in a candidate for glory, a sin. Very often, we rise early to manage our temporal affairs, but what of eternal? "He that loveth sleep," though in worldly things may not lose much, yet in spiritual things "shall be a poor man." When we have a long trip to take, we rise early in the morning and set our day before us. Yet every soul is on a more momentous and immensely longer journey to eternity, which cannot be delayed a day. Therefore, we have a great need to rise early and seek the Lord.

When we are older and look back on our lives, how many healthy hours will be lost in superfluous sleep? These hours, no doubt, will stare us in the face. Will we look back with sorrow on vigorous youthful hours lost in sleep—hours which might have been improved for eternity, and spent in directing our prayers to God? Did a friend, whom you dearly love, ever come early in the morning to visit you? Did you not rise to entertain him, not knowing how soon he would go away? Shall you then give the Beloved of your soul any less than your friend? Metaphorically, sleep is a kind of death; when asleep, how can I have communion with God? Out of sovereignty, He may speak to man in a dream, in a vision of the night (like Zachariah); and sometimes the dreams of His people have been divine, so that, when they awoke, their sleep has been sweet. But the duty of saints is to seek Him with all the activity of their soul, in the full exercise of all her powers. With the psalmist, believers should awake themselves early, that they may praise Him. David arose early to secret prayer, as did our Lord.

But as for me, I will come into thy house in the multitude of thy mercy: and in thy fear will I worship toward thy holy temple.

—PSALM 5:7

It is generally believed that David was the author of this psalm. If this is the case, the temple was not built yet. Only the tabernacle existed, so he must mean the tabernacle. The word "temple" here probably represents the Holy of Holies, the place where the divine Shechinah dwelt. It is here where David will prostrate himself.

It is with humility, not pride, that the psalmist contrasts himself with the fate of the wicked. "But as for me, I will come into thy house." His argument for attendance is not that he is better than they, but that he has received mercy. We must never think we can come to the house of God with our own works, our own labors, our own righteousness. No, David realizes that he brings with him a multitude of sins. His ground for coming, though sinful as he is, "is in the multitude of thy mercy." It is as if he is saying, "I will approach the house of God with confidence because of Thy boundless grace." God's laws are all numbered, as are the sins we commit. But in Christ, these numbered sins are met with innumerable mercies.

"And in thy fear will I worship toward thy holy temple." This is not a servile fear. Many worship God out of drudgery, but not the true believer. The fear here is a filial fear, a respect and adoration for the wonders of grace in exchange for great sins. When the soul is freed from the curse of the law, the only response is true worship from the heart.

"But as for me." We should care nothing about how the world might view our worship, but make devout promises to attend upon the great love wherewith we are loved. Doesn't this temple also foreshadow redemption in Christ? In Him, God reconciled the world to Himself. In Him dwells all the fullness of the Godhead bodily. In every age, in every dispensation, Christ was always the Temple where the covenant God was met with and worshiped. The human nature of Jesus was the real temple of the divine. Nowhere else can God be found.

Shiggaion of David, which he sang unto the LORD, concerning the words of Cush the Benjamite.
                                                            —PSALM 7:1

We often overlook the preface of a psalm and get right into the text itself. In doing so we forget that the preface is also part of Holy Scripture, and we often inadvertently gloss over some helpful thought and food for the soul.

The Word "Shiggaion" is only used one other time in the entire Bible. In Habbakuk 3:1, we find these words, "A prayer of Habakkuk the prophet upon Shigionoth." In both instances of the word, we find great meaning for the believer. The word itself seems to describe a deep flow of inward feelings. It is akin to a spontaneous song or poem that expresses the heart—not so much with words of precision and forethought, but by spontaneous emotion. Very often we are concerned with the words of our prayers rather than the prayer in our words. Here, the psalmist is not outlining his song with wondrous phraseology, or with systematic precision, but with utter sincerity. Here we find David exemplifying this strain of prayer in a Shigionoth.

Sometimes it is good for us to order our prayers in such a way that we are giving full thought to their content. There are times we pray and "receive not, because we ask amiss, that we may consume it upon our lusts" (James 4:3). For this we need to pray with understanding that is according to the will of God. Other times we know not what we ought to pray, and the Spirit therefore intercedes "with groanings which cannot be uttered" (Rom. 8:26). However, we should also notice those times when we, like David, are so overcome by the wonders of the Lord that we speak out of spontaneous rapture.

It reminds us of the words of Thomas Brooks, when he said, "God looks not at the elegance of your prayers to see how neat they are, nor the geometry of your prayers, to see how long they are, nor yet the arithmetic of your prayers to see how many they are, nor yet the sweetness of your prayers, nor the logic, but the sincerity of your prayers, how hearty they are." May the Lord give us some Shiggainon prayers today!

How long wilt thou forget me, O LORD? for ever? how long wilt thou hide thy face from me?

—PSALM 13:1

What do we do when the promises of God seems to contradict His providence? When the withdrawing presence of the Spirit makes us feel as if He will hide Himself from us forever? We must see that even in this there is purpose. Not one feather of affliction is laid upon the heart of the believer that is not set there with great purpose by God. Even when God appears to withdraw, He never does so completely. He is causing us to let go of the ropes and tethers that strap us to this earth. To wait in silence for our God, then, is our object. A delay in answer is only a perception on our part, all the while being taught by the school of silence.

Have we then any reason to complain of days and months of apparent loneliness? No. God has appointed a set time, and at the set time He will return to you. These seemingly absent days are good for us. Though the time seems long in our mind, to wait with patience for Him creates an expectancy through serious meditation and confession of sin. God has always dealt this way with His people for growth in grace. And these trials, like the tilling blade of the farmer, break up the fallow ground of the heart, bringing forth a rich crop of ripened fruits. This brings an increase of glory to God, and unspeakable joy to the soul, through the ages of eternity. Isn't this worth more than all that might come from a speedy answer?

Then sit still, dear soul, and calmly wait for the return of your Lord. He is not far. And while you wait for the sense of His presence to return, wonder more why justly deserved judgments are not executed against you rather than His promise never to leave you. "I will never leave thee, nor forsake thee" (Heb. 3:5).

The LORD is my shepherd; I shall not want.
—PSALM 23:1

Who is the LORD, and what qualifies Him to be my Shepherd? The word LORD here is in capitals. This means YHWH, the covenant-keeping God. It is not speaking of the Father, in distinction from the Son and the Spirit, but God in His three Persons and one substance. And yet this statement was best fulfilled in the incarnation of Christ who said, "I am the Good Shepherd."

Christ says four times in the New Testament that He is the Bread of life, four times the Light of the World, twice the Door, once the Vine, three times the Son of God. Yet over thirteen times, Christ refers to Himself as a Shepherd. It is the clearest self-portrait of the Son of God. That is why Peter, an eyewitness to Christ's earthly ministry, in all the titles He could have afforded to Christ, described Him as the "Shepherd and bishop of your souls" (1 Pet. 2:25).

How is the Lord like a shepherd? A shepherd leads sheep out and in so that they find pasture and safety. So it is with Christ. Isaiah 42:16 says, "And I will bring the blind by a way that they knew not; I will lead them in paths that they have not known: I will make darkness light before them, and crooked things straight."

A shepherd watches over his sheep and keeps them from being destroyed by ravenous beasts. So it is with Christ. Ezekiel 34:28 says, "And they shall no more be a prey to the heathen, neither shall the beast of the land devour them; but they shall dwell safely, and none shall make them afraid."

If any sheep have strayed, the shepherd brings them back to himself. So it is with Christ. Psalm 119:176 says this: "I have gone astray like a lost sheep; seek thy servant; for I do not forget thy commandments."

A shepherd brings his sheep to the shade in times of scorching heat; in times of persecution and affliction, he finds asylum for them. So it is with Christ. Isaiah 4:6 reads, "And there shall be a tabernacle for a shadow in the daytime from the heat, and for a place of refuge, and for a covert from storm and from rain."

This is our Shepherd. He is the Lord Christ!

The LORD is my shepherd; I shall not want.
—PSALM 23:1

A remarkable feature about revivals is that they have normally occurred among people of humble origins. That reminds us of the words spoken of Christ when he preached, "And the common people heard him gladly" (Mark 12:37). The Bible itself is written by and large to a nomadic, earthy people. Christ, Himself, although completely uncommon in every way, came from humble origins, was known as a carpenter's son, born in a lowly stable. But who is the Lord here in our text? The word LORD in the King James version is in capital letters, meaning Jehovah, the covenant God. It is not speaking of the Father, in distinction from the Son and the Spirit, but God in His three Persons, and one substance. Yet this text is best fulfilled in the words of Christ, "I am the good shepherd" (John 10:11).

"The LORD is my shepherd." The relationship here is deeper than mere formal possession. It is one of personal possession—you yourself are possessed. It is like a child saying with pride, "This is my father," when in fact the child belongs to him. It is a term of endearment and love as if to say, "Who do you belong to? A king? A prince? A ruler? I belong to Christ. The Lord is my shepherd."

Further it says, "I shall not want." The word for "want" in the Hebrew is not desire but signifies a lack or need. In effect, the text is saying, "The Lord is my shepherd, I have everything I need." A sheep of Christ will lack no good thing, for He has promised to supply all our needs "according to his riches in glory" (Phil. 4:19). When the sheep is under the care of the Great Shepherd, while we may suffer at times in the body, there is a promise to provide soul nourishment and spiritual food.

Is Christ the Shepherd and Great Bishop of your soul? In the old days, after a sheep had been purchased by a shepherd, it was marked for ownership by the shepherd cutting a special notch in his ear with a sharp knife. This special mark was on the ear of every sheep the shepherd owned. Thus the word "earmarked." "The Lord is my Shepherd, I shall not want." Is He your provider, your sustainer, your all? Do you bear His mark by faith?

He maketh me to lie down in green pastures.
—PSALM 23:2

Green pastures is significant in that "pastures" means not only grass, but new grass. Coupled with "green," this means a meadow of abode, bringing together a fullness of meaning in an abode of tender grasses. The shepherd brings the sheep to the place of sustenance with both purpose and authority.

What are these "green pastures" but the Scriptures of truth—always fresh, always rich, and never exhausted for the lambs of God? A sheep left to feed itself will find a patch of earth and eat it to the ground. Yet there is no fear of biting the bare ground where the grass is long enough for the flock to lie down in it. Sweet and full are the doctrines of the gospel—food for the soul, as tender grass is for the sheep. When we are enabled by faith to find rest in the promises, we are like the sheep that lie down in the midst of the pasture; we find at the same moment provision and peace, rest and refreshment, serenity and satisfaction.

These green pastures are not only the Word, but also the ordinances. God's ordinances are food for all believers; the Word of life is the nourishment of the new man. It is milk for babes, pasture for sheep, never barren, never parched, but always a green pasture for faith to feed in.

God makes His saints to lie down; He gives them quiet and contentment in their own minds. Whatever their circumstances might be, their souls dwell at ease in Him, and that makes every pasture green. Are we blessed with the green pastures of the Word as they are preached and displayed in the ordinances? What good would it do a sheep to walk right through the best of fields if he never took the time to eat and rest? Sadly, so many believers do this with the Word. Let us not think it enough to pass through the green pastures, but let us lie down in them and abide in them; this is our rest forever. It is by a continual use of the means of grace that a soul is fed.

He leadeth me in the paths of righteousness.
—PSALM 23:3

The phrase "the paths" in the original is a masculine noun, which primarily means "encampment or circle of a camp." But in our text it also means "track or path." Our way is led by Christ, and that is wonderful to His own. But what is more, a shepherd will cause the sheep to follow a track well-known to him. This is what we have in Christ, who came, as the book of Matthew says, "to fulfill all righteousness." He leads the sheep in paths of His own making.

So what does this mean to us? For a sheep, it means the shepherd is always watching where the sheep are going. He knows that a sheep left to himself will follow the same path he has always known until it becomes a rut, or in some cases, an actual crevice, where he can become stuck. Isaiah 53:6 says, "All we like sheep have gone astray; we have turned every one to his own way," which means turning into sin and wandering away from the good path.

Notice here that David does not say, "He leadeth me into paths of righteousness," as if to say, "There is the path over there; go and walk in it alone. I'll watch from a distance, I hope everything turns out alright for you." No, the text says, "He leadeth me in the paths of righteousness." This means Christ is going before us in righteousness. What we are expected to do by way of righteousness has already been done before by Christ.

He is our Elder Brother, He is our Mediator, He has walked the path of righteousness perfectly, with no wandering or straying. His perfect righteousness leads us not into the way, but in the way.

Observe, that the plural is used in this text: "the paths of righteousness." There is a plurality of commandments set before us in Christ. "If you love me," says our Lord, "keep my commandments." Whatever God may give us to do, we desire to do, led by His love. Some Christians overlook the blessing of sanctification. And yet, to a thoroughly renewed and restored heart, this is one of the sweetest gifts of the covenant: to walk in righteousness.

He restoreth my soul.

—PSALM 23:3

Because of who we are by nature and what we know of ourselves experientially, we know that we are liable to fall. We are prone to wander. Wandering from Christ can take on many different forms. When David says, "Why art thou cast down, O my soul? and why art thou disquieted in me?" he is expressing sorrow of heart. Sorrow can cause any one of us to drift away from the Great Shepherd. For some, it is seeing a loved one in pain. Or perhaps a situation at work or even at home draws your attention away from the presence of the Shepherd's love. We stop grazing on the Word, and before we know it, we are like a lost sheep unable to move ourselves from that place of sorrow and despondency.

Let us remember that when our soul grows sorrowful, Christ revives it by diligent seeking. This restoration is not only a recovery from despondency, but also a rescue from what caused our drifting. This text is telling us that the same hand which first rescued us from ruin reclaims us from all our subsequent failures. There is, as 1 John indicates, a time when we stumble into darkness and sin, but He, the Great Shepherd of the soul, is there to bring us back to Him. Chastisement itself is blended with tenderness, and the voice which speaks reproof, saying, "They have perverted their way, and they have forsaken the Lord their God," utters the kindest invitation, "Return, ye backsliding children, and I will heal your backslidings" (cf. Jer. 3).

So when the soul wanders, be it into sin, disparaging circumstances, or the trials of life, the great restoring Shepherd brings us back. Added to the return is a restoration of the very relationship that was lost through our own wanderings. So then it is all of grace that we might not boast in ourselves, but in the One who brings us to restoration. Can you admit this for yourself? Have you been sullied by the sinfulness of self, the world, or the devil? Can you not also be restored by the Shepherd Jesus Christ?

APRIL 14

*Yea, though I walk through the valley
of the shadow of death.*

—PSALM 23:4

When we think of this portion of Scripture, we often have in our minds a wide valley of darkness. But this is not the case. In fact, these valleys were narrow and deep gorges where the sun never shone. They were dangerous because they were often home to many predators during the daylight hours as well as the night. They often contained thick underbrush where, if a timid sheep was to fall, it would be next to impossible to get out. It refers to a ravine overhung by high precipitous cliffs, filled with dense underbrush, designed to inspire dread in the timid.

If we were to translate this passage literally, the text would read, "Even though I pass through the shadow of the deep gorge of darkness, I will fear no evil." The passage is not speaking of death as much as it is speaking of the fear of death. It speaks of peril and danger that could be associated with death as a shadow.

What is a shadow? It is the harmless outline of an object. If I were to put my hand up against a wall where a light was cast, what harm could come to you from my shadow? None. The shadow is the image that the thing itself casts. So here, death is looked upon as a shadow. Why only a shadow to David? Because the Shepherd, Jehovah, is with him. He is secure in his Shepherd's care.

Is this not the place we should seek for in Christ? We live in a world bent on avoiding the inevitable—death. Creams, diets, pills, exercises, operations, augmentations, are all designed to delay what will inevitably come. There is a real fear in the natural mind of death, even for believers, at times. But here, David is saying that death has no power over him. Should the sheep get too close to the edge of that gully and run the risk of falling to his death, he will not fear because the Shepherd is near.

Dear reader, should you draw close to the grave and the sorrows of death surround you, and should you be upon the very border of eternity, hold fast to Christ, and sing, "O death! where is thy sting? O grave! where is thy victory?"

*Thou preparest a table before me in the
presence of mine enemies.*
—PSALM 23:5

The context of this passage, written by David, probably speaks of his conflict with either Saul or Absalom and the violent encounters against his person. It is, no doubt, painted against the backdrop of very trying circumstances. Yet the whole tenor of this psalm is not first and foremost tactile. It's not dealing with physical food and drink, but spiritual.

The vast majority of the Christian life is hidden. It has outward manifestations to those around us, but it is primarily a spiritual life. And so the application here is first to the spiritual man. This table is a spiritual banquet for the nourishment of the soul. In the Scriptures, when a table is employed as a metaphor, it is representing provision or bounty. And here this table is furnished for the guest in the presence of his enemies. What a strange place for a banquet!

The word "preparest" in the Hebrew is a long verb, which tells us that the activity of preparation is slow, methodical, and organized. When a soldier gets hungry, he quickly grabs some bread or some water, eats as quickly as possible, and returns to the fight. But here we have a table set before the enemy, right in front of their eyes. Picture it. There stands the enemy of your soul, ready for a war against you. And just before they are ready to attack, they stop in their tracks. "What is this?" they say. "Is that a table coming out? Do I see a tablecloth? Is that drink I see being poured, and do I smell roasted lamb? What is happening over there?" What a picture! Further, the Hebrew indicates that the enemy can only observe this banquet at a distance. They cannot approach you. That is embedded in the root "before my enemies."

Is this not what we have in Jesus Christ? Because of the provision made through His shed blood, through His active and passive obedience, through the merits He has won and the alien forensic imputation of that righteousness to us, we have spread before us a banqueting table of gospel provision where sin may not touch us!

APRIL 16

*Surely goodness and mercy shall follow
me all the days of my life.*
—PSALM 23:6

How could David, in all seriousness, say these words? His life was marked by trials, internal fighting, strife, and war. Was not David's life sought by Saul? Was he not driven to the wilderness, pursued by vengeful forces? And yet he writes in full confidence, "Surely goodness and mercy shall follow me all the days of my life." He prefaces it with a "surely," which is an emphatic "indeed." David is saying, "Surely, surely goodness and mercy will follow me all the days of my life!"

We have a tendency to think of goodness and mercy in very worldly terms. Some would argue that an uneventful Christian life is a good Christian life. To have everything that you desire, no temporal problems, and a full bank account is God's goodness to the believer. Yet when this word is used in our text, it means *spiritual* bounty and sweetness. David is taking stock of his life, and as he assesses it, he is not measuring the quality of his life by temporal blessings, but by inward graces. As Christians, we often want God's goodness and mercy to become evident in the wrong way! As frail and weak people, we look for the good as measured by time, not eternity. And so here, to keep the eye of faith on Christ, on His dealings with us, is His goodness towards us in mercy and grace.

Notice also that His goodness and mercy shall not precede us, but "follow." "Follow" here could rightly be interpreted as "pursuing and chasing after" the believer for the remainder of his earthly tomorrows. As we pass through the storms of life and walk through the valley of the shadow of death, as a table is prepared before you in the presence of all your faults and sins (enemies), you will look back on your life and say, "Surely God's goodness and His mercy are evident in all that has happened."

If you are in Christ, you have been pursued by His goodness, pursued by His mercy—not just a few times, but "all the days of your life." What a reason to praise your Shepherd today!

*I have not sat with vain persons, neither
will I go in with dissemblers.*

—PSALM 26:4

Under the Old Testament law, anyone who touched a dead carcass or had a running sore was to wash his clothes, bathe himself in water, and be considered unclean until the sun had set. To the church of the Old Testament, this represented the contamination of sin under the ceremonial law. If this was the picture or the shadow, how much worse is the reality, when we are friends with the world? Yet I fear that this pollution is more permanent than for a single day. We are defiled, not only by sin rising in our own heart, but by being with those who openly sin as well as witnessing the sin of others. The corruption of our nature is so great that we are ready to catch the contagion; and if we do not detest, hate, and abhor it as we should, then we are polluted by it.

Out of a sense of sanctified thanksgiving, David says here, "I have not sat with vain persons, neither will I go in with dissemblers." Can you also say this?

Our great difficulty is that we must live in a fallen world full of those that are relishing their sin. We must walk through this Vanity Fair, but on our way, our pace should quicken and we should be making sure that our dealings with the world are only of the general sort, to be done with as little expense of precious time as possible, unless we have in view doing good to other men's immortal souls. We must be on guard against this, as the world seems to be entering the church at an alarming rate. Listen to the similar words of James: "Know ye not that the friendship of the world is enmity with God? whosoever therefore will be a friend of the world is the enemy of God" (James 4:4). If we find that we have been defiled by the world's enticements and temptations, let us remember to cleanse ourselves in the holy laver of washing. "Wherefore come out from among them, and be ye separate, saith the Lord, and touch not the unclean thing; and I will receive you" (2 Cor. 6:17).

For I have heard the slander of many: fear was on every side.
—PSALM 31:13

For the man after God's own heart, in the darkest days of his distress, slanderous words probably felt like volleys of stones. Yet David, this great king of earth, was never more like the King of Heaven than when he was wrongfully slandered. Our own trials often cause us to be identified with Christ.

Matthew 5:11 says, "Blessed are ye, when men shall revile you, and persecute you, and shall say all manner of evil against you falsely, for my sake." Oh, how sweet is the testimony of a good conscience before the Lord in the face of slander; it is an impenetrable shield against all the poisoned arrows of reproach. The soul can call to the heart-searching God to witness her innocence. But how difficult is it to be of a meek and forgiving spirit, when spoken against! To love an enemy and forgive a foe is a higher calling than most Christians achieve. Yet we must strive. Christianity in theory and Christianity in practice are two very different things. It is easy to talk of Christian forbearance, love, and patience among friends, but to practice it with our enemies proves us indeed. The evil language of slanderous times should not greatly disturb us since, in the Day of Judgment, all that is dark shall be made light before the omniscient Trinity.

Our grief should never be greater for our own slander than the malicious slander against Christ, against His character, and against truth. John 15:18 says, "If the world hate you, ye know that it hated me before it hated you." Every time a military man enters a battle, he must either stand his ground or retreat in disgrace. Likewise, under every trial, our graces either grow or suffer loss.

Therefore, our present task is neither to slander our slanderers, nor to meditate on revenge, or rejoice when evil finds them, but to justify God in all things. Then, we must forgive, pray for, and love our enemies, taking the opportunity to study in ourselves what may be reproved or even chastised. Never forget that every grace (faith, patience under the rod, humility of mind, and meekness towards all) must improve under present providences.

The transgression of the wicked saith within my heart, that there is no fear of God before his eyes.

—PSALM 36:1

The wicked flatter themselves with the false hope that all shall be well with them "till their iniquity be found to be hateful" by the Searcher of the thoughts and intents of the heart. Many delusional people flatter themselves that they are not so bad after all, and could be saved on a whim—as if salvation comes lightly and their sins are trivial. True, salvation is offered to the chief of sinners, but sinners must be saved *from* sin, not saved *in* sin. This is the error David is exposing: that some are convinced that mercy trumps all of God's other attributes, as if God should trample on His holiness, truth, and justice to exalt His mercy in saving a sinner, or in pardoning sin without any satisfaction to follow. Others flatter themselves that, because God is loving and merciful, He could never allow many to go to hell. Yet they refuse the living way God has pointed out, by which they must be saved.

Again, there are others who, because they have given up the bigger, more obvious, and excessive sins and now live a more sober life, believe that they are converted. They think heaven is theirs by some exchange of greater sins for lesser. Yet they have never felt one pang of the new birth; they do not know what it is to be born again.

Lastly, there are some who count themselves believers and would not question their salvation for all the world because they have been serious all their lives. They have hated the great sins of the world, loved religion and religious talk. These have a form of godliness, but they have denied the power thereof. They know nothing of union and communion with the Son of God. These are all dead while they live—dead before God, though alive in their own opinion and in the opinion of others. How fatal such self-flattery is. Oh, that we would be kept from this kind of self-deception and that we would work out our own salvation with fear and trembling, by the power of the Holy Spirit!

I said, LORD, be merciful unto me: heal my soul; for I have sinned against thee.

—PSALM 41:4

Suffering and sin are like a body and its shadow: they are inseparable. We must never think that our violations against the law of God are anything less than a sin against God's person: "for I have sinned against thee." David expresses in Psalm 51:4, "Against thee, thee only, have I sinned, and done this evil in thy sight." He had sinned against Bathsheba, against Uriah, against his generals, and against his nation, but it was against God first and foremost. His confession of guilt, then, is given in an appeal to the highest court, God Himself. So must our confessions be. Though we have sinned against self, friend, or enemy, more than this, we have sinned against light, knowledge, and love. For the believer, the recognition of guilt should drive him to the wonderful attribute of God's mercy.

Mercy and healing are also inseparable. Here, there is no pleading to God's justice, but an immediate petition to mercy for the soul. The godly person, while having many things in his life in need of healing (body, family, finances, etc.), will be more concerned with the soul than anything else: "heal my soul." We hear much of the cure of souls, but we often forget the reason for its sickness: "For I have sinned against thee." Here then is the root of sorrow and the essence of true repentance. And where true repentance is discovered, so is mercy. God's mercy never cools, wanes, or weakens. Yet there is a condition found here in our text, well expressed by Thomas Watson: "Mercy is not for them that sin and fear not, but for them that fear and sin not." What better evidence is there of God's mercy than a healed soul; where not only is the guilt of sin removed, but the sense of guilt as well. The healed soul is a mended soul, a cured soul, repaired and made new.

Lead me to the rock that is higher than I.
—PSALM 61:2

There are times we feel like David in the middle of a stormy sea. The water is up to our knees, and we do not falter. Up to our waist, and we do not shake. Up to our neck, and we begin to despair, yet not without hope. But what about when life seems over our heads? When the trials of this life choke us? Oh, this is when David cries out, "Lead me to the rock, that is higher than I"—higher than our troubles, above the storms of our circumstances. Even though the top of it is out of our reach ("higher than I"), we can still say, "Lead me."

What is firmer than a rock? Waters may topple the mighty oak and tear them up by their roots. But my Rock shall stand fast forever. Do rocks defend us from storms on every side? So does this Rock. Is the blast from hell itself? Christ has the keys of hell and of death. Is it from sin? Christ is your righteousness. Is it from Satan? He has conquered principalities and powers. Is it from afflictions? He is your sympathizing and feeling High Priest. Is it from losses? He is your exceeding great reward. Is it from heavy providences? He makes all things work together for your good. Is it from anguish? He is your joy. Is it from darkness? He is your sun. Is it from doubts? He is your Counselor. Is it from deadness? He is your life. Is it from enemies? He is your shield. Is it from temptation? He is your deliverer. Is it from false friends? He will never leave you nor forsake you. Is it from death? He is the resurrection and the life. What a high rock is Christ, what a glorious refuge! Here we defy the worst storm that earth and hell can bring us. Here we must cling by faith to the Rock that is made of God, a hiding place from the storm, a shelter from the tempest until every blast blows over, and there is not a threatening cloud in the sky. Until our heaven is established with an everlasting calm, cry with a loud voice, "Lead me to the rock that is higher than I!"

*To see thy power and thy glory, so as I
have seen thee in the sanctuary.*

—PSALM 63:2

How did the psalmist see the glory and power of God in the sanctuary, if God is a most pure Spirit? If we could ask David how he saw Jehovah in this text, what would he say?

First, we would see the table of shewbread, literally, the "presence bread." It consisted of twelve unleavened loaves, said traditionally to have been laid in two piles of six. This bread was designed to be a symbol of the full and never-failing provision of Christ who is the bread of life, the manna that came down from heaven. Next we see the lampstand, sometimes known as the candlesticks, which represents the Holy Spirit's illumination. It was the only light of the sanctuary which revealed the beauty of the tabernacle. So it is with the Holy Spirit. Oh, how His warm inward light makes beautiful the Word, the church, the preaching, and the prayers of the service! We then see the altar of incense, a symbol of intercessory prayer. It points to Christ the Son of God always praying for us before the Father.

If we could look into the Holy of Holies, we would see God's dwelling place among men. In the Ark of the Covenant would be a pot of manna, Aaron's blossoming rod, and the unbroken tables of the law. In these we see our Provider, our High Priest of authority, and our Lawgiver.

Finally, we would see the mercy seat where no judgment is found, but only mercy for the penitent. Here, annual atonement was made for the sins of God's people through the shed blood of sacrifice. Oh, it is all a picture of Christ in His fullness! David saw Jehovah in the sanctuary, in provision, illumination, intercession, and forgiving mercy. We have all of these in Jesus Christ, who is the fulfillment of all these shadows, and who tabernacled with men. We need not look far to see Christ in the Old Testament. He is on every page, in every shadow, for "beginning at Moses and all the prophets, he expounded unto them in all the scriptures the things concerning himself" (Luke 24:27).

Reproach hath broken my heart; and I am full of heaviness: and I looked for some to take pity, but there was none; and for comforters, but I found none.

— PSALM 69:20

Spurgeon once said, "Our Lord died of a broken heart, and reproach hath done the deed." We often think that Christ succumbed to His injuries on the cross, but this is not true. When our Lord suffered upon the cross, He did not die as a result of His pierced hands and feet, exposure to the elements, thirst, or the loss of blood. Mark 15:37 says, "And Jesus cried with a loud voice, and gave up the ghost." The Greek word used for "loud" is *megas*, where we get our English word "mega." It was with a "mega cry" that He gave up the ghost (John 10:18). The instrument of death was reproach. In the original, it means "scorn as upon an enemy." It was not simply the scorn He faced from enemies—those who scourged His back, pressed thorns on His head, and plucked out His beard. The reprehension here was the manifestation of a deeper, providential reproach, a deeper disgrace. It was the reproach of the Father that pressed so hard upon Him that it broke His heart.

"I looked for some to take pity, but there was none, and for comforters, but I found none." The word "looked" in this passage means "to wait or look longingly." Notice the text does not say "onlookers," or even "friends." We know that Mary, Martha, John, and perhaps even Peter witnessed His death on the cross. Were they not comforters? The word "comfort" here in our text means not simply a consolation, but an identification of the soul. It is speaking about not simple empathy, but sympathy. This is the kind of comforters for which Christ was scanning the horizon. He did not find such a comforter in His beloved John, or even His mother. No, in this regard Christ was all alone. He did not even find this comfort in the Father. "My God, my God, why hast thou forsaken me?" (Mark 15:34). Why? Because Christ was to bear the reproach and the curse due to us for sin. He was comfortless so that we might have comfort.

During your day today, take comfort that, while sin may buffet us, while the flesh might condemn us, "the sufferings of Christ abound in us, so our consolation also aboundeth by Christ" (2 Cor. 1:5).

And thy thoughts are very deep.
—PSALM 92:5

By nature, we admire a man or woman who is even just a little wiser than we are. Yet the wisdom of all the nations and all the angelic hosts combined are but folly before God. Before His infinite knowledge, all our thoughts are laid open, and all our conceptions are swallowed up as if they never were. How divinely glorious is His limitless knowledge! We could not possibly know or retain every thought that has flowed from our heart or every word that has dropped from our lips, much less those of our neighbor. But it is not so with God. There is not a word spoken, sung, written, typed, thought, or heard that God has ever forgotten. He presides over every purpose, guides every step, terminates every action, and governs every individual. What amazing knowledge is this: that not only nations and regions in their rising and falling are governed by Him, but every person in his particular place and circumstance, is minutely ruled by Him. It is hard to understand how the actions, words, and thoughts of so many billions of people on this earth are all known to Him as clearly and distinctly as if there were but one person on earth. Nor are the equally great number of men, women, and children who have departed from this world into the next less known by Him.

Even if these thoughts, words, and actions of all men or all time were multiplied infinitely, still everything would be as clearly, plainly, and distinctly known by Him as if only one angel, one man, one insect, or one atom existed. Hence, we may understand how infinite His power must be, for it is of the same extent with His knowledge, as are all His divine attributes.

In a word, dear reader, what joy ought to fill your heart, seeing His love is of the same extent and duration as His knowledge. His love to you, if you are in Christ, is just as deep. It is "very deep." What a mighty God we serve!

For my days are consumed like smoke, and
my bones are burned as an hearth.

—PSALM 102:3

What is all the struggle in the world for? Why do we spend our time trying to be something in the sphere of nothing? Our days are "consumed like smoke," like the foaming bubbles in a rapid stream, here for a moment and then no more. Let's look at the generations past—heroes, politicians, celebrities, writers, and poets, who commanded the attention of thousands and tens of thousands. Now they are but a brief thought in our memory, a quick conversation over dinner. And how soon, like them, will we also be forgotten? How frail is our life! It is like a pile of grass, a withered leaf, some dry stubble, a wilting flower, a cold breath. Consider how short our life is on earth. It is nothing but a long exhaled breath. No sooner do we weep for a departed loved one than death suddenly seizes on us, transferring our mourning to another. In a little while, we must follow them into the silent grave.

Surely we should not be so anxious about a life so short, a home so temporary, and a world so vain where we are only strangers, pilgrims, sojourners, flying away from everything below. Let the world spend itself on itself. This should not trouble those to whom life is but a continual death.

Then how should we spend this short life we are given, our few winged moments, which are all numbered to us? Surely, in nothing better than in looking out and laying up for eternity. Our Lord said that while we are in this world we should look to the next: "But lay up for yourselves treasures in heaven, where neither moth nor rust doth corrupt, and where thieves do not break through nor steal." Is that not David's point as well, to be far more concerned with the eternal than the temporal? Oh, that the Lord might give us a daily reminder of the psalmist's words, "My days are like a shadow that declineth; and I am withered like grass. But thou, O LORD, shalt endure for ever" (Ps. 102:11–12).

APRIL 26

Let his days be few; and let another take his office.
—PSALM 109:8

The disciples never suspected Judas to be the betrayer, even after Christ dipped the sop and handed it to Judas, who left to do the wretched deed, as John 13:28 says, "Now no man at the table knew for what intent he spake this unto him." We have no indication even in the writings of the four Gospels, which were written in perfect hindsight, that the disciples were thinking of Judas. The response is altogether different—"Lord, is it I?" This seems to indicate that each of the disciples thought it might be he himself before another, even Judas. Judas appeared to be a holy man to look at and to know. These twelve had been together for almost a thousand days. How well could you get to know someone in one thousand days? To eat, sleep, walk, talk with eleven others—how well would you get to know them? Quite well, I suspect. Yet the disciples knew nothing of an unfaithful Judas.

Oh, how unfaithfulness can boil just under the surface of our skin! The carnal professor, as the Puritans put it, is impossible to spot, until he shows himself. For what reason we do not know, Judas looked upon the Light of the World as a burning fire. It exposed Judas for what he really was, a hypocrite. The New Testament calls these people unwise virgins, fruitless branches, goats, and chaff. Whatever the name, these are they who abide within the company of believers, yet never come to a saving knowledge of the truth.

And how often did Christ open the door of opportunity for Judas to repent? On the night He was betrayed, He looked at Judas and said, "Friend, wherefore art thou come?" So many times Jesus laid the way open for Judas to say, "I am a betrayer at heart! My hypocrisy, my hidden hatred, it is not hidden to Thee." But he did not.

We would be sorrowfully mistaken if we would not admit that within each and every human heart lies a Judas. Judas was not unique. "The heart is deceitful above all things, and desperately wicked: who can know it?" (Jer. 17:9). The irony is that when we deny this fact, we invariably walk down Judas's path.

I called upon the LORD in distress: the LORD answered me, and set me in a large place.
                                                        —PSALM 118:5

Some people are not easily comforted in distress. They are often of a sad disposition, what the old writers called melancholy; they are prone to depression and pessimism. This can be the result of looking inward instead of looking upward. Yet the ones who follow after Christ are known by another characteristic: they seek God amid troubles. It is always amazing to see how the grace of God will enable a soul to call out to Him for help amid great pain. He can be laid aside by sickness, grieved by death, his pains multiplied, pursued by the devil to break his heart and spirit, and yet he is able to say, "I called upon the LORD in distress: the LORD answered me, and set me in a large place."

Nothing can keep the head above the waters of distress better than to cry, "Bless the Lord, O my soul, and all that is within me, bless his holy name." The Devil would like to defeat us. He would like to have us tried like Job. His greatest desire is that we would "curse God and die" in the trials of our lives. Yet after all that he was able to do to Job, God won the victory, and the Devil ran like a beaten dog with his tail between his legs. Why? Because the tried and hurting soul cries out amid despair and is "set in a large place."

When a soul will bless God for the bitter dregs given in hardship, the Lord sends in return the sweet wine of comfort. Dear reader, if we can praise God in the night season, daybreak is not far off. No, there never was a soul who desired to call upon God in affliction whose prayer was not answered. Our Psalmist knew of this help, for he concludes, "The LORD is on my side; I will not fear: what can man do unto me?" (Ps. 118:6). Many times, during distress, when we are heavy of heart, would it not be good to do what Luther said to do, "Come, let us sing a psalm, and startle the Devil"?

It is good for me that I have been afflicted;
that I might learn thy statutes.

—PSALM 119:71

A converted soul may walk with God in close communion, as Enoch did, captivated with the glory of His countenance and lifted above the world by the outlet of His love; but this is not the ordinary path of most believers. No, we must live out our lives here on earth, awaiting our final transport to glory. Enoch had a blessing, and so do we. Ours is another mercy, another kind of "walking with God." Our mercy is to be driven near the throne of grace and made earnest in prayer by the rod of affliction. A good man will learn much by sitting under the means of grace, finding great instruction there, but affliction gives an edge to his devotions and an urgency to his petitions, making him draw nearer to the throne. It seems under affliction he stays longer and cries louder. "It is good for me that I have been afflicted."

Among the many precious fruits of affliction, I will mention only one: "that I might learn thy statutes." "Learn" here means to be taught like a student. It presupposes that there is a general ignorance in us, like a child in kindergarten, of the great lessons of faith. There is a Latin phrase that speaks loudly here: *experientia docet*, that is, experience teaches. Very little is to be learned without affliction. If we would be students of Christ, we must be sufferers with Him. Spurgeon once said, "There is no royal road to learning the royal statutes; God's commands are best read by eyes wet with tears." How often we mistake affliction for a curse when it is meant for a blessing! Take heart, dear reader; we learn more through our trials than our triumphs. The design of affliction is this, that when pressed upon by affliction, we press upon the promises, plead for intervention, and are earnest with God. A loving parent never keeps back what is needful for the child, be it praise or discipline. God deals with His own in the same way, even in affliction. It is here that His ways become precious, His laws not grievous, His leading more satisfying. David is telling us that affliction is the school of sanctification, where we go on learning until our graduation into glory.

I cried with my whole heart; hear me, O LORD.
—PSALM 119:145

We do not often think of prayer as crying. We usually think of it as dignified communication between man and God. But consider this. There is a famous Covenanter painting found in J. A. Wylie's *History of Protestantism* of a Puritan minister leading his people in conventicle prayer in a field service. He is kneeling with a straightened back, hands folded, and crying eyes lifted toward heaven. The people around him are similarly in varying positions of prostration, seeking the Lord for help. It was earnest prayer; it was praying in their prayers. Over fifty times in the Psalms alone, David mentions crying as a form of prayer.

So what do the words "I cried" mean? These two words actually make up a single Hebrew verb meaning to "utter a loud sound." It usually signifies someone in distress, in great need of divine help. We are reminded of Romans 8:26, "Likewise the Spirit also helpeth our infirmities: for we know not what we should pray for as we ought: but the Spirit itself maketh intercession for us with groanings which cannot be uttered."

In this text, David desires that his cry would not die en route, or be crowded out by sin, but that God would hear and answer. True prayer is not satisfied with the formality of the exercise. If God does not hear our prayer, we pray in vain. The term "hear" is often used in Scripture to express attention and consideration. In one sense, every breath on earth is heard by God, as well as every heart's cry. But David goes beyond this. He desires a gentle, sympathetic ear, like a doctor gives to a moaning patient.

There may be no beauty of delivery in your prayers, no length of expression, no depth of doctrine, or precision in diction; but if your whole heart be found in your prayers, they will find their way to the throne of grace, sanctified by Christ our Mediator and High Priest. "Hear me, O Lord!"

They that sow in tears shall reap in joy.
—PSALM 126:5

We often think that our immediate trials will last forever. Our tears are not the end, but only a means to the end—*joy*! This text is teaching us that if we never sow in sorrow, we will never reap joy. If godly sorrow is our seed, spiritual rejoicing will be our harvest. However, keep in mind that while sowing is short and reaping is short, the time in between is long. It is a full season. And remember, this sorrow is not so much a temporal sorrow, but spiritual. It has everything to do with the bondage of sin and the discovery of forgiveness. If we were never captives to sin, Christ could not free us. Here is one of the great *antimonies* of Scripture: tears shall bring joy. And the joy they shall bring is something the world knows nothing of. It is a spiritual lesson that tears of earnestness beget tears of joy for "deep calleth unto deep."

Let us then endure the night of weeping. Though weeping endures for a time, joy comes in the morning of eternity. We must fight while on this field of battle called life to gain the crown of eternal life. We are not to be as a hired hand. We must not lie down and rest until the evening shadows cover the weary lambs. The world is too barren a soil to bring true joy to the heart. Why do we so often mistake this thorny wilderness for a garden of flowers, this place of danger for a palace of delight, and this howling desert for an enchanting forest?

Our ultimate joy shall be in heaven, not on earth. Every believer has a harvest waiting for him there. For this very reason our own Savior "went forth weeping." He was "a man of sorrows and acquainted with grief," yet "bearing precious seed." He sowed that seed around Himself on the cross, died, and rose again that we might have this comfort: "And ye now therefore have sorrow: but I will see you again, and your heart shall rejoice, and your joy no man taketh from you" (John 16:22).

MILK  HONEY

from Ecclesiastes

ROY MOHON

The words of the Preacher, the son of David, king in Jerusalem.
—ECCLESIASTES 1:1 (read Ecclesiastes 1:1–7)

Ecclesiastes is from the Greek. It parallels the Hebrew *Koheleth*, which means a leader who gathers and addresses an assembly. "Preacher" is thus a reasonable translation. The connection with Solomon is unmistakable: the Preacher is "the son of David," a king in Jerusalem over the undivided kingdom of "Israel" (v. 12), with "great experience of wisdom" (v. 16). Professor Edward J. Young considers the connection to be that wisdom is "presented as embodied in a person, and that person is Solomon" (*An Introduction to the Old Testament*, p. 348). Ecclesiastes exhorts us to practical godliness in our world of mixed experiences.

The words of the Preacher come as a challenge from God. "Vanity of vanities, all is vanity" strikes a chord in all, even hardened sinners. This emptiness burdens Ecclesiastes, compelling him to address our human condition by spiritual exhortation to transform heart and life.

The message of unprofitable labor is unwelcome. It pricks the bubble of man's false optimism with the uncomfortable reality: "for what shall it profit a man, if he shall gain the whole world, and lose his own soul?" (Mark 8:36). We put so much effort into life to get it to work, but what is the gain? If we look only at things under the sun, what hope is there?

As one drives to the delivery room, the hearse from the retirement home is heading to the graveyard. The Preacher, like the graveside, has a message men would rather forget: "for what is your life? It is even a vapour, that appeareth for a little time, and then vanisheth away" (James 4:14). You die, but the local scenery remains the same.

Our scientific age is preoccupied with the physical universe but misses the important lessons from the world around us. Look at "the sun" (v. 5). It "hastens" to its place with mechanistic and tiring activity, like the treadmill character of human life. Look at "the wind" (v. 6). Its arbitrary fluctuations result in no lasting change as it whirls about continually just as you do. Look at "the rivers" (v. 7). They maintain continuous motion in a fixed direction without altering the status quo.

Do not be depressed by Ecclesiastes's worldview, but use it like your spectacles cloth to remove accumulated dust in your heart and gain a clear view of life.

...and there is no new thing under the sun.
—ECCLESIASTES 1:9 (read Ecclesiastes 1:8–11)

The author of Ecclesiastes found the physical world instructive as he observed its strenuous, repetitive activity without any real progress. Surely intelligent humans can do better and achieve things of enduring significance. Ecclesiastes would have you realize that this is not so.

We are so actively engaged in our small sphere of life that we forget that the stars follow their courses, the hills are watered, and the lions are fed. How little we see of, or contribute to, the continuous activity that maintains the universe! Like mice in a vast museum of working exhibits, we scurry about, oblivious to the ceaseless activity that takes place.

The anthropologist, Richard Rudgley, explains that our generation has rewritten history to promote its own doctrine of progress. He writes: "In this new mythology the notion of civilisation…replaces Eden and this novel paradise exists not at the beginning of time but, if not right now, then just around the corner" (*Lost Civilizations of the Stone Age*, p. 1). This is our great success story, but Ecclesiastes disagrees: "there is no new thing under the sun." When we consider the nature of things, as opposed to their form, progress is an illusion because what appears to be new has been already. The Tower of Babel seemed new but it was the same as former and subsequent activities—a social enterprise, employing technology and vast resources, directed to the honor of man and civic glory and rendered insignificant by the intervention of God.

The myth of novelty can be maintained because of the shortness of man's communal memory. He is afflicted with a convenient amnesia. The present agenda necessitates the exclusion of past events. Not to know Joseph was convenient for a Pharaoh who wanted to persecute the Israelites (Ex. 1:7–8). History shows that each generation is preoccupied with the whirl of its own achievements.

Do not view these thoughts as the meanderings of resigned pessimism. Ecclesiastes wants some realism from you. Our generation needs to wake up and see the truth about itself and so get on to a better track. The preacher's words are not the lament of a disappointed soul, dealt some rough blows in life, but a convincing way of urging you not to overlook spiritual values in life.

I have seen all the works that are done under the sun; and, behold, all is vanity and vexation of spirit.
> —ECCLESIASTES 1:14 (read: Ecclesiastes 1:12–18)

Children enjoy a puzzle until they become frustrated by lack of progress in joining the pieces together. We can put a jigsaw away, but we must persevere with the puzzle of life.

Ecclesiastes gave his heart to "search out by wisdom" all things "under heaven." This strikes us as exciting, for all men "even if they know not God, feel a deep compulsion or inner urge to discover the truth." (H. C. Leupold, *Exposition of Ecclesiastes*, p. 53). We are used to questions such as: Why am I here? What is the meaning of life? To be significant, the search must be exhaustive and embrace all things. Consequently, we find the task exacting, but, if we are serious about life, we are compelled to try and make sense of it all.

The search is a wearisome toil, a "sore travail." There are so many contradictions. The crooked cannot be made straight and the data that we lack cannot even be numbered. Attempted shortcuts do not work. Humanistic optimism looks for a manmade utopia but ignores the unpleasant realities of life until a terrorist attack puts "depravity" back in the politicians' speeches. Bleak pessimism causes some to face life with a kind of desperate courage. The British philosopher Bertrand Russell believed the world was doomed to destruction and despair. Escape from reality through drugs, mysticism, sensuality, or suicide, like all other shortcuts, leaves the knots tied!

By telling us that God has given to us our exacting task, Ecclesiastes restores relevance, proportion, and reality. We must come to the One who breaks the chain of relentless vanity. What a relief it is when you have struggled with a puzzle and then everything falls into place! Trusting God got Ecclesiastes moving in the right direction. "When the fulness of the time was come" (Gal. 4:4) and the eternal Word came in the flesh, vanity was displaced by a life of true worth and a sacrifice of infinite value.

Follow the Preacher in giving your heart to know wisdom. Recognize foolishness and do not be deterred when you get sadder as you grow wiser (vv. 16–18). Accept the awesome realism in this book and look beyond the "under the sun" mentality to see God, righteousness, and true comfort.

> *I said in mine heart, Go to now, I will prove thee with mirth, there-*
> *fore enjoy pleasure: and, behold, this also is vanity.*
> —ECCLESIASTES 2:1 (read: Ecclesiastes 2:1–11)

We think of mirth as involving gladness, excitement, pleasurable feelings, and gaiety. Ecclesiastes wanted to put such enjoyments to the test.

The gap between legitimate enjoyment and sin narrows considerably in pleasure seeking, so Ecclesiastes determined that his heart would still be led by wisdom. He was not proposing moral abandonment but would remain in control. Righteous Noah got drunk; circumspection in life's pleasures has its place. Neglect of self-control is the fast lane to sin whether by over-consumption of food, ostentation concerning possessions, immodest dress, or illicit passion. "Let your moderation be known unto all men" (Phil. 4:5).

The test had to be comprehensive or Ecclesiastes would always be thinking that there were other things to try and we would doubt the value of his experiment. He attempted on a large scale the things that most pursue to some extent in search of happiness: houses, gardens, woods, possessions, animals, precious things, entertainment, and hobbies. He had to examine them thoroughly because Satan's trick is to put some new trinkets on the horizon to consume five more years of the life of the unwise saint or sinner—by which time its silver gleam has tarnished.

The conclusion is bleak. All these pleasures are "good things" but, of themselves, they yield nothing. What are they accomplishing? The emptiness remains. It is a fruitless endeavor. However, the absence of any "profit under the sun" is not equivalent to all of these activities being useless charades that deceive us. The rich fool was deceived because his wealth was his total world. The Christian can see that when all things are done as unto the Lord, then even the most mundane activities have significance for eternity. Ecclesiastes approaches the problem from the negative side to woo us away from unrealistic expectations about our pleasurable activities.

The life of Christ demonstrates that sin is not necessary for personal fulfillment and true joy. Keep Christ central in your life so that good things do not become traps to ensnare you. Be sure that without the Savior the yield will be zero even if you should gain the whole world!

And I turned myself to behold wisdom, and madness, and folly: for what can the man do that cometh after the king? even that which hath been already done. —ECCLESIASTES 2:12 (read Ecclesiastes 2:12–17)

Having discovered the emptiness of acquisition and amusements, Ecclesiastes turns to intellectual pursuits to escape vanity.

Ecclesiastes proves the excellence of wisdom by comparison. There is a spectrum of wise, wiser, and wisest, but folly is not on the spectrum. To be foolish is not just to be less wise; we are not to think of a dimmer switch, which gradually reduces the amount of light, but of the on-off switch. The fool is not in some twilight zone, but is in utter darkness. The practical effect is that he cannot see where he is going. The fool is driving with his headlights off. While the ambient light is good, he gets along, but as soon as external beneficial influences are gone the result is disaster. He is in the broad road that leads to destruction.

Death is the one certainty in life and any wisdom that fails to address it must be woefully inadequate. Science cannot grapple with it and a philosophy of death becomes mere speculation. Death, however, levels all. The wise man and the fool lie side by side in the earth. Does this mean that death has rubbished wisdom? Logically it looks as if wisdom did not help, and even is vain.

Ecclesiastes found this devastating. It is bad enough that death is common to the wise and foolish; it is worse that one's contemporaries will not even bother to conserve the memory of better men. The pieces of the jigsaw puzzle of life cannot even be forced together. It is grievous or "all wrong." This is frustrating and demoralizing. Today's achievements are tomorrow's archive on the way to the recycling bin. If you have high expectations of intellectual pursuits, Ecclesiastes wants you to face up to the fact that it is vanity and vexation of spirit. You need something more.

Feel the full weight of your vanity, futility, vexation, and grief. Despairing of your own intellectual achievements, look for higher wisdom. The Christian knows that this higher wisdom is in Christ. He is the eternal Wisdom, the Conqueror of death, and the One who gives His own a new and enduring name and memorial.

For all his days are sorrows, and his travail grief; yea, his heart taketh not rest in the night. This is also vanity.
—ECCLESIASTES 2:23 (read: Ecclesiastes 2:18–26)

Job had to recognize the obvious, but he did so with submission and praise: "Naked came I out of my mother's womb, and naked shall I return thither: the LORD gave, and the LORD hath taken away: blessed be the name of the LORD" (Job 1:21). How can we get to such a disposition in the light of depressing circumstances? Ecclesiastes has further thoughts on this.

A last will and testament focuses our attention on how much the deceased left behind. From his point of view, he left everything behind. The hard working entrepreneur's epitaph might be: "I accumulated but another spends" or "I toiled but another enjoys." It is particularly discouraging to think of a man who has been diligent to be wise and to dispose of his resources in a just and efficient way having to leave his wealth to a fool.

When Solomon passed away, a few days of folly on the part of Rehoboam ruined a lifetime's work and the kingdom was divided (1 Kings 12:12–14). How can all the sacrifices be worthwhile? We labor with effort and exhaustion. It goes to the very core of our being with vexation of heart. We have many sorrows that pain the soul. Our travail and fatigue is a grief to us. The mind is turbulent and uneasy and we cannot sleep. Despite our labor, all our accomplishments slip away like sand in an hourglass. We cannot bestow durability upon our labors.

To make one's soul enjoy good in his labor seems to be impossible in such circumstances, but the things that are impossible with men are possible with God. When we give thanks for our food and ask God's blessing, we acknowledge His provision and necessary blessing of it to us. After a bout of sickness, we are well aware that there is nothing automatic about the body's reception of food. God would have us enjoy what He gives. There is a place for fasting and prayer, but we are not to be morose ascetics continuously afflicted with discontent, bitterness, or disdain of enjoyment.

Flee the pleasures of sin and seek the wisdom, knowledge, and joy that come from the hand of God. It will then be well with your soul.

To every thing there is a season, and a time
to every purpose under the heaven.
—ECCLESIASTES 3:1 (read Ecclesiastes 3:1–11)

Initially, we might think that this passage is about us matching our conduct to what is appropriate at particular times. When we bury our friend we mourn. When a child is born we rejoice. There is a duty of appropriate response (James 5:13–14). Ecclesiastes leads us to think about our duties but his primary reference is to why we have to do so—we are not in control. There is a time to be born, and a time to die. We do not control either our beginning or end or anything in between. To everything there is a season because God is in control. Life is full of mixture and opposites. The Jews referred these verses to the changing fortunes of Israel as a nation. It is true enough that God's sovereignty applies to individuals, families, nations, and the apple of His eye, the church, for which all things work together for good (Rom. 8:28).

Life's changes involve travail. Ecclesiastes could rightly say: "I have seen the travail, which God hath given to the sons of men to be exercised in it" (v. 10). Like the disciples, we are often toiling in rowing but making no progress (Mark 6:47–48a). God gives to us such exercise that we might understand our limitations. The mixed nature of life necessitates submission to the highest will. We have storms and tranquility, chastening and blessing, and we are humbled as well as honored. Through these changes we learn that it is futile to strive against God's providence, and we no longer labor in vain.

I once sat opposite a couple on a train journey and had given up the prospect of any profitable conversation with them. How wrong I was! We ranged from fox-hunting to the Arab-Israeli conflict in a few minutes, then to the mixed nationalities in our church, and from that to a serious conversation about how sinners can be saved. We often forget that serious questions hover just beneath the surface in the hearts of unconverted people. They cannot find out many things but insistent questions remain.

The sun shining through your blinds convinces you that it is a beautiful day. Get a glimpse of the excellence of God's ways to convince you of His glorious sufficiency.

I know that, whatsoever God doeth, it shall be for ever: nothing can be put to it, nor any thing taken from it: and God doeth it, that men should fear before him.
— ECCLESIASTES 3:14 (read Ecclesiastes 3:12–15)

When we understand God's sovereignty, our hearts are humbled before Him and we know how to live and to draw comfort from His control of all things. Though we have real wills and make real decisions, it is God who controls the times and seasons. We must adjust to this. Here are three responses. (1) We must rejoice. The unconverted man anticipates happiness by taking control; the godly man is happy knowing that God is in control. (2) We must do good. Jesus went about doing good, and He is our great example of effective and fruitful living. (3) We must enjoy what God has given. The covetous soul enjoys nothing. Godliness with contentment is great gain. The godly man's daily portion, large or small, comes in a beautiful wrapper and the card reads, "With love." What love (John 3:16)!

"I know" emphasizes certain, personal knowledge. Ecclesiastes would have you assured of the following. (1) God's works are of eternal duration. Whatsoever God does is forever. He who has begun will perform it to the end. However painful the grinding in these mixed times, God brings His jewels to a perfect sparkle to be fit for Christ. (2) God's works are complete in themselves. An unbearable burden is lifted from the shoulders of the person who understands the completeness of God's work. The Pharisee would add to Christ's righteousness and, by the mass, the pope would supplement Calvary, but David says: "The LORD will perfect that which concerneth me" (Ps. 138:8). (3) God's works cannot be frustrated. It looked as though Haman would destroy all but he was hanged on his own gallows!

There is an impress of divine sovereignty upon life's seasons that men might revere God. Mortal clay despises the Creator and denies His providence but "the fear of the LORD is the beginning of knowledge" (Prov. 1:7). The sovereignty of God is a mystery but this intellectual conundrum is notwithstanding spiritual balm.

Do not make divine sovereignty an excuse for abdicating personal responsibility. Even in these mixed times, see it as the guarantee of rejoicing, fruitfulness, and enjoyment through a life of reverent submission to His will.

I said in mine heart, God shall judge the righteous and the wicked: for there is a time there for every purpose and for every work.
—ECCLESIASTES 3:17 (read Ecclesiastes 3:16–22)

He who feeds on the Living Bread will be transformed. A right view of life results in a right kind of life.

Perversion in the courts is devastating because society's bedrock is the "place of judgment," where objective judgment should be without partiality, and the "place of righteousness," where judges should be subjectively upright. But when it is not so, providence is not defeated, for "there is a time" to straighten out distortions. Even if we do not see it here, the proving process is already going on as God, who sees the heart, "manifests" or "winnows" the sons of men to separate the wheat from the chaff.

The afterlife is not apparent. What is observable seems to support the evolutionary hypothesis: "a man hath no preeminence above a beast...all turn to dust again." However, struggles for vindication in court bring home to men their impotence in a timely way because soon it will be evident in a final way. On his deathbed, a man may seek to set right the wrongs that never troubled him for half a lifetime. As he sinks away, he has deep forebodings about the reality of ultimate justice. This is a bleak prospect but there is a distinction after all, for "the spirit of man...goeth upward." For the righteous, death is a gateway to joy. The body perishes like a beast but "the spirit shall return unto God who gave it" (Eccl. 12:7). Our only hope before God's judgment throne is the blood and righteousness of Jesus Christ.

The right attitude is "that a man should rejoice in his own works." Get on with what falls to you to do and do it with your might (Eccl. 9:10). Do not live in a morbid frame of mind but with a glad heart. Now is your time to live for God. He is in control—you do not need to fret about what you cannot change (Eccl. 9:1–2).

Injustice is painful and you should not ignore it; but remember that no one ever suffered injustice as Christ did. Take heart and remember: what you cannot straighten out, God will in His time.

So I returned, and considered all the oppressions
that are done under the sun.
—ECCLESIASTES 4:1 (read Ecclesiastes 4:1–3)

Our world furnishes many examples of desperate need especially as a result of man's inhumanity to man.

Ecclesiastes "returned and considered." It was time to consider. The events demanded it. Some were intentionally making life unbearable for others. The Hebrew word for "oppression" covers both fraud and force in taking advantage of others. Ecclesiastes took time to consider. Many do not! It is uncomfortable to discern the signs of the times that call us to an urgent assessment of the true situation, and it is a terrible aggravation when those with the power to remedy the problems do not.

What a terrible point to come to! Of the dead, living, and unborn, Ecclesiastes states that the "living" are the worse off! This could have been said in a concentration camp full of skeletal prisoners. This is an "under the sun" (vv. 1, 3) assessment that does not work for eternal things. The worst living condition in a day of grace gives time for repentance and consequent eternal salvation. When battle was imminent on July 22, 1680, Richard Cameron prayed, "Lord, spare the green, and take the ripe." Let the casualties be those who are ready to die.

What a heartbreaking scene. There was oppression and no comforter. We have often seen the weeping child comforted by a loving parent. How dreadful to be bereft of help, alone, and forsaken. It was so for the Savior when the foundation of lasting comfort was laid: "My God, my God, why hast thou forsaken me?" (Ps. 22:1). The Christian finds comfort through the Savior's blood. The Father comforts us, the Son comforts us, and the Holy Spirit comforts us (Ps. 103:13–15; John 14:1–3, 15–18). Ecclesiastes could not see this through our eyes, but his blunt words do not deny spiritual things and the resurrection of the dead. It is the opposite. It is because he believed in things "above" the sun (Eccl. 5:1–2) that he had found the key to avoiding emptiness.

Let your life speak to a pleasure-seeking generation full of many sorrows of the higher life that has its roots in heaven.

Better is an handful with quietness, than both the hands full with travail and vexation of spirit.
> —ECCLESIASTES 4:6 (read Ecclesiastes 4:4–16)

We can learn by counsel or we can learn by experience. Learning by our own mistakes is both painful and costly. It is better to listen to what the wise man advises.

The work environment is highly competitive, the ambitious advance their careers at the expense of others, and "a man is envied of his neighbor." What a "vanity" it is! Even the world calls it a "rat race." This is what happens when vocation is undervalued. The fool or sluggard prefers to opt out of the hassle. He has no zeal for lawful endeavor and his talents are wasted to his own loss. Contentment excels both envy and sloth for "better is an handful with quietness, than both hands full with travail and vexation of spirit." Contentment can coexist with true diligence and protect us against worldly cares.

"One alone" can be a self-inflicted loneliness. The miser is alone because he does not want to share. He never sees anyone warm, fed, and happy as a result of his labors. He is utterly selfish. He acquires riches but to no good end. What a vanity it is! Companionship is to be preferred because the stresses and strains of life can be shared. A fall is not so bad when help is at hand: "a sure friend is made known when in difficulty" (Ennius). In cold times, two can have heat, as even sheep know. Spiritual sheep should know the same lesson: in danger, we need the friend that sticks closer than a brother to withstand the enemy.

When we become successful and achieve prominence, there is a danger of pride and refusing to be admonished. When instruction is considered expendable, we are as a headstrong mule. The poor and wise child is better than this. Any former political leader, no longer in power, can verify Ecclesiastes' observations: the new king comes from obscurity; he has great popularity that strengthens and peaks before disappearing altogether. This world is full of fragile castles and ruined fortresses. Surely this also is vanity and vexation of spirit except if we humble ourselves to seek heavenly wisdom.

Learn these obvious lessons and live them out, keeping close to the Friend of sinners to support you in life's way.

Keep thy foot when thou goest to the house of God....
—ECCLESIASTES 5:1 (read Ecclesiastes 5:1–3)

We are surrounded by vanity and it is easy to lapse into the ways of the world. We may avoid the gross iniquities of adultery and murder but be casual about approaching God. Here are three guidelines to avoid sins in the sanctuary.

First, joy is important in worship but many today equate joy with an emotional "feeling good" where one's energies are released in spontaneous "sacred" dancing and the like. Here is a word of constraint: "Keep thy foot." We have nothing against our child's enthusiasm when she is prancing along the cobbles, but we see the inappropriateness of it relative to the uneven surface. "Watch your step," we say. The house of God is not a place like every other. It is not a place for bold expressiveness but for being ready to hear. The Preacher's exhortations are often scorned until it is too late, but the sacrifice of fools never pleases God. Vain worship was the great sin of the Pharisees.

Second, there is a great difference between the wise man and the fool in their depth of understanding. The fool does not care to see beyond the end of his nose, whereas the wise man accepts the responsibility to know and understand (Eccl. 1:13). The Queen of Sheba sought the superior wisdom of God at great cost. Do you treasure what is in the Bible and earnestly search it? What do you forgo for quiet time, family worship, prayer meetings, and Sabbath worship? At the heart of the house of God is Christ. For many Jews, the sacrificial lamb was enough, and they never got to the Lamb of God. They had too little awareness of sin and too much confidence in their own works.

Third, make your prayers significant. Jews and Gentiles sinned in prioritizing quantity over quality. Neither the heathen nor the hypocrite is to be our model (Matt. 6:7; 23:14). What is necessary in prayer is not length but relevance. "Father, into thy hands I commend my spirit" (Luke 23:46) was enough. Just as a flurry of business will generate a dream, a profusion of words will reveal the fool. Remember, God is in heaven and we are but dust.

It is said that Whitefield's exclamation "Oh!" could stop sinners in their tracks. The Savior's "It is finished" (John 19:30) summed up in one word the most significant event that has ever taken place.

Suffer not thy mouth to cause thy flesh to sin....
—ECCLESIASTES 5:6 (read Ecclesiastes 5:4–7)

This passage is a proof text for the Westminster Confession's section on vows, which states: "A vow is of the like nature with a promissory oath, and ought to be made with the like religious care, and to be performed with the like faithfulness." We are familiar with the vow in Holy Matrimony. The time for consideration is before the vow is taken; afterwards, it is sinful not to keep it.

The presence of God is not something commonplace. The inconsiderate vow is evidence of a low view of God where reverence and awe are absent. What are your views of the God of heaven today? Do you see that He is infinite, eternal, majestic, sovereign, holy, and gracious? Do you stand in loving awe of Him? Where a vow is not necessary, "avoidance" is better than default. Moses' law was: "if thou shalt forebear to vow, it shall be no sin in thee" (Deut. 23:22). However, once a vow has been taken, it is binding and it is a serious sin not to fulfill it.

The tongue must be mastered or its rashness brings the whole man under guilt. You cannot disown what your mouth utters. It is a great folly to excuse as an error a rashly made vow and then carry on as usual. The sinner might expect to continue enjoying the privileges of church membership, but failure to confess sin leads away from God and He is angry. When the knocker of the cathedral in Durham City was seized, the supplicant was granted sanctuary from even the king's anger. So must we sinners seize upon the cross of Christ or our sins will consume us.

We cannot escape vanities for they are in our many words as in our dreams. There is, however, a corrective to our natural flippancy—fear God. It is proposed to us as the preferable course—"but fear thou God." If only we would do so, how many sins we would be preserved from! Think of Christ's reverence for His Father. He would not go along with the profanation of the Temple.

Lay hold upon the promises made to those who fear God: acceptance, mercy, goodness, instruction, and help in trouble (Acts 10:35; Luke 1:50; Ps. 31:19, 25:12; Isa. 50:10).

He that loveth silver shall not be satisfied with silver; nor he that loveth abundance with increase: this is also vanity.

—ECCLESIASTES 5:10 (read Ecclesiastes 5:8–20)

We live in a materialistic age. "Money talks," does it not? Surely possessions cannot be an illusion like some desert mirage? We need to be careful: "He that loveth silver shall not be satisfied with silver." Here are guidelines concerning possessions.

Paul warns us that "the love of money is the root of all evil" (1 Tim. 6:10). It results in apostasy because it becomes the object of desire. For Judas, thirty pieces of silver outweighed the possession of Christ as Savior. Ecclesiastes mentions only silver, not gold, for we must not imagine that greed is only the rich man's sin. Those with less might be more grasping. However, the love of money does not work for anyone. As our estate grows, our dependants increase. As riches increase, we have more of the same to look after. The laborer sleeps soundly while excess of living keeps the rich awake. The spiritual void remains. It has been told that in the pocket of a corpse they found a suicide note and $50,000.

In the good times few think how fleeting riches are, but when the banks are writing off billions the nation trembles. Job could withstand his losses because he had faith. He lost a fortune but loved his Redeemer more. For many, it is otherwise and riches hurt them. They become disappointed and embittered. Egyptian burial chambers witness how much of this world the pharaohs wanted to take into the next. But each left as naked as he came! Only in Christ will death lead into eternal riches (1 Tim. 6:6–9).

Must we then become ascetic monks? Must we be miserable people feeling guilty that we have some wealth? Should we sell all and give to the poor? No! Labor is toilsome and to enjoy its fruits is morally unobjectionable—indeed, it is comely and fitting. Each under his vine was a token of the blessing of heaven. The possession of goods and the opportunity and power to enjoy them is God's gift. You look back and see that you had what you needed and were better off than you realized. This was God answering your prayers so that you might live a quiet and peaceable life in all godliness and honesty.

Work while it is day. Shun fretful anxiety. Avoid selfishness and be generous. Thankfully rejoice in God's goodness.

All the labour of man is for his mouth, and yet the appetite is not filled.
—ECCLESIASTES 6:7 (read Ecclesiastes 6:1–12)

Ecclesiastes has already shown us that riches cannot truly satisfy but can harm us. Proper use of what God gives is consequently important (5:10–18). Further analysis and counsel is in place.

The expression "under the sun" begins and closes this chapter. We are living in this world, and many religious people settle for paying their dues to heaven on Sunday and getting on with life the rest of the week with scarcely a thought for biblical principles. God is active, however, in the Monday market. The acquisition of wealth attributed to shrewd dealings, or from what the world calls "Lady Luck," actually results from God's sovereign giving of riches and honor, which consequently accumulate to our advantage. The age of the billionaire has come but there is another side to divine sovereignty. God gives so much but then "a stranger eateth it," and the man who spent his life in avaricious acquisition loses all, if not in life, then in death. Thus, man without higher values is inferior to the untimely death that escapes all such bitterness.

Spurgeon's John Ploughman spoke of the drunkard who has a hole below his nose and pours all his money into it. There is also a deeper meaning in Ecclesiastes' observation. Beyond the mouth is the "appetite" or soul without contentment always wanting more. Do not assume that this is the rich man's sin. It is the unbeliever's sin. The "wandering desire" or soul roves around looking for something new, something more, or something else.

It is time to get things into proportion. However far back we look, the situation is the same. Each man is dust before his Maker. However much more is brought into the situation it will not help. If the bucket has no bottom, however much is poured in, it will never be filled. What is needed is not a greater quantity of liquid, but a new bucket. So it is with man. More possessions do not improve him because he needs a new heart. Without Christ, our life is but a shadow.

Heed Him who said, "Learn of me" (Matt. 6:19–34). He is the absolutely reliable Counselor and teaches us how to handle possessions.

The heart of the wise is in the house of mourning; but the heart of fools is in the house of mirth.
—ECCLESIASTES 7:4 (read Ecclesiastes 7:1–10)

The Preacher seems to be gloomy and some depict him as a brooding sceptic who can find no value in life and extols death. Nothing could be further from the truth. Someone having a good time might find Ecclesiastes' words an unwelcome challenge, but those suffering find comfort in them.

The translation "better is a name than nard" preserves the play on words in the Hebrew. "Nard" (as in "spikenard") is used to reflect the similarity of the Hebrew *shem* ("name") to the Hebrew *shemen* ("ointment"). Anointing with oil was a sign of good times (Eccl. 9:7–8) but the godly man still has what is best—a good name—even in bad times. As it is with Christ, so it should be with us; when troubles come and our perfumes are gone, our spiritual fragrance should remain (Ps. 45:1–2, 7–8; Song 1:3; 2 Cor. 2:14–16).

We adopt the view that "the day of death" is better than "the day of one's birth" when we speak of a "merciful release." When the burden of suffering for a particular saint gets too great, we understand death is a blessing for him; but can we say that it is better to be at the funeral than at festivities? We know which people prefer. Only a bold preacher can take such a text. I was glad it was used at the funeral of a Christian colleague when many staff members were present. Pleasures have their place, but funerals compel us to face our end. The "house of mourning" is good if we are ready to be instructed and face our personal need for an answer to death.

We are not worse for mourning. Consider Jesus' astonishing teaching: "Blessed are they that mourn, for they shall be comforted" (Matt. 5:4). You cannot get true happiness eating and drinking to be merry. Sadness improves the heart. The song of fools is an emotional bubble that soon bursts, a short, loud "crackling of thorns" without enduring warmth. It is the "rebuke of the wise" that brings godly sorrow and salvation. Pride and passion are best forsaken for, as one has put it, "to lengthen my patience is the best way to shorten my trouble."

Don't be looking back, thinking times were better then, but move forward to what Christ has in store.

Consider the work of God: for who can make that straight, which he hath made crooked?
—ECCLESIASTES 7:13 (read Ecclesiastes 7:11–14)

If we have the wrong values for life, we are in for a tough time spiritually. Worldly responses do not really work. Consider the value of each of the following.

Skin cancer reminds us of the sun's danger. Shade is necessary. In the same way, money is a "defense" and saving for a rainy day is a wise precaution. We must not, however, expect money to solve all our problems. It is more important to pray for an understanding heart. Wisdom is more than a problem-solving capacity. It "gives life." It goes beyond preserving us in trouble to bestowing upon us real, spiritual, abundant, and eternal life, for at the heart of true wisdom is Jesus Christ and His atoning blood.

There are many crooked things in life that we have to straighten out. When we have offended our brother, it requires prompt confession and reconciliation (Matt. 5:23–24). It is, however, the height of arrogant folly to imagine that we can solve all problems. Many things that happen in God's providence, according to His permissive decree, defeat our understanding, ingenuity, and resources. It is our place to consider, not complain. We must submit and reflect as Mary did, who "kept all these things, and pondered them in her heart" (Luke 2:19).

The God-fearing have a heavenly Father. We are not in the grip of a cold and impersonal destiny to which we must be resigned. In life's changes, the rule is simple: rejoice in prosperity and reflect in adversity, for both are from God. In fact, it is of particular relevance that God has designed mixed times for us in this way. He has "set the one over against the other" in order that we might not have certainty about our earthly future but trust in Him. We cannot predict with any certainty what will come and "nothing" earthly is sure, but when we trust in God we have peace.

Be glad that you are not in control. What confusion would result if we were in control! Look rather to God's infinite power, wisdom, and love, and you will have peace, composure, and confidence.

It is good that thou shouldest take hold of this; yea, also from this withdraw not thine hand: for he that feareth God shall come forth of them all.
—ECCLESIASTES 7:18 (read Ecclesiastes 7:15–18)

The politician's middle way supposedly lies between dominant social control and uncaring capitalism focused on economic priorities. The moralist's middle way turns out to be one of gross compromise of biblical ethics. Is there a real middle way? Ecclesiastes thinks so.

Too many, like Job's friends, make absolute assumptions on the basis of the general principles of divine government. Promises made to the righteous are true, but the temporal aspect is subordinate to the eternal aspect. Enoch's life was shorter than his contemporaries but to be translated was better. The ways of sin often shorten life. Drugs, drink, promiscuity, and gang wars all take their toll, but we are not to imagine that providence is so mechanical that there are no exceptions. The just man may perish while the wicked man's life is prolonged. The middle way is not a mechanism to secure temporal advantage.

The Savior speaks of self-righteousness as "righteousness" (Luke 5:32). Man regards it as righteousness but it is an abomination to God. The conceit of adding to God's law is self-destructive. It climaxed with the Pharisees who strained at a gnat and swallowed a camel. True religion must never be reduced to a code of conduct. We must beware, however, of going to the opposite extreme of unbridled license. Even in the New Testament church there were those who crept in unawares and turned the grace of God into lasciviousness, expecting forgiveness without separation from "wickedness." They have many followers today.

We are to "take hold" of the wise man's middle way. Christ is the Lord our righteousness and in Him we trust that we might be justified by faith alone. Our obedience is of love, not merit. We are pained by our own continuing sins. We do not want to be self-righteous or licentious, but we must do more than make a good start. Having "taken hold," we must keep hold because there are many discouragements to true godliness.

Come to the sufficient Christ. He has everything for our every need in every way. We need nothing to the left of Him or to the right of Him. He is our middle way. Trust in Him, delight in Him, rest in Him, commit your way to Him, and follow Him today!

Wisdom strengtheneth the wise more than
ten mighty men which are in the city.
—ECCLESIASTES 7:19 (read Ecclesiastes 7:19–29)

We are all sinners and good at finding faults in others. We have a high sensitivity to the faults of those about us, and it is helpful, when we are about to criticize, to remember our own transgressions. Man's city is full of "mighty men" but real strength comes from wisdom. "Wisdom strengthens the wise," but, in pursuing wisdom, we are not to have unrealistic expectations about our potential progress (vv. 19–22).

The commonsense proverb is that "a little knowledge is a dangerous thing." The Preacher did not share the self-confidence of the unlearned who confidently expect "to set the world to rights." He enthusiastically threw himself into his research as a man with a map to buried treasure. From the harbor, all looked like smooth sailing, but once he had launched into the deep and spent long nights and days without sighting land or seeing sun or stars, his mood was more sober. The treasure is far off and buried exceedingly deep.

Though we must be content with imperfect knowledge, we must never stop searching. There is a treasure hid in a field and we must dig for it. The heart must be set upon this intellectual enterprise. In engaging in it, there are similar activities to studying for a Master's degree such as reading, remembering, and reflecting, but the whole business is qualitatively different. Ecclesiastes's search is for wisdom, not merely knowledge. It is about life, not livelihood. It concerns moral and spiritual realities.

In our expedition for truth there are real dangers. (1) There is the danger of being distracted. We must be on our guard against sensual impulses and the seductiveness of the wisdom of this world with its moral laxity. (2) There is the danger of disappointment. When we seek again and again and do not find, we are discouraged. At this point, the Preacher is not being offensive about women, just honest about his findings.

As one created in the image of God with intelligence, the potential of which is unknown to us, cease from clever devices and speculations to deny God and indulge sin, and diligently pursue the wisdom that produces godliness through faith in Christ.

Whoso keepeth the commandment shall feel no evil thing: and a wise man's heart discerneth both time and judgment.

—ECCLESIASTES 8:5 (read Ecclesiastes 8:1–5)

Although true wisdom originates with the teachings of Jesus Christ, our *intelligentsia* treat Him with scorn. As in natural things the wise man builds upon the rock, so in spiritual things we must have the right foundation (Matt. 7:24–25; 1 Cor. 3:10–11).

The face is the mirror of the soul. When the faces of the boy and girl in our children's reading books changed from sweet and handsome to tough and rough, it was not cosmetic but reflected a change of character. Their lifestyle had become more aggressive. The wise man has also changed from within, but in the opposite direction. He has gone from boldness to brightness. Rebirth results in an inner glory that must necessarily shine out (2 Cor. 3:10–18). The wise man is friendly, not fierce. Jesus was resolute but not rough—meek but not weak.

We must not be deceived by demands to avoid authoritative preaching. Satan's arrow is not aimed at authoritarianism but at the authority of God. However meekly you tell the sinner he must obey God, he will not have it. The wise man's life is one of submission to authority and he renders to Caesar the things that are Caesar's. We can sum up the wise man's conduct as submissive but not servile. The powers that be are not absolute and the godly man must be ready to stand as John the Baptist did regarding Herod. Our taxes must be paid and speed limits observed, so that when we resist abortion, euthanasia, or fornication our rulers understand it is not insubordination but moral conviction that motivates us.

The wise man knows what he ought to do and the best times for doing it. The lives of Joseph and Daniel remind us that good men can be kept from evil in corrupt systems. Places of employment contain many pitfalls these days; we must be circumspect to avoid accusations, but we must not compromise God's standards.

We have our example. Follow Him! Although "his visage was so marred more than any man" (Isa. 52:14), as the prudent servant of the Lord, Christ lovingly served Him.

Because to every purpose there is time and judgment, therefore the misery of man is great upon him.
—ECCLESIASTES 8:6 (read Ecclesiastes 8:6–8)

Not to know what a day will bring is a great exercise of soul to us. What will be on the morrow? How will we handle uncertainty? The Preacher has some helpful thoughts on this.

However much we control, much is beyond our control. Management theorists introduced a theory of chaos to help executives to manage in an ever-changing scene. The Preacher does not see the universe as chaotic. It might look that way, but things are actually ordered and precise. This is not the mechanistic order of the Deist with his divine watchmaker, but the precision timing of the divine Surgeon actively involved at each stage of the operation. It is not only exactness of timing, but moral ends that characterize the works of God. There is judgment. People prefer the evolutionist's chance world because morality involves responsibility and accountability, but to resist things as they really are brings "misery." Submitting to God's way brings blessedness.

The future defeats the proudest of men. The insurance industry engages in detailed estimates of future risk, but it does not stop heavy losses through unexpected floods. People yearn to know about their personal future and also what is going to happen in the world. What desperate raking about in the entrails of a beast to foresee what might be, when an ancient king consulted his astrologers! In our modern scientific age, lines still form to consult Gypsy Lee with her crystal ball! The believer sees things differently. All goes according to God's plan. The future is as definite as the past to Him and all is under control.

Only a fool makes no preparation for death. Death is something we can be sure of. Ecclesiastes is not being fatalistic. He wants us to be realistic about human impotence. It is your spirit, but you cannot hold it back from an appointment that you did not make. However much power a man has exercised in his life, he has no power here. The godlike are found to be mortal, whether Pharaoh, Goliath, or Nebuchadnezzar. There is no discharge in this war. Demobilization brings great jubilation, but once this battle is engaged there is no way out!

Be realistic, not pessimistic, and prepare for death through wisdom centered on Jesus Christ, the Conqueror of death.

Though a sinner do evil an hundred times, and his days be prolonged,
yet surely I know that it shall be well with them that fear God, which
fear before him.
—ECCLESIASTES 8:12 (read Ecclesiastes 8:9–17)

Every earthly love will come to ashes and we need to know how to handle various specific situations. Matthew Poole comments: "There are some kings who use their power tyrannically and wickedly, whereby they do not only oppress their people, but hurt themselves, by bringing the vengeance of God and men upon their own heads." When we see injustice, it wearies the soul as it is remembered again and again. We are in danger of fretfulness, evil speaking, sinful courses, inner bitterness, and backsliding (see Ps. 37:1–5; Ex. 14:11–12; Heb. 12:4, 14–15; Ps. 73:1–3).

Death is the great leveler, for all are prostrate in death. The oppressing dignitaries were often seen parading to and fro and Ecclesiastes saw them buried with great magnificence, but who remembers them now? Death ends the sinners' glory but is the beginning of a fuller glory for believers.

Whatever the oppressions, doubt not the stability of the moral order. What would you have thought at the cross where Christ's lovely life came to such an end? God's sovereign control gave the New Testament church confidence that the crucifixion was not justice overturned but justice satisfied (Rom. 3:23–26). Men who lack faith are hardened by the longsuffering of God and are fully set or "filled up" to do evil, but such sinners overlook the crucial ingredient of the moral order—beyond this life there is ultimate justice. Whatever crimes the sinner has got away with to date, when the reckoning comes he will account for them all!

Remember the link Ecclesiastes makes between conduct and deserts. This presents a problem from our horizontal vantage point—what happens to the just belongs to the wicked and what happens to the wicked belongs to the just. However, there is a higher principle: "it shall be well with them that fear God." Remember the lifestyle Ecclesiastes recommends. Enjoy what God has given in home, vocation, and community despite perplexing providences. Remember the limits Ecclesiastes recognized. Though Ecclesiastes loved wisdom, he recognized limits. To "play God" and seek ultimate and comprehensive understanding will result in bitter disappointment. "Stand in awe, and sin not; commune with your own heart upon your bed, and be still" (Ps. 4:4).

> *...the righteous, and the wise, and their works, are in the hand of God: no man knoweth either love or hatred by all that is before them.*
> —ECCLESIASTES 9:1 (read Ecclesiastes 9:1–3)

We must recognize the preciousness and advantage of life in days of grace. There are things that we cannot fathom. James the brother of John was killed with the sword while Herod flourished in his palace (Acts 12:1–2). We must lay to heart the fact that, although God's sovereignty extends to the wicked, the righteous are eminently in His hand. We cannot discern God's disposition to us by events. As a father leads his formerly lost child back to safety, the passage through briars will still hurt but it is on the way home. Events are not to be our ultimate guide. In his worst sufferings, the believer is safer than the impenitent sinner.

The Hebrew noun translated "event" is from the Hebrew verb "to meet." Events are happenings we meet day by day. The Preacher is not being fatalistic but is reminding us that we are passive in the face of much in life. Things happen to us. We do not generate them. These happenings do not distinguish between the righteous and the wicked. Illness, unemployment, bereavement, and the like are the same for both. Looking at it from a human standpoint, under the sun, this is an evil and it drives the natural man deeper into his degeneracy.

You have in you the evidence of your need to be saved. The natural man concludes that, if the sacrifices of a religious life give him no more security in life than the next man, he may as well get the most out of life, eating, drinking, and being merry. This is, however, a terrible fullness. What a thing to be "full of evil" (Rom. 1:29–32)! It is also madness. Ecclesiastes is not lapsing into the same mold. He sees things as they really are. This madness is the blindness of the man who, seeing a gleaming object before him, rushes to seize it, not realizing it is a sword pointed to his heart. Such are the pleasures of sin for a season. They tighten the noose around the sinner's neck. "To the death" is the King's command and the sinner goes instantly to the execution block.

Repudiate the fantasy of seeking life through material enjoyments and flee to Christ for true life and salvation.

Whatsoever thy hand findeth to do, do it with thy might; for there is no work, nor device, nor knowledge, nor wisdom, in the grave, whither thou goest.
                          —ECCLESIASTES 9:10 (read Ecclesiastes 9:4–10)

"A living dog is better than a dead lion." In one masterly stroke, we are faced with the privilege, opportunity, and urgency of life. The meager mongrel excels the stuffed lion by that inexplicable quality called life. The dead are out of things "done under the sun." What a challenge to the only appropriate lifestyle!

The world's assurance is self-confidence. This is a woeful attitude. There are too many hard knocks for such a thing. The Christian life involves warfare against the world, the flesh, and the devil. It is a grueling combat with forces of evil (Eph. 5:12). We need to be more than self-assured. True assurance involves knowing that God accepts our labors irrespective of how circumstances are going. You are to keep on doing what is right because it is right, just as Christ did.

Hollywood's attractiveness is physical and lustful and panders to sin. It invades homes with its destructive lifestyle using televisions and computers. How different this biblical attractiveness is. (1) There is a right attitude. Christians are not to be morbid ascetics treating the material side of life as evil. The gifts of God are good and we should enjoy them. (2) There is a right appearance. The Christian should not be messy, untidy, or unkempt. Even when we feel desolate or are brokenhearted, our dress and demeanor should reflect our highest interest and reveal our inner glow. We have the fine linen of Christ's righteousness and share that oil of gladness with which He has been anointed. (3) There is a right affection. May our spouses and Christian brothers and sisters forgive us for our morbid times when we took no joy in their company because we were too preoccupied with sorrow. Hardships cast a long shadow, but we must still live joyfully.

Melancholy stifles action, but true joy unleashes it. Take each day's opportunities and engage heart and soul and mind and strength in activities to honor God. How the activities of Reformers, Puritans, and others have changed the world! Our kaleidoscope of life ends at death. All of its different colors and shapes will have been fashioned through our activities here.

Work while it is day. Christ has risen from the grave and has conquered death. He is seeking and saving sinners. The Light is shining and the new dawn is near. Live joyfully while you work.

...but time and chance happeneth to them all.
—ECCLESIASTES 9:11 (read Ecclesiastes 9:11–18)

In the fable of the hare and the tortoise, the hare lost despite its speed. Outcomes in life are unpredictable and we need wisdom.

In our enterprises, we expect achievement to follow endeavor. Such expectation would be irrational in a world of chance. Our adjustment of means to ends involves design and witnesses to an orderly creation. The general rule is not, however, an invariable rule. The relationships between resources, endeavor, and achievement do not operate like the fixed law of gravity (Luke 14:28–32). Often outcomes do not match the resources and effort put in.

In saying "time and chance" happen to all, the Preacher is looking at things as they appear under the sun. According to the Hebrew, chance is not fortune, but that which occurs or meets us. Time and chance affect our control but not God's ultimate control. This was evident in the life of Christ. Under the sun, He controlled waves, illness, demons, and death, but God is not obliged to match our achievements in life to our resources and efforts. This is an unwelcome truth to the ungodly man but it is full of consolation to the believer, who confesses: "My times are in thy hand" (Ps. 31:15).

Sinners are lax about judgment because they imagine it will not overtake them soon. There is no such guarantee! The youth who thinks he has his whole life before him might hit a tree on his motorbike and suddenly his life under the sun is gone! To be unready is fatal. The unsuspecting fish or bird is suddenly caught. The end of the impenitent is terrible. It is an evil net and they are snared in an evil time like Sodom, Babylon, or Herod.

Have confidence in heavenly wisdom. What little estimation is placed upon true wisdom even among believers! Yet it works, even if soon forgotten. It is better than strength. You will find true wisdom in quiet, away from the clamor of this world.

Be cautious about destroying good. One sinner can quickly sweep away much painstakingly established good in family, church, or state. Heavenly wisdom is pure, gentle, kindly, impartial, and sincere (James 3:17).

Folly is set in great dignity, and the rich sit in low place.
—ECCLESIASTES 10:6 (read Ecclesiastes 10:1–7)

"Dead flies cause the ointment of the apothecary to send forth a stinking savour." We are reminded by these words that small departures from true wisdom contaminate the sweet savor of Christ in us with the stench of death. We consequently need objectives in life that are consistent with the best overall strategy. Ecclesiastes has lots of good advice in the remainder of this book.

This is a memorable illustration. The perfumed ointment is so pleasant, elevating, and refreshing. But flies of death, being deadly flies as well as dead flies, alight upon it from the dunghill or rotting carcass. You cannot even see the bacteria, but the subsequent stench betrays their effect. The refreshing ointment has become repulsive. No one can afford to ignore even a little folly. When the heart is hardened to even one sin, a festering process is set that will corrupt the whole man.

This is something that you must do. You have no control over the position of your biological heart, but it is different in spiritual things. The spiritual heart is the fundamental core of man's life and it must be at his right hand, in the place of honor. Each has his heart where it is because of inclination and purpose. The wise man loves what is right and positions his heart accordingly, at his right hand. The fool loves what is evil and positions his heart at his left. You can see the result of this in the way he lives.

The proud spirit is a retaliatory spirit. It is not just given to righteous indignation at supposed faults. It is also given to unrighteous indignation at real faults. There is a need for godly composure, forbearance, and peacemaking in life. There are many real provocations in employment, courts, legislation, and executive decisions. Providence permits many reversals under the sun. Things are apparently not as they should be. The wrong people are in the places of influence. It was so at Christ's trial. The unworthy condemned the only One who is worthy in the sight of God.

Keep your heart in the right place, being humble and peaceable, for better times will come.

...but wisdom is profitable to direct.
—ECCLESIASTES 10:10 (read Ecclesiastes 10:8–15)

Life is very complicated. The events, relationships, and challenges defeat us. We cannot tell which way to turn. How sufficient the Lord Jesus Christ always was, and what weak failures we seem to be in comparison! How can we do better?

The hunter, farmer, and lumberjack know that the common enterprises of life involve danger. The tree surgeon has to think about which side of the branch to saw as he sits on it. Circumspection and vigilance are necessary in life. What is presented with respect to our simplest activities applies to our greatest endeavors. Complex endeavors involve great hazards. It is not that the worst always happens, but it is always possible. Risk assessment is not an optional extra. If being carefree means being careless, it is sinful. Like the ax, the spiritual mind is blunted by diversions and sharpened by rigorous effort.

If you would avoid being bitten, the snake must be charmed. The tongue, too, can be venomous, and foolish words cause much pain (James 3:5–10). How different are gracious words! What a challenge it is to be like Christ (Luke 4:22). The wise man, like the Lord Jesus, can stoop in kindness to counsel inferiors. Those who have experienced grace should have no difficulty being gracious. The alternative is mischievous madness. If you have lost a forgiving spirit, you have spent too little time at the cross.

The fool is full of a sense of his own importance and what he is going to do. He has grand plans and he multiplies words in extolling them, but he never submits to God. He is like some architect who has so much to say about his latest drawings but fails to submit them to the chief architect who could, in a moment, have told him of the dangers of his project (James 4:13–15). How can he do anything but weary himself when he cannot even follow a sign-posted road to the city?

Let wisdom from Christ direct you or you will be like a mariner without his compass. However hard you row, it will be wasted labor.

> *By much slothfulness the building decayeth; and through idleness of the hands the house droppeth through.*
>
> —ECCLESIASTES 10:18 (read Ecclesiastes 10:16–20)

There is a direct relationship between conduct and real prosperity. Material prosperity can continue after moral prospering has disappeared but cash cannot stave off the retribution of God: "Woe to thee, O land when thy king is a child." There is money to sustain wining and dining, but there is a deep, terminal cancer within.

Leadership is the manager's buzzword. He knows the four types: the autocratic, the benevolent dictatorship, the consultative, and the participative. The ancient world had its intricacies and intrigues of organizational life, and quality of leadership was important even then.

(1) The case negatively stated: Immature leadership results in misery.

(2) The case positively stated: Noble leadership results in blessing. King Lemuel was brought up to focus upon a life of service (Prov. 31:1–5). The perfect example is the Lord Jesus Christ. Though of the noblest origin, He came to serve and to give Himself, even unto the death of the cross, to clear away guilt that sinners might be saved through faith in His Name.

Scripture contains many warnings against the evils of slothfulness (Prov. 6:6–11). The life of our Lord was always one of strenuous spiritual endeavor. He was much in prayer, in living and maturing, in His temptations, miracles, and travails for us. Ecclesiastes' statement of the evils of laziness serves as an exhortation to labor. This life is to be seized as a precious opportunity to serve God. When it is, each day has its own radiance in consequence.

"Curse" is literally "to speak lightly of" and includes flippant comments. We must guard our tongues because we are to give an account of every idle word. Guarding the tongue begins in the heart and Ecclesiastes cautions against cursing in thought. What festers in the mind will burst out of the mouth. The evil man will catch one word and bend it to his own prejudices; it is wise to guard against putting a sword into the hand of the enemy. Maintain circumspection at all times and in all places. In evil times there are evil networks, and tyrannies thrive on informers, who, like birds, will "carry the voice."

Be ready to suffer for Christ but let it not be for your own folly (1 Pet. 4:14–16).

Cast thy bread upon the waters:
for thou shalt find it after many days.
—ECCLESIASTES 11:1 (read Ecclesiastes 11:1–10)

Ecclesiastes is not concerned with some culturally oriented lifestyle that is rendered redundant by changed circumstances. On the contrary, he has solid help for difficult times. The worldly say, "Life goes on," but Ecclesiastes would not be content with such passive resignation.

In hard times, we are tempted to look after "number one." It is easy to be generous when the harvest has been plentiful, but when the "seven ears, withered, thin, and blasted with the east wind" come, it is easy to lapse into selfishness (Gen. 41:23). In such a day, Elijah was sent to the widow of Zarephath, who had a sharing spirit. Generosity is commended in the words "cast" and "give." Both involve goods leaving us. The Preacher's message is, if there are real needs, meet them. Seven is the number of completion, but the message is that if an eighth comes along, still give. The miser thinks he loses by giving, but the Preacher sees personal gain in it. Dickens's Scrooge had to learn that companionship was more valuable than cash.

A higher hand superintends life as we know it. The laws of nature reflect the divine decree and created order, and we cannot alter what we find. If it rains, we still have to go to work. If the storm brings the tree down, it is where it is, and you have to work with that. You cannot change the fixtures. It is your plans that have to be changed. The storm is a reminder of God's judgment. The awesome thunder and lightning are a guarantee of the ultimate fixture.

Adversity can stifle activity. Too close observation of wind and clouds deter from possible labor. The gospel preacher must be "instant in season" and "out of season" (2 Tim. 4:2). Many things we are anxious about never materialize and we are ignorant of what outcomes might be. The farmer has to sow in hope (James 5:7–8). Our ignorance reminds us that the potential of what we do can exceed our expectations because God is at work. In pregnancy, mysterious developments result in birth. You must get on with what belongs to you to do.

Be a good steward of the Master's goods undeterred by unpromising circumstances or a hidden future. Remember your end (vv. 7–8), rejoice in right things (v. 9), and remove fretful anxiety (v. 10).

Remember now thy Creator in the days of thy youth, while the evil days come not, nor the years draw nigh, when thou shalt say, I have no pleasure in them. —ECCLESIASTES 12:1 (read Ecclesiastes 12:1–7)

Ageism is discrimination against older people in employment, healthcare, and so on. The *American Association of Retired Persons* has secured legislation against ageism covering working conditions of forty- to sixty-nine-year-olds. That such legislation has been necessary indicates the lack of appreciation of the benefits of maturity.

Youth is the springtime of life with vibrancy, vigor, and vitality. The summer is yet to come and autumn and winter seem far away. Whatever the task, enthusiasm and energy can be poured into it. These advantages of youth can be squandered if not properly regulated, as is vividly seen in the Prodigal Son (Luke 15:13). Greater energy misdirected results in greater catastrophe. The advantages of youth are best utilized and preserved by serving one's Creator in a godly way.

Our generation despises old age, identifying it with weakness, incapacity, and incompetence. Old age is preoccupied with infirmities and is devoid of former pleasures. The light of life is in decline. The godless feel cheated and want their time over again, but the life focused upon Christ cannot wither and disintegrate because there is a spiritual springtime in the soul. In the metaphor of the house, the "keepers" (arms) tremble, the "strong men" (legs) weaken, the "grinders" (teeth) diminish, the "watchers" (eyes) darken, and the "doors" (ears) shut. The aged are up with the skylark, heights frighten, and normal paths contain hazards. The hair, like the "almond," turns white just before petals fall. The slightest thing is a "burden" and the appetite declines. The "mourners" are ready at hand.

The Christian has more knowledge of the afterlife and this produces a wonderful assurance. To die is "gain" (Phil. 1:20–24). The Preacher, however, has no doubt that there is more to come. When the body is committed to the dust, the spirit has an appointment elsewhere. Death is not the end, though it represents a very significant terminus. The gold lamp suspended by its silver cord is fragile and breaks. Functioning ceases. The wheel is broken. The mysterious union of body and soul is terminated and the spirit goes to God.

Make your life a significant testimony to youngsters like the girl who wrote: "I am fourteen years old and already feel my life has been a waste of time."

Let us hear the conclusion of the whole matter: Fear God, and keep his commandments: for this is the whole duty of man.
—ECCLESIASTES 12:13 (read Ecclesiastes 12:8–14)

We expect closing words to be significant and feel cheated when a book sputters at the end. Ecclesiastes does not disappoint us in this regard.

Ecclesiastes ends where he began. All his searching has confirmed the vanity of sensuous enjoyment, human wisdom, human labor, earthly endeavor, acquisition of riches, high position, formalistic worship, and material goods. Christ also taught the vanity of earthly things if made our goal (Matt. 6:31–33).

Diversions will not help. We need spiritually wise men who will persevere in giving "good heed," pondering these things, making diligent search in order to impart spiritual truth. The Preacher "still taught the people knowledge." The wise man realizes that sinners need "words of truth," even "the words of the wise." The Lord Jesus was a teacher and we still need "acceptable" (pleasing and delightful) "words." Oh, to so preach Christ!

(1) Accept the admonition: It is the Shepherd who speaks through His ministers. Goads spur to godliness and nails are supports on which to hang our thinking. (2) Avoid distractions: There are "many books," the Internet, and other alternatives to consume our time. (3) Available resources should be used wisely: study is tiring. Truth yields soul-refreshment whereas substandard wisdom is a weariness of the flesh.

We cannot improve on Ecclesiastes' conclusion: "Fear God, and keep his commandments: for this is the whole duty of man." (1) This conclusion is theological: "fear God." God is the fountain of life and through faith in Christ we can know Him. (2) This conclusion is moral: it concerns God's "commandments." Justification is by faith in Christ, but God's commands remain the absolute moral standard. Morality is not merely about values (what we esteem to be right); it is about virtue (inner righteousness that accords with God's standard). (3) This conclusion is practical: "keep his commandments." He who loves God will serve God.

The final judgment is the ultimate day of reckoning. The Preacher has left us on the very brink of eternity, face to face with God, the Judge of all the earth who shall do right. Do you see who He is? Do you see what you are? Do you see your need of Jesus Christ, the Way, the Truth and the Life, without whom all is vanity?

MILKHONEY

from Isaiah

DIRK J. BUDDING

Come now, and let us reason together, saith the LORD: though your sins be as scarlet, they shall be as white as snow; though they be red like crimson, they shall be as wool.

—ISAIAH 1:18

How exceedingly great is the mercy and compassion of the Lord! However sinful you are, whatever you did, there is hope for you. Hear the voice of the Lord Himself to you now: "Come now...." The Lord did not say: "Go away into everlasting fire." He could have done that. We, and the people to whom Isaiah prophesied, deserved that. When the Holy Spirit shows us the reality of our sinful nature and life, then there is no hope in ourselves. The provocations against the Lord were terrible. He compares them with Sodom and Gomorrah. He condemns their vain religion and their empty prayers. Their whole life is one ruin. And are we better? No!

Yet the Lord in His mercy speaks to them and to us now. He calls, "Come now." Not tomorrow, but now. It could be your last day. It could be the last call of the Lord.

Why does the Lord call us? "Let us reason together." Let us see everything in the light of God's holy law: your thoughts, your lusts, your words, your actions, your religion—everything, your whole corrupt life. What do you see then? Sins as scarlet. You cannot wash them away. Even your repentance and tears cannot wash them away. They are like crimson, and it is totally impossible to wash them away yourself. But hear the promise of the Lord: "they shall be as white as snow...they shall be as wool." You shall be white and bright, without any blot or spot. How is that possible? It is possible because the Lord gave His only begotten Son; the blood of Christ cleanses of every sin. When you are washed in the blood, your sins disappear. Your terrible scarlet sins are washed away. You are so beautiful in the sight of the Lord it is as if you never had any sin. Come now, to Christ, the only Fountain, opened for all uncleanness. That is the command of the Lord Himself.

But how can I be washed? Only by faith, not by works. Believe that you are totally guilty, wretched in yourself. Believe that the Lord Jesus shed His precious blood for you at the cross. That blood applied to your heart by the Holy Spirit creates peace in your soul, peace which goes beyond all understanding. "Therefore being justified by faith, we have peace with God through our Lord Jesus Christ" (Rom. 5:1).

And many people shall go and say, Come ye, and let us go up to the mountain of the LORD, to the house of the God of Jacob; and he will teach us of his ways, and we will walk in his paths. —ISAIAH 2:3a

The "mountain of the LORD…the house of the God of Jacob" is a wonderful place. Everything in this house shows us the love of God, the beauty of Christ, the way of peace and holiness. It is an example of the heavenly sanctuary. We all must come there, and we can only come in a spiritual way to see the holiness and righteousness of God when the lamb is killed.

The Lamb of God was given by the Father unto the death on the cross. God did not spare His own Son. What proof of the all-surpassing love of God in giving His own Son for our salvation!

There we see the love of Christ which goes beyond all knowledge. He is the Lamb who takes away the sin of the world. Out of His sacrifice and blood comes forth the fountain of all blessings, forgiveness, peace, and eternal life.

There we see the high priest, coming out of the holy of holies with the blessing of the eternal love and peace of the triune God. He is an example of our great High Priest, Jesus Christ. Out of His fullness, we receive grace for grace: grace sufficient for all our needs, life for our death, light for our darkness, hope for our hopelessness, a full redemption and forgiveness.

Many people are drawn to that wonderful place, the house of God. They see their need of Christ with the eyes of faith. They are hungry in their souls to be taught the way of salvation. They see the beauty of Christ, and they trust in Him that He will show them the way of holiness and happiness. They are made willing to go down the narrow way, and so they enjoy the peace of God in their hearts. They spread the fragrance of Christ to others.

They also take others with them. Their life is one continuous call, "Go with me. Enjoy wonderful and eternal blessings." Thus they are a blessing for their own wife or husband, for their friend or neighbor. They are used and blessed by the Lord to save others. Is your life such an invitation? When the love of Christ is a reality in you, then you want to share it with everybody. It is your loving desire to bring sinners to Christ as much as you can. What did Andrew do with his brother Simon? "He brought him to Jesus" (John 1:42). Do the same!

When the LORD shall have washed away
the filth of the daughters of Zion....
—ISAIAH 4:4a

There is only one thing really important in your life. Nothing else is as important. Within a short time, you will stand before the holy judgment throne of God. The Father has given all judgment to His Son, Jesus Christ. When you stand before Him, He will search you—your whole life, your heart, your feelings, your thoughts, your words, and your actions. All will be compared with the holy law of God. Nothing is hidden before Him who sits on the throne.

Your sins will appear, without any exception. They all will be punished in eternal fire, with complete honesty and justice.

But if your sins are washed away, you shall stand there without any spot or blot. It will be as if you never had any sin, because the Lord will have washed away all your filth.

You cannot wash yourself. Do not try to deceive yourself. So many people forgive their own sins and live in a false rest and a vain hope. Only the Lord Himself can wash away your sin. You have so many sins! If you had upon you all the sins of the whole world, the Lord is able and willing to wash away your sins. Never think that your sins are too many and too great, for in Zion, the Lord has opened the fountain of blood, which washes away all sins.

The Father Himself gave up His only begotten Son to open this fountain. The Son Himself gave His precious blood as the only fountain, in which your sins are washed away. The Holy Spirit applies the blood of Christ to your guilty conscience.

He convicts you of your sin. He shows you your filthy heart and life in the light of the holy law of God. He makes you cry, "O God, be merciful unto me, a sinner." He shows you the beauty and the fullness of Christ. He makes your soul thirsty for the blood that washes away all your sins. He creates in you the faith that Christ died for your sins; yes, for yours. And so He fills your heart with the peace that is beyond all understanding. He gives you the continuing desire to be holy, to give your whole life to the Lord. So you follow after perfection and you reach your goal in eternal glory. Nothing can be compared with the washing away of your sins. Seek that!

Then said I, Woe is me! For I am undone; because I am a man of unclean lips, and I dwell in the midst of a people of unclean lips: for mine eyes have seen the King, the LORD of hosts.
—ISAIAH 6:5

Have you ever seen God? The Lord Jesus teaches us, "Blessed are the pure in heart, for they shall see God." Only by the grace of God can we know and see God. Before the Lord called Isaiah to be His servant, He revealed Himself to him. He saw the Lord sitting upon His throne. He heard the seraphim crying, "Holy, holy, holy is the Lord of hosts." The holiness of God was deeply impressed upon his soul. In this divine light, he saw himself. "Woe is me! for I am undone." "I am nothing more than a filthy rag. I am worthy to be cast out. I cannot stand before the holy God. In His light I am sin, nothing but sin. I am undone."

This is the lesson which we all need to learn when confronted with the holiness of God. "I am a man of unclean lips." I cannot bring forth one clean work. I cannot utter one word by which God is magnified. I am totally unworthy and unable to be a child of God, to be a servant of the Lord. Thus we are cut off of all our own possibilities and righteousness. This is the way of the Lord when He calls us from darkness into light and calls us in His service. The Holy Spirit opens our eyes to see ourselves and to see the Lord. It is only because of God's free, sovereign grace that He sends a messenger to the people. By this He shall receive all glory, and that is the purpose of all His works.

But then one of the seraphim comes with a live coal in his hand, taken from off the altar. The altar is the place of the sacrifice, the place of blood. Here is a glorious example and prophesy of Christ. His blood washes away every sin. By the application of His blood and righteousness, we become totally clean. We receive a clean heart, a clean mind, and clean lips. We receive a true, loving, remaining, and growing desire to magnify God, to be used to the extension of His kingdom, to work and speak according to His holy will. The coal is laid upon his mouth. The word sounds in his soul, "Thine iniquity is taken away and thy sin purged." He hears it from the Lord Himself, and is therefore willing and able to give himself to the Lord. Do you know His voice, too?

Therefore the Lord himself shall give you a sign; behold a virgin shall conceive, and bear a son, and shall call his name Immanuel.

—ISAIAH 7:14

What is your greatest sin? It is your unbelief; that is the most terrible sin. This is the sin we started with in Paradise. We believed Satan, the liar. We did not believe God. And now we are so deceitful. We hide our unbelief behind a cloak of piety. Like Ahaz, we by nature reject the goodness of God, and we abide and die in our sin. The Lord comes to Ahaz the king of Judah. "Ask thee a sign of the LORD...." Ahaz is in great trouble, and the Lord will show him His might and love to save him. But Ahaz refuses. "I will not ask, neither will I tempt the LORD." By this statement he hides his great, awful sin behind the pretence of humility. Man, by nature, is hypocritical. If you think you're better, you don't know yourself at all.

What does the Lord say? "I shall reject you"? He certainly would be righteous in doing so. But no, the Lord says, "Therefore the Lord himself shall give you a sign." Salvation does not depend on us, or on our choice; it depends completely on the Lord. Salvation came forth out of His eternal, one-sided love. "Behold a virgin shall conceive." He, by His Holy Spirit, unites Himself with our nature. God out of God, Light out of Light, sanctifies our nature in His Son.

"She shall bear a son." The Son of God and the Son of Man: two natures in one unique Person. "And shall call his name Immanuel"—"God with us." He shall take away all our sins, also our greatest sin, unbelief. Out of His fullness we receive His Spirit and He convicts us of our unbelief. He creates in us true repentance and a deep sorrow for our unbelief. He reveals Christ in all His beauty and fullness to us. He enables us to embrace Christ as our Savior. And so we are saved by faith, united with Christ by true faith. Therefore, we hate what He hates. We walk by faith. We fight against our unbelief and all other sins. And we are more than conquerors in and by Him. Do you fight that good fight every day?

Behold, I and the children whom the LORD hath given me are for signs and wonders in Israel, from the LORD of hosts, which dwelleth in mount Zion.

—ISAIAH 8:18

"Behold," or, give me your full attention. We must see the wonders that are revealed here, the wonders of the Lord. "I and the children whom the LORD has given me." "I" refers here to Christ, speaking to those who wait upon the Lord (v. 17). The Lord hides His face from the house of Israel. They can miss, if necessary, everything and everybody, but they cannot miss the Lord. They cannot miss His face shining upon them. And the more they have experienced the great wonder of His love, the less they can miss Him.

The Lord comforts you. He says, "Behold, I...." The Lord reveals Himself in Christ and by Christ. He is the only way to the Father. For the sake of His righteousness, the Father shines His face upon us, and we enjoy His unspeakable love and peace. God is reconciled in Christ. The Father Himself loves you. You are given to Christ by the Father in the eternal counsel of peace between the Father and the Son in the communion of the Holy Spirit. He loves you from eternity to eternity. Nothing and nobody can separate you from His love.

The children of God are the signs and the wonders in Israel. A child of God cannot be hidden. His children are the city set upon the hill, the salt of the earth, the recipients of God's electing, irresistible love. In the true children of God, Christ becomes visible. There is a big difference between a child of God and all other people. This is the difference between life and death, between darkness and light. They are also "wonders," for there is no greater wonder in human life than to be called from darkness into God's marvelous light. There is no greater wonder than to be a child of God, a letter of Christ, visible for everybody to see and read. Yes, that is a wonder of the Lord of hosts. He is the Father in His electing love, the Son in His redeeming love, the Holy Spirit in His sanctifying love. To Him be all the glory. He dwells in mount Zion in the midst of His people. He dwells in the midst of the sacrifices. That mount was an example of the heavenly sanctuary from which all blessings come down, so that we become "a sign and a wonder." Are you a sign and a wonder?

For unto us a child is born, unto us a son is given: and the government shall be upon his shoulder: and his name shall be called Wonderful, Counsellor, The mighty God, The everlasting Father, The Prince of Peace.

—ISAIAH 9:6

Do you know this Child? Did you see Him with the eye of faith? Is this Child given to you? In the free offer of the gospel He is offered to you. But did you receive Him in your heart, by the Holy Spirit, in true faith? If so, then you see His beauty, His glory. Then you love Him and follow Him. He is your King, for the government is upon His shoulder. In each of these precious names, Christ's beauty and glory is revealed. His name is "Wonderful." He is fully God and fully man in one Person. The mystery of godliness is great. He is "Wonderful" in His love, in His perfect righteousness, in His miracles. Who is this, that the winds and the seas obey Him?

His name is "Counsellor." Is there a question which He cannot answer? Is there a problem which He cannot solve? No! When we don't know the way, He is the way. When we don't know how we can be saved, He is the answer.

His Name is "the mighty God." Yes, He is the Almighty. There are no limits in His power to love, to save, and to seek the lost. By His divine power He took away the sin of the world while in His human nature. Are you dead? He makes you alive. Are you blind? He gives you your sight. Are you the chief of sinners? He takes away the burden of your soul and brings you back to the Father. He is "the everlasting Father." He could say: "I and my Father are One. He who hath seen me, hath seen the Father."

He is "the Prince of Peace." He is our Peace. By His perfect sacrifice, He merited peace with God. By His Holy Spirit, He brings this peace in your heart—a peace which goes beyond all understanding. In this peace we enjoy a foretaste of heaven.

Oh, what a perfect, precious Savior! Knowing Him is eternal life. To miss Him is eternal death. For this Child is God's only begotten Son, in whom He is well pleased. Hear Him!

*They shall not hurt nor destroy in all my holy mountain: for the earth
shall be full of the knowledge of the LORD, as the waters cover the sea.*

—ISAIAH 11:9

"The rod out of the stem of Jesse" is the King of Peace, our Lord Jesus Christ.
His kingdom is coming. He brings the peace of God into your heart. When
you come to Him, laboring and heavy laden, He will give you rest and peace
with God. This peace is beyond all understanding. And when you are living
in peace with God, you are looking forward to the coming of His kingdom.
The Belgic Confession says so beautifully, "Therefore we expect that great
day, with great desire." That is why the Lord Jesus teaches us to pray, "Thy
kingdom come." One day, this wonderful promise will be fulfilled totally. In
the holy mountain of the Lord, there shall be no more pain. Here you may
have to suffer, if you love the Lord. Here people hurt you because you follow
Him. Here the devil is busy in vain to destroy the Lord's people, to destroy
the church of God. But the gates of hell shall not conquer them. When His
kingdom has come, that time is past, forever and ever, for the earth shall be
full of the knowledge of the Lord. Every man in the new heaven and the
new earth shall be totally full of His knowledge. There will be no room for
anybody else other than the Lord, the Father in all His glory, the Son in all
His love, the Holy Spirit in His full eternal communion. The triune God
shall fill you. The few drops of that knowledge and love are so sweet here.
They cannot be compared with anything else. Oh, what shall the fullness be,
the eternal fullness of that knowledge?

All the Lord's people shall be united in that perfect love and knowledge.
What in this world gives a deeper tie than fellowship in the Lord? What
sweeter communion is there in this world than the sweet communion of the
saints? Here on earth is a small part of the fullness of joy and unity which we
shall have hereafter with and in the Lord. The question is, do you truly know
and love the Lord? The beginning is here, the fullness hereafter.

Oh, seek this wonderful Lord! In Christ Jesus, He stretches His arms
out to you. "Look unto me, and be ye saved, all the ends of the earth: for I
am God, and there is none else" (Isa. 45:22).

Behold, God is my salvation; I will trust, and not be afraid: for the LORD
JEHOVAH is my strength and my song; he also is become my salvation.

—ISAIAH 12:2

There no greater blessing than to know that "God is my salvation"—God Himself. God the Father is my eternal, perfect, loving Father. God the Son is my loving Redeemer. God the Holy Spirit is living in me and is my dear Comforter. There is profound happiness in God. There is a deep fullness of love and peace. He is so wonderful and beautiful! He is altogether lovely! We shall need an eternity to know Him and to love Him.

How precious the little word "my" is—salvation received from the Lord Himself, out of the fullness of the sacrifice of Christ, applied by the Holy Spirit in *my* heart. Then we can honestly say, "I will trust, and not be afraid." God is so perfectly faithful and trustworthy. There are no limits to His love and His might to protect you and to save you. When you belong to Him, there is no reason to ever be afraid. All things in your life must work for good; all trials and tribulations bring you nearer to the Lord. He rules your whole life by His perfect wisdom and love. You have no strength in yourself to conquer any enemy, but you don't need it, for the Lord Jehovah not only gives you strength, He is your strength, your Almighty strength. By His strength, He created heaven and earth in six days. By His strength, He carries you through all your tribulations. With His everlasting arms underneath you, He guides you and brings you home with Him.

Therefore, He is your song. When your heart is filled with His love, your only desire is to praise Him and to magnify Him not only with your words, but with your whole life. Your whole life is one song of praise to His glory. Here on earth it is still in part, but yet true and wonderful. But within a short time, you will receive your deepest wish which is to sing His praise perfectly in eternity, united with the whole church of Christ. The wonder is so great: "He is also become my salvation." This salvation is not only for others, but "my" salvation, too. I can never understand that a wretched sinner as I am received Him as my salvation. I need eternity to thank Him, to adore Him, to glorify Him. Is that your desire and future?

Behold, the day of the LORD cometh, cruel both with wrath and fierce anger, to lay the land desolate: and he shall destroy the sinners thereof out of it.
—ISAIAH 13:9

Babylon was a strong empire. It seemed invincible. Her inhabitants lived in false rest and trust. It is dangerous to trust yourself and to trust in man. To not trust in God and Christ is really dangerous, for only by faith in Him can you be saved. Only in losing all trust and hope in yourself and putting all your trust in Christ alone can you have rest.

The destruction of Babylon is an example of the last day of this world. "Behold": let it have your daily and deep attention. Let it be in your thoughts and hearts, continually. "The day of the Lord cometh." Nobody can hinder that. The day of the Lord's wrath and anger comes. It comes at the Lord's time, and in His way. Then, if you are still an unbeliever, you will know God as a consuming fire. You will know Christ as your terrible Judge to condemn you for all eternity. Then you will lose all your properties, all your idols, all your pleasures. Then you will have nothing and your place will be in eternal fire. You will be eternally lost, unless you flee from the coming wrath. This serious warning comes to you. God has no pleasure in your destruction, but in your conversion.

There is a refuge for the coming wrath, but only one: Christ Jesus. He bore the whole wrath of God against the sin of the world. In Him is a full redemption, a perfect righteousness. In Him is an eternal refuge. If you are hidden in Christ, you have nothing to fear, but everything to hope.

The Lord shall lay the land desolate. Nothing shall be left of all the pleasures and glories of this world. Everything shall be consumed in the holy fire in which heaven and earth shall perish. He shall destroy the sinners out of it. If that day, the last day of your life, shall find you as an unsaved sinner, it shall be too late to repent and believe the gospel.

But this terrible message for sinners is at the same time a glorious gospel message for God's people. No sinner shall be found in the new heaven and earth. The saints alone shall inhabit that glorious place, united in one heart, love, and desire to magnify, to praise the Father, the Son, and the Holy Spirit unto all eternity. Will you be there?

What shall one then answer the messengers of the nation? That the
LORD hath founded Zion, and the poor of his people shall trust in it.
—ISAIAH 14:32

There is an enormous, eternal difference between the Lord's people and all other people—not by nature, but by free, sovereign grace. Here is a serious prophecy against the Philistines. "Howl, O gate, cry, O city; thou, whole Palestina." "Howl and cry," sinner, living without Christ and without hope, deceiving yourself with a false hope and a vain rest. There is no life, no rest, no hope, but in Christ. You shall perish without true faith in the Savior.

But what is the answer to the messengers of God's people? They are hungry to hear God's Word about them. Their heart is thirsting for God, the living God. They know that they are not better; they know themselves as the chief of sinners. But their souls are thirsting after the righteousness which saves from death—the full righteousness of Christ revealed in the sacrifices in the Old Testament. Christ's righteousness comes forward in full and glorious reality in His sacrifice on the cross.

What is God's answer to His poor, afflicted people? His answer is that He has founded Zion. Zion is an example of the church of God of all places and all ages. The Lord Himself has founded His church in His eternal love and free choice. He has founded Zion in the perfect righteousness of Christ. He has founded Zion in His faithful promise, His holy, infallible Word. This is a wonderful, solid foundation which no one can remove. "And the poor of his people shall trust in it."

This refuge is for those who only have guilt. They can only sin and nothing more. They increase their guilt daily and can never pay anything, for all their righteousnesses are as filthy rags. Therefore, they flee to Zion; they flee to the sacrifice of Christ and trust in Him. They find in Him all their salvation. He fills their heart with His wonderful peace. And so they enjoy the foretaste of eternal salvation. They rest in the love of the Father and the righteousness of the Son, by the wonderful working of the Holy Spirit. They receive the inheritance of eternal glory.

The poor are rich. Are you among them?

At that day shall a man look to his Maker, and his eyes shall have respect to the Holy One of Israel.
—ISAIAH 17:7

The Lord often uses tribulations to bring His people back to Himself. "For whom the Lord loveth he chasteneth, and scourgeth every son whom he receiveth" (Heb. 12:6). It is far worse if the Lord lets us go without chastening. But He will never let His people go in their own ways: "At that day...," the day of sorrow, the day that the glory of Jacob shall be reduced, and a man shall "look to his Maker." That is the great turn in a man's life. That is the new birth, the work of grace in our heart. By nature, we seek ourselves. We listened to the devil: "Thou shalt be as God." We look to our idols, we trust in our false hope and vain religion. But the day that the Lord begins His good work in us, we look to our Maker.

Our soul is thirsting for God, the living God. We cannot be filled and satisfied with anybody and anything else but God. He is our Maker. He has a right to our whole heart, love, and life. We realize how far away we are and our heart breaks in true repentance. Only our Maker can fill our heart and life. He is the purpose of our life. We begin to see His beauty, His glory, and the choice grows in our heart to seek Him. We come back, with the Prodigal Son, to our heavenly Father. We see Him as "the Holy One of Israel." We cannot stand before Him. We are not worthy to be called His child. We cannot imagine that He still loves us and shall receive us. And yet we go to Him, our Father.

Our hope is only in Him; in His mercy and in His promise. We read in His Word that His hands are spread out wide to coming sinners and we throw ourselves by faith into the everlasting, ever-loving arms of the prodigal's father. We read that he "fell on his neck and kissed him" (Luke 15:20). And so we receive the kiss of reconciliation by faith in Christ. He is the Way by which we return. Only out of the fullness of His righteousness, the Father kisses our soul. It is on His account only that we are saved and comforted. Therefore, He receives all the glory. We look on Him and live for Him. He is our Maker, our Redeemer, and our Bridegroom. "Behold the Lamb of God, which taketh away the sin of the world" (John 1:29).

*Whom the LORD of hosts shall bless, saying, Blessed be Egypt my peo-
ple, and Assyria the work of my hands, and Israel mine inheritance.*
—ISAIAH 19:25

The blessing of the Lord makes us eternally rich. This blessing is His love,
His nearness, yes, He Himself. When you are blessed by the Lord, you are
His child. He loves you, He protects you, He makes you ready to be with
Him in eternal glory. There is no reason in you for which the Lord can bless
you. On the contrary, you deserve His curse. But that is the wonder of free
grace. The Lord blesses people who are cursed in themselves. Because of His
free grace, Christ became a curse on the cross. The Lord can bless you for
Christ's sake, and He does. Hear this wonderful gospel message: "Blessed be
Egypt my people." In the Bible, Egypt is the example of darkness, enmity,
and filth. And yet the Lord calls them, "my people."

Amazing grace! Christ fled to Egypt soon after His birth. Then His gospel came to Egypt. For many years, Egypt became an important Christian
country. Until today, the Lord has His blessed people there. How faithful
and trustworthy is His Word!

Assyria is also a big region in the Middle East. The Lord calls it "the
work of my hand." His good work in the heart of Assyrians seemed so
impossible because they were very cruel enemies of Israel. But the work of
God is a work of love. The work of God is irresistible. The work of God
changes us totally.

This word is a source of hope and light. For us, when we see our own
hard heart, when we feel ourselves so blind, when we see the enmity in our
heart, it seems so impossible to be saved. But it is the work of "the LORD of
hosts." Enemies are reconciled with God. What is impossible with man is
possible with God. All His promises will be fulfilled.

Israel is the third nation mentioned. Sadly, most of the present-day nation
of Israel rejects the Lord Jesus. But we are looking forward to the fulfillment
of this rich promise when their eyes shall be opened. God's promise will be
fulfilled and they shall see Him whom they, and we, have crucified. Then they
will embrace their Savior in large numbers. Let our prayer be for Israel.

JUNE 14

O LORD, thou art my God; I will exalt thee, I will praise thy name; for thou hast done wonderful things; thy counsels of old are faithfulness and truth.
—ISAIAH 25:1

What precious words: "thou art my God." If that is true in your life, you are the most happy and rich person in the world. God is your everlasting Father. No one can separate you from His love. He is your loving Redeemer, your Bridegroom, your Lord and God. Thomas could say when he saw Jesus in His divine glory: "my Lord and my God" (John 20:28). He is your eternal Comforter who dwells in you and will stay with you forever. God, the triune God, my God!

It often seems too wonderful to be true, and yet He makes it true by His Holy Spirit. You can know that it is true by whether you have one great desire: "I will exalt thee, I will praise Thy name." That is the purpose of your life. It is the pleasure of your soul to exalt and to praise God with your whole life. At the same time, it is your daily sorrow that you fall so short of it. And that makes you long for the day when you will exalt and praise Him perfectly in eternity.

Why are you longing to praise and exalt the Lord? "For thou hast done wonderful things." He has done wonderful things in the life of His people. "For thou hast made of a city an heap.... Thou hast been a strength to the poor, a strength to the needy in distress, a refuge from the storm, a shadow from the heat...." What wonderful things! The Lord has destroyed all that rebelled against Him. That is what He did in your life. By His love, He destroyed your enmity. When you cried to Him, He became your strength. You were so poor, so guilty, so full of distress, and He revealed Christ in your soul. The strong God! He took away the sin of the world. He conquered all the powers of sin, devil, and hell. And He became your strength, your righteousness, your life, and your joy. By faith you could say, "My Lord and my God."

Why you? Are you better than others? No, you knew that you were the most unworthy, the chief of sinners. But it is because of His counsels of old. It is His faithfulness and truth. It is His eternal, electing love. Therefore, He implants and augments the desire in your heart: "O LORD, thou art my God, I will exalt thee, I will praise thy name"—here and to all eternity.

Thy dead men shall live, together with my dead body shall they arise. Awake and sing, ye that dwell in dust: for thy dew is as the dew of herbs, and the earth shall cast out the dead. —ISAIAH 26:19

This is a gospel promise with a double blessing: "Thy dead men shall live." By nature, we are dead in trespasses and sin. Our spiritual death is an active enmity against God. We do not know Him rightly, we do not love Him, and we do not praise Him. And so we miss the purpose of our life and are lost for eternity, unless dead men live.

"Thy dead men shall live" by the almighty, powerful love of Him who is the Life. It is an eternal wonder when this prophecy is fulfilled in our own life. "But God..., hath quickened us together with Christ (by grace ye are saved)" (Eph. 2:4–5). When He lives in us and we in Him, we are changed from death into life. Then we shall awake with Him. We are looking forward to the great day of His coming.

What an eternal difference will appear when we have lived and died in Christ! Our dew shall be "as the dew of the herbs." The dew of the Holy Spirit will make us beautiful. We will be made conformable to the glorious body of Christ, we shall see Him as He is, and we shall be like Him. We will receive such a glory as no eye has ever seen, nor ear ever heard, which was never thought of in any human mind. We will be eternally full with God and, together with the whole body of Christ, have only one goal — His praise and honor. We will have one heart and one mind, being united in perfect love for the Lord and for one another.

But the earth shall cast out all the dead. The dead are they who hardened their heart and rejected Christ in unbelief or deceive themselves in their self-made faith and vain hope. They will arise to shame and everlasting contempt, being conformed to their father, the devil. It is one or the other. Therefore we are warned and called unto repentance. We are called by and to the Savior. He is the Life. He has promised to give His sheep eternal life. That life begins here, when we are quickened with Him. That life shall never end but shall come to fullness and glory at the day of His coming.

Are you ready? For "the Spirit and the bride say, come" (Rev. 22:17).

Therefore thus saith the LORD GOD, Behold, I lay in Zion for a foundation a stone, a tried stone, a precious corner stone, a sure foundation: he that believeth shall not make haste.
                                                        —ISAIAH 28:16

Your heart is more deceitful than anything else in the world (Jer. 17:9). By nature, we have made lies as our refuge and under falsehood we have hid ourselves (v. 15). Unless the Truth comes in our heart and life, we live in a false rest and perish forever. "Therefore thus saith the LORD GOD" is a wonderful gospel message in the Word. His Word is the remedy against our wicked heart and depraved nature. By His Word, He changes everything. "Behold I lay in Zion for a foundation a stone."

"I lay": it is His work, coming out of His eternal love. Nobody can hinder it. "I lay in Zion"—that is, in the midst of His people, a wicked, a corrupt people. He lays "a foundation," the only foundation on which we can build, an eternal foundation.

This is a wonderful prophecy of Christ. He is such a sure foundation! He is the Truth, the Way, and the Life. He finished everything on the cross for our salvation. His sacrifice is more than sufficient for the sins of the whole world. He is a "tried" stone. He has appeared and He is able to bear the whole building of His church. He is absolutely faithful and able; therefore, He is such a sure foundation.

When you build on this foundation by true faith, you are assured by His Holy Spirit of eternal life. You are assured of His eternal love for you. He makes you happy and assured. You can then say by grace, "I am persuaded that no creature shall be able to separate me from the love of God, which is in Christ Jesus our Lord." Do you believe in Christ alone for salvation? That is the only way to become united with this sure foundation.

By faith, you are cut off from Adam and united with Christ. He lives in you and you in Him. He is your life, your only hope, your Bridegroom. You know that He is faithful. You know that He will fulfill all His promises in His time. That's why you wait for Him more than the watchers for the morning. Within a little time He shall come and take you up, and you shall be where He is. Your deepest wish will be fulfilled! To be with Christ is by far the best.

The meek also shall increase their joy in the LORD, and the poor among
men shall rejoice in the Holy One of Israel.
                                                    —ISAIAH 29:19

The Lord will always have His people. Among all the thorns, He creates His lilies. His Word works powerfully and irresistibly in the hearts of sinners. The deaf shall hear and the eyes of the blind shall see; they shall hear the Word with power, and their heart will break in true repentance. Their eyes will see the King in His beauty. Their heart will thirst for God, the living God. By faith in Christ, they shall be made conformable to His image, for He says, "Learn of me; for I am meek and lowly in heart" (Matt. 11:29).

"The meek shall increase their joy in the LORD." The meek know their sorrow, but also their joy, a joy which is unspeakable. We experience this unspeakable joy when the Lord speaks to us personally and says, "Your sins are forgiven." Then we enjoy a true and sweet communion with Him by Christ in the communion of the Holy Spirit. We can then believe with our whole heart that He loves us and we love Him. He opens for us the gates of heaven and we receive a foretaste of eternal joy.

The joy of the meek is in God the Father, and His eternal, electing love; in God the Son, and His wonderful, redeeming love; and in God the Holy Spirit, and His applying and comforting love. Outside the Lord, there is no true joy. All the joy outside of the Lord ends in eternal sorrow. But the meek shall have true, increasing joy, which no one can take away. In the Hebrew language, it is literally written that they shall have joy after joy—a joy that is ever increasing in depth and height, until we are in eternal joy and forever full of joy in the Lord.

"The poor among men shall rejoice in the Holy One of Israel." The poor among men are they who have only guilt. They only increase their guilt. And yet, they are blessed. "The Holy One of Israel," Jesus Christ, paid all their debt and took upon Him all their guilt. They can stand before God as if they never had or did any sin. Who shall describe this joy in Christ? And when the foretaste is so wonderful, what shall be the eternal fullness? Do you know that joy already?

And a man shall be as an hiding place from the wind, and a covert from the tempest; as rivers of water in a dry place, as the shadow of a great rock in a weary land.
—ISAIAH 32:2

This text is a beautiful and precious prophecy of Christ. He is the only "man" who is the real and eternal hiding place when the hurricanes of the judgments of God go over the world. When His wrath and anger against sin are revealed, to whom shall we go? There is only one hiding place, this "man" who is God Himself. This Man, the "man of sorrows," fulfilled all righteousness. To whom else shall we go? He is calling us. He is inviting us. "Come unto me, all ye who labour and are heavy leaden" (Matt. 11:28). There is eternal safety in Him. There is a wonderful rest in Him, in His perfect righteousness, in His eternal, perfect love.

Therefore, He is also "a covert from the tempest." The word "tempest" can also mean "flood." At one point, the flood of the wrath of God went over this sinful world. No one was spared except those who were in the ark: Noah, his sons, and their wives. Therefore, we are called to hide ourselves in the only place of safety against the tempest, the flood of God's eternal wrath. We can only escape by faith, believing that we are eternally lost outside this covert and that we are safe in this covert God has given. "This is my only begotten Son, in whom I am pleased; hear Him!" What an eternal wonder that God loved the world so much that He gave His only begotten Son to be our only refuge and covert. How terrible to deny and reject such a wonderful covert!

But this "man" is also as rivers in a dry place. Our soul is so dry, fruitless, and barren. But when this Man pours out His waters on our soul, everything changes. The fruits of the Spirit become visible in our life. We will be green and verdant to proclaim that the Lord is good. Even in old age we will bear rich fruit.

Christ is also "the shadow of a great rock in a weary land" when the sun is burning in full heat. We cannot stand before the holy anger of God, who is a consuming fire, but here is the Rock. In His shadow, you shall sing joyfully. There you experience safety and love. There you hide yourself, until you are with Him in eternal glory.

And Hezekiah received the letter from the hand of the messengers, and read it: and Hezekiah went up unto the house of the LORD, and spread it before the LORD.
                                                                —ISAIAH 37:14

This was a terrible letter! It was Hezekiah's death sentence. If you look at it from the human side, there was no hope to be saved. This is an enormous army against a small flock. This is what the Lord allowed His children to feel. That is where He brings us, again and again. We must be cut off from all human hope, that is, from all our own righteousness. This opens the way to be saved only by divine grace and divine strength.

Hezekiah read the terrible, blaspheming letter. The letter was full of human pride, and it was totally empty of any knowledge and fear of God. That is man by nature. In the depth of our being, everyone is the same. Only free, sovereign grace makes a difference between us all. By grace, we know God. By grace, we see the almighty power and faithfulness of God and His love revealed in Christ.

"And Hezekiah went up unto the house of the LORD." He fled to the only refuge, for everything in the house of God spoke of Christ. There was the sacrifice, there was the blood, and there was the blessing. There was the presence of God reconciled in the blood. There was the cloud, the visible sign of His loving presence. And the heart of Hezekiah was there, too. Christ alone has the answers to all our questions. In Him is the solution of all our problems. He is God's answer for all our impossibilities.

Hezekiah spread the letter before the Lord. He gave the whole problem over into the hands of the Lord. It was no longer his problem, but it was the concern of the Lord. It gives a wonderful rest in our soul when we submit ourselves totally to Christ and give all our sins, all our needs, and all our enemies into His hand. His rich promise is, "I care for you." He is the Lord; He does what seems good in His eyes. Faith gives away everything to Christ and trusts Him with our whole salvation. He has all power in heaven and on the earth. The mouth of the mocker shall be stopped.

The love and power of God shall appear, as it did for Hezekiah. An army of 185,000 men died in one night. So it shall always happen with all the enemies of God. Whose side are you on?

Behold, for peace I had great bitterness: but thou hast in love to my soul delivered it from the pit of corruption: for thou hast cast all my sins behind thy back.

—ISAIAH 38:17

The most troublesome times in the life of the Lord's people are often the best spiritual times in their life. The Lord uses and blesses the ways of tribulation to make us more and more conformable to the image of Christ. He brings us deeper into the suffering of Christ. He gives us a clearer knowledge of Christ, which is the desire of our soul. We want to know Him, and to know Him more and more. The way to this knowledge is the cross of Christ.

Hezekiah had peace. The Lord had done mighty miracles; Hezekiah had been released from his mighty enemies. There was such a demonstration of the might and love of God for him. But now things became worse. He received a deadly illness and a discouraging message: "Set thine house in order: for thou shalt die and not live." And, until now, he didn't have a son, so the promise of salvation was not fulfilled. Without the Savior, he could not meet God. That's what we have to feel, too. Without Christ we cannot live, and without Him, we cannot die either.

But how wonderfully the Lord turned Hezekiah's bitterness! "But thou hast in love to my soul delivered it from the pit of corruption." The Lord filled his heart with His lovingkindness and everlasting goodness, which is better than life. The Lord delivered him from the pit of corruption. He cast all Hezekiah's sins behind His back. His soul was crying for the Surety, that is, for Christ (v. 14), and in Christ, the Lord embraced his soul in love. In the arms of his Lord, he found peace, forgiveness, and everlasting love. All his sins were cast behind God's back. The Lord would remember them no more. All his sins were blotted out by Christ, and now there was no condemnation for him, for Christ bore his condemnation on the cross. How good the Lord is for a sinner! He is still the same. In all our needs and sins, there is only one Way, and that is Christ.

In Christ, God stretches out His hands to us. And for Christ's sake, He will embrace and kiss a sinner and fill his heart with the foretaste of eternal joy. How worthy is the Lord to be loved and praised into all eternity! Do you agree, with your whole heart?

But they that wait upon the LORD shall renew their strength; they shall mount up with wings as eagles; they shall run, and not be weary; and they shall walk, and not faint.
                                                                —ISAIAH 40:31

Are you waiting upon the Lord? If you belong to the Lord's people, you are always waiting upon Him; you cannot live without Him. He is your life, your purpose, your most beloved One. You can only be fulfilled and satisfied with the Lord. Everything and everybody but Him leaves you empty. Only the eternal love of your heavenly Father can make you happy. Only the redeeming love of your heavenly Bridegroom, Jesus Christ, can give you rest. Only the applying and sanctifying love of your only Comforter, the Holy Spirit, can change you from glory to glory. So you are always waiting upon the Lord. When you are in sweet communion with Him, you are the most happy person in the world. When He hides His face from you, it is more bitter than death.

If you are waiting on the Lord, He shall renew your strength. We are so weak in ourselves. We have no power to fight the enemies of our souls. But He shall give us renewed strength, again and again. When we cannot go farther, He carries us. When we lose all our hope, He revives our hope and strength. When we are tempted, He shall overcome all our temptations. His strength is a divine strength. He who created heaven and earth by His Word is at your side.

You shall "mount up with wings as eagles," the wings of faith and prayer. You cannot stay and live here. Your habitation is in heaven. You are attracted by the Sun of righteousness. You will run the race. You follow after perfection. You have to overcome many troubles, you have to fight strong enemies, but you shall not be weary, for eternal love sustains you and perfect wisdom guides you. You are kept by the power of God unto salvation. Therefore, you shall walk with the Lord and not faint.

Spiritually, you are of the family of Enoch and Noah. They walked with God. How soon was Enoch at home! He did not see death, for Christ died for him. Noah, also, was strong through his walk with God. He could stand alone in the midst of a wicked generation and he was safely hidden in the ark—an example of our hiding in Christ.

*To open the blind eyes, to bring out the prisoners from the prison, and
them that sit in darkness out of the prison house.*
—ISAIAH 42:7

The power and the love of Christ to release sinners is without limits. He is
"the mighty God." He is given of the Father "to open the eyes of the blind."
By our falling into sin, we are all spiritually blind. We make a god after our
own image, but the real God we cannot see. We walk according to our own
ways and opinions, but "the Way" we cannot perceive. And so we hasten to
eternal darkness unless Christ opens our eyes.

Since it is God's pleasure to open blind eyes, you can expect it from Him.
Everything changes in your life when He opens your eyes. For the first time
in your life, you see the reality of your sinful state and nature, which is the
same as the reality of your lost eternity. You see very clearly how impossible it
is to save yourself. You see yourself totally hopeless and lost while He reveals
to you the beauty of God. Your soul is thirsting for God, the living God, and
you long to be reconciled with Him; to belong to Him is your highest goal.
He reveals Himself to you, as He did with the man born blind. He says "It
is I," and your eyes see the King in His divine glory and beauty. He reveals
Himself to you as your Redeemer. He creates in you the faith that He took
away all your sins on the cross, and now you see the chief reason and purpose
for your life, which is to glorify God. Now you see God, because your heart
has been made pure by His blood. Now you follow after to become mature
in Christ, and you see the kingdom which is coming and has come in your
soul. You are brought out of your prison. You were imprisoned with not only
a life sentence, but also an eternal sentence. You could never free yourself, but
Christ delivered you from eternal prison and brought you into the liberty of
the children of God. You no longer live in the darkness of the prison house
of Satan, but your name is written in heaven. And soon you shall live in the
eternal light of the glorious presence of God. Then you have eternity to love
and praise Him, thereby reaching your goal.

What a precious, almighty Savior is Christ! He calls you, sinner. Flee to
Him, and expect these wonders from Him. They all flow to us out of His
fullness. He expects nothing from you. He is all, and gives all.

Thus saith the LORD, thy Redeemer, the Holy One of Israel; I am the LORD thy God, which teacheth thee to profit, which leadeth thee by the way that thou shouldest go.
— ISAIAH 48:17

When the Lord speaks, we have to listen with our whole heart. It is such a privilege to hear His voice when the Lord speaks to us by His Word. He reveals Himself as "thy Redeemer." You need a Redeemer. By nature, you are bound by Satan. You are dead in trespasses and sins. You are gathering to yourself wrath unto the Day of Judgment. It is totally impossible for you to redeem yourself. And now the Lord is coming to you as "thy Redeemer."

The Father sent His only begotten Son to seek and to save the lost. The Son of the living God came in our flesh to redeem us from Satan, sin, and death. By His perfect sacrifice, He took away the sin of the world and merited a righteousness that is more than enough for the whole world. God the Holy Spirit comes into your heart to convict you of your sins and to make you feel your need of the Redeemer. He applies the righteousness of Christ to your soul, so that you enjoy peace in your heart by the precious blood and the wonderful blessing of being reconciled with God.

But if you reject this only Redeemer, you are lost, yes, doubly lost, to all eternity. This Redeemer is "the Holy One of Israel." He is holy, pure, and spotless. He revealed Himself as "the God of Israel"—of a people sinful in themselves, and yet chosen by Him. He comforts His people mightily: "I am the LORD thy God." What an eternal wonder when He applies that to us personally! Then we can respond, "My Lord and my God!" Then we adore Him and admire Him and love Him with our whole heart.

The Lord God will teach you to profit day by day and in all your needs and circumstances when you ask Him to show you the way. To profit is to do what is according to His holy Word. You have the desire to know His will, and to do His will. He leads you by the way that you have to go. Jesus Christ is the Way and He shows you Himself. You live and move and have your being in Him in the way of continual prayer, and so He prepares you for eternal glory.

He will take you home to heaven forever with God, the Father, the Son, and the Holy Spirit. God is all in all.

Can a woman forget her sucking child, that she should not have com-passion on the son of her womb? yea, they may forget, yet will I not forget thee. Behold, I have graven thee upon the palms of my hands; thy walls are continually before me.

—ISAIAH 49:15–16

Millions of times each year in our terrible age women forget their children or permit them to be killed by abortion. By this we can see that natural love is disappearing. This is a sign that our Lord Jesus Christ is coming soon. Yes, the natural man is hard and cruel, and inclined to all evil. And still, there is no end to the Lord's goodness. He is full of compassion for His people.

Zion complains: "The LORD hath forsaken me, and my Lord hath for-gotten me." That's how Zion feels, but it is not reality. Sometimes we can feel far away from the Lord. Job said, "Behold, I go forward, but he is not there; and backward, but I cannot perceive him" (Job 23:8). What a difference there is between our feelings and reality! A woman can forget her child, but not the Lord. He will never forget His child. He loves you from eternity to eternity with a perfect love. You have been in His heart always and you shall always be there. He showed His love by giving His Son for you. He poured out His love in your heart by the Holy Spirit, so that you love Him.

"Behold, I have graven thee upon the palms of my hands." Oh, to see your name there in God's hands! The hands of Christ were pierced on the cross for your sin. In Christ, you see the great love of the Father for you. In Christ, you see His great love for you, giving Himself unto death.

"Thy walls are continually before me." Zion, God's city, the church of the living God, has walls that are always before the Lord. All the events in Zion, all that happens in Zion, all your sorrows, all your tears and sighs, are continually before Him. And now He comes to you and He takes you up so that you are where He is. And He shall wipe away all your tears. Christ has really been forsaken so that we should be taken to the Lord and never be forsaken by Him. We are always before Him, always with Him. Is that the desire of your soul?

But he was wounded for our transgressions, he was bruised for our iniquities: the chastisement of our peace was upon him; and with his stripes we are healed.

—ISAIAH 53:5

"Our transgressions": how can we express how infinitely terrible they are! One sin brought all of mankind into death and misery. This shows us the holiness and pureness of God. The least sinful thought separates us from God and makes us worthy of death and hell. And what an innumerable number of sins we have! Every day the number is growing and the burden is heavier. What shall our burden be when we come to our last day, the Day of Judgment? The Holy Spirit convicts us of these sins, and then we see and feel it. By nature, we want to excuse ourselves and accuse others, but desperately we need divine light to see how serious sin is. Our sin is transgression, a willful rebellion against God. The more we become convicted of this truth, the more we admire the unspeakable love of God in giving His Son. He made Him to be sin. All the transgressions of all His people were pressed upon Him.

"He was wounded for our transgressions." In all His wounds, He did not only feel the physical pain, but much more than that—the spiritual pain. He felt the pain of the holy wrath and anger of a righteous God against sin. He felt the fire of God's holy wrath in every wound. That is what made it so exceedingly heavy. That pressed the blood out of His holy body. That is what "bruised" Him. It was unbearable. It caused Him to perish; He was bruised to death.

Who can bear the full wrath and anger of the God who is a consuming fire? Jesus could. His human nature was supported by His divine nature, otherwise He would have been crushed under such a burden. He would have been consumed in such a fire. What an eternal wonder when we can say by faith, "He was wounded for my transgressions. He was bruised for my iniquities." Does that not break our heart and fill us with unspeakable joy and love?

And yet, that joy is often mixed with sorrow, and we think to ourselves, "I am the cause of all His sufferings." His chastisement made me whole. By His suffering and death, He merited a full redemption and eternal salvation and, out of Him, the living waters flow into my soul. The Holy Spirit, by whom I am born again, applies the merits of Christ to my heart. Then I can stand before God as if I never had or committed any sin. I am made whole in Him, by Him, and with Him.

For the mountains shall depart, and the hills be removed; but my kind-ness shall not depart from thee, neither shall the covenant of my peace be removed, saith the LORD that hath mercy on thee. —ISAIAH 54:10

Truly, the kindness of the Lord is better than life! His lovingkindness is from eternity to eternity upon them that fear Him. He shows His kindness by His love, being reconciled in Christ with me. All the merits of Christ are accounted to me as well as all the love of the Father that I experience, through Christ, in the communion of the Holy Spirit. This is an eternal love, an unchangeable love, a perfect love, a love that makes you happy forever. Nothing can be compared with God's kindness for His people.

The Lord comforts His people, "afflicted, tossed with tempest and not comforted" (v. 11). "For the mountains shall depart, and the hills be removed." That shall happen on the great day of God's judgment. Nothing of this world will remain, and nothing will stay as it is. Even though this world seems strong and sure, it will be removed by the hand of the Almighty. Everything in which we trust, and on which we build, will one day be no longer. But the kindness of the Lord will never be removed.

His covenant of peace will not be removed, for it is an eternal covenant. It has its roots in God's eternal love and pleasure. It is founded on the Rock of ages, Jesus Christ, and on His blood and perfect righteousness. If we are built on this rock, we are saved forever. This is the Word of the Lord who cannot lie. The Lord's Word is sure. Oh, blessed are we, when His Word sounds deep in our soul! What a comfort in the midst of our afflictions and temptations. Everything can be lost in this world, and I can and will lose all the world, but I will never lose the lovingkindness of my Lord. Many will leave me, but He will never leave me nor forsake me. And that is only because of His mercy, and not any goodness in me. I only have sin and guilt. There is nothing in me and there shall never be anything in me for which the Lord can love me. His peculiar love is from all eternity. It is His free mercy for me a sinner. And when I enjoy that mercy, I have only one desire: to praise, love, follow, and obey Him. I stay "tossed with tempest" in this world, but soon I will be with Him. Then I will enjoy Him forever; I shall know even as I am known.

Seek ye the LORD while he may be found,
call ye upon him while he is near.
—ISAIAH 55:6

The time of grace is brief. Once it is gone, it can never be retrieved. When you stand before the judgment throne of Christ, when the books of your life are opened, it will become clear how you spent the precious time that God gave you to seek Him. For that is the purpose of your life: to seek your Creator, to seek your Redeemer, to seek your Comforter. In Paradise, you lost God, His image, His favor, and His fellowship. You are doomed! But now the Lord, in His mercy and goodness, comes to you and commands you, "Seek ye the LORD, while he may be found." Now is the time of grace and mercy. Now is the time when He can be found.

The means of grace, which is the glorious gospel in which the way of salvation is preached to us, are so great. We need to be present in the place where Christ is lifted up and offered to us as a perfect Savior. There His Holy Spirit is working, graciously renewing sinners. There we are offered Christ as the Way to be reconciled with God, by His blood, so that we experience His forgiving love. If you find Him, you find eternal life. You find true joy and a foretaste of eternal joy. You find everything you need for time and eternity. You find God the Father, your loving Father in Christ; God the Son, your loving Redeemer and Bridegroom; and God the Holy Spirit, your Comforter, who dwells in you and abides with you. He witnesses with your soul, that you are a child of God. Oh, call upon Him, the triune God, while He is so near!

He speaks to us by His Word. He calls us by His servants. His Spirit works in us true repentance and a broken heart, but also true love, peace, and joy in believing. Call upon Him. His arms are open to receive you. His mouth is ready to kiss you. His might and love surpass all your understanding. And when you find Him, you seek Him more and more, for the Lord's people can only be satisfied with God. "My soul thirsteth for God, the living God." Soon, we shall be satisfied with Him in eternal glory. For they that seek Him shall find Him—here in part, and soon in perfection.

> *For thus saith the high and lofty One that inhabiteth eternity, whose name is Holy; I dwell in the high and holy place, with him also that is of a contrite and humble spirit, to revive the spirit of the humble, and to revive the heart of the contrite ones.*
> —ISAIAH 57:15

There is an enormous chasm between God the Creator and a sinful creature. We begin to realize that when the true knowledge of God comes into our soul by the Holy Spirit. We feel it in the depths of our soul. He is "the high and lofty One" and I am sinful dust. He inhabits eternity, and I am of few days. His name is Holy, and I am so unholy. That's how we experience the wonder of our text.

It sounds unbelievable, but yet it is true. The high and lofty One dwells in the high and holy place. The whole endless universe is full of His glory, but the fullness of His majesty is in heaven. There the Son of God is in our flesh at the right hand of God. Thousands of angels sing His glory. The souls of the saints love and praise Him in perfection. And still, the Lord has other dwelling places, so many dwelling places no one can count them all. Does He dwell in your heart? How would you know? He dwells with Him that is of a contrite and humble spirit.

By nature, we are proud and hard. We want to be God; we are totally self-centered in our thinking, feeling, words, and actions. There is nothing in us but sin. But when God, by His Holy Spirit, comes in our heart, everything changes. We see who we are and what we have done. Our heart breaks in true repentance. The contents of Psalm 51 are living in our soul: "Have mercy upon me, O God, according to thy lovingkindness…. For I acknowledge my transgressions; and my sin is ever before me." We acknowledge what we deserve: "that thou mightest be justified when thou speakest, and be clear when thou judgest."

Our heart is crying for the cleansing power of the blood of Christ; "wash me, and I shall be whiter than snow." We want to be clean and new. "Create in me a clean heart, O God, and renew a right spirit within me." The angels are filled with joy and the Lord hears our cries, "to revive the heart of the contrite ones."

God Himself revives us. We cannot do it ourselves. We are and stay totally dependent. The hypocrite helps himself, but God's child can only be revived by the Lord Christ Himself. His righteousness, applied to our souls, fills us with life, love, and joy.

*I will greatly rejoice in the LORD, my soul shall be joyful in my God;
for he hath clothed me with the garments of salvation, he hath covered
me with the robe of righteousness.*
                                                        —ISAIAH 61:10a

There is a joy that is unspeakable, a joy in the Lord that no one can take away from us. A thousand worlds together cannot give us this joy. This joy is the beginning of eternal joy. In heaven, this joy will be perfect, continuing, and endless. We enjoy a foretaste here. It is a joy in God the Father when the Word of Christ becomes reality in our soul. It is a joy in God the Son. The apostle Peter wrote about this love, "Whom having not seen, ye love; in whom, though now ye see him not, yet believing, ye rejoice with joy unspeakable and full of glory" (1 Pet. 1:8).

What is the reason of this joy? "He hath clothed me with the garments of salvation." He put off my clothes, for they are filthy rags. I stood naked before God with nothing to cover my shame, and the Lord Himself clothed me with the garments of salvation, just as He did with Adam and Eve in Paradise. He clothed them Himself with "the garments of salvation." This refers to the full forgiveness of all my sins. It means to be clothed with the perfect righteousness of Christ. It is to be clothed with the perfect holiness of Christ. It is to be filled with perfect love, glory, and happiness.

We shall enjoy the fullness of Christ's garments when we are with Him in heaven. We begin to enjoy the reality here, since we are covered with the robe of His righteousness. This robe of righteousness was woven during the life of Christ, in which He glorified the Father completely, and in His suffering and death, by which He totally satisfied the righteousness of God. He paid my whole debt. He bore my whole guilt. He was wounded for my transgressions, and all that He did is given to me by faith. The Holy Spirit applies all these blessings to my soul, and then I can confess, "I will greatly rejoice in the LORD." All other joys end in eternal sorrow. Only the garments of salvation can make us ready to enter salvation. They bring the foretaste of salvation here in our heart in this life. Do you know this unspeakable joy?

For behold, I create new heavens and a new earth: and the former shall not be remembered, nor come into mind.
—ISAIAH 65:17

How infinitely great is the future which the Lord has provided for His people! It is beyond our understanding and all our expectations. This future will soon be here. We already hear the footsteps of the heavenly Bridegroom and we see the signs of His coming. Let our heart be longing with great desire for this day when He comes to judge the living and the dead. The Devil, and all who served him, will be cast into the bottomless pit, and then this wonderful prophecy shall be fulfilled, "For behold, I create new heavens and a new earth." In the beginning, God created heaven and earth by the Word and it was all very good. Nevertheless, there was a possibility of sinning. There was the serpent who could enter and affect God's creation. That all had to happen according to the perfect, wise counsel of Him with whom we have to do. But in the new creation, there is no sin, devil, or hell.

In the new creation, there will be eternal happiness with no threat of evil. There will be no thought of evil, for the former things will not be remembered. They can never come into our mind because our mind and heart will be eternally full of God. God will be all in all. We shall love Him perfectly. There cannot be any thought which is not totally filled with His love. We will admire and adore Him, and we will be so busy that we have no time for anything else. It is our greatest joy, our eternal pleasure, and our deepest wish that this will never end. Our wish will be fulfilled; this is eternal joy, this is eternal life.

The former things shall not be remembered anymore and the things which are then shall fill us to all eternity. We will be united with Christ in the fullness of the Holy Spirit. The love of the Father will dwell in us in all perfection. The love for each other shall unite us unto all eternity to the same goal. And Christ's prayer shall be heard: "and the glory which thou gavest me I have given them; that they may be one, even as we are one" (John 17:22). We can share in this glory by a true faith in Christ.

MILKHONEY

from Hosea

DAVID P. MURRAY

I will avenge.
—HOSEA 1:4

The "I will" of God dominates the book of Hosea. The phrase appears over seventy times in fourteen chapters. A few times, it appears in the negative "I will not," and tells us what God will not do. Mostly it is stated positively and tells us what God will do to and for His people.

There are two main classes of "I will" statements in Hosea. The first class is judgmental and reveals God's resolute determination to chastise His erring people. The second and largest class is redemptive and reveals God's emphatic determination to restore His chastised people to the fullest possible experience of His love.

God's people need both of these divine "I wills" in their lives. Both are rooted in God's love, both reveal God's love, and both result in God's love being shed abroad in the heart. Without the "I will avenge," we would become complacent and cold. Without the "I will allure," we would give in and give up. Sometimes we need to hear the solemn "I will avenge." Sometimes we need to hear the soothing "I will allure." The Christian's life oscillates between these two poles. Indeed, it might be said that we are constantly experiencing either "I will allure" or "I will avenge."

Here, Hosea is promising God's vengeance on Israel for King Jehu's brutal role in Ahab's gruesome death at Jezreel (2 Kings 9–10). Though Jehu had obeyed God's commission to execute, he had displayed trickery, butchery, and hypocrisy in doing so. And, in calling his child by the name of this site of murderous bloodlust, Hosea was reminding Israel that though this event had happened over a hundred years previously, it had still not been repented of, that the attitudes behind it were still prevalent in the land, and that God would punish them for this.

Dear Christian, are you experiencing the "I will avenge" of God? Are you under the rod of His anger? Are you mystified as to why? Could it be that there is a specific sin, perhaps committed many years ago, which you have not honestly faced up to and repented of? Or are some of the sinful attitudes behind such a sin still lingering and still poisoning your soul? If so, then be thankful for the "I will avenge" of God. Mercifully, He will not leave you to perish or pine away in your sin.

I will go after my lovers.
—HOSEA 2:5

God's "I will" is always coming into conflict with our "I will." Instead of, "Not my will, but Thy will be done," we assert, "Not Thy will, but my will be done." Instead of asking, "What wilt Thou have me to do?" we, as it were, look God in the eye and wonder, "What will I have Thee to do?"

Hosea's repeated re-assertion of the "I will of God" was rendered necessary by the daringly disobedient "I will" of Israel. Here, Hosea portrays Israel as a wife with a perfect husband. He lovingly brings her home all she needs. He opens the door and puts bread, water, wool, flax, oil, and drink on the table. She takes all these gifts and packs them away in her cupboards. But then she walks straight past her loving husband without so much as a "thank you," and walks out the door, saying, "I will go after my lovers, that give me my bread and my water, my wool and my flax, mine oil and my drink." Israel took the loving gifts and ignored the loving Giver. Worse, she attributed the loving gifts to the enemies and opponents of the loving Giver. And then, as if that was not bad enough, she turned her back on the loving Giver, and went to praise and party with "lovers" who were actually enemies not only of herself but also of the loving Giver.

Confused believer, surely you must confess that you have reenacted this scene many times in your life. The Lord has been a perfect Husband to you and has richly blessed you in His love. But, instead of saying "I will go after my Lover," you have said, "I will go after my lovers." You have taken His gifts and ignored Him. How many times have you bypassed opportunities to worship and pray in order to go after worldly pastimes and pleasures? Are these your lovers? What has TV ever done for your soul? Did sport die for you? Does music ever live to make intercession for you? Does your investment portfolio love you with an everlasting love? Have your friends laid down their lives for you? Turn away from what is turning you away from Christ. Resolve by His grace, "I will go after my Lover."

I will hedge up thy way with thorns.
—HOSEA 2:6

When God cursed the ground on account of the first sin, He promised that it would bring forth thorns. Thorns, then, are an emblem of difficulty resulting from sin. But, there is often mercy even in God's harshest judgments. Without the "thorns" of difficulty that scratch us, pierce us, and pain us, would we ever hate the sin which caused them? Would we ever want to be free from the sin of this world? Would we ever cry out for our wounds to be healed and our pains relieved?

Israel had strayed from God's path and sought her own path. She had broken down God's fences and was wandering in her own way. But, instead of just leaving His people to wander farther and farther away until they were out of sight and out of mind, God promised, "I will hedge up thy way with thorns, and make a wall, that she shall not find her paths." In mercy God would send difficulties into Israel's life that would scratch, pierce, and pain her so that she would be stopped in her tracks, and prevented from going any farther.

Many Christians have come up against the thorn-filled hedges of God in their lives. They have strayed from God's path, jumped God's fences, and traveled far from Him, often without serious, immediate consequences. They have said, "I will follow my lovers." But, after watching from afar for a time, God eventually responds, "I will hedge up thy way with thorns."

Our great and good Shepherd sends pain-filled difficulties into our lives to frustrate our sinful desires and directions. Perhaps your ambition made an idol of your job. But now you have lost your job. God has hedged up your way with thorns. Perhaps you were proud of your family. But now a son has rebelled against you. God has hedged up your way with thorns. Perhaps vanity was puffing you up. But now God has sent disease into your body. God has hedged up your way with thorns.

These are painful experiences which pierce deep into our hearts and minds. But they are sent in love to stop us from going farther away, to make us examine our wounds, to cry for help and healing, and to turn us back to God's pathway. Whatever we do, let's stop trying to get through the hedge!

I will allure her.

—HOSEA 2:14

Our "therefores" are so different from God's "therefores." In the previous verse, Israel's sins are listed and then climaxed with "she went after her lovers, and forgat me, saith the Lord." After such a litany of iniquity, we expect the Lord to say, "Therefore I will forget you." That's what we would say in a similar situation. However, God's "therefores" are different from our "therefores." Instead of using the greatness of Israel's sins to demonstrate the greatness of His justice, He uses them to display the greatness of His mercy. "Where sin abounded, there did grace much more abound" (Rom. 5:20). So, in response to "she forgat me," the Lord says, "Therefore, behold, I will allure her."

The Hebrew word behind "allure" is used in Exodus 22:16 to describe a man's overt and obvious romantic wooing of a young lady. In Judges 14:15, the same word describes a woman's subtle and secret attempts to entice a man to divulge confidential information. So the process of "alluring" may be either overt or covert.

The Lord allures in both senses of the word. Sometimes He will woo His people obviously and openly. He will set His charms before the believer and challenge the world to outbid Him. The believer clearly sees what God is doing, how God is powerfully and irresistibly attracting the soul, and he consciously responds to His offers of grace. Or, the Lord may work more secretly in the heart, slowly but surely turning the soul back to Him so that the believer hardly notices the work of God until it is done, when she responds with surprise and wonder that the Lord has healed her backsliding and loved her freely.

O straying sheep, forget human "therefores," take this divine "therefore" to God, and plead this sublime heavenly logic as you seek to return to His warm embrace. Take the greatness of your sins to God and plead the greatness of your sins as a powerful argument for His mercy. "For thy name's sake, O Lord, pardon mine iniquity; for it is great" (Ps. 25:11). And, if you are conscious of the Lord's alluring, then believe His romantic overtures are sincere and be happily seduced by His love. Or, perhaps you should examine your heart to see if God is wooing you more subtly. Let us trace all to this great and all-conquering "I will allure her."

I will...bring her into the wilderness and speak comfortably unto her.
—HOSEA 2:14

Most of us would prefer being taken to a palace with all its comforts rather than a wilderness with all its dangers. But here God promises His people a wilderness which is full of comforts—comforts that cannot be enjoyed in any palace.

God was promising Israel that they would be conquered and taken captive by foreign powers as a punishment for sin. This was to be a wilderness experience with many dangers and sufferings. The people would be hungry, harmed, far away from home, and especially far away from God and His Temple. Surely nothing good could come out of this! But wait; God says He "will bring her into the wilderness and speak comfortably to her." He will combine the uncomfortable wilderness with comfortable words.

This was Israel's experience in the wilderness of foreign exile. There, in the midst of their sin-caused sorrow, God spoke words of promise and hope to the repentant. How often this is the Christian's experience. When we are in comfortable situations, we become increasingly deaf to God's voice. We do not need to hear it, we think. So God brings us into the most uncomfortable situations in order to speak to us in a way we will hear.

You are told you have cancer. As you leave the clinic, you feel like you are in a waste-howling wilderness. You sense great danger. Fear of pain and death overwhelm you. A lonely path of surgery and chemotherapy stretches ahead of you. The world feels so bitterly cold and hostile. You get home and fall on your knees as you sob and cry out, "Lord! Lord! Help, help, help!" And there, in the midst of that wilderness moment, God begins to draw near. Comforting verses of Scripture begin to circulate in your mind and filter down to your troubled heart. As He soothes and reassures, you sense the intimate love of your heavenly Father. And, for moments, you think that this feels more like a palace than a wilderness.

If only it wasn't always so necessary for us to be brought into the uncomfortable wilderness to desire and delight in God's comfortable words!

I will give her her vineyards from thence, and the valley of Achor for a door of hope.

—HOSEA 2:15

Vineyards in the wilderness? A door of hope in the desert of despair? Achor means "trouble" and was so named because Achan's idolatrous greed there resulted in the "trouble" of defeat for Israel, and the trouble of "execution" for Achan and his family (Josh. 7:24–26).

Achan's sin was a challenge to Israel. How would they react? Would they trace their defeat to sin? And how would they deal with it when they found it? By searching out the sin in their midst, and by dealing with it so decisively and comprehensively, they found a door of hope to lead them out of Trouble Valley. But they only found the door because God gave them the door; their repentance was God's gift.

This is what God promises the greedy and idolatrous Israel of Hosea's day also. In the desert darkness of foreign exile, God would give them the refreshing wine of repentance and the enlightening hope of forgiveness. What mercy and grace!

Perhaps idolatry and greed have got the better of you, and you lie defeated and despairing in Trouble Valley. The Lord is troubling your health, your family, your work, or your church. Thus the divine gauntlet is laid down, and the divine challenge is posed. What will you do? Will you trace your trouble to your sin? And, if you have found the cause of your trouble, are you dealing with it decisively and comprehensively? Are you "stoning" it and its ungodly associates to death? If so, then God is opening a door of hope in your Trouble Valley. Perhaps the door has only opened a little, but it is enough to encourage you to persevere in your sin-stoning work. And, as each stone of repentance strikes the evil hidden in your heart, the door of hope creaks open more and more, until the light of God's love and favor floods in, and you begin to hope once again in His mercy. Hallelujah! God has given you the valley of Achor for a door of hope.

Praise God for Christ, the Giver of door-opening hope in the valley of Achor. "Him hath God exalted with his right hand to be a Prince and a Saviour, for to give repentance to Israel, and forgiveness of sins" (Acts 5:31).

I will take away the names of Baalim out of her mouth.
—HOSEA 2:17

God's Old Testament people were taught so many of God's names: Jeho-vah-jireh (the LORD who provides), Jehovah-nissi (The LORD our banner), Jehovah Rophi (the LORD who heals), Jehovah Ra-ah (the LORD who sees), etc. They had been entrusted with so many profound and precious divine names. And yet, what names did they take up in their lips but the names of Baalim ("lords"), the names of the heathen gods and deities. They forsook the name of the one LORD and spoke the name of many lords. As God listened to Israel day by day, it was not His own name He heard but rather those of false gods.

Despite this, here God promises that He will one day come and take away the names of Baalim out of her mouth. He will do it, and it will hap-pen. The names of heathen gods which dominated their conversation and even their worship would be heard no more. God will put a new song in their mouth to magnify Him. It may seem impossible. How can Israel break the habit? How can they simply stop what they had gotten so used to doing? The great secret is in the divine "I will."

Was there not a time, Christian, when your mouth was full of the names of Baalim? Despite your godly upbringing, your conversation was full of the Baalim of this world. You spoke of football and baseball, of supermodels and singers, of celebrities and millionaires. These were your lords, your Baalim. When God came down to listen for His name in your life and home, all He heard were the names of Baalim. Where was the name of Jesus Christ, the Name above every name?

But God, who is rich in mercy, came down to your mouth and took away the names of Baalim. You have no interest in them anymore. You don't want to talk about them anymore (Ps. 16:4). Instead, the precious names of the LORD are your meat and drink.

And what if your mouth is still full of Baalim? Bring your mouth to God and say, "I can't stop this. I can't save myself. Come and take away the names of Baalim out of my mouth. Take away the lords and make me confess that Jesus Christ is LORD."

And in that day will I make a covenant
for them with the beasts of the field.
—HOSEA 2:18

The lions ravage us, the sparrows flee us, and the scorpions bite us. All these things are against us. Fear and hostility pervade the whole creation. How different from Genesis 1:28: "And God said unto them, Be fruitful, and multiply, and replenish the earth, and subdue it: and have dominion over the fish of the sea, and over the fowl of the air, and over every living thing that moveth upon the earth." What a contrast to Genesis 1:31: "And God saw every thing that he had made, and, behold, it was very good." Lions, sparrows, scorpions, man, and woman—the whole creation and every creature—lived in perfect "matrimonial" harmony.

What happened? One sin. One sin divorced us from the creation, from one another, and from God. Hatred, fear, suspicion, and hostility fill the air and every breast. We run after one another and from one another. Every barking dog, every roaring lion, every hissing serpent on this earthly realm reminds us of the discord, division, and divorce that exist in the spiritual realm. Does this grieve you? Do you hate the sin that has caused it all, and groan with the whole creation for deliverance (Rom. 8:19–23)?

Exiled Israel longed to return home. But the people were deterred by the frightening wild animals and warring nomads that had filled the land in their absence. So, here God reassures them, "And in that day will I make a covenant for them with the beasts of the field, and with the fowls of heaven, and with the creeping things of the ground: and I will break the bow and the sword and the battle out of the earth, and I will make them to lie down safely." God covenants to create conditions of peace and safety.

All this is but a pale shadow of what God will ultimately and climactically do in the final "new heavens and the new earth, wherein dwelleth righteousness" (2 Pet. 3:13). God has made an unbreakable covenant to reverse the estranging and acrimonious effects of sin. And when God covenants to do something, it will be done. He cannot lie or break His promise. Fellow creature of God, will you be among those who He "will make to lie down safely?" Or will you know enmity-filled eternal separation and division?

I will betroth thee unto me.

—HOSEA 2:19

Three times in two verses, the Lord says, "I will betroth thee." Some commentators believe that this reflects the involvement and commitment of each Person of the Godhead in this betrothal. In other words, the Father, the Son, and the Spirit are each saying, "I will betroth thee." It is, however, more likely that the threefold repetition of "I will betroth thee" is for emphasis. It emphasizes the eagerness of the Lord to unite with those who have divorced Him and are now separated from Him. Israel did the separating, but God does the uniting.

Betrothal went further than the courtship alluring of verse 14. It was also more decisive than our Western ideas of engagement. Betrothal involved handing over a bride-price to the young lady's father, whose acceptance of it finalized the commitment. Sometimes, especially if there was no living father, the bride-price was passed to the bride herself. This is what we have here: the Lord comes to betroth His bride to Himself with a six-fold bride-price of foreverness, righteousness, judgment, lovingkindness, mercies, and faithfulness.

What is different here is that the proposer is already married to the bride-to-be! The Lord was already in covenant union with Israel. But Israel had divorced Him by covenant disobedience. Yet the Lord comes and proposes all over again. In effect, He is saying, "Let's start over. You will be as a virgin-bride to me, as though you had never committed any unfaithfulness to me. Let us enjoy the warmth of a new beginning with all the freshness of first love."

Unfaithful Christian, distant "divorcee" full of regrets, you long to return to your Lord, yet fear that your relationship with Him will never fully recover and be as it once was. Listen to what He says as He graciously proposes all over again: "I will betroth thee unto me." Come then and start afresh with all the excitement and thrill of first love. Your relationship can recover. It can be the same again—yes, even better than before. And if you doubt His sincerity, look at the six-fold bride-price He is offering you: foreverness, righteousness, judgment, lovingkindness, mercies, and faithfulness.

I will betroth thee unto me for ever.
—HOSEA 2:19

So, dear believer, you are encouraged by this betrothal proposal, and you are excited about beginning afresh and starting over. But you hesitate! What if I cannot keep it up? What if I fall again and break my promises again? Surely, I won't be given another chance. There will be no way back then. You ask, "Is it worth the risk?" What's the point of beginning again when I know I will fall and break my promises again? There is no "what if" about it.

Well, consider the first element of the bride-price which the Lord is offering you: foreverness. "I will betroth thee unto me for ever." This is not just for a time, not even for a long time, but forever.

This foreverness can be viewed in two ways. The first way is experientially. When God's people are chastised, it has a curative effect. Before, their relationship with the Lord was characterized by fits and starts—betrothal one day, divorce the next, and so on. Divine chastisement changes that start-stop relationship into a "forever" relationship. Painful though the chastisement is, it produces a much steadier relationship. So, rod-marked friend, your heavenly Father is bringing you from temporariness to foreverness, from start-stop to steady-as-she-goes, from betrothed-divorced to betrothed forever.

The second way to view this foreverness is objectively—that is, to see it as referring to the unbreakable union between the Lord and His people. So, fallen believer, the Lord hears all your hesitating "what-ifs?" and replies, "However many what-ifs on your side, on my side there is only foreverness!" The Lord is promising you that the union is unbreakable. As He said in the days of His flesh: "And I give unto them eternal life; and they shall never perish, neither shall any man pluck them out of my hand" (John 10:28). Jeremiah Burroughs put it this way: "The bond of union in a believer runs through Jesus Christ, is fastened upon God, and His Spirit holds the other end of it so that it can never be broken." Therefore, when the Devil whispers, "You've really done it now. That's it. It's all over!," take these precious divine words and rebuke him with them, "I will betroth thee unto me for ever."

I will betroth thee unto me in righteousness.
—HOSEA 2:19

The second part of this generous bride-price is righteousness. Righteousness can be either threatening or comforting. Martin Luther spent many years terrified by Paul's description of the gospel as a revelation of God's righteousness (Rom. 1:17), which he understood as the righteousness with which God is righteous and punishes the unrighteous sinner. So terrorized was his conscience that he came to hate the "righteousness of God." However, one day he came to realize that the righteousness being spoken of was not a divine demand, but a divine provision; not a revelation of God's condemnation, but of God's salvation; not something God required of him, but something God offered to him. His whole life was instantly transformed. This was how he put it:

> At last, by the mercy of God, meditating day and night, I gave heed to the context of the words, namely, In it the righteousness of God is revealed, as it is written, "He who through faith is righteous shall live." There I began to understand that the righteousness of God is that by which the righteous lives by a gift of God, namely by faith. And this is the meaning: the righteousness of God is revealed by the gospel, namely, the passive righteousness with which merciful God justifies us by faith, as it is written, "He who through faith is righteous shall live." Here I felt that I was altogether born again and had entered paradise itself through open gates. There a totally other face of the entire Scripture showed itself to me.... And I extolled my sweetest word with a love as great as the hatred with which I had before hated the word "righteousness of God." Thus that place in Paul was for me truly the gate to paradise.

You may ask, "But what if I cannot meet His standards? What if I am a disappointment to Him?" Here in our verse, God promises all His covenant people, "I will betroth thee unto me in righteousness." He will not condemn and reject you but will acquit and accept you. Though you specialize in unrighteousness, He specializes in righteousness. Let His righteousness be your comfort, not your terror. As He betroths you to Him, He clothes you in pristine, pure, divine righteousness. He sees no spot in you.

I will betroth thee unto me… in judgment.
—HOSEA 2:19

Judgment? Surely this cannot be good for me! The last thing I need is judgment. Surely, this word of danger is out of place among all these other words of encouragement. Well, the context is one of encouragement and comfort. So it is unlikely that the word carries its common meaning of guilt, sentence, and execution.

There are three possible ways to look at "judgment" positively. First, it can describe God's intervention for His people against their enemies. In this sense, God is the "Judge" of the widow (Ps. 68:5). If that is the meaning here, then God is promising His covenant people that He will intervene on their behalf against their enemies, thereby better securing them to Himself.

Second, "judgment" can describe the process of re-ordering what has been disordered. Therefore, perhaps here God is promising not only that He will remarry Israel but will re-order the chaos of the Israelites' lives. He will put things back in their proper place.

Third, we might say of someone, "We respect his judgment." What we mean is that this is not someone who acts rashly or thoughtlessly, but, rather, acts wisely after due deliberation. This is the most likely meaning here. Some people marry hastily, later regret it, and try to escape. However, God is saying that His people need not fear this of Him. His marriage proposal is well thought out—an eternity of planning! "I will betroth thee unto me in judgment." He knows all about Israel and He knows all about you, your past, present, and future. He weighs it all, thinks it all through, and after due consideration of all the factors involved, still says, "I will betroth thee unto me"!

Some people may wish they had waited longer or had known certain things before they decided to get married. They might not have proceeded if they had. However, God knows everything and has known us longer than we have known ourselves; yet He says, "I will betroth thee unto me."

Doubting Christian, the Lord did not make a mistake in the day of your espousals. He does not regret His decision to propose to you. Lost and lonely soul, here is a divine Husband who knows everything you've been or will be and yet deliberately and determinedly proposes marriage. What do you say?

I will betroth thee unto me…in lovingkindness.
—HOSEA 2:19

We commonly speak of love or of kindness. However, the Bible speaks much of God's "lovingkindness." There is a multiplication of good things here. God's love is being multiplied by God's kindness and the blessed result for His people is lovingkindness. This is no cold, intellectual love. Neither is it cold, practical love. It is a warm and affectionate love which results in thoughtful acts of kindness.

When the mother and wife of the Roman Emperor Alexander Severu incited him to severity and objected to his mildness and readiness to yield to his subjects, saying, "You have made your power more contemptible by your kindness and compliant spirit," his answer was, "But more secure and lasting."

This leads us on to the deeper meaning of "lovingkindness." The Hebrew word here is often used to describe the gracious motivation behind God's covenants with sinners. All such covenants are started by grace and sustained by grace. This, says the Bible, is lovingkindness. The initial betrothal is gracious, but so is the ongoing divine commitment. This is lovingkindness. The Lord does not start these relationships because of what He can get out of them. And neither will He end them even if oftentimes the relationship is so one-way. This is lovingkindness. His betrothal to His people was not begun because He was attracted to them, and neither is it sustained by any such attraction. This is lovingkindness.

This lovingkindness was vividly demonstrated by Hosea in his relationship with his prostituted wife, Gomer. How shiveringly horrific such a betrothal was! But this was a betrothal in lovingkindness. And this repulsive relationship was designed by God to illustrate His relationship with Israel. This was a betrothal in lovingkindness. And, however much you shudder at this thought, be glad God doesn't; your only hope is the same lovingkindness of God. Your only hope is that God does not love as you do, that God will say, and continue to say, "I will betroth thee unto me in lovingkindness." When you experience this kind of betrothal you will stop shivering and shuddering at the thought, for the repulsive has become your redemption.

I will hear.

—HOSEA 2:21

"I will hear, saith the LORD, I will hear the heavens, and they shall hear the earth; and the earth shall hear the corn, and the wine, and the oil; and they shall hear Jezreel" (vv. 21–22). Here, the sky asks God for clouds, and God gives it. The earth asks the sky for rain, and the sky gives it. The corn, the wine, and the oil ask the earth for fertility, and the earth gives it. Jezreel, or Israel, asks the corn, wine, and oil for sustenance, and they give it. This chain of giving encourages Israel to trace the links all the way back to God. The success of every request to supply need encourages Israel to bring her own requests to God. Verse 18 spoke of the restored harmony of the animal world, and here a picture of agricultural harmony is added.

One of Israel's great sins was the worship of Baal, the heathen god of fertility. They prayed to him for fruitful fields and also attributed the results to this idol. For too long, God could say, "I don't hear." Israel failed to bring their requests and their thanks to Him. He did not hear them. As He waited over Israel, listening—nothing. Nothing but deafening silence. For this, Israel was to be judged.

However, this infliction would restore the golden chain of God's providence to their lives, both national and personal. They would again recognize their need of and debt to God. So, God predicts, "I will hear." Israel would once again pray for divine provision and recognize it with thankful worship. And with satisfaction, God says, "I do hear."

Has God been hovering over your life and hearing nothing? He is listening but saying, "I don't hear." "I don't hear prayer for daily bread. I don't hear thanks." You are attributing your blessings to your own strength, to luck, or to sheer coincidence. You are patting yourself on your back rather than praising God with your lips. The golden chain of prayer, providence, and praise has broken down. But God is saying, "I will hear." He is coming to break your Baal. When it lies shattered before you, you begin to look heavenward, prayer is stuttered and stammered heavenward, and heaven replies, "Now I hear. And you will be heard."

I will sow her unto me in the earth.
—HOSEA 2:23

What's the point of a land full of fruit if there are no people to eat it? Having promised to fructify the land in the previous verses, God now promises to populate it. He will not only sow corn, wine, and oil, but people. Because of sin, Israel's fields and towns lie empty and still. But that barren and empty land will be filled with produce and people by God's great "I will." He will take the remaining seed of His people—few and weak as they are—and sow them in the land again. Onlookers might scoff at the dim prospects for such a seed in such a land. But in God's time and with His blessing, that handful of seed will flourish and fill the land again to the astonishment of all. "Look!" says the now startled scoffer. "Look at what God has produced! What a farmer!" Weak seed plus almighty sowing results in glory for the Sower rather than the seed. I will sow her "unto me" in the earth. When the Lord sows, it is unto Him, it is unto His praise and honor.

Barren soul, frail seed of humanity, the divine "I will sow her unto me" is your great and only hope. Plead with the heavenly Agriculturalist to sow you unto Him in the earth. You look at yourself and see deadness and dryness, and you conclude that God can find better seed to work with. This is true. But He is looking for weak and worthless seed. That should be your hope, not your despair. Reverently argue your poor condition with Him: "Lord, I am poor and needy. Many scoff at me. I scoff at myself. For I am truly hopeless and helpless. But if Thou wilt sow me in the earth, all scoffing will be silenced. Think of what they and I will say if Thou wilt sow me in the earth with Thy divine benediction. No more will they mockingly say, 'What pathetic seed!' But, rather, 'What a great Sower!' O sow me unto Thee in the earth. Make me an exhibit of what divine sowing can accomplish with the least promising of materials." God always rises to the challenge of this persuasive argument.

I will have mercy upon her that had not obtained mercy.
—HOSEA 2:23

"I will not have mercy" are the most terrifying words a sinner can hear from the mouth of the Lord. These words will destroy the souls of the unrepentant sinner on the Day of Judgment. These words will echo round the chambers of hell forever: "I will not have mercy." And who can argue with them? Those who spend their earthly days saying, "I don't want mercy," can hardly complain when at the end of their days God grants them their request eternally, "You didn't want mercy, and so you will not have mercy." These words dash every dream and quash every hope, "I will not have mercy." Oh, mercy-spurning sinner, will this be your death-sentence? Will you ever hear these "No Outlet" words?

Oh my soul, woe is me! Have I not rejected God's offered mercy time and again? How many times I have whispered in my soul, "I will not have mercy." How many times I have stubbornly insisted, "I want merit, not mercy. I want to be a creditor who is owed, not a debtor who can never repay." And now, here I am hastening to judgment and eternity with neither merit nor mercy. Oh woe, woe is me!

But here is hope, despairing soul. Israel was just like you; she refused mercy time after time. She was judged by the removal of mercy in foreign exile (Hos. 1:6). But God looks down in pity on her merciless condition and says, "I will have mercy upon her that had not obtained mercy." What a turning point! What tear-drying, heart-rejoicing, dream-fulfilling words of hope!

Go to the Lord and say, "I have not obtained mercy because I did not need nor want mercy. But now I desperately need it and earnestly want it. I abandon all my imagined merit. Oh Lord, be merciful to me, the sinner." And wait, what do you hear? Can it be, "I will have mercy upon her that had not obtained mercy"?

And dear Christian of many years, recall what turned your life around. It wasn't your merit or will; it was God's mercy and God's will. It was when He said—oh, blessed moment—"I will have mercy upon her that had not obtained mercy."

I will say to them which were not my people, Thou art my people.
—HOSEA 2:23

When we look out on this world, we see innumerable differences between peoples and nations. We see different nations, different languages, different skin colors, different cultures, different clothing, etc. Who could possibly catalogue all these differences? Within one country or even one city, there are so many different personalities and characters. No two are alike and each one demands its own unique file.

When God looks out on the world, He sees more and He sees less. He sees more differences than we ever can, both national and individual differences. But, in some ways, He also sees less difference than we do. Because for all the incalculable variety, God sees just two people groups: "My people" and "not My people." That's it. As simple and stark as that. The Lord Jesus had a similar "filing system." "He that is not with me is against me; and he that gathereth not with me scattereth abroad" (Matt. 12:30).

When the Holy Spirit is working in your soul, you will begin to see the world as God sees it. You will get past all the many external differences in people and you will see that there are but two ultimate categories: "My people" and "Not my people." When this crystallizes for you, alarm bells will begin to ring in your soul as you see that you are in the wrong group; you are not one of God's people. God looks down on you and says, "Not my people." What must you do to be saved? "Believe on the Lord Jesus Christ, and you shall be saved." He is the Passport to heavenly citizenship. He gives you title to belong to God's people. When God looks down and sees Christ is your hope and sees Christ is in you, He re-classifies you: "My people." "I will say to them which were not my people, Thou art my people, and they shall say, Thou art my God." And do you say this? If He owns you as His, will you be ashamed or hesitant to own Him as yours?

Because thou hast rejected knowledge, I will also reject thee.
—HOSEA 4:6

God gave Israel more knowledge of Him than any other nation in the world. He gave them His law, His history, His poets, and His prophets. They had hundreds of chapters and thousands of verses. And yet, here God accuses them of "lack of knowledge." How could they know so much and yet know so little? It was because they had rejected knowledge. They had received it but had rejected it.

Now, there is some knowledge we can do without. There are many subjects in the world that we can be totally ignorant of and yet live safely and happily. The knowledge of God through His Word is not one of them. The consequences of lacking knowledge of God are horrific and horrendous. God laments, "My people are destroyed for lack of knowledge." Israel's deliberate choice to reject the knowledge of God and instead to be ignorant of God had catastrophic effects. And their rejection of knowledge resulted, eventually, in God's rejection of them. "Because thou hast rejected knowledge, I will also reject thee."

Sadly, Israel's experiences are still being repeated in many nations which God has blessed with His knowledge. The knowledge of God has been rejected, and these societies are in the painful process of inevitable self-destruction. This truth-rejection, self-destruction, divine-rejection cycle can also be seen in many Christian churches, schools, and universities.

But let's make it personal. Has God given you His truth and are you rejecting it? Are you neglecting to read it? Are you disobeying it? Are you doubting it? This is not just geography or history or biology. This is eternity at stake.

Your schoolteacher imparts knowledge. You receive it. Your lecturer imparts knowledge. You receive it. Your boss imparts knowledge. You receive it. Your President imparts knowledge. You receive it. Your God imparts knowledge. You reject it. God says, "My people are destroyed for lack of knowledge: because thou hast rejected knowledge, I will also reject thee." In fact, this also has grave consequences for your children. Hosea goes on, "Seeing thou hast forgotten the law of thy God, I will also forget thy children." Look into the eyes of your children and see the eternal effects of your ignorance. Listen to these solemn words, "I will reject thee." And He will.

Therefore will I change their glory into shame.
—HOSEA 4:7

Material and spiritual prosperity rarely go hand-in-hand. Apart from some happy exceptions, as a person increases in financial wealth, they usually decrease in spiritual health. So it is with churches and with nations. So it was with Israel: "As they were increased, so they sinned against me" (v. 7). As the nation grew and expanded under the skilful economic management of Jeroboam, so did their sins. As men and women grew more self-sufficient, they grew away from dependence upon God. Places of idol-worship multiplied and flourished. They gloried in their shiny golden calves at Dan and Bethel which were much more impressive than the blood-stained temple at Jerusalem! And what about our priests and our ceremonies?

"I will change their glory into shame." God zeroes in on what they especially boasted of and gloried in. He targets what was the greatest source of their pride—their man-made religion—and warns, "I will turn their glory into shame." God can take what is the greatest source of pride and turn it into our shame. Hanging Haman, grass-eating Nebuchadnezzar, and worm-eaten Herod testify loudly to God's abilities in this area.

Do you glory in your beauty? God can take glamorous supermodels and change them into bald models of the latest sackcloth (Isa. 3:16–24). Oh, how many beautiful women are in hell, their glory turned into their shame. Do you glory in your wisdom? God says, "I will destroy the wisdom of the wise, and will bring to nothing the understanding of the prudent" (1 Cor. 1:19). How many clever men are in hell lamenting the glory they gave to their now shamed degrees.

How easily God can change your glory into your shame. So glory not in your children, your career, your church, or your nation. "But let him that glorieth glory in this, that he understandeth and knoweth me, that I am the LORD which exercise lovingkindness, judgment, and righteousness, in the earth: for in these things I delight, saith the LORD" (Jer. 9:24).

How easily God can turn your shame into glory. He can take you from the lowest and most shameful condition and, through the grace of the Lord Jesus, transform you from glory to glory (2 Cor. 3:18).

For I will be unto Ephraim as a lion.
—HOSEA 5:14

What would you most like to meet, an angry lion or a peaceable lamb? That's the choice we all face. The Lord Jesus is revealed in Scripture as both the Lion of the Tribe of Judah (Rev. 5:5) and the Lamb of God (John 1:36). To His enemies He will be an angry lion, and to His friends He will be a peaceable lamb.

Hosea foresees this and predicts that, for Ephraim and indeed the whole of unrepentant Israel, the Lord will be as a lion who will tear them and then take them away without hope of rescue. "For I will be unto Ephraim as a lion, and as a young lion to the house of Judah: I, even I, will tear and go away; I will take away, and none shall rescue him." Terrifying! To be torn apart by a lion is surely one of the great human horrors. So, here, the Lord takes this most frightening of fears and says, "This is how bad it will be." And it was. The brutal Assyrians came, tore them in pieces, and carried them away captive without hope of rescue. And it could have been so different. Through the annual Passover and the daily sacrifices, God was pointing Israel towards the Lamb of God who would take away their sins and give them peace with God. But because they did not want the Lamb, He changes into a soul-tearing Lion.

We will all meet the Lord Jesus one day, either at the day of our death or on the Day of Judgment. So, the question is not, "Will you meet Him?" but "How will you meet Him?" or, rather, "How will He meet you?" Will He be as a Lion or a Lamb to you? Will it be anger or peace? Will the Lion want your blood, or will the Lamb give you His blood? Will you spend eternity being torn asunder without remedy, or will you spend eternity celebrating "the Lamb slain from the foundation of the world" (Rev. 13:8)? "Behold the Lamb of God which taketh away the sin of the world."

I will go and return to my place till they acknowledge their offence, and seek my face.
—HOSEA 5:15

In the previous verse, Israel is ravaged by the divine Lion. The nation is torn and taken away, and none can rescue. Now the angry Lion is portrayed as returning to His lair with its prey in His mouth. He drops the faintly breathing body and lies down in His place. His fury is partly assuaged; His prey is barely alive. And He says, "I will go and return to my place, till they acknowledge their offence, and seek my face: in their affliction they will seek me early." After some time, the body begins to groan and stir; the eyes open and slowly and fearfully focus on the angry adversary. Eyes meet. Time stands still. "I'm so sorry," stutters and stammers the aching body. "I provoked your anger. I understand and accept your just response. Thank you for sparing my life. Please pity me. Please help me." The Lion slowly rises and walks round the pitiful sight. He moves towards the face, pauses, opens His mouth, and...begins to lick the wounds and warm the fear-frozen limbs. The eyes open in wonder and, instead of seeing a bloodthirsty lion, behold a blood-shedding lamb!

Wounded, bleeding, barely breathing believer, has the Lord ravaged you? You provoked and provoked until His anger was justly roused. He tore you and took you away. Bodily disease, family disaster, business failure, or dark depression has left you barely alive. But you sense there is now a lull in the storm, some welcome days of relative peace. This glimmer of comfort enables you to lift your eyes heavenward. And there you sense the root cause of all your troubles—the face of your God, justly angered by your backsliding and compromising. Eyes meet. Time stands still. Fight or flight? Or faith? Faith neither fights nor flies but rather repents and casts all on the Savior's mercy. Such faith and repentance transforms the bloodthirsty Lion into a blood-shedding Lamb. Look at the very next verse, "Come, and let us return unto the LORD: for he hath torn, and he will heal us; he hath smitten, and he will bind us up" (Hos. 6:1).

I will not execute the fierceness of mine anger.
—HOSEA 11:9

What is your best hope of salvation? Some people hope that God will be just like them (Ps. 50:21). They hope that God is a compromiser like them, that He is a kind of changeable character, and they just hope that they will catch Him on a good day rather than a bad day. But God says our hope should instead be based on His unlikeness to man. "I will not execute the fierceness of mine anger, I will not return to destroy Ephraim: for I am God, and not man; the Holy One in the midst of thee: and I will not enter into the city." It is God's dissimilarity that is our best and only hope. "For I am the LORD, I change not; therefore ye sons of Jacob are not consumed" (Mal. 3:6).

Do you really want someone like yourself to be your only hope? What are you like? Are you not unpredictable, capricious, and changeable? Do you not judge one way one day, and another the next? Have you ever been fiercely angry and yet possessed the self-control not to execute the fierceness of your anger? Have you ever found a technique to turn away and exhaust your anger? No, you haven't, because you are man and not God. Too much weakness and too little wisdom means that you will usually execute the fierceness of your anger.

Only God has the power and the wisdom to find a way of not executing the fierceness of His anger upon you. His power and His wisdom is found in Christ crucified. He is the power and the wisdom of God (1 Cor. 1:24). Having executed the fierceness of His anger upon Christ, God can then turn to you and say, "I will not execute the fierceness of mine anger." And because He is God and not man, once He executes His anger, it is gone. He does not harbor a grudge or bear secret and bitter resentment against you. He is God and not man. Let God's dissimilarity be your hope, your only hope of salvation.

I will place them in their houses.
—HOSEA 11:11

God's judgment of foreign exile for Israel was intended to have the same effect as a lion's roar. It was to restore the fear of the Lord in them, and then to restore them to their land. As Hosea puts it, "When he shall roar, then the children shall tremble from the west. They shall tremble as a bird out of Egypt, and as a dove out of the land of Assyria: and I will place them in their houses, saith the LORD" (Hos. 11:10–11). The people of Israel were exiled to Egypt and Assyria because of their spiritual deafness and insensitivity. God said, "I will place them in foreign lands." There they would hear God's roar in this painful providence and begin to tremble before Him again, as a dove would upon hearing a lion nearby. Trembling is mentioned twice (v. 10, 11) in order to emphasize the predominant characteristic of God's repentant people. This double trembling at God's word would hasten their flight from captivity. Having returned to God, He would again "place them in their houses," the place of security, comfort, and rest.

Our churches and nations are ripe for God's roar. We have covered our ears and hardened our hearts. The fear of God is not before our eyes. Sometimes we hear the divine roar in the distance through terrorist attacks, floods, tsunamis, or earthquakes. We stop for a moment, listen for a moment, fear for a moment, then get on with our lives. Gradually, we grow harder and harder. How near does the roar have to get before we tremble as a bird, until we fly to Him as a dove? Oh, for more trembling in God's people!

God's roars are not intended to frighten us away from Him but to draw us to Him. Perhaps God is roaring in your life and you are beginning to tremble before His omnipotence and your impotence. Your life is all upside down, and everything is falling apart. Oh, may your trembling draw you out of sin and its disordering consequences to Christ and His order-restoring salvation. He can make all things well again for you. Peace, harmony, safety, and a sense of belonging are restored. "I will place them in their houses."

I…will yet make thee to dwell in tabernacles.
—HOSEA 12:9

Listen to this for a proud boast: "Yet I am become rich, I have found me out substance: in all my labours they shall find none iniquity in me that were sin" (Hos. 12:8). It was for such proud self-confidence that Israel would be once again removed from its land and suffer Egypt-like bondage. And yet, here Hosea holds out hope for an Egypt-like exodus by promising a new celebration of the Feast of Tabernacles which commemorated that event: "And I that am the LORD thy God from the land of Egypt will yet make thee to dwell in tabernacles, as in the days of the solemn feast."

Israel's festivals were all times of rejoicing, but the Feast of Tabernacles was especially marked by joy (Lev. 23:40; Deut. 16:15). This was partly because the feast celebrated the harvest of corn and grapes, but mainly because, by spending time in homemade tents in the desert, they were reminded of God's miraculous provision for them when they lived as desert-nomads for forty years. What a comfort Hosea's promise of restored festivals must have been to God's people in exile. What hope this holds out to the repentant! God will restore our festivals and our joy if we repent.

Proud unbeliever, you have resisted God and rejected His mercy. You are self-confident and independent. You have no sense of your own sinfulness. But God is bringing you down. Your life has turned sour. You are not so sure of yourself as you once were, and you wonder if there is any hope for one who is so proud and defiant as you are. Be encouraged with this promise of mercy: "And I that am the LORD thy God from the land of Egypt will yet make thee to dwell in tabernacles, as in the days of the solemn feast."

Perhaps you are a believer who has been walking in your own strength and at a proud self-sufficient distance from God. But now you are miserable. You wish you could experience total dependence on the Lord again. Listen to God's gracious promise: "I…will yet make thee to dwell in tabernacles, as in the days of the solemn feast." There is no frivolity or superficiality at the Lord's feasts; this is serious and substantial joy.

I will be thy king.
—HOSEA 13:10

Who wants to be a King of self-destroyed people? God does. Who wants to be King of people who consistently rejected Him and chose many inferior kings? God does. "O Israel, thou hast destroyed thyself; but in me is thine help. I will be thy king: where is any other that may save thee in all thy cities? and thy judges of whom thou saidst, Give me a king and princes?" (Hos. 13:9–10). He does not say, "You have achieved a lot, therefore I will be your king," but, "You have destroyed yourself, therefore I will be your king." He does not say, "You have chosen me to be your King, therefore I will be your King," but, "You have rejected me, therefore I will be your king." What grace and favor!

Do you not need a mighty King? Who can bring order into your chaos? You can't; no one else can but God. Who can subdue your unruly passions and regulate your anarchic thoughts? You can't; no one else can but God.

And yet, how much you resisted, didn't you? Do you remember how many times you said, "I will not have this man to reign over me"? How many times the King drew near, and you said, "I will be king." You resisted and rejected with all your might. But then the day came when you heard with irresistible power, "I will be your King, I will be your King." Your will bent, broke, and at last surrendered. You fell down in your soul and said, "Lord, what wilt thou have me to do?" You worshiped and said, "O Lord, thou art my God and King, Thee will I magnify and praise." And what a King He has been to you! Has He not guarded you? Has He not led you in many spiritual victories? Has He not brought you into His banqueting house and His banner over you was love? Do you not look forward to the day when you arrive in His heavenly Kingdom and He will say, "I am thy King"?

Remaining rebels, lay down your arms. You cannot win. He will be your King. He will eventually rule you. He will rule you in heaven or He will rule you in hell. "I will be thy King."

I will ransom them from the power of the grave.
—HOSEA 13:14

Hosea 13:1–13 sets forth the death of Israel in stark and graphic terms. Israel "died" at Baal Peor (v. 1). They pass away "as the morning cloud, and as the early dew that passeth away, as the chaff that is driven with the whirlwind out of the floor, and as the smoke out of the chimney" (v. 3). Wild beasts tear them limb from limb (v. 8). And yet in the midst of this deathly, funereal atmosphere, the prophet is given a glimpse of the nation's resurrection: "I will ransom them from the power of the grave; I will redeem them from death." What a death, but what a resurrection! What a ransom which delivers from death and the grave!

Sometimes, when God begins a saving work in a soul, He shows the sinner how his soul "died" through various sins he committed. We all have our "Baal Peors." Then He impresses on the grieving sinner the brevity of life and the imminence of death. Wherever the soul looks, it sees life rapidly passing and death accelerating towards him—the morning cloud, the evaporating dew, the wind-blown chaff, the chimney smoke, all so brief, all so eloquent of life and death. The terrifying grave opens its ghastly mouth for young and old. The soul is dead, the body is dying, the grave is gaping. But prayer is rising, "Have mercy upon me, O LORD; for I am weak: O LORD, heal me; for my bones are vexed. My soul is also sore vexed: but thou, O LORD, how long?.... Return, O LORD, deliver my soul: oh save me for thy mercies' sake. For in death there is no remembrance of thee: in the grave who shall give thee thanks?" (Ps. 6:2–5). "Then he is gracious unto him, and saith, Deliver him from going down to the pit: I have found a ransom. His flesh shall be fresher than a child's: he shall return to the days of his youth: he shall pray unto God, and he will be favourable unto him: and he shall see his face with joy" (Job 33:24–26). What a resurrection! And what a ransom! "The Son of man came not to be ministered unto, but to minister, and to give his life a ransom for many" (Matt. 20:28).

O death, I will be thy plagues.
—HOSEA 13:14

Disease brings death, and the grave destroys. But here God promises a radical reversal. Death will be diseased and the grave will be destroyed. Israel's enemies will themselves be defeated and Israel will be released.

Paul borrows this language and the principle behind it to anticipate the ultimate victory of the Christian over death: "So when this corruptible shall have put on incorruption, and this mortal shall have put on immortality, then shall be brought to pass the saying that is written, Death is swallowed up in victory. O death, where is thy sting? O grave, where is thy victory?" (1 Cor. 15:54–55).

This great climactic victory will be seen in all its glory on the day of the general resurrection of all God's people. As the Lord Jesus comes to claim the precious dust of His saints and to transform them to be like unto His glorious body, He shouts, "O death, I will be thy plagues; O grave, I will be thy destruction."

But we need not wait until then to see foreshadows of this victory. Every time a Christian defeats the fear of death and its soul-paralyzing power by trusting in Christ to save his body and soul from death, the victory shout is heard, "O death, I will be thy plagues; O grave, I will be thy destruction."

Every time a Christian faces terminal illness and death with faith and confidence in Christ, death is plagued and the grave's power is destroyed.

Every time a persecuted Christian faces the firing squad and looks heavenward with peace and confidence, all heaven celebrates the victory, "O death, I will be thy plagues; O grave, I will be thy destruction."

As you face your own end in this world, may this great divine "I will" make death and the grave weaken and wither before you. May you look forward to the day of full and final victory when "[w]e shall all be changed, in a moment, in the twinkling of an eye, at the last trump: for the trumpet shall sound, and the dead shall be raised incorruptible, and we shall be changed" (1 Cor. 15:51–52).

I will heal their backsliding.
—HOSEA 14:4

One word describes Israel's history: backsliding. Two words describe God's response: chastising and healing. Most of Hosea's message was about the backsliding and the chastising, but here his theme moves on to the healing.

Hosea's prophecies tell us that backsliding is very common. Octavius Winslow said, "There is a tendency to secret, perpetual, and alarming departure from God." Backsliding requires no effort. You don't need to do anything to slip away; it is such a gradual process that it is usually unnoticed until it is too late. And this despite preachers like Hosea pointing it out so clearly. It usually begins in the heart. Love for God and His people diminishes. Reverence for the Bible decreases. Enjoyment of prayer evaporates. Delight in the Sabbath fades. It is like an ant removing sand, one grain at a time, from one side of a set of scales to the other. No change is noticed until suddenly the scales tip. Church activity and service may cover up the worrying inward reality for a time, but when the scales eventually tip, outward moral catastrophe is usually imminent. And, as Israel discovered, backsliding and its eventual chastisement is a miserable experience. Remember Bunyan's erring pilgrim who had to go back for his mislaid scroll—he ended up covering the same road three times, and it was dangerously late and dark when he finally arrived exhausted at his lodgings. Ask Naomi how bitter backsliding is (Ruth 1:20–21).

But, and here is great encouragement, backsliding can be healed—not by the backslider but by the Lord. "I will heal their backsliding." No one can return from backsliding except through the merciful intervention of Christ. Look at Peter weeping bitterly over his declension and desertion. Who can restore him? "Go tell the disciples, and Peter..." (Mark 16:7). The Lord intervenes to heal his backsliding.

So Israel, and so you, backslidden one, look to Christ as the great Healer of backsliding. True grace is indestructible. It may decay but it can never die. Bring your faint embers and remaining sparks to the Lord and say, "Heal my backsliding. Fan my embers into flame."

I will love them freely.
—HOSEA 14:4

How much does your love cost? How much do you extract from someone in return for your love? How many diamonds must he buy to secure your love? How beautiful does she have to make herself to guarantee your continued love? How obedient do your children have to be to ensure your love? How many toys do your parents have to buy you to make you love them? How much does your love cost?

How much does God's love cost? How much do we have to give Him? How much do we have to pay Him? How much do we have to do or say? How many laws do we have to keep? And for how long? The answer to all these questions is zero—nothing—nil. "I will love them freely."

This is written over every page of God's dealings with sinners. When we look at Abraham or Moses or David, we hear God saying, "I will love them freely." When we look at Peter or Thomas or Saul of Tarsus, we hear, "I will love them freely." When we see God's people restored to God's land, we hear, "I will love them freely." When we see Christ with arms outstretched on Calvary's cross, we hear, "I will love them freely." When the Holy Spirit is poured out on Christ's crucifiers at Pentecost, we hear, "I will love them freely." Throughout all church history, the church has heard, "I will love them freely."

And what about your own life, child of God? Is not "I will love you freely," written above it? How much did God's love cost you? How much did you pay for a godly upbringing? How much did you pay for faithful pastors? What was the price of your justification? How much for your adoption? Sanctification? Zero—nothing—nil. "I will love them freely."

If freely you have received, then freely give.

I will be as the dew to Israel.
—HOSEA 14:5

Dry, dry, dry. Have you ever felt like that? Has your soul ever seemed like a desert? You look at the wastelands within your soul and you can't find any bud or blossom, never mind any fruit. There is no refreshing, encouraging oasis anywhere. It wasn't always like that. You can remember a time when there was bud, blossom, and fruit everywhere. There was a little oasis here and a little stream there. Spiritual life and liveliness flowed in your blood and all was well with your soul. What happened? Well, many things happened, didn't they? But the more important question is, how do you get out of this? We turn to Hosea to find the answer.

God gave Israel the land of Canaan as promised, a land which flowed with milk and honey. Under His blessing, they had known many years of fruitfulness and fertility. However, their disobedience had brought them and their land under the divinely promised curse. God withheld water from the land and the result was desert-dryness everywhere.

But, when this divine chastisement had humbled Israel and brought her to see her need of the Lord, He promised He would return with His dew. "I will be as the dew to Israel." This is sovereign dew; God creates it, sends it, and controls it. This is softening dew; it soaks into the hardest soul and breaks the hardest clods. It is stimulating dew. It refreshes and invigorates. It is saving dew; it is God Himself who will be the dew. "I will be as the dew to Israel: he shall grow as the lily, and cast forth his roots as Lebanon."

So, dry soul, look up. It is the Lord alone who can refresh you and reinvigorate you. He can make the desert sand blossom into a rose. Each of His three Persons can drench you with dew. Even one of His attributes can saturate your soul. Just one of His words can break the hardest clod. "Lord, come and beautify and fructify me with Thyself."

"I will...."

"I will avenge" (Hos. 1:4).

"I will hedge up thy way with thorns" (Hos. 2:6).

"I will allure her" (Hos. 2:14).

"I will...bring her into the wilderness and speak comfortably unto her" (Hos. 2:14).

"I will give her vineyards from thence, and the valley of Achor for a door of hope" (Hos. 2:15).

"I will take away the names of Baalim out of her mouth" (Hos. 2:17).

"I will make a covenant for them with the beasts of the field" (Hos. 2:18).

"I will betroth thee unto me" (Hos. 2:19).

"I will betroth thee unto me forever" (Hos. 2:19).

"I will betroth thee unto me in righteousness" (Hos. 2:19).

"I will betroth thee unto me...in judgment" (Hos. 2:19).

"I will betroth thee unto me...in lovingkindness" (Hos. 2:19).

"I will hear" (Hos. 2:21).

"I will sow her unto me in the earth" (Hos. 2:23).

"I will have mercy upon her that had not obtained mercy" (Hos. 2:23).

"I will say to them which were not my people, Thou art my people" (Hos. 2:23).

"Because thou hast rejected knowledge, I will also reject thee" (Hos. 4:6).

"Therefore will I change their glory into shame" (Hos. 4:7).

"For I will be unto Ephraim as a lion" (Hos. 5:14).

"I will go and return to my place till they acknowledge their offence, and seek my face" (Hos. 5:15).

"I will not execute the fierceness of mine anger" (Hos. 11:9).

"I will place them in their houses" (Hos. 11:11).

"I will make thee to dwell in tabernacles" (Hos. 12:9).

"I will be thy king" (Hos. 13:10).

"I will ransom them from the power of the grave" (Hos. 13:14).

"O death, I will be thy plagues" (Hos. 13:14).

"I will heal their backsliding" (Hos. 14:4).

"I will love them freely" (Hos. 14:4).

"I will be as the dew to Israel" (Hos. 14:5).

What will you do?

MILK  HONEY

from The Gospels

MAURICE J. ROBERTS

And the Word was made flesh, and dwelt among us, (and we beheld his glory, the glory as of the only begotten of the Father,) full of grace and truth.

—JOHN 1:14

The most wonderful event of all history is the coming into this sinful world of Jesus Christ, the eternal Son of God. That God should create man and place him in a paradise is amazing kindness. That God should save lost and fallen man by His grace is more amazing still. But no words can adequately convey the amazement due to this supremely wonderful act—that God became man!

We must be careful to understand correctly what the Bible means when it tells us of the incarnation of Christ. God is a Trinity: Father, Son, and Holy Spirit. The Son of God, the second Person of the blessed Trinity, took to Himself our human nature two thousand years ago and became the God-Man. "He became what he was not without ceasing to be what he was," said an early Christian writer.

We must be careful to understand correctly what we are taught by the doctrine of the Incarnation. We do not mean that Christ laid aside His divine nature when He became man. He did not "empty Himself" in the sense of losing any aspect of His godhood.

Before the Incarnation, Christ was God. After the Incarnation, Christ became also man. Since the Incarnation, Christ has been one Person in two natures. His human nature consists of a body and soul, like us. He therefore has two natures which are united to each other, but which do not become mixed one with the other. He has two natures. But He is one Person and will be one Person in two natures forever.

It was a stupendously great act of God's love to give us His dear Son. Jesus Christ came to save our souls by His perfect life and by His atoning death on the cross. If Jesus had not become man, we could not be saved. Sin was committed by man, and it had to be atoned for by man. Jesus Christ is the last Adam. He came to put right all that the first Adam had put wrong.

There are plenty of things in this world to make us sad. But the coming of Christ into this world is the happiest and best news possible. Oh my soul, bless God for this unspeakable gift of a Savior!

Wist ye not that I must be about my Father's business?
—LUKE 2:49

These are the words of our Lord at the tender age of twelve. They show that He knew Himself to be the Son of God and the promised Savior of the world. Such was the union of the divine and the human nature in Christ's person that He was all along conscious of the unique relationship which He bore to God the Father and the unique mission which He had to fulfill as the Messiah. Much as our Lord loved both His mother Mary and His adoptive father Joseph, He did not hesitate to put His duty to God first in life.

Here we see both how a perfect child naturally behaves and how fallen and ruined our own nature is as sinners. The whole duty of man is to love God with all the heart and soul, and to love his neighbor as himself. If sin had not entered into the world, both we and our children after us would naturally do so. The child Jesus is the one exception to the rule that "all have sinned."

How wonderful a child Jesus Christ was! He alone of all children never had Adam's sin imputed to Him. He alone was born morally, physically, and spiritually perfect. He alone went through every stage of development without abnormality, blemish, or blame. The child Jesus "increased in wisdom and stature, and in favour with God and man" (Luke 2:52). He at no time broke God's moral law in thought, word, or deed. He did not experience what it means to have a guilty conscience. Christ's mind, body, and soul were all through His growth and development radiantly pure and spotlessly holy. Never was there a child on earth like Him, and never will there be.

The Lord Jesus is here our example. Much as we are to love father and mother, we are under obligation to love God still more and to put God first in life. "He that loveth father and mother more than me is not worthy of me," said Jesus (Matt. 10:37).

This lesson is of great practical importance to us all. If we put the claims of God first in our life, God will take care of the rest. God's work and God's "business" must come first. Oh my soul, your happiness is to love God above all creatures.

*Then cometh Jesus from Galilee to Jordan
unto John, to be baptized of him.*
—MATTHEW 3:13

Jesus lived a private life for thirty years, but after His baptism, He suddenly shot into public notice with the brilliance of a meteor. For thirty silent years, our blessed Savior quietly waited until His "hour was come." The prophet Isaiah compares this period of Christ's life to a hidden weapon. "He made me a polished shaft; in his quiver hath he hid me" (Isa. 49:2).

When Jesus reached the age of thirty, God's time had come to manifest to the world the glory of His incarnate Son.

Baptism for Jesus Christ had a unique significance. For us sinners, it is a sacrament appointed by Christ for His covenant people illustrating by an outward washing what God's Spirit does inwardly in the heart. But for Christ, baptism had quite another significance. It was the voluntary expression of His readiness to be the Savior of the world. He was baptized with our guilt and sin, to suffer the penalty due to us, and so to ransom us from death and hell by His obedience and blood.

At the baptism of Christ, the Holy Spirit came upon our Lord to equip Him for the work He came to do. There was from this moment on a joint-ministry of the Son and Spirit. All the miracles of Christ were done in the power of the Holy Spirit. Also, when Christ offered Himself to God on the cross as our sacrifice, He did so "through the eternal Spirit" (Heb. 9:14).

Before His baptism, Christ did no miracles and preached no sermons. But after His baptism, He entered upon His glorious God-honoring ministry. As we study the ministry of Christ, we come to see more and more clearly that He is the God-given Savior who came in fulfillment of the Old Testament Scriptures to die for us. "Thou shalt call his name Jesus: for he shall save his people from their sins" (Matt. 1:21).

Commit your life to this Savior and He will give you sufficient grace. God has given to Him the Holy Spirit "without measure" (John 3:34).

Get thee hence, Satan: for it is written, thou shalt worship the Lord thy God, and him only shalt thou serve.
—MATTHEW 4:10

These words of Christ were addressed to the devil at the great moment when our Lord was about to begin His world-shaking ministry. The world was almost entirely ignorant of who Jesus was and what He had come to do as our promised Redeemer.

But Satan understood very well who Jesus was and why He had come into the world. In an all-out frontal attack on our blessed Lord, the devil attempts to lure Him into sin as he did to our first parents. But in vain. Where Adam failed, Jesus Christ is victorious.

We need to note carefully the circumstances of our Lord's temptations. First, we see that He was led by God into this conflict (Matt. 4:1) in order to face the foe and to vanquish him. Then, we are to see that the one weapon used by our Lord was the Word of God, the Bible. "It is written," says the Son of God three times.

Satan is expert at tempting men and women to disobey God. His subtle art is to present the bait and hide the hook. He seeks to persuade us that there is good to be had in sin. He is a liar and a murderer (John 8:44). His aim is to draw us into committing sin against God. Then, when we too willingly yield, he accuses us and tells us that we deserve God's punishment. Hence, he is called "the accuser of our brethren" (Rev. 12:10).

The devil is a real person. His great aim is to ruin our souls by luring us into sin, if he can. Satan cannot force our will but he can present sin to us in ways which appeal to our fallen nature and appetites: the lust of the eyes, the lust of the flesh, and the pride of life.

Our defense is to quote God's Word to counter the assaults of the devil. Those who do not know their Bible are defenseless against this deadly enemy. Oh, then let me read God's Word daily! And let me be ever alert to the ensnaring whispers of this unseen enemy of my soul. May God help us to put on the gospel armor spoken of in Ephesians 6. Then, when his dangerous voice urges me to enjoy some sin, I shall be ready to say to him: "Get thee behind me, Satan."

Follow me, and I will make you fishers of men.
—MATTHEW 4:19

Here are our Lord's words spoken early in His "Great Galilean Ministry." Christ's ministry lasted a little more than three years. It may be divided in this way: (1) the Early Judean Ministry, (2) the Great Galilean Ministry, (3) the Perean Ministry, (4) the Cross. The lengthiest period was this one in Galilee. Here our Lord spent some eighteen months. What sermons He preached there! What miracles He performed before men's eyes! But tragically, all too many rejected His claims to be the Savior!

Jesus' words above were spoken to two fishermen, Peter and Andrew, as they were fishing in the Sea of Galilee. These two brothers heard Christ's call and they followed Him immediately to become "fishers of men." There is no sin in following a lawful secular profession. But if we hear the call of God to spiritual service we should follow Him in order to learn the great "art of man-fishing," as Thomas Boston called it. One way is the pulpit, another the mission field. But whatever our forms of service, we should above all aim to catch men for Christ and bring them to hear the blessed gospel that they may be saved.

Man-fishing means working to bring sinners to know the Savior. It is to go forth with the gospel net and cast it out into the sea of mankind in the expectation of catching the lost and bringing them home to Christ. "He who winneth souls is wise" (Prov. 11:30). The devout Samuel Rutherford said that if one soul from his parish would meet him in glory, his heaven would be "two heavens." Let us all, as far as we can, seek to catch men for Christ.

Much as we rejoice in God's sovereignty and power, we must never neglect our duty to seek to save souls. It is right and good for us as God's people to seek by all lawful means to get people to hear the gospel and to come under its influence.

It is a wrong-headed form of Christianity that teaches believers to sit still and do nothing until God brings people to us. A fisherman has to go after his fish; they will not go after him. God's sovereign grace is not dishonored when we use biblical means to seek to win lost sinners for Christ.

How long has it been since you attempted to evangelize someone?

AUGUST 6

> *No prophet is accepted in his own country.*
> —LUKE 4:24

Christ uttered these words in His home synagogue in Nazareth, where He had been brought up and where His family was known. He was recently come into Galilee and was now full of the power of the Holy Spirit (v. 14). Here our Lord is seen preaching to His fellow townsfolk. Their eyes were all fastened on Him. They marveled at His astonishing gift of preaching. They were evidently deeply impressed with His person and presence. But they quickly found an excuse for dismissing His message: "Is not this Joseph's son?"

Our Lord rebukes their unbelief: "No prophet is accepted in his own country." They were dismissive of His claims and of His doctrine on the grounds that they "knew him"—or rather, they thought so. To them, He was just "Joseph's son" and no more!

How quick people are to find some excuse or other for rejecting Christ's message! As it was then, so is it still. In much the same way do men and women despise Christ's people and Christ's servants. They flatter themselves that they "know all this" and "do not need us to tell them." Oh, how much they did not know about Christ! Had they but humbled themselves to listen to Him, they would have found that He is the eternal Son of God and the Savior of the world.

Sad to say, hell will be in the end full of people who lightly dismissed the claims of Christ and of Christ's faithful witnesses. Sin blinds men to their need of religious instruction. They are willing to go to college and to learn about science or mathematics, but they are contemptuous of any who would attempt to point them to heaven and to explain to them the way of forgiveness and peace.

The first step to heaven is when men begin to ask the question: "Who will show me how to find God?" The tragedy with those who despised Jesus Christ was that they failed to see who He was. Jesus, whom they called "Joseph's son," was no other than the eternal Son of God! Why do people not stop to think what they are doing when they speak slightingly of the Savior who offers them eternal life and pardon? Could it perhaps be sheer pride?

*The people were astonished at his doctrine: for he taught them as one
having authority, and not as the scribes.*
                                        —MATTHEW 7:28–29

This explains how the crowds felt after hearing our Lord's Sermon on the
Mount recorded in Matthew 5–7. No doubt the crowds who heard Christ
on the occasions whenever He preached would have felt the same. They were
simply amazed and astounded. There was something in Christ's preaching
that they recognized as special. There was an "authority" in it.

Our Lord, of course, is unique and His preaching uniquely wonderful.
Yet it is true to say that others who preach ought to seek to have some of
this "authority" in their preaching. It is a quality which leaves the hearer
amazed—almost stunned—because it comes home personally to the heart
and to the conscience.

This effect in preaching, when it is real, is the gracious work of God's
Spirit. Christ was full of the Spirit of God and people felt this "authority" in
His preaching and teaching. It registered with them as a word to them from
God. The same effect of preaching is felt in days of revival and blessing.

Let us never forget there is such a thing as revival. Again and again
in the past, God has revived His cause on earth. The Reformation in the
days of Luther and Calvin was the greatest such revival since Pentecost. But
there have been many other revivals, such as those with Jonathan Edwards
and George Whitefield in the United States during the eighteenth century.
Again, one of the greatest revivals was that which took place in the years
1857–1860 in the New York area. Thousands of sinners were brought to
Christ in those blessed years. At that time, the Spirit of God worked powerfully also in Northern Ireland, Scotland, and Wales.

In times of revival, preaching takes on new authority and lost sinners are
humbled to repentance and newness of life. How good would it be if congregations felt more of God's blessed power under the preaching! It is what
causes men to cry out, "What must I do to be saved?"

Oh, let us pray for a fresh baptism of God's power on all true, God-sent
preachers of the Word. May God give them this wonderful "authority." And
let us pray regularly for another God-sent revival.

Therefore the Son of man is Lord also of the sabbath.
—MARK 2:28

Overdoing always leads to undoing, as the Puritans used to say. This is a problem that religious people always have to keep an eye on. The temptation is to take "a good thing too far." The Pharisees were experts at this, especially in the issue of Sabbath observance. They were ready to make it a sin to pluck and eat ears of corn on God's holy day. But Christ, as ever, rebuked and corrected them for their excess.

The Ten Commandments are God's rule of life for the believer and as such Christ endorsed them (Matt. 5:17–19). The Christian Sabbath was altered providentially by God after Christ's resurrection from the last to the first day of the week. Our Sabbath now is "the Lord's Day" (Rev. 1:10), which we, as Christians, are to keep special. It is the day on which we are to attend God's house and get food for our immortal souls. We should love and cherish it.

The Lord's Day is badly kept when men are content to go only to one church service in the day. It is badly kept when professing Christians feel a liberty to enjoy their secular pleasures and sports on that day. It is badly kept when people unnecessarily travel and allow themselves to do unnecessary work on that day—or simply to idle away the day in trivial pursuits.

The Lord's Day is well kept when men make it their practice to attend, so far as health permits, the two services of God's house. It is well kept when professing Christians discipline themselves to do extra Bible reading and to have extra prayer. It is well kept when we lay aside the ordinary secular things of life and spend time in meditating about the world to come, and in speaking with our friends and teaching our young families about the great truths of God.

Let us not, as the Pharisee's did, spoil God's Day with a sour spirit. But let us rejoice on this day because it prepares us for the eternal Sabbath which is to come (Heb. 4:9).

Thy faith hath made thee whole; go in peace.
—MARK 5:34

Christ loved to help and to heal all who came to Him. He delighted to serve sinners and to save them. All bodily illness is a fruit of man's fallen state. Our miseries all flow from the fact of our being sinners. Christ frequently healed the illnesses of men who came to Him. But those who came to Him in faith got more than healing. They got salvation, pardon, and eternal life for their souls.

Both are true in the case of the "woman with the issue" of whom we read here in the Gospels. She came with a physical ailment and yet, more still, she came believing in Jesus as the glorious Son of God. In her timid heart, she said, "If I may touch but his clothes, I shall be whole."

She had, like many others, tried many human helps before this in her longing to be healed. But when she came to the Lord Jesus in faith, she came to the One who truly could heal her in both body and soul.

It is most important to know that we can only be saved in one way. That is by faith and faith alone. The big mistake which multitudes make is to think that we are saved by a mixture of faith and works. But, until we are saved by faith alone, we cannot do even one single good work. Salvation is by faith alone because Christ's work is perfect and needs no addition from us. The function of faith is to reach out, like an empty hand, to receive the gift of Christ's perfect righteousness.

The touch which the woman gave to Christ was an act of faith. It brought her the blessing which she sought. Christ gave her assurance: "Thy faith hath made thee whole: go in peace."

If we want to know God's pardon in our lives and to feel the peace of God in our souls, we must seek God's forgiveness by faith alone in Christ. Our own righteousnesses are as "filthy rags" (Isa. 64:6).

No wonder God's Word tells us: "By grace are ye saved through faith—not of works, lest any man should boast" (Eph. 2:8–9)!

> *Take these things hence.*
> —JOHN 2:16

Christ cleansed the Temple at Jerusalem twice, once at the beginning of His ministry and again at the end of it (see John 2:16 and Matt. 21:12). He did so out of zeal for God and the purity of God's worship. In the course of cleansing God's house, Christ drove out the money-changers who were making gain from those who came to worship God. He also drove out those who were selling oxen, sheep, and doves for sacrifice.

Sadly, in the Middle Ages there was also this tendency in sinful man to abuse God's worship and to use it as an opportunity to get money out of the poor! Sinners commercialized God's worship and so turned God's house into a market. With all such behavior our Lord is most displeased. "Take these things hence!," He cried in indignation.

The lesson here must not be lost on us all. We must do nothing in God's worship but what God Himself has authorized. Too many churches today are ignorantly prepared to bring elements into church worship which have no warrant in Scripture: orchestras, bands, dance, drama, and the like.

Worship is a scriptural and a heavenly thing. What God looks for in us is reverence, awe, humility, and a contrite heart. The best things in worship are serious attention to the preaching of God's Word, concentration on singing His praise, and a sincere desire to pray to Him for His gracious blessing. Do you have this zeal for God's house that Christ had? Do you seek out a church to worship in which social and theatrical gimmicks are not allowed any place in the worship? Or do you secretly hanker after forms of worship that are easygoing on the conscience and make God's house as much like the world outside as possible?

Let us all remember that in the great Day of Judgment, Christ will purge out of His church all that is worthless and worldly. "Take these things hence," He will say. What will stand up to Christ's scrutiny is what is "gold, silver and precious stones" (1 Cor. 3:12). The "wood, hay and stubble" will be burnt up with fire.

In matters of His own worship, God is very jealous. "God is a Spirit: and they that worship him must worship him in spirit and in truth" (John 4:24).

Wilt thou be made whole?
—JOHN 5:6

The words of Christ here were addressed to a sick and infirm man beside the pool of Bethesda in Jerusalem. Evidently a miracle occurred there at certain times. "An angel went down at a certain season into the pool, and troubled the water: whoever then first after the troubling of the water stepped in was made whole of whatever disease he had" (v. 4).

There were very many frail and ill persons lying there around this pool with a great variety of infirmities. This particular man had lain there for as long as thirty-eight years, hoping to be cured. But someone else had always got into the pool before him and up until this hour he had missed his chance of being cured. It was a sad sight!

But Jesus Christ now performs a miracle on him. Immediately, at the command of Christ, he is healed and is able to carry away his bed!

This wonderful event reminds us that in the Gospels we read of all sorts of miracles performed by Christ. We may classify them in this way: (1) miracles of healing, (2) miracles in which devils are cast out, (3) miracles over nature, (4) miracles of raising the dead. They all have this message for us: Jesus Christ is God, with power over the whole universe of men and other created things.

But Christ sought out this man a little later and gave him this message: "Sin no more, lest a worse thing come unto thee" (v. 14). There is something worse than sickness. It is *sin*. Many people are concerned for their health as if it were supremely important. But God's Word teaches us that ill-health and recovery are comparatively small matters compared to having our sins forgiven and getting our soul right with God.

Let us look at the subject fairly and honestly. If our bodily illnesses are healed they will someday come back. We must all die sooner or later. But if we have our sins forgiven, we shall have eternal life both now and forever with God in heaven. Let us therefore get our priorities right. To live a healthy life without Christ is to die in our sins forever. But to have Christ as our Physician is to be in the care of One who can turn death into a mere "sleep."

But I know you, that ye have not the love of God in you.
—JOHN 5:42

It is hard to imagine more devastating words being uttered by the Son of God to anyone. This is all the more so when we see that the people to whom our Lord was speaking at the time were deeply religious people—indeed, they were among the most religious people on earth. They had the Old Testament Scriptures. They had divine ordinances of worship. They had sacraments. They had learned theological scholars. Yet, for all these privileges, Christ has this to say to them: "I know you, that ye have not the love of God in you."

How could our Lord say this to such respected and educated Jewish men? It is because God looks not at the outward appearance but at the heart (1 Sam. 16:7). For all their traditions of religious knowledge and worship, these devout critics of Christ were at enmity with God.

Knowledge is not necessarily truth. Devout people can be devout merely on the outside. This is what Christ elsewhere means when He calls the Pharisees "whited sepulchres" (Matt. 23:27). Whitewashed graves are fresh and clean to look at, but inside they are full of death and decay. So, our Lord means, are those whose religion does not change the heart.

Reader, is your heart cleansed by the blood of Christ? Has your pride before God been humbled? Do you bow the knee gladly and willingly before your blessed Maker? These are questions which are resented by many people. But they are the most important questions of all.

Christ reads the heart of every one of us and He well knows those who love God and those who do not love God. We cannot see into men's hearts; our assessment of men's character must be based on what we see in their outward life and conversation. But Jesus' eyes are "a flame of fire" to read every one of us for what we truly are.

Let us then make sure that before we meet Christ in the Day of Judgment we have been truly converted. Only in that way shall we avoid hearing Him say to us also: "I know you, that ye have not the love of God in you."

Labour not for the meat which perisheth, but for that meat which endureth unto everlasting life.

—JOHN 6:27

Jesus' mission and ministry did not begin and end with material blessings. He came above all to give people eternal life. This should always be reflected in the life of the church here on earth. Important as material things are, they must never become the primary concern of Christians. The material blessings must lead on to the spiritual.

This is exactly what we see in the chapter from which the above words of Christ are taken. The previous day, our Lord fed the five thousand with five loaves and two small fishes (v. 9)! This was another of His astounding miracles, proving that He is the very Son of God. So impressed had the huge crowd been that they had wanted to make Jesus a king (v. 15). But our Savior did not come to earth to be given such earthly honors. After all, He eternally is the King of heaven and earth.

On the day after the miracle, the people came to Christ enquiring of Him how He had crossed the Sea of Galilee. Then came this stern voice to them: "Ye seek me, not because ye saw the miracles, but because ye did eat of the loaves, and were filled" (v. 26). Then follow the words which form our text above: "Labour not for the meat which perisheth...."

Christ's meaning must be this: "Get your priorities right in life. Important as food and drink and other such things are, they are not the most vital things in man's life. It is far more important to be feeding on the Bread of Life, that is, on Me."

How sad it is to see people spend so much time and energy on the trivial pursuits of life and so little time and effort seeking to know God, to enjoy God's blessing in our soul, to be in fellowship with Christ as the Son of God.

We must eat to live; but we must not live to eat. May God make us hungry for that heavenly manna which feeds the soul eternally! They who hunger and thirst after Christ and His righteousness in this present life will be given the right "to eat of the hidden manna" (Rev. 2:17) in the world to come.

For neither did his brethren believe in him.
—JOHN 7:5

Jesus Christ had no human father. Joseph was His adoptive father. God was His Father. Mary was the virgin-mother of our Lord's human nature. In short, we say that Christ had no father as to His human nature, and no mother as to His divine nature. So great a mystery is the Person of our Lord. No wonder He is called "the mystery of godliness" (1 Tim. 3:16)! That Mary was not a virgin after the birth of Christ is shown from these words of the Apostle Matthew: "Then Joseph…knew her not till she had brought forth her firstborn son" (Matt. 1:25). Normal marital relations were established after the birth of Jesus.

Jesus clearly had brothers and sisters, whether born to Joseph and Mary or else born earlier to Joseph. We cannot be certain, nor do we need to know. The remarkable fact mentioned in our text is that these "brethren" did not believe in Him. The names of some or all of these brothers are given to us: James, Joses, Simon, and Judas (Matt. 13:55). We know that there were "sisters," too (Matt. 13:56). But the matter which concerns us now is what our text tells us about these brothers: "They did not believe in him."

This is at one and the same time surprising and comforting. It is surprising because they lived and grew up with One who was perfect in His life and behavior. Yet, for all that, they did not know who He was! How blind is fallen human nature! How incapable man is without God's grace of recognizing or appreciating what is spiritual!

But this strange fact is also comforting. Our blessed Savior knew what it was like to grow up in a home where there were unbelievers. As our great High Priest now in glory, He can understand and sympathize with His people who often in this life have to live in the same home with unbelievers.

The happy fact, however, appears to be that His brethren, either some or all, were converted after His resurrection. James and Jude were among Christ's brothers and were the authors of the two short Epistles which are in the New Testament. Let us pray and work for the salvation of all in our own families!

If any man thirst, let him come unto me, and drink.
—JOHN 7:37

The above words were cried out in a loud voice by Christ on the last day of the Jewish Feast of Tabernacles referred to in Leviticus 23:34. It is a wonderful gospel invitation, explained more fully in the verses that follow: "He that believeth on me, as the scripture hath said, out of his belly shall flow rivers of living water. (But this spake he of the Spirit…).""

There is such a thing as spiritual thirst. This is what Christ is referring to. Many are quite content, seemingly, to grow up, go to school, then to work, then to marry, then to retire, then to die. Sadly, such people are quite happy not to know God, not to read the Bible, not to pray, and not to prepare for what lies beyond the grave. But such a "life" is, in God's view, a living death. Since they live only for worldly satisfaction and pleasure, such people are "dead while they live" (1 Tim. 5:6).

Men and women were created to "glorify God and to enjoy Him forever" (*Westminster Shorter Catechism*, Q. 1). Sadly, sin has made us all carnal and worldly. From this sleep of worldly death Christ here summons us all to know the spiritual things that are infinitely more important than worldly things.

"If any man thirst" is a challenge to us all. Do we really wish to know God, to have union and communion with Christ? Do we feel the emptiness of a life lived without God? Then let us take careful heed to Christ's words here: "Come unto me, and drink." To "come" to Christ is to believe in Him as the gracious Savior of the world sent by the God of love to save us. To "drink" is to seek our deepest satisfaction, not in things of the world, but in knowing Jesus Christ as our Lord.

There is an infinite fullness in Christ. Let no one suppose this Well could ever run dry! The broken cisterns of human pleasure will all prove worthless at last (Jer. 2:13). But those who believe in the Lord Jesus will find in Him an endless supply of joy and inward satisfaction. Have you found it so for yourself?

Before Abraham was, I am.
—JOHN 8:58

These words were uttered by our Lord to His critics. They are very remarkable words indeed, bearing in mind that the Jewish patriarch Abraham had been then dead for some two thousand years. There is no doubt about the way His critics understood these words. They judged Him to be a blasphemer, worthy to be put to death. For this purpose they took up stones to stone Him and would have killed our Lord there and then, had it not been that His time had not yet come.

The "I am" sayings of Christ are all unique to our blessed Lord. No prophet or apostle of Christ ever presumed to assert the things that Christ affirms of Himself over and over again: "I am the bread of life" (John 6:35); "I am the light of the world" (John 8:12); "I am the good shepherd" (John 10:14); "I am the resurrection and the life" (John 11:25); "I am the way, the truth and the life" (John 14:6).

Each of these "I am" sayings points us to one or other of the aspects of our Lord's fullness and glory. Taken together, they are like a magnificent rainbow of many colors, each one reminding us that "Christ is all."

When our Lord informs us that He is before Abraham, He refers to the fact that in His godhood He is eternal, "without beginning of days or end of life" (Heb. 7:3). As to His human nature, our Lord was in His early thirties (although He seems to have looked more like a man of nearly fifty, perhaps because of all the stress and strain which He underwent for our salvation—see v. 57). But as concerning His deity, Jesus is ageless. His eternity knows neither beginning nor end. To convey this, the Book of Revelation says of Christ that He is "alpha and omega" (the first and last letters of the Greek alphabet).

Let us bless God that our Savior is eternal, before all things and above all things. What an honor to know the love of One who is "the Ancient of days" (Dan. 7:9)! And what a privilege to be among the disciples of this eternal Son of God who, in all ages of mankind, has been gathering His beloved children into His spiritual family!

Lord, I believe.
—JOHN 9:38

Nothing is sweeter than true faith in Jesus as Savior. This is what we see in the blind man's confession, which forms our text above. This dear man of God had recently been healed of his blindness by our Lord and he knew therefore by personal experience of Christ's healing power.

His simple faith contrasts markedly with the unbelief of the religious "experts" who interrogated him to discover how he had been healed. Much as these "experts" argued to the contrary, the blind man (now cured) stood his ground as he spoke up for Jesus. They struggled hard to explain away the miracle; he argued straightforwardly that if Jesus were "not of God, he could do nothing" (v. 33). For his faithfulness the blind man was promptly excommunicated: "They cast him out" (v. 34).

Learning and theological scholarship, higher degrees from universities and seminaries, extensive reading, and a knowledge of Hebrew and Greek are all excellent things in themselves. But better still is to have a true, genuine faith in Jesus. More still, scholarly learning will profit nothing in the end if the scholar in question, however great or famous, has never been "born again" (John 3:3).

That the scholars in this passage were extremely able and learned men, we need not doubt. But that they did not have "the one thing needful," love for Christ and trust in His finished work, is all too obvious. Faith in Christ and love for His Word, the Bible, are the most important things in religion. It has been well said that "Christ was crucified under Hebrew, Greek, and Latin." Many a scholar since Christ's day has been "buried" under these languages without having a true saving faith in Jesus. How else can we account for the large numbers of liberal scholars who teach their students to treat the Bible as if it were "myth and legend"? Do not misunderstand this point. Study and learning are excellent things—when they are found in a real man of God. But learning without godly love for Christ as our Savior puffs men up and only makes them more ripe for God's punishment in hell than they were previously.

Before we handle this Bible we must first be able to say of it, "Lord, I believe."

I and my Father are one.
—JOHN 10:30

The profoundest of all mysteries is God Himself. There is one God, but there are three Persons in the godhead. When we speak of the "oneness" of God, we refer to His essence or substance. When we speak of the "threeness" of God, we refer to the Persons. This is too deep for our little minds to comprehend. But it is the way God has revealed Himself to us in the Bible. It is absolutely correct to speak of God as the "Holy Trinity."

Jesus makes clear to us that He is the Son of God in many places of His teaching, but perhaps nowhere more clearly than in our text: "I and my Father are one." What He means is that He and the Father are not one Person, but one God. The gospels show us the evidence for this unique and staggering claim. The miracles are the evidence that Jesus' lofty claim is true.

As we learn from the Bible, the Persons of the godhead are these three: the Father, the Son, and the Holy Spirit (or Holy Ghost). Each Person is equally God; each Person equally has the divine essence and the divine attributes. Each Person is active in creation, providence, and redemption.

Yet there are passages in Scripture also which indicate that there are "works" distinct and peculiar to each divine Person. These are as follows: the Father's distinct work is to "beget" the Son; the Son's distinct work is to be "begotten" of the Father; the Holy Spirit's distinct work is to "proceed" from the Father and from the Son. We refer to these "works" of the Persons of the Trinity as the "works which are within God Himself."

These "works" are not the result of God's will, as other works of God are, but they are necessary works and belong to the nature of God as God.

We should often meditate on the being, Persons, and works of God. Everything about God is "matchless, godlike, and divine." How privileged we are to know Him in Christ, and what blessedness it will be eternally to enjoy Him in heaven at last! No wonder the Bible speaks of God in this way: "Of him, and through him, and to him, are all things: to whom be glory for ever. Amen" (Rom. 11:36).

Jesus wept.
—JOHN 11:35

"Jesus wept" famously makes up the shortest verse in the whole Bible. The occasion of them was at the grave of Lazarus and in the company of Lazarus's two sisters, Mary and Martha, and other mourners.

Ever since our first father Adam disobeyed God by eating from the fruit of the Tree of the Knowledge of Good and Evil, death has brought sorrow and tears into man's life on earth. Either the wife must lay her husband's remains in the dust, or else the husband must perform this last service for his wife. From the earliest days of banishment from Paradise, man's life has been lived in a "vale of tears."

It is a beautiful and a lovely thing to read here that "Jesus wept." It shows that our Lord's human nature was real. Like us, He had feelings and emotions. Like us, He sympathized with those who were in trouble and distress.

There is another occasion in the life of our Lord in which we read that He wept: "He beheld the city, and wept over it" (Luke 19:41). The tears shed by our Lord on this occasion were because He foresaw the terrible judgments that were to come upon Jerusalem when the Romans would destroy the city in AD 70.

True Christianity is a feeling religion. It tells us to "weep with them that weep" (Rom. 12:15). It urges us to "be kindly affectioned one to another with brotherly love" (Rom. 12:10). It reminds us that our duty is to "be pitiful" (1 Pet. 3:8). The language which God uses in Scripture when referring to His love for His believing people is the language of pity and of love: "Can a woman forget her sucking child, that she should not have compassion on the son of her womb? Yea, they may forget, yet will I not forget thee" (Isa. 49:15).

As Christians, let us never despise or even overlook this aspect of our faith. There is a place for tears and for deep pity. Our Lord here shows us that. Wonderful as it is to relate, our Savior, now in heaven, is still "touched with the feeling of our infirmities" (Heb. 4:15). Christ loves His own dear people. In the end, He will "wipe away all tears from their eyes" (Rev. 7:17).

Lord, teach us to pray.
—LUKE 11:1

If the apostles of Christ needed to be taught how to pray, how much more do we! Two factors prompted the above request. First, Christ Himself was observed to be deep in prayer. When He completed His prayer, they approached Him with their request. Second, evidently it was known to them that John the Baptist used to teach his disciples to pray. These are very good reasons why we should all seek to improve in our prayers.

In response to the apostles, the Lord Jesus Christ gives us some choice lessons to lead us to greater maturity in prayer. For one thing, we do well in prayer to give first place to God, His kingdom, His glory, and His sovereign will. Then we bring our petitions for ourselves and for our families. In prayer, we must avoid being wordy or long-winded. God knows what we need before we ask. Furthermore, God delights to hear His children pray to Him. He will give us what is best for us, even as a father does to a child.

We all tend to be too easily discouraged in prayer. For this reason, Christ here gives us wonderful assurances that our praying is not in vain: "Ask, and it shall be given you; seek, and ye shall find; knock, and it shall be opened unto you" (v. 9). This is one great encouragement. And another follows on after it: "If ye then, being evil, know how to give good gifts unto your children: how much more shall your heavenly Father give the Holy Spirit to them that ask him?" (v. 13). Our duty then, when we approach God in prayer, is to remind ourselves of these great assurances which Christ here gives to us. It glorifies God when we believe in His gracious promises. And it strengthens our faith to experience how real and true God's promises are.

The Bible tells us of mighty prayers and how they changed history: Abraham pleading over Sodom (Gen. 18); Jacob wrestling with the angel (Gen. 32); Joshua calling for God to make the sun to stand still (Josh. 10); Hezekiah defying the king of Assyria (Isa. 37); the Ancient Church in prayer so that the "place was shaken" (Acts 4).

May God make us all more mighty in prayer and more believing of His promises to those who pray!

*Yea rather, blessed are they that hear
the word of God, and keep it.*
—LUKE 11:28

To correct an unfortunate and ill-timed exclamation by a woman in the crowd, these words of Christ were spoken. In her zeal to show some respect to Jesus, she had cried out, "Blessed is the womb that bare thee..." (v. 27). It is noteworthy that Christ, as on all similar occasions, dampens down any attempt to elevate His mother Mary. No doubt He foresaw the superstitious worship which would be offered to her in coming ages.

True blessedness, affirms our Lord, does not consist in any physical or natural relationship with Jesus but in something very different. If we wish to be blessed in time and in eternity, we must get to know, understand, and obey the Bible, which is God's holy Word. It is in the Bible that we find the real Christ. It is in the Bible that we hear God's voice. It is in the Bible that we have the light that leads safely to heaven.

The attitude of Christ towards the Bible is of the very highest importance to us all. Did Jesus Christ treat the Word of God as liberal scholars today do? To our Lord, was the Bible just "myth and legend"? Certainly not! Christ everywhere and in every way endorsed the Bible as the inspired revelation of God.

Hear our Lord's words: "Thy word is truth" (John 17:17); "The scripture cannot be broken" (John 10:35); "It is written" (Matt. 4); "Heaven and earth shall pass away, but my words shall not pass away" (Matt. 24:35); "Search the scriptures...they are they which testify of me" (John 5:39); "Then opened he their understanding, that they might understand the scriptures" (Luke 24:45).

The Bible is God's inspired, verbal revelation. If we wish to be wise, blessed, and happy, we need to make the Bible our companion and our joyful study night and day. As people read and obey God's holy Word, they become more blessed in all aspects of their life. We read that the "blessed man" makes the Bible his study night and day (Psalm 1). The apostle Peter tells us to regard the Bible as the one and only sure light which now shines in this dark world (2 Pet. 1:19).

Wherefore, if God so clothe the grass of the field, which today is, and tomorrow is cast into the oven, shall he not much more clothe you, O ye of little faith?

—MATTHEW 6:30

Worry is a ghost that haunts every man in this life. Our Lord Jesus Christ here in His wonderful Sermon on the Mount analyzes, confronts, and exposes worry for what it really is: lack of faith in God on our part.

The antidote to worry is to have faith in God. This is to have a lively day-by-day confidence in Him that He knows what we need and is well able to supply it when we need it. To train us up in this lively exercise of faith, our Lord points our minds to familiar things all around us: the birds of the air, the flowers in the field. The argument our Savior makes is, or ought to be, very obvious to us. If God feeds the birds, will He not feed His own children in this life? If God gives beautiful petals to the flowers, will He not give adequate clothing to His own dear Christian people?

Beneath each worried fear and anxious thought there lies the seed of Atheism. But if we believe in God, does not that mean too that we believe in His perfect knowledge of us, His perfect care for us, and His perfect provision for us? Though we do not see God, yet He sees us and is well aware of all our needs before we feel them. When we wake up to this wonderful truth we shall be ready to cry out, as did Hagar in her hour of need, "Thou God seest me" (Gen. 16:13).

Oh, let us seek grace to become more like our Savior, who never worried. Even when He had fasted forty days and nights, He still waited patiently and trustingly on His Father until provision arrived: "Angels came and ministered unto him" (Matt. 4:11). When in the hour of His arrest, our Lord was defended rashly by the hasty use of a sword, He cried out, "Thinkest thou that I cannot now pray to my Father, and he shall presently give me more than twelve legions of angels?" (Matt. 26:53).

Let us repent of our "little faith" and strive to take God more at His Word.

Judge not, that ye be not judged.
—MATTHEW 7:1

These famous words of Christ are found towards the end of the Sermon on the Mount. They are words of immense practical relevance and importance in our life. Unfortunately, they are words which are all too often misunderstood and misinterpreted.

It is tempting to take these words of our Lord in an absolute sense, as though it were always and in every situation wrong to pass any kind of judgment on persons or actions. But it is impossible to believe that this is what Christ meant by the words, "Judge not." The obvious reason for saying so is found in the very chapter where the words are written: "Give not that which is holy unto the dogs, neither cast ye your pearls before swine" (v. 6). Again, we see these words a little later on: "Beware of false prophets" (v. 15).

Obviously, we must make a judgment about persons and behavior so as to be capable of recognizing people who are "dogs," "swine," or else "false prophets." Indeed, Christ teaches us to "judge righteous judgment" (John 7:24). We must, as Christians, make a just and fair assessment of men and of their characters. Our Lord is not here discouraging that.

"Judge not" here means that we are not to be unkind, unjust, or uncharitable in the way we think of other people. Kindness and love for others should lead us rather to believe the best of them as far as we possibly can. It means to give people the benefit of the doubt and to put the best construction possible on other people's character and actions.

After all, this is how we would wish ourselves to be treated. And God will see to it that if we are unloving in our attitudes we shall suffer for it: "For with what judgement ye judge, ye shall be judged" (v. 1).

Do we not all fall very short at this point? Oh, let us seek grace to think and to speak generously of others as far as possible! But we must not press Christ's words too far. When we have evidence that some men really are "false prophets" or "dogs" or "swine," as many are, we have to protect our souls from them. The key is found in Christ's words: "Judge righteous judgment" (John 7:24).

They that be whole need not a physician.
—MATTHEW 9:12

It is, at first reading, strange to find that Christ can say these words: "They that be whole need not a physician." This initial surprise arises from the obvious fact, well understood by all readers of the Bible, that we have all sinned and so are all in need of Christ as our Doctor, or Physician. But if all are sinners, who are those to whom He refers as being "whole" and as "not needing a physician"? The question is a most important and profitable one to ask.

Obviously, there are no sinners who possess a sufficient righteousness that they can stand in God's presence without any help from Christ. Obviously, too, there are no sinners who can heal their own diseases unaided by God. So what does our Lord mean by the phrases, "They that be whole" and "need not a physician"?

Christ uses these expressions ironically. He means that, sadly, many people do not feel they are sin-sick, lost sinners. They do not realize that they need Christ to attend to their tragic condition. They are not conscious of how depraved they are or how much they would be benefited by coming to Jesus to have their soul put right.

That this is Christ's meaning is all the more clear when we notice that those to whom He was speaking were Pharisees, who were notorious for their religious pride, self-righteousness, and contempt for "ordinary mortals" whom they regarded as far beneath them. It was, after all, a Pharisee who prayed, "God, I thank thee that I am not as other men are" (Luke 18:11). It is this religious pride that God exposes and condemns in the words of Isaiah 65:5, when he quotes the arrogant man as saying, "Stand by thyself, come not near to me; for I am holier than thou."

We shall have no benefit from Christ as the great Physician of souls if we fail to realize our wretched, sinful condition. It is as we are deeply conscious of our own faults, failings, sins, and depravity that we shall flee to Christ for the "balm of Gilead."

Self-righteousness kills thousands who go to church. Have you yet learned that your condition is hopeless eternally—unless you come by faith to Jesus to cure you?

The harvest truly is plenteous, but the labourers are few; pray ye there-fore the Lord of the harvest, that he will send forth labourers into his harvest.
—MATTHEW 9:37–38

What need there is in this world for faithful preachers! The cities and the country-places could happily take ten thousand men of God, all ready to feed the churches and to gather in the lost to Christ.

This fact clearly moved our Lord deeply as He cast His eyes upon the multitudes who passed by in His own day. He saw these multitudes, we are told, "as sheep having no shepherd" (v. 36). Our Lord sorrowed to see how these crowds of men and women struggled with their problems: some with ill-health, others with poverty, others with alcoholism or some other addiction. Our Lord saw the irreligious multitudes unable to cope with their sinful habits and temptations. He saw the sad eternity that lay ahead for all who would die without faith in Him.

We in our own day need to look at life in this way. It should move us with compassion to see the thousands who know nothing of the gospel, groping their way through life in this world. Poor, ignorant sinners do not know even the simplest things about the world in which they find themselves. "Why am I here on earth?" "Where did I come from?" "Is there anything after death?" Sadly, until they hear a faithful preacher, they scarcely know how to face up to such deep and serious questions.

There are all around us many thousands of immortal souls who, if God's Word were to be preached to them, might become, by grace, a ripe harvest for God's kingdom. But there are so few laborers. For one reason or another, the number of men who devote themselves to the work of preaching the everlasting gospel seems to be small in most ages and in most places.

Here then is a duty for you, reader. Pray to God that He will raise up laborers to go forth into the harvest fields of the world, both at home and abroad. "He that reapeth receiveth wages and gathereth fruit unto life eternal" (John 4:36). Not all are called to preach; but all can and should pray for more laborers.

The very hairs of your head are all numbered.
—MATTHEW 10:30

We do not apply our minds as we should to the absolute perfection of all God's works. All believers would readily acknowledge that God cares for His own people. But we are too content with a vague approximation. What we need to do is to raise our thoughts of God's fatherly protection to the highest possible level.

This is what our blessed Lord is doing for us in the words which form our text above: "The very hairs of your head are all numbered." This is a startling statement, when you stop to think of it! God is in possession of a comprehensive, perfect, and fully detailed knowledge of our body, our mind, and our soul. He has His eye on every faculty of our soul and body all the time.

We must admit that we do not all always live in the conscious, or even the half conscious, realization of this revealed truth. If we did, we would be less concerned about what unkind and unspiritual people think or say of us. We would be less anxious about the hatred of this world towards us because we are the people of God.

It seems certain that such factors as the above were present in our Lord's mind as He gave this teaching to His disciples. Just a little earlier He had said to the disciples, "Fear not them which kill the body, but are not able to kill the soul" (v. 28).

So long as we suppose God to be remote and far off, we shall be terrified by the thought of martyrdom. But if God is in control of all events and is watching every breath we draw and is aware of every time we blink, we gain courage to face the fiercest of enemies. God's grace will be sufficient for us in every fresh trial of life. And when our time, as believers, comes to leave this life, we shall experience God's help as we cross the river of death.

We may not in our country be facing blatant persecution for our Christian faith today, but we may face it someday. How good to know that God is infinitely present always to all His children! With this thought we should be "as bold as a lion" to confess Christ before men.

Jesus…was transfigured before them.
—MATTHEW 17:1–2

The human nature of Christ veiled His Godhead during the years of His humiliation in this life. Most who met our Lord and who saw Him made the mistake of supposing Him to be a mere man like themselves. It was in the nature of our Lord's self-abasement that He should be "despised and rejected of men" (Isa. 53:3) and that His critics, turning a blind eye to the miracles and the spotlessly holy life of Christ, should sneeringly say, "We know that this man [Jesus] is a sinner" (John 9:24).

We might correctly say of Christ that while He was here among men He was "in disguise." His human nature acted as a veil, as it were, to conceal the true glory of His divine Person. However, on one very remarkable occasion, the glory of His Person was permitted to show through and to illuminate the human nature.

This was on the occasion of the Transfiguration. On this one occasion, which only three of the disciples were permitted to witness, our Lord appeared in transcendent glory. "His face did shine as the sun, and his raiment was white as the light," says Matthew's account. "His raiment became shining, exceeding white as snow; so as no fuller [a bleacher of cloth] on earth can white them," says Mark's account. "They [the three disciples] saw his glory," says Luke 9:32. "He received from God the Father honour and glory," declares the apostle Peter, who saw it with his own eyes (2 Pet. 1:17).

The Transfiguration was very clearly appointed by God the Father to give honor to His obedient and faithful Son, who was soon to give His life for the world by dying on the cross. These circumstances were all ordained to raise the minds of all believers ever since to cherish the highest adoration for Christ. The glory of His Person shone forth. The voice of God the Father identified Him as the only-begotten Son. The presence of two Old Testament worthies indicated that the saints of all ages have a profound interest in Christ's sufferings and death.

Oh, let us gaze on Christ now by faith—until we see Him face to face in the glory above!

What therefore God hath joined together, let not man put asunder.
—MARK 10:9

Here is Christ's pronouncement on the importance of marriage in human society. It is very much for the good of the human race that we should know and be clear about how Christ viewed marriage. The devil has in different periods of history attempted to undermine marriage in one way or another. Sadly, this is very much the case in our own day!

It cannot be doubted that Christ defines marriage as a coming together of a man and his wife such that they have a new relationship one with another. They are now "one flesh," says our Lord. Clearly our Savior teaches here that marriage is a creation ordinance: "From the beginning of the creation God made them male and female." Then again, as our text above shows, our Lord viewed marriage as a lifelong relationship, one which no man ought to "put asunder."

Happy is the society in which Christ's view of marriage is welcomed and cherished by the people. A stable marriage is a blessing to all who are connected to the family. A stable and affectionate marriage is a great blessing to the children of the home. It is in no small measure the backbone of a healthy society and the wealth of the nation as a whole. When stable marriage decreases, sorrow and sin increase. That there are legitimate grounds of divorce cannot be denied. That legitimately divorced persons may lawfully remarry is most certain. Christ's teaching, when properly understood, makes due allowance for divorce and remarriage under certain circumstances. But the basic concept laid down here by our Lord is that marriage is an ordinance of God which, when entered into, should be for life.

The unmarried should never enter into marriage without the most serious intention to be faithful within it. And those who are married should pray daily for their wife or husband that God would grant mutual faithfulness and richly bless them.

All who are wishing to enter into marriage should do so prayerfully. God's Word should be carefully consulted and considered by persons intending to marry. And once people are married, they should pray daily to be given grace to live affectionately and lovingly with the one whom they have married. After all, in marriage we wish above all to help one another, and our children, to get safely to heaven.

He took them up in his arms, put his hands
upon them, and blessed them.

—MARK 10:16

There are some dignified and religious persons in this world who appear to have no interest in children. Such was not our Lord Jesus Christ. It is possible that the disciples imagined Jesus to be above showing affection to mere children. At least, we read here, they "rebuked" the people who brought young children to Him. But, if so, they were entirely mistaken. He was "much displeased" with those who sought to stop children being brought to Him.

The behavior of Jesus Christ should be an example to us all. Children are quick to realize when they are loved and welcomed, or when they are not. As Christians we wish to show love to children so as to win them to listen to the gospel which we believe.

What more perfect example of love to children could we ask for than this, in which we read that our Lord took them up in His arms and laid His hand on their head to bless them? "Suffer the little children to come unto me, and forbid them not," says this gracious Savior.

Our Lord's example and His words are the only warrant we need to encourage us to do all in our power to lead, teach, and instruct children and young people towards a real faith in God and in the gospel.

Our Savior goes even further. He says of the little children: "Of such is the kingdom of God." These words of our Lord surely mean that children, even at a young age, may become, by God's grace, true and sincere believers and members of God's spiritual kingdom. Further, Christ's words also surely teach that a childlike spirit is a gospel spirit. All true Christians are childlike in that they, with a humble believing faith, have received the gift of forgiveness and everlasting life, while the haughty and high-minded utterly fail to get these gifts because of their pride.

If you are not a child of God, you need to humble yourself. Those who get into heaven must all be of a childlike spirit. Those who exalt themselves will sooner or later be humbled by God. But those who humble themselves will in the end be exalted. Happy are they who cultivate a child-like, self-effacing spirit!

*And they were in the way going up to Jerusalem; and Jesus went before
them: and they were amazed; and as they followed, they were afraid.*

—MARK 10:32

Here we see Christ and His twelve disciples on the way to the place where
He was to suffer and die for His people. What animated our Lord to go on
"before them" with such zeal and alacrity? It was love for God and for God's
will. "Lo, I come…I delight to do thy will, O my God: yea, thy law is within
my heart" (Ps. 40:7–8). These prophetic words of the psalmist were fulfilled
in every part of our blessed Savior's life and ministry.

But why were the disciples "amazed"? The answer is easy to see: "As they
followed, they were afraid." They had seen all too often how great was the
opposition to their Master of the powerful religious hierarchy in Jerusalem.
To their amazement, they were now witnessing the Lord striding briskly
towards the place of crucifixion. Christ was determined to do all His duty to
God and man and, as He prepared to give His "back to the smiters," He now
set His face like a flint (Isa. 50:6–7).

In this, as in all else, Christ is our example. When duty, however painful,
faces us, we must hasten to meet it and steel ourselves by God's grace to do
what needs to be done for God's glory. It was this spirit which stirred in the
apostles after Pentecost and led them to devote their very lives to the spread
of Christ's gospel. This was the spirit which moved Wycliffe, Luther, Calvin,
and Knox, the Covenanters and the Puritans, and a host of other Christian
worthies, to risk all for Christ.

The truth is great and it will prevail. But we, as followers of Christ, must
rise to the call of duty when God summons us to it. May God give to us all
the grace of courage when this call to duty comes. When good men keep
silent, evil will prevail. Too often, good men prefer peace when God's providence is summoning them to painful conflict against error and falsehood.
Let us recall Luther's courageous words: "Here I stand. I can do no other. So
help me God."

It is finished.
—JOHN 19:30

All false religion presses man's conscience to look for acceptance with God from what we as men can offer to God to placate and please Him. The theory is easy to understand. Man's conscience tells him that he is not in a right condition of soul with his Maker. Surely then, says the logic of man, we must earn God's mercy by extra efforts and additional devotions. Professing Christians themselves, past and present, have sometimes gone wrong on this very point. The whole story of the Middle Ages and of the pre-Reformation church especially is amply illustrative of this deep-seated tendency in man to attempt to make himself good enough for God by efforts of his own.

It comes as a shock to those who are ignorant of God's Word, the Bible, when they hear that nothing man can do of himself is able to please God or to earn His love or favor. The condition of mankind is such that we cannot satisfy God's justice by efforts of our own. Neither strictness in religion nor scrupulosity in attending to spiritual duties has any merit in the sight of God. The Bible puts it in this way: "They that are in the flesh cannot please God" (Rom. 8:8).

What man cannot do to appease God, however, has already been done for us by the Son of God, Jesus Christ. This is what His cry here on the cross means: "It is finished." It is a glorious, triumphant cry. It tells us that He has done all that is necessary to bring us pardon and peace with God.

Christ has fulfilled all the demands of God's law. His holy life has actively fulfilled the law for us. His death has paid the price of our disobedience. Christ now offers to us a perfect righteousness. In order to enter into the benefit and enjoyment of what He has done, we need do nothing except repent and believe in Him as Savior and Lord.

To believe savingly in Christ is to become right with God at once. God imputes to the believer the whole obedience and righteousness of the Redeemer. We are justified by His blood and are at once and forever admitted into the family of God. Here is the profound wonder and glory of the gospel: it is not of works but all of grace. When we see and believe in Christ as the One who for us has fulfilled the law's demands we are brought from death into life.

Do you have this blessed faith in Him? Do you worship Christ as the One who has fulfilled all God's demands for us sinners?

MILK & HONEY

from The Gospels

DAVID H. KRANENDONK

And when he was come nigh, even now at the descent of the mount of Olives, the whole multitude of the disciples began to rejoice and praise God with a loud voice.

—LUKE 19:37

Earlier in His ministry, the Lord Jesus had avoided publicity. However, when He went to Jerusalem a final time, He entered the city amid the throngs of Passover worshipers in a way that drew attention to His messianic kingship. See Him come as the fulfillment of Zechariah 9:9: "Rejoice greatly, O daughter of Zion; shout, O daughter of Jerusalem: behold, thy King cometh unto thee: he is just, and having salvation; lowly, and riding upon an ass, and upon a colt the foal of an ass." His requisitioning of the donkey showed He is the King of power and meekness, authority and humility. The time had come to confront the people with His greatness. Each one had to show how he or she stood toward His claim to be the Messiah.

When Jesus began to ride to Jerusalem, the people were constrained to honor Him. As He descended the Mount of Olives, which faces Jerusalem, the crowds thickened, their excitement grew to fervor, and their praises swelled in volume. They sang of His works as God's works. They sang of Him as the King coming in the name of the Lord. They sang of "peace in heaven" as the divine peace that flows from heaven to earth. They sang of "glory in the highest."

"But," you may think, "a week later they were crying out, 'Crucify Him!' This was all superficial." We can even be prone to say, "Master, rebuke them!" But the Master replied to the Pharisees who demanded that, "if these should hold their peace, the stones would immediately cry out." He must be praised as the Messiah. Sinners must know and confess who He is then and now. When He rides before us in the pages of Scripture as the King of salvation, we may not stand silent on the sidelines only looking down on the superficiality of others whose lips praise Him.

See Jesus ride forward! He knew what awaited Him in Jerusalem. Yet He went forward because He is the King of redemption from sin. This King is so approachable in His meekness and mercy and yet so glorious in His might and majesty. See Him ride! Is He not the King for us to fall down before with "Hosanna" cries for mercy and "Hallelujah" songs of praise?

SEPTEMBER 2

And when he was come near, he beheld the city, and wept over it.
—LUKE 19:41

Here is a great contrast. The closer the crowds came to Jerusalem, the louder their joyful praises became; but, when the Lord Jesus rode down the Mount of Olives and saw the city stretched out before Him, He wept. His all-seeing eye surveyed the city and the throngs ahead of Him. He saw what was in their hearts and foresaw what would happen to them in the future. His eye was filled with tears and His heart with pain. Never before had He received such praises as this day, yet never before do we read of Him weeping like He did here.

He foresaw the inexpressible suffering and utter destruction that would come on this religious city. Multitudes of its inhabitants would die in their sin, stand guilty before God, and be condemned to everlasting destruction because they did not believe in Him as the Prince of Peace. Their very songs indicate they were more focused on the miracles He performed than on what He declared about Himself as the Messiah through those works. Theirs was a temporary excitement, not rooted in a change of heart. Their lips praised God, but they never learned to cry out to God for deliverance from their burden of sin and bondage to Satan. Enmity against God still reigned in their hearts. Therefore, despite all their praises, a just condemnation awaited many of them. No amount of praises with our lips can make up for a lack of true faith in our hearts. Enthusiasm in song, sincerity in religion, and zeal in keeping God's law outwardly cannot please God if we remain strangers of true conversion in our hearts.

See the compassion of Christ Jesus for such sinners! The sight of unbelief melted His heart and drew sobs of sorrow from Him. He knew how God-dishonoring and foolish neglecting such a great salvation is. He knew what awaited them because He knew what awaited Him: the wrath and curse of God. He wept. There is no compassion like Christ's compassion. If He wept over unbelieving sinners like me, how can my eyes remain dry? If His compassion moved Him to shed His blood for sinners like me, must I not be moved with compassion for those around me as well? May a sight of His eyes of compassion melt our hearts and give us eyes like His.

Behold, I have prepared my dinner: my oxen and my fatlings are killed, and all things are ready: come unto the marriage. —MATTHEW 22:4

The gospel proclamation is so amazing. No wonder it begins with a "Behold!" Look! Listen! Here is a wonderful message! The message is first about what God has done and provided for sinners. The invitation does not speak about what the guests are to do, but what the King has done in preparing the dinner. The gospel feast is not a potluck but a feast prepared by the divine Host alone. The gospel message is not that God has done His part and you must do yours, but that "I have prepared my dinner...all things are ready." The entire feast of good things is prepared by the triune God. With Him is a feast of every grace for your every need. God has enlightening, humbling, pardoning, reconciling, renewing, guiding, strengthening, restoring, assuring, sanctifying grace. The cost of this provision was nothing less than the death of His only-begotten Son.

Because Christ has purchased every item in this feast, the call may freely sound today, "Come unto the marriage." This call now extends beyond the borders of Israel to the farthest reaches of the world, including where we live. What a mercy it is that we hear this call! He knows how much you need Him and commands, "Come!" You can wonder whether there is grace for you, but He calls, "Come!" If you question His willingness, only hear that call, "Come unto the marriage!" Does something keep you from this feast? Is it your "farm" or "merchandise" (v. 5)? Do you still value your pleasures more than this gospel feast? Are you seeking your happiness in earthly things? Are you concerned about earthly loss and gain more than eternal loss and gain? Are you still satisfied with yourself? You do not know if you will hear this call tomorrow, but today He still calls you, "Come unto the marriage." There is no feast like this feast.

The *Canons of Dort* (Head III/IV, Art. 8) confess, "As many as are called by the gospel, are unfeignedly called. For God hath most earnestly and truly declared in His Word, what will be acceptable to Him; namely, that all who are called, should comply with the invitation. He, moreover, seriously promises eternal life, and rest, to as many as shall come to Him, and believe on Him."

*Come, ye blessed of my Father, inherit the kingdom prepared for you
from the foundation of the world: for I was an hungred, and ye gave
me meat…I was a stranger, and ye took me in.*

—MATTHEW 25:34–35

Soon, Christ will return and the great division will take place. The welcome
word "Come" will be a word of pure grace to those on His right hand. They
are not called servants who merited heaven, but ones "blessed of my Father."
The blessing of the Savior's Father made them citizens of heaven. They will
not earn their place there, but inherit it freely. This inheritance was prepared
for them before creation. Entrance into the everlasting Kingdom is rooted in
the Father's eternal and gracious election.

At the same time, the reason for their entrance is said to be their care,
feeding, hospitality, and compassion toward Christ. We would expect Him
to say, "For you were hungered, and I gave you the bread of life; you were a
stranger to God, and I took you into my family." But the actual words are the
reverse. Is entrance into the kingdom then dependent on works? Yes, in the
sense that every heir who walked on earth will have performed them. James 2
argues that true faith shows itself in works of charity. Justification gives birth
to sanctification. First John 3:14 confesses, "We know that we have passed
from death unto life, because we love the brethren. He that loveth not his
brother abideth in death."

As a believer, you may not see these works in yourself, but Christ sees
them. You do not keep a log of good works, but Christ does. You see the self-
centeredness in your generosity and the lack of love in your help of others,
but He sees His own work in you. That is why on the final day, with amazement you will hear your works confessed.

Christ's teaching shows us that Christian compassion is not just for dea-
cons or certain believers, but every person renewed by God—though some
may have more opportunities and abilities than others. Do we show practical
compassion? Do we do so out of love to Christ? In light of the final day, a life
of love arising from God's free grace is essential. On that day, none will regret
the sacrifices love led them to make in service to others. They will realize that
service to Christ's body is service to the Savior who gave Himself for them.

Peace I leave with you, my peace I give unto you: not as the world giveth, give I unto you. Let not your heart be troubled, neither let it be afraid.

—JOHN 14:27

In a peaceful room, your heart can still churn with troubles. Troubled hearts gathered with the Lord Jesus in the upper room. The disciples had argued in pride and been humbled by their Master washing their feet. They had been warned that one of them would deny Him and they all would forsake Him, and that He would die and leave them. Believers are no strangers to heart-trouble about past sin, fear about future dangers, and confusion about present circumstances.

But, amid this all, Christ gives His peace. His peace belongs to Him and is in His heart. He has peace because He is right with God, knows God as His God, and has perfect trust in and submission to God. We are the opposite by nature. Therefore, His soul was troubled under the load of God's curse to reconcile His sinful people to God.

The way to receive His peace is to be restored into a right relationship with God and receive the knowledge of God. If God is then for you, who can be against you? If God has given His Son to die for you, shall He withhold any good thing from you? If His hand holds the reins of world history, can anything past, present, or future escape His control? Knowing these things gives a peace that is not dependent on your circumstances.

He has left this peace behind as His church's inheritance. No greater inheritance exists. His death has secured it as the continued possession of His church. When His people are troubled, He asks, "Have you forgotten what I have left you as an abiding bequest? I have not taken it back."

What a mercy that He also gives this peace. He is risen to be the Executor of His own will and distribute His legacy to those who dare not take it. He gives it freely as a personal gift. The world may speak empty wishes or sincere yet powerless words, but He gives effectually by His Spirit. The world's peace is an empty, fleeting illusion that cannot stand up in the light or under assault. His peace is a real and everlasting peace. With this peace alone, you need not be afraid on the churning sea of life. With Him, you will reach the harbor of perfect peace.

SEPTEMBER 6

I am the true vine.
—JOHN 15:1a

How can I live and flourish spiritually? "I am the true vine," the Lord Jesus said. The great "I am that I am" compared Himself to a humble vine that rises from the ground to support and nourish the fruitful branches above it. That same night, men would seek to uproot and destroy Him as a useless vine. But through being cut off in the place of His unfruitful people, He became the vine that is so deeply rooted that it will never be uprooted. Those who abide in Him never need fear that they will be destroyed. In stating "I *am* the true vine," He teaches that He will always remain the vine and will always have branches.

As the vine, He now lives to nourish the branches united to Him. He came, died, arose, and ascended to send His Spirit as the sap that enlivens and fructifies barren branches. He is the only source of life and blessing. "I am the true vine" calls us to seek life in Him alone through union with Him.

A grape branch exists to bear fruit. If it misses that purpose, it is useless. If we belong to the church as a fruitless branch belongs to the vine, we miss the purpose of our existence. Branches which have no sign of life or only some leaves of profession but no fruit of the Spirit will be cut off. To bear fruit, we need to receive the Spirit as the vital bond with the living Savior. Is our main concern in life to be a fruitful branch to the glory of the Father as the Husbandman?

To bring forth more fruit, we must learn to increasingly abide in this Vine. Growth in grace is not becoming stronger and better in ourselves, but more dependent on Christ's grace received by the Holy Spirit and through His Word. Growth is learning more that "He that abideth in me, and I in him, the same bringeth forth much fruit: for without me ye can do nothing" (v. 5). If He is the Vine, rest in Him, yield all to Him, and receive all life and fruitfulness from Him. Apart from Him we have no life. In Him is all we can desire. He says, "I am the true vine." There is no other source of life and we need none other. He exhorts, "Abide in me and I will make you fruitful."

And when he is come, he will reprove the world of sin...of sin, because
they believe not on me.
—JOHN 16:8a, 9

The world's misery is that it lives in bondage to sin and in separation from God. Its greatest misery is that it does not perceive its misery. The gospel of pardon for the guilty and healing for the diseased meets dead ears. The natural man is so diseased he thinks he is healthy and so blind he thinks he sees. God's law also means little to him because he has his own standards of right and wrong.

What will break through this misery? The Holy Spirit. He has come to expose sin. Like the Jews who heard Stephen preach, some are "cut to the heart" by God's Word and yet resist the Holy Spirit (Acts 7:51, 54). Some may feel reproved and yet harden under it. We may never build our hopes on our convictions of sin; hell itself is filled with an awareness of sin.

What a mercy it is that the Comforter also reproves to bring to true repentance. The Holy Spirit exposes sin's character. Sin is coming short of God's glory, which is the purpose of our existence. Sin is rebelling against heaven's King and violating God's law. The Spirit shows that sin arises from unbelief. Unbelief refuses to believe what God says about His glory and worthiness to be trusted, loved, and served. Unbelief refuses to admit that God's description of man is true. Unbelief refuses to trust in Christ alone for salvation. By revealing something of who God is, the Holy Spirit convicts of the presence and character of sin.

When the Spirit's reproof leads to true repentance, you become honest before God, confess your sin and misery before Him, sorrow over your sin and unbelief, hate and turn from it, and can no longer do without God and His deliverance from sin. Your ears strain to hear a gospel of pardon and healing.

Rather than simply lament the general lack of a sense of sin today, let us ask ourselves, "Has the Holy Spirit reproved me? Is He still doing so?" The question is often asked: Have you been comforted by the preaching? Another question to ask is: Have you been reproved by it? Both reproof and comfort are gracious blessings worked by the Holy Spirit. Pentecost is proof the Spirit does both and the pledge that He will continue to do so, as the gift of the Father merited by the Son, today.

SEPTEMBER 8

He shall glorify me: for he shall receive
of mine, and shall shew it unto you.
—JOHN 16:14

Must the Lord Jesus not be glorified? He is all-glorious as the eternal Son of God, the only Mediator, and the King over all. All the attributes of God sparkle in Him. Through Him, the Father performs His wondrous deeds. In verse 15, He confesses, "All things that the Father hath are mine." Paul wrote, "In him dwelleth all the fulness of the Godhead bodily" (Col. 2:9). None can be compared to Christ in His fullness, sufficiency, preciousness, power, and beauty.

Do you long to see His glory and glorify Him? To share in His riches and live out of them? To know Him? Listen to what Christ Jesus said about the Holy Spirit: "He shall glorify me." The Spirit makes Christ's glory known to sinners. The Spirit causes His disciples to see His greatness. He humbles them and exalts Christ in their minds, hearts, and lives. He makes the glory of man fade away like starlight fades before the rising sun. The knowledge of Christ is at the heart of all true spiritual life. The Spirit's deepest desire is not to magnify some unique gifts of the Spirit but God's singular gift of His Son.

In doing so, the Spirit does not simply make sinners spectators of Christ's glory, but they share in Christ's work. He receives words of instruction from the chief Prophet and brings them to the heart of His ignorant people. He receives the treasures of grace from Christ, the Treasure-house, and brings them to His poor people. He receives the garment of salvation and clothes guilty ones with it. In showing Christ's glory, He causes sinners to share in His glorious grace and to be led into greater devotion to Christ.

The Lord Jesus said, "He shall receive of mine." The Spirit receives and shows only a portion of Christ's fullness. The more you see in Christ, the more you realize how much more there is of His person and work. The more you know of Him, the more you realize how little you know of His infinite beauties. The more you receive of Him, the more you long for more of His riches. The more He works, the more you long for glory where sin is no more and Christ is all. The Lord Jesus must be glorified and He shall be. The triune God will ensure it. Is that your hope and longing?

This do in remembrance of me.
—LUKE 22:19

As the Lord Jesus broke bread at the first Lord's Supper, He lovingly instructed His disciples: "this do in remembrance of me." These words raise the question: Do we know Him? To remember Him, we must first know Him. If He is a stranger to us, we cannot remember Him. We can think about some facts recorded in the Gospels, but that is different from remembering Christ Himself. The Lord's Supper is for those who know Him.

These words direct their focus to the Lord Jesus, the whole focus of the Supper. The Supper is not primarily about your sorrow, but His sorrows; not your desire, but His desire; not your faith, but His faithfulness; not your works, but His works; not your life, but His life; not your love, but His love; not your vows, but His vows; not your joy, but His joy. The Supper is about His beauty, His grace, and His righteousness.

Remember Him who came into the world to save sinners, of whom I am chief. Remember Him who was a man of sorrows and acquainted with grief. Remember Him who was wounded for our transgressions and bruised for our iniquities. Remember Him who went from the Lord's Supper table to Gethsemane, to Gabbatha, and to Golgotha, all for the sake of your sin. Let the scenes of His sufferings pass through your mind and may their substitutionary character fill you with humble awe, amazement, and adoration. Remember Him who also entered the grave only to rise again, ascend into heaven, and pour out His Spirit. Remember Him who ever lives to make intercession for them that come unto God by Him. Remember Him who will one day gather His bride to Himself to be at the marriage supper of the Lamb. The bread and wine point to all these things about Him, who says, "This do in remembrance of me!"

Amid all you lack, meditate on what He has! At the Table, He reveals Himself as the fully sufficient and suitable Savior and calls the weakest in faith to think of and remember Him. There is no end to the riches in the Supper's Lord as they are displayed at the Lord's Supper. Does that make you look forward to the Lord's Supper? When the Supper is administered, may His people have such a remembrance of Him that all else is forgotten and they are left with Him alone!

But I say unto you, I will not drink henceforth of this fruit of the vine, until that day when I drink it new with you in my Father's kingdom.
—MATTHEW 26:29

The cup of blessing at the Last Supper spoke to the disciples of remission of sin, but to the Lord Jesus of indescribable sufferings for sin. "This is my blood…which is shed," He said. Yet, as He gave the cup, He saw beyond the depths of His suffering to the heights of eternal communion, like a man descending into a deep valley looks to the mountain tops on the other side.

Christ confessed He would "not drink henceforth of this fruit of the vine." Wine, and every good and refreshing gift of God, would be taken from Him. The communion expressed by this cup would be withdrawn when His disciples would flee and His Father would forsake Him.

But hear Him confess, "I [will] drink it new with you in my Father's kingdom." For that joy set before Him, He endured the cross. He longed for that day out of love for His unworthy people, zeal for His Father's honor, and desire for the final restoration of His fallen people into full and harmonious communion with Him. That day will come.

As He entered the night of desolation, what a day of light He held before His disciples! On earth, that communion with Christ is so often broken by backsliding, hindered by dimness of sight, and weakened by unbelief. However, Christ has secured the day when He will be the host at the eternal communion feast. There, nothing will come between Christ and His bride. They shall see Him as He is and their "joy shall then unbounded be."

Do you long for this eternal communion with Christ Jesus? Do you long to be in that kingdom of the Father where all is holy and to His glory? Have you experienced a taste of that communion with Christ, perhaps also at the Lord's Supper? Every taste of communion is only a small foretaste of the fullness to come. Is it your grief that you so often spoil that tender communion? May that grief stir up more desire for the unhindered communion to come. May your lack lead you to the Savior whose blood secured that future for those who deserve to be cast away. Remember that a foretaste of communion is a pledge and guarantee of the fullness to come.

That they all may be one....
—JOHN 17:21a

In John 17, we reverently enter the sanctuary of the Lord Jesus' holy prayers on the eve of His sacrificial death. In them, He requests from His Father the fruits of His mediatorial service to His Father. He prays for all the elect whom the Father has separated from the world and given to Him (vv. 2, 6, 9). He gives eternal life to them (vv. 2–3), manifests the Father's name to them (v. 6), and gives faith to receive His words (v. 8). He prays the Father to keep them (v. 11) and sanctify them through His truth (v. 17). He prays, "I will that they also, whom thou hast given me, be with me where I am" (v. 24).

In this context, Christ prays "that they all may be one." His prayer for spiritual unity is rooted in the reality that God has given all His people as one gift to His Son. This unity is realized through the Holy Spirit's work of drawing them to Christ by faith. The more the Spirit sanctifies and leads believers to live out of Christ, the more this unity becomes evident.

Are there not far too many church members with whom you experience no real bond? Are there rifts and tensions within your congregation? Is there a lack of love? Are there strained relationships between congregations? Is the church broken into many denominations that go their separate ways? Does the world mock at the fragmentation, contention, fighting, and coldness of the church? What reason for brokenness of heart these realities are!

How we must listen to this request of the dying Savior, "That they all may be one." Breaking denominational walls down alone is not the remedy. Neither is some training in how to be polite to one another sufficient. True healing flows from above in the form of true conversion. It comes in answer to this High-Priestly prayer. The next day, Christ shed His blood to secure that answer. Amid all the brokenness, let us look to this great Intercessor to pour out His Spirit to unite us to Himself by saving faith, sanctify us, and keep us. Let us not only listen to His prayer but begin to echo His prayer for this profound unity to bind us together as churches and individuals. To be united to Christ is to be united to one another. The more communion with Christ, the more communion of the saints and true church union there will be.

> *I have prayed for thee, that thy faith fail not.*
> —LUKE 22:32a

The devil loves to work in secret. He is glad that a veil conceals so many spiritual realities from our view. The chief Prophet alone can lift a corner of that veil and expose the devil at work behind it. He warned Peter, "Simon, Simon, behold, Satan hath desired to have you, that he may sift you as wheat" (v. 31). Satan fixed his eye on Peter, set his heart on having him, and opened his lips to ask to have him in his sieve. He wanted to toss Peter about until Peter was exposed to be nothing but chaff.

The sieve of Satan's assaults within you and temptations around you can be so severe. He draws to sin and has arguments to keep you from God. Whether he comes as a roaring lion or angel of light, his purpose is always to blow you away like chaff. All God's people know this sieve of Satan. Satan is most concerned to demonstrate that there is no spiritual life in those he fears there is.

This is a frightening reality. Who is a match for this foe? If Christ only lifted the veil to show Satan, everyone with a measure of self-knowledge would despair. But Christ also reveals Himself as the one who opens His mouth. He says, "I have prayed for thee, that thy faith fail not." The word "pray" here is an intense form of beseeching. With great earnestness, Christ prays to His Father on behalf of His Peter who does not even realize the danger he is in.

Christ's prayers are stronger than Satan's desires. After Peter denied his Master, why did he not hang himself in despair like Judas? When he saw the death of the One he confessed to have the words of eternal life, why did he not give up all hope? "I have prayed for thee, that thy faith fail not" is the only reason. Christ knows all that goes on behind the veil concealing so much from our view. He knows Satan's every move. He even grants Satan's request to place God's people on the sieve. That can be so painful and distressing.

Yet, through Christ's intercession, Satan's sieve becomes God's means of trial to demonstrate the genuineness of His grace in His people. If it were not for His grace, they would fail; but they never shall, because Christ never ceases to intercede "that thy faith fail not."

Pray that ye enter not into temptation.

—LUKE 22:40

Prayer is more important than sleep. When the Lord Jesus led His disciples through the darkness into the garden of Gethsemane, He did not simply pray with them and then let them sleep. He exhorted, "Pray! Now is not a time for sleep but prayer!"

When is prayer more important than sleep? When temptation is near. They had been warned that one of them would betray Him and all would forsake Him. Should that warning not have stirred them up to pray, "Let me not fall"? Jesus had warned the disciples, "Satan hath desired to have you, that he may sift you as wheat" (v. 31). What reason they had to pray that Satan would not succeed! Preserving grace is needed because mere human resolve will melt before temptation's power. Therefore, pray!

The Lord Jesus had also encouraged them: "Ye are they which have continued with me in my temptations. And I appoint unto you a kingdom" (vv. 28–29). He had given them endurance under temptation before and promised to continue to do so. That promise is an encouragement to pray for continued grace and for temptations to serve as trials to purge and drive us closer to Him.

Exactly when you think that other things are more important than prayer, that it is a time to sleep and not pray, or that you need not pray because you think you can manage, Christ exhorts, "Pray that ye enter not into temptation!"; "Let him that thinketh he standeth take heed lest he fall" (1 Cor. 10:12). He says, "Pray without ceasing" (1 Thess. 5:17).

Is God binding that call to pray on your heart? You may not know what lies in wait for you down your path, but when you feel the need for prayer pressed on you, God must have a reason for it. He is preparing you for what is to come in your life through prayer. He calls you to pray for your own good. He knows how quick you are to be silent. But when you are silent, He exhorts, "Pray!"

Let your silence be broken by prayer to God. Let your weakness and sin as well as His assurances of help impel prayer that you enter not into temptation. Around you are a thousand snares. How will you be kept from them? Pray! All the love of Christ moves Him to call you to pray.

Father, if thou be willing, remove this cup from me: nevertheless not my will, but thine, be done.
—LUKE 22:42

The greatest display of self-denial exists in the sufferings of the Savior who prayed, "Not my will, but thine, be done." Everything in His sinless human will shrank from drinking this cup. All the vengeance of an infinite God was poured into it. All God's holy anger against sin filled that cup. A larger or more bitter cup never existed.

Jesus saw this cup and prayed to His Father. He did not question His Father's love, but asked, "Father, must love give gall to drink? Must I be forsaken by Thee, the God I love?" He did not push the cup away, but humbly asked whether there was a way for His Father to take it away. His petition already reveals His submission. He desired nothing that His Father did not desire. Instead, He desired His Father's will. He confessed, "I have a natural aversion to suffering and an intense aversion to being forsaken by Thee, but let Thy will and eternal counsel be done." He requested God's will to be carried out because He knew God's will is best. God's will would lead Him through sufferings to the glory that awaited and thereby would deliver sinners from having to drink the cup of fury eternally and secure for them the cup of salvation. "Let that will be done," He prayed.

Do you find self-denial and submission to God's will difficult? You may ask the Lord to remove the cup of sufferings, if He is willing. But you have no reason to resist Him. See the Savior receive that cup of fury. It was far worse than any cup you can receive in this life. We deserve to drink His cup forever. Anything less than that cup is a cup where bitterness is still mingled with sweetness. If the sinless Savior drank the undiluted cup of God's punishment, can I, a sinner, resist the mixed cup of affliction? If He denied Himself for me, can I maintain my own will? He calls out, "If any man will come after me, let him deny himself, and take up his cross, and follow me" (Matt. 16:24). Following Christ, you will discover that where He leads is best. On His path, He will be with you to strengthen you, comfort your soul, and sanctify affliction for your good. That is the Father's will. His will is best.

Be ye come out, as against a thief, with swords and staves?
— LUKE 22:52

The Lord Jesus addressed this question to Jewish leaders who knew the Scriptures and heard Him preach. What were these men doing on this solemn Passover night with a rough band of soldiers? Should they not have been meditating, praying, and singing about the mysteries of redemption? Instead, they were coming against Jesus as if He were a thief.

The Lord Jesus had just rebuked those who sought to defend Him with weapons and healed Malchus's severed ear. This last action makes His question so penetrating: "Be ye come out, as against a thief?" Does a thief present himself to his captors and heal them? The word "thief" is used for highway robbers, like the ones who left a man half dead in the parable of the Good Samaritan. Is this what the Lord Jesus had been during His ministry? He had not hurt and stolen, but healed and given.

Christ is no thief, yet many still treat Him as if He were. We are too orthodox to ever call Him a thief, yet we can live as if He is. Some are afraid His service will rob them of their pleasures, fun, and friends. Some do not want to think too seriously of His teaching for fear it will take away their presumptuous comforts. Keeping Christ at a distance and resisting Him and what comes from Him is treating Him as a thief.

The Lord Jesus asks, "Am I really someone who has come to harm you? Do you have a good reason for your resistance?" Hear the longsuffering patience in that question! He reminds us of His goodness so that we would break down before Him with the confession, "I have been living as if Thou art a thief, but I am the thief who has stolen Thy good gifts and used them to resist Thee! I thought Thou would take good things from me, but I have nothing good for Thee to take away. Take what is wrong from me and give me what is good!"

Christ was numbered among the thieves not only by the Jews but also by God Himself. He was punished as a thief in order to merit every blessing for those who have robbed God of His honor. He is the One to supply in our deepest needs and deliver from our greatest hurts. He is the gracious Giver whose hand opens wide to supply.

But Jesus held his peace.
—MATTHEW 26:63a

Christ Jesus was silent in court. His silence was not an implicit admission of His guilt; it was a witness against the guilt of the Sanhedrin who conducted an unlawful trial and of the High Priest who asked Him to defend Himself against an invalid charge of two witnesses whose testimonies did not agree. His silence solemnly testified against their unbelieving injustice.

In His silence, He also went forward to fulfill His own saying that the temple of His body would be broken. He did not resist. He could sing to His Father, "I suffered silently because Thy will is best." He fulfilled the prophecy of Isaiah 53:7: "he is brought as a lamb to the slaughter, and as a sheep before her shearers is dumb, so he openeth not his mouth." Why? He knew "the LORD hath laid on him the iniquity of us all" (Isa. 53:6). He knew that when one stands before God with guilt he cannot open his mouth to defend himself or complain of God's punishment. He stood there in the place of those who had misused their tongues and whole beings to exalt themselves against the God of heaven. He stood guilty with nothing to plead.

If He was silent, can we still protest against God's just punishment of our sin? Can we still excuse, minimize, or shift the blame for our sin? Seeing the silent Savior laden with iniquity, there is reason for every mouth to be stopped and all to become guilty before God. One confession remains: "Behold, I am vile; what shall I answer thee? I will lay mine hand upon my mouth" (Job 40:4).

If you must be silent before the heavenly Judge, listen to the message of the Savior's silence: sin must be punished and I will bear that punishment for those who are inexcusably guilty. I will take their sin on Myself so that they may be delivered forever.

By His silent suffering, He has earned the right to speak. By His Spirit, He still silences sinners before God and opens their ears to hear Him speak, "Father, forgive them! As Thy Lamb, I have given Myself as a sacrifice for them!" He is the effectual advocate for speechless ones. When He speaks, accusers must shut their mouths. "Who is he that condemneth? It is Christ that died" (Rom. 8:34). When He speaks of His pardon, you may open your mouth to sing, "Worthy is the Lamb that was slain to receive honor."

And the men that held Jesus mocked him, and smote him. And when
they had blindfolded him, they struck him on the face, and asked him,
saying, Prophesy, who is it that smote thee?
　　　　　　　　　　　　　　　　　　　　　—LUKE 22:63–64

During His trial, Jesus was silent while the noises of mockery and blasphemy
assaulted His blessed ears. His captors turned His prophetic ministry into
an object of ridicule. With cruel smirks they approached a blindfolded Jesus,
struck Him with their fists, and taunted Him with the call, "Prophesy, who
is it that smote thee?"

They exhibited great contempt of Him. He had spoken with power and
performed signs to demonstrate the truth of His words, but they treat this
Prophet's words as worthless. How terrible is trifling with God's Word, treating it as man's word, dismissing its message, and living in contradiction to it!
Such responses make a mockery of the chief Prophet.

What sufferings He endured! He had declared that He came to fulfill
Isaiah's prophecy of opening the eyes of the blind, but now they mock Him
as one so blind that He cannot tell whether Zadok or Elnathan is smiting
Him. He had heard the voice of the Father declare, "Hear ye him," but now
they reduce His prophetic office to a guessing game. He endured this blas-
phemous mockery.

We easily choose to be silent rather than be mocked for what we said.
We can be so afraid of a sneer, smirk, barbed remark, or mocking taunt.
However, if He, the Master, was mocked, His servants should expect the
same. "If they have called the master of the house Beelzebub, how much
more shall they call them of his household?" (Matt. 10:25).

Suffering the reproach of Christ with Christ is far better than siding
with His mockers. God's Word will stand: because "ye have set at nought all
my counsel,…I will mock when your fear cometh" (Prov. 1:25–26). God's
holy mockery will pop the balloon of their inflated pride and eternally show
the vanity of their attempts to oppose Him.

Those who belong to Christ may know He took their place as ones who
deserve God's mockery. Thereby Christ has earned the right to be the Prophet
whose words have power to enable His servants to endure man's mocking
words. Hearing His blessed voice causes fear for the breath of mockers to
fade, even though the pain their words give may remain. Our honor is secure
with the Savior whose prophetic word will prove true.

Then came Jesus forth, wearing the crown of thorns, and the purple robe. And Pilate saith unto them, Behold the man!
—JOHN 19:5

Pilate's men had made a mockery of Christ's kingship. After scourging His blessed back, they crowned His head with sharp thorns, placed an old robe on His shoulders, assaulted His ears with a mocking "Hail, King of the Jews," and struck His body with their hands.

Pilate then brought Him before the crowd and called out, "Behold the man!" Literally, he says, "Behold! The man…" without finishing his sentence about this man. He seems to say, "Make up your own mind about Him. Is this a king to reverence and fear? He is so powerless! Why do you bother to demand the death of such a man? Pity him instead!" But the rejection of the crowd shows that no one will ever rightly understand who Jesus is by simply looking at His bleeding form or pictures of it.

Whatever Pilate intended, God uses Pilate to draw our attention to "the man." Through Pilate, God calls out, "Behold, the man!" "Behold, man!" "Behold, mankind!" With His crown of thorns and faded robe over His bleeding back, He shows what has become of man. God created the man, Adam, crowned with glory and in His image, but we have exchanged honor for shame, royalty for slavery, and blessing for curse and suffering. We must complete the sentence and say, "Behold, mankind is in misery!"

What an amazing sight it is to see this misery embodied in the incarnate Son of God! The glorious Son humbled Himself so low. As the second Adam, He took the place of the fallen first Adam. Like the first Adam, He stood there as the representative of a new humanity. Behold, this man is the King to take away the crown of thorns and give the crown of life and honor! Behold, this man is the Savior to deliver from the misery that fills a fallen race! God Himself finishes Pilate's sentence with these words: "Behold, this man is the Savior of fallen men!"

Behold! Here is a wonder. No human or angelic mind could ever devise it. No redeemed heart will ever weary of it. Here is a wonder to behold, adore, and break down before: the Son of God was a man with a bleeding back and a crown of accursed thorns to secure eternal glory for fallen humanity. "Behold, the man…." Do words not fail to describe Him?

His blood be on us, and on our children.
—MATTHEW 27:25b

During the Lord Jesus' trial, Pilate had repeatedly declared he could find no fault in Him. Pilate had just washed his hands to show he wanted nothing to do with the shedding of Jesus' innocent blood. He did not want to be responsible for what would happen to Jesus.

In response, the Jewish crowd before Pilate shouted, "His blood be on us, and on our children." They were confessing, "God may hold us responsible for this man's blood!" They knew that if it was innocent blood it would cry out for divine vengeance, as did the blood of Abel. But they thought His blood was worthless. They rejected and despised Him.

God heard their cries and granted their request. The Lord Jesus had told them the parable of the wicked husbandmen who were destroyed for shedding the blood of their master's son. How many of these shouting people died with the guilt of Christ's blood upon them? How many of their children died in the Roman siege some decades later? Many children followed in their parents' footsteps of rejecting the Messiah and perished with them. We live in families, not in isolation. How we live affects others, especially our children. If we despise the Savior, we not only make ourselves guilty but also lead our children to destruction. It is so important for young people to seek the Lord and to seek a spouse who does as well. Parents have a great responsibility in raising their children.

Must we then not cry, "His blood be on us, and on our children" in a way so different from what the Jews meant? We cannot enter marriage, raise children, or live without the Surety's blood on us to cleanse us and our children from guilt. We are also guilty of despising and rejecting the Savior. We have pierced Him by our sin. The prophet Isaiah had to confess, "we esteemed him not" (Isa. 53:3). We cannot wash our hands of what we have done in our own bowl of water. We can only plead, "His blood be on us, and on our children by Thy Spirit to cleanse us from our sin." Peter preached to those who had crucified the Lord and were pierced in their hearts, "the promise is unto you, and to your children" (Acts 2:39). That promise of cleansing is sealed in the baptismal water administered to us and our children. God works from generation to generation.

> *And they gave him to drink wine mingled*
> *with myrrh: but he received it not.*
> —MARK 15:23

Throughout His sufferings, Christ Jesus received blows, scourging, and a crown of thorns. However, when He arrived at the place of crucifixion, He refused a cup of relief. Behind Him lay Gethsemane's agony, the trial's intensity, and His loss of blood, which would have caused His body to crave a refreshing drink. Before Him lay His crucifixion and dereliction, that would induce a man to cry out for any pain relief. Myrrh was a bitter substance used for pain relief. The hand of mercy seemed to offer Him this cup of relief.

Why did He reject it? He knew He was not a victim to be dulled, but the Servant of the Lord, who had the most important work to perform. This work required His full alertness. With full consciousness, He was to bear the full burden of wrath against sin. No myrrh was to dull the experience of the intensity of hellish agony. What love moved Him forward to drink the cup of His Father's fury as a real and fully alert Man!

His refusal reminds us that there is no myrrh, aspirin, or even a drop of water to cool the tongue of those in the torments of hell. The Savior who endured these sufferings without any relief warns us most seriously about that reality. Let us not be dulled by sin and drugged by the devil's apparent mercy into believing there is no need to worry. May what Christ endured awaken us to this reality.

Greater yet, this action proclaims the substitutionary love of the Savior who remained alert to drink every last drop of His Father's cup. What more could He do to convince you that His heart is filled with saving mercy? He did this to open up streams of true and full relief for those worthy of none.

This Savior is the compassionate High Priest. Believer, remember Him who refused the cup of relief to purchase the relief you may receive in your afflictions: medication, anesthetic, and other pain relief, as well as food and drink. Think of Him when the doctor says, "We can't do anything to help you." This Savior can be touched with the feeling of your infirmities. When God draws your eye to Him, even in affliction, your heart may be filled with amazed adoration that He should have no relief from pain to secure eternal relief.

*Then the soldiers, when they had crucified Jesus, took his garments...
now the coat was without seam, woven from the top throughout. They
said therefore among themselves, Let us not rend it, but cast lots for it,
whose it shall be: that the scripture might be fulfilled.*

—JOHN 19:23–24

We might turn our eyes from this scene in reverence for the One so humili-
ated. Indifferent soldiers "took his garments." His last possessions were taken
from Him. What is more degrading than for enemies to strip a person of
everything and hoist him up for all to see him in his shame and pain? Christ's
enemies seem to be in control, but in reality they are only means in God's
hand to fulfill the prophecy of Psalm 22:18: "They part my garments among
them, and cast lots upon my vesture." Right through human indifference and
enmity, God fulfills His Word then and now.

His garments needed to be taken away because He needed to become
poor. We have forfeited every gift down to the clothes on our backs. Whether
you are richer or poorer in material possessions, you see in a naked Savior
what you deserve.

The Lord Jesus also needed to suffer shame. The Fall has made public
nakedness a shame, however much society may increasingly try to glory in
it. What a contrast to all the obsession with bodily beauty is Christ on the
cross, bleeding, broken, and without a covering before the people. The worst
is that He hung in the shame of a sinner who appears before God without
anything to cover himself. He endured the shame of the cross (Heb. 12:2).
Have you come to see in Him your picture? Has He led you to throw away
your filthy rags of self-righteousness and appear before a Holy God covered
only in shame?

The gospel is that His nakedness was not His own. He bore the shame
and poverty of others because He bore their sin. An uncovered person and
a naked Savior fit together. Looking to Him as the Substitute, you see that
He gives riches and a covering which is not your own. He gives you clothes
to cover your shame before others. Let that guide what clothes you wear and
how you wear them. Far greater, He gives the song: "my soul shall be joyful
in my God; for he hath clothed me with the garments of salvation, he hath
covered me with the robe of righteousness" (Isa. 61:10).

And he said unto Jesus, Lord, remember me
when thou comest into thy kingdom.
—LUKE 23:42

We do not know this man's name. We only know he was a malefactor or doer of evil; his crimes made him deserve death. A long life of sin lay behind him. He was using his waning strength to mock the One who hung beside him. What greater picture of wickedness and hopelessness can there be? However, on the cross something changed. He began to tremble before the holy God whom he was soon to meet. He came to confess that he justly deserved to die and that Jesus had done nothing wrong. He recognized that Jesus was a great King who was on His way to His glorious kingdom. What a change!

Listen! As he hung powerless before a rapidly approaching death, he called, "Lord, remember me when thou comest into thy kingdom." He dared to ask Jesus who was going to heaven to remember him who was going to hell. He had nothing to commend himself to Christ, but he knew Christ was able to think of him in grace. He knew he deserved to be forgotten but could not do without being remembered.

Listen! As Christ hung under the curse, He cried, "Verily I say unto thee, Today shalt thou be with me in paradise" (v. 43). There is no room for doubt. Because Christ was entering the thief's hell, He and the thief would enter His paradise. He declared, "Today, I will call you into My holy presence to rejoice in My everlasting salvation from sin, delight in My sovereign love, and enjoy the bliss of unbroken communion with Me. You, a criminal, and I, the King, will never part again."

How this account sparkles with the glories of sovereign grace! Grace gives conviction, confession, petition, expectation, and salvation. We or our loved ones cannot be too close to death to receive this grace, if this thief received it in his dying hours. With the thief, there is every reason to despair of human help, but no reason to despair of mercy for anyone living, even if he or she has lived so long in sin and unbelief that we think it is too late. There is every reason to cry today, "Lord, remember me," "Remember him," or "Remember her." Christ is now in paradise as the Savior who hears prayer and speaks through His Word and by His Spirit. God "forgetteth not the cry of the humble" (Ps. 9:12).

It is finished.
—JOHN 19:30

God needs only to speak one word to save a sinner or comfort a distressed heart. *Tetelestai* is such a word: "It is finished." As Christ Jesus hung in the painful torture and humiliating shame of the cross, the people thought, "*He* is finished. His life is over." Instead, Jesus cried, "*It* is finished! The work My Father gave Me to do on earth is finished!" No one else had perfectly obeyed God's law and fulfilled God's will. Jesus could confess, "My meat is to do the will of him that sent me, and to finish his work" (John 4:34). He kept God's law on behalf of those who do not even begin to keep the law by themselves. He also finished His task of offering Himself up as a sacrifice to God. The Old Testament priests were never done, but Christ offered Himself up "once for all." He satisfied God's justice as the sin-bearing Surety of His people (Heb. 10:10).

"It *is* finished" is a shout of certainty at the center point of history which secures the final end of history. His work ensures that God will have His ruined creatures back again—an eternal Sabbath's rest where God shall rejoice in the work of His hands and His redeemed shall rejoice in His work is coming. This is because "by one offering [Christ] hath perfected for ever them that are sanctified" (Heb. 10:14).

You can add nothing to Christ's finished accomplishment of redemption. You may rest in nothing apart from it. Our moral decency, doctrinal orthodoxy, earnest sincerity, religious diligence, and covenant privileges can form no part of the basis of our salvation. God is only satisfied with the perfection found in the One who cried, "It is finished." You need add nothing to His work. You need not despair when you realize you cannot contribute to your salvation. He cried, "It is finished!" That one word is enough to lead you to let go of everything and sink upon this only foundation by faith. May this one word enter our hearts and go with us today and all our days so that we confess, "Therefore we always hold fast this foundation, ascribing all the glory to God, humbling ourselves before him, and acknowledging ourselves to be such as we really are, without presuming to trust in any thing in our selves or in any merit of ours, relying and resting upon the obedience of Christ crucified alone" (*Belgic Confession*, Art. 23).

And he took it down, and wrapped it in linen, and laid it in a sepulchre that was hewn in stone.

—LUKE 23:53a

If you have stood by a grave, you know how graves and grief go together. The grave confirms the truth of God's declaration, as a consequence of the Fall, "to dust shalt thou return." Unless the Lord returns soon, we are all headed for a grave. On the way, we are told of the singular grave of the Prince of Life. His burial was not a matter of course. The bodies of crucified criminals were often left on their crosses or on the ground to be eaten by beasts and birds, or at best thrown in a shallow, common grave. God's hand of providence brought Christ to an unused sepulcher.

Christ was buried to fulfill prophecy. For example, Isaiah 53:9 prophesies, "he made his grave with the wicked, and with the rich in his death." That is why 1 Corinthians 15:4 confesses He was buried "according to the scriptures."

In being buried, He also confirmed He truly died. His entire body was wrapped tightly in linen. Spices were put in His mouth, ears, and nose. His burial was the "amen" of His death in the place of His people who deserve to die.

His burial was also a step of His humiliation. Who can understand that the eternal Son of God who came in the flesh should lie in the dust of death? The grave proclaims the repulsiveness of God's once beautiful creation. Our bodies are sown there in corruption. The power of Jesus' divine nature preserved His body from corruption, yet He entered that realm.

May the fearful thought of your grave lead you to His grave. If you belong to Him, His grave is the seal that He took your death on Himself. In doing so, He made your grave a bed upon which you may await the eternal day. As surely as you follow Him into the grave, you will follow Him out of it into eternal life. He has gone before you.

If you have stood at the grave of a loved one who is beloved of God, you know grief, but not as those who have no hope. Through the tears, God may give grace to sing, "O grave, where is thy victory?... But thanks be to God, which giveth us the victory through our Lord Jesus Christ" who died, was buried, and rose again. (1 Cor. 15:55–57).

And, behold, there was a great earthquake: for the angel of the Lord descended from heaven, and came and rolled back the stone from the door, and sat upon it. His countenance was like lightning, and his raiment white as snow.

—MATTHEW 28:2–3

No one saw the Lord Jesus arise, but the signs of His resurrection displayed His glory. As God stretched out His arm to raise His Son, the very earth leaped and shook before Him. God opened the heavens and sent an angel to the closed tomb. He came with heaven's brilliance on his brow. His face shone as a ball of continuous lightning. His clothing was "white as snow," pure and righteous. This showed he came from God's holy presence. Soldiers became like dead men before the Lord's servant. If a servant of the risen Savior has such glory, how much more glorious must his Master be?

The angel came to the sealed stone. What use were battle-hardened guards? What could Pilate, a seal, or a stone do to keep the grave closed? All these insurmountable obstacles were obstacles no longer. The angel rolled away the stone to reveal an empty tomb. He did so not to let Jesus out, but to let people see inside the sepulcher and know, "He is not here, for he is risen." See the angel publicly display Christ's victory!

The permanence of that victory is shown in the angel sitting on the stone. He did not leave the stone standing ready to seal the entrance again. He turned it on its side and sat on it. The tomb stone symbolized the power of death. An angel sitting on it before an empty tomb proclaims that a way out of the grave has been opened. Grace has triumphed over sin and death. Nothing could or will ever overturn that victory.

Christ no longer suffers as the Sin-bearer but lives as the righteous Life-giver. Those who cannot open their own spiritual grave and roll away the stone that seals their death may hear the message of His empty tomb: He "was raised again for our justification" (Rom. 4:25). Nothing can stop Him from giving life to those who lie in their spiritual graves. Nothing will stop Him from raising them in the final day. If in your spiritual grave you find the living Savior and follow Him into your physical grave, you will also follow Him in His triumph over the grave. Nothing will stop Him, the risen, conquering King.

Jesus saith unto her, Mary.
—JOHN 20:16

Love cannot endure separation from its beloved. Mary's tears rose from the pain of missing the One she loved. She owed everything to Him. He had expelled seven devils from her and showed her His love. Now He was gone. How could she continue on without Him? As the *Canons of Dort* confess, "His gracious countenance...is to the godly dearer than life, and the withdrawal of which is more bitter than death." This pain is an evidence of God's grace.

Yet, Mary lacked something. The promise that Christ would rise again echoed in the empty tomb that morning, but Mary never heard it. Later she saw two heavenly messengers, but turned away before they could proclaim Jesus' resurrection. Jesus Himself met her, but she turned from Him as well. She had drawn her own conclusions that He was dead and turned away from all the comfort offered her. If finding Jesus had depended on Mary, she would have never found Him, even though she desired Him.

If you seek and do not find Him, could your problem also be that your own conclusions and feelings keep you from receiving the comfort contained in God's Word for seeking souls? Could you be turning away from Him who is coming through His Word and messengers to comfort?

The wonder is that Christ lives to find those who cannot find Him. All the while, Jesus had His eye on Mary with a resolve to reveal Himself to her. She could not do without Him, but much less could He do without her, because He died and rose to save her and all His people. When you miss Him, you may know that He longs far more for those who seek Him than they long for Him.

He came to Mary because all other voices and events failed to comfort her. He spoke one word, "Mary!" Hearing His voice, she knew He was alive—for her. He remains the Good Shepherd who calls His sheep by name. He still lives today as the Rabboni or Master of those who seek Him. He lives to stir up that love and dependence to such intensity that they cannot do without Him. He lives to remove the clouds of ignorance and unbelief. He lives to reveal Himself. Be assured that He is risen to seek out those who can neither find Him nor do without Him. His love cannot endure separation.

And Thomas answered and said unto him, My Lord and my God.
—JOHN 20:28

What distress Thomas had kept himself in by his absence from where the risen Jesus met His disciples! That first week they walked in the light, but he walked in darkness. They could not make him share in the light they received. "Unless I put my finger in the nail holes, I will not believe," he said. He longed for this message to be true, but didn't dare believe it unless it passed his self-made test. Do you also dare not believe He has risen for you? Are you prescribing your own spiritual remedies?

Eight days later, Thomas could not stay away from the disciples' gathering. Neither could the Lord Jesus. He came and called Thomas to follow through with his prescriptions, but Thomas could not. When God comes to us by His Spirit, our own prescriptions to Him fall away. Then Jesus prescribed His remedy, "be not faithless, but believing." The remedy is faith: taking the Lord Jesus at His word and embracing what He declares, even when all our senses tell us His Word cannot be true.

Faith led Thomas to confess, "My Lord and my God." Gone were the tossing waves of disquiet and the dark clouds of doubt. In a moment, all was calm and bright. He knew, believed, rejoiced, and adored. As impossible as the joy of faith seemed before, so impossible was the sorrow of unbelief now. He knew the Jesus who died is the mighty, sovereign, redeeming "Lord" over all. He who overcame death is able to overcome all else. Greater yet, He is "God." Here Thomas rose above the other disciples. He who struggled in greater darkness now spoke with greater light than they all. Thomas also knew this Savior was his own: "my" Lord to deliver me and "my" God to be with me. Thomas had nothing to say about himself but everything about his Lord. When faith is exercised, we fall away, and He is our whole focus.

The Lord Jesus no longer reveals Himself to our physical eyes. Yet, His word to Thomas remains: "blessed are they that have not seen, and yet have believed." By faith, we may have the same certainty and assurance that Thomas had. His Lord and God may be ours because his Lord and God still lives to give the same grace He gave Thomas. Do not prescribe to Him, but hope in Him. "Be not faithless, but believing."

And he said unto them, Cast the net on the right side of the ship, and ye shall find.
—JOHN 21:6

Skilled fishermen fishing at the right time and in the right way did not catch a single fish. After an entire night of fishing, a stranger on the shore called out if they had any fish. They had to reply, "No." What a humbling confession this was for the disciples! Yet it was very instructive. We need to be delivered from self-reliance and pride through the discovery of our own inability. God may give an empty net in our daily work or in our home, in the church or in our soul; all our toil appears to be in vain. Yet, pulling in empty nets is not in vain when the Lord uses fruitless efforts to teach that "without me ye can do nothing" (John 15:5). Then an empty net is a blessing from the One who stands on the shore, watching you toil, ensuring you catch nothing, and preparing you to receive His provision.

The Lord Jesus issued a command and a promise to these helpless disciples: "Cast the net…and ye shall find." They were not to stop because they were unsuccessful and expect the fish to jump into the boat. They were to act at the Master's command and according to His precise prescription: on the right side. Following the command is the promise: "Ye shall find." They would not find because of their skill but because of His promise.

Command and promise often go together in Scripture. Ecclesiastes 11:1 exhorts, "Cast thy bread upon the waters: for thou shalt find it after many days." Galatians 6:9 encourages, "Let us not be weary in well doing: for in due season we shall reap, if we faint not." Continue on, not in self-reliance or in discouragement because of your weakness, but becoming more dependent on God and hoping in His Word. Jesus said, "Seek and ye shall find" (Matt. 7:7). However unable you may be, this word remains true. His command and promise go together and both are true. The command constrained the disciples to obey and the promise was fulfilled in a full net.

Through an empty net, Christ proclaims "without me ye can do nothing." Through a full net, He calls, "Trust Me to use and bless you in My way." If Christ teaches you both of these lessons, you can thank Him for both of these nets.

And he said unto them, Go ye into all the world, and preach the gospel
to every creature. He that believeth and is baptized shall be saved; but
he that believeth not shall be damned.
—MARK 16:15–16

Meditate on salvation and damnation. Can you weigh them? Can you comprehend the torments of hell and delights of heaven? Damnation is being forever separate from God's blessed presence and submerged in God's infinite wrath. Salvation is to be separate from every trace of sin and pain and to be forever with the God of infinite beauty.

Christ Jesus came into this world to obtain salvation for those who deserve damnation. Therefore, when He left, He commanded, "Go ye into all the world, and preach the gospel to every creature." "Gospel" means "good news." The gospel is that the Son of Man has come to lay down His life for sinners and to seek and save the lost. We have a great gospel!

This gospel calls for faith. "He that believeth and is baptized shall be saved." Do we have this faith which trusts in the Savior alone for pardon and renewal? If we do not believe, we "shall be damned." Our having the gospel is a serious thing, and trifling with it ends in damnation. There is no middle ground between faith and unbelief, salvation and damnation.

To believe is to be saved. If we are enabled to believe, we will never come under condemnation. Then we also desire the gospel to be spread and know God's Spirit is able to use it to make unbelievers believers. The more we live out of the gospel of free grace, the more we will be burdened for others to hear and receive it.

Having experienced the power of that gospel herself, the church is to be God's mouth to the world, declaring that gospel with clarity, zeal, and love. She is to go into a world lying under the curse not to learn from and conform to it, but to be a witness of gospel grace in it. This gospel must be preached to "every creature"—us, our families, acquaintances, and neighbors, our nation, and all the nations of the world.

We owe our hearing of the gospel to Christ's commission. That gospel must continue to spread according to that same commission. Shall the immeasurable weight of man's salvation and damnation and God's glory not fill our hearts with concern, prayer, and zeal for this commission today?

While he blessed them, he was parted from
them, and carried up into heaven.
—LUKE 24:51

Have you not thought before, "I wish I could have been there with the disciples?" Words of exhortation and grace poured out of the Lord Jesus' blessed lips. His hands stretched out over them to bless them. As He did so, His feet rose from the ground and He ascended up toward heaven until a glorious cloud took Him from their sight. This scene is filled with quiet majesty and tender love.

Those outstretched hands proclaim the whole purpose of His work on earth. He was born, He lived in perfect obedience, He died a sacrificial death, and He rose as the Prince of Life to be able to stretch out His hands of blessing over His disciples and church. The people He stretched His hands over were sinful, but His hands were pierced. From His wounds stream all the blessings of salvation from sin, reconciliation to the Father, conformity to Christ, and communion of the Spirit—the blessings for body and soul, in life, in death, and throughout eternity. The last view of Christ on earth was of Him blessing.

As He blessed, He was carried up into heaven. He did not storm the gates of heaven; His Father carried Him into heaven as the One who blesses. The Father delighted to see His Son stretch out His hands to bless. This was the whole purpose of the Father in sending His Son. With joy the Father received the blessing Mediator and set Him at His right hand. The blessing Christ gives His church is the joy of the Father.

He who entered heaven blessing His church still lives to bless His church. What hope would there be for you, if that were not the case? If He would lower His hands and cease to bless, none would be added to the church and every living member would still perish. But His hands remain stretched out. Christ Jesus is the same yesterday, today, and forever. He still pronounces His blessing upon the poor in spirit who hunger and thirst after Him. He still sends His Spirit to convey His blessing. That is why we may share already or still come to share in the same blessing the disciples received. When He gives His blessing today, it is no less real, full, or gracious than if we had stood with the disciples on Mount Olivet.

OCTOBER

MILK & HONEY

from Acts

DAVID SILVERSIDES

The former treatise have I made, O Theophilus, of all that Jesus began both to do and to teach, until the day in which he was taken up, after that he through the Holy Ghost had given commandments unto the apostles whom he had chosen.
—ACTS 1:1–2

Under the inspiration of the Holy Spirit, Luke had written the gospel of Luke. This was his "former treatise." The book of Acts is his second work. The first tells us of what "Jesus began both to do and to teach" until His ascension to the right hand of the Father, and this book tells us what He continued to do and teach from the Father's right hand by the Holy Spirit. So the book of Acts tells us of what our exalted Savior was doing in the early part of the New Testament age of the church. It tells us of how He replaced Judas among the twelve, of His outpouring of the Holy Spirit and showing by this sending of "another Comforter" that He had not left His disciples, but was with them still (John 7:39, 14:16–18, Acts 2:33).

The book of Acts shows us how our Lord Jesus was fulfilling His promise to build His church by enabling His apostles to preach with all boldness and by adding to the church such as should be saved through His Spirit opening their hearts to receive the gospel preached to them (Acts 2:47, 16:14).

Do we live as those who, by faith, believe that we have an almighty Savior at God's right hand "whom having not seen, ye love" (1 Pet. 1:8)? Is He our chief joy? Do we convey the truth that it is a blessed thing to belong to Him, to be redeemed by Him, and to serve Him ungrudgingly as the most glorious, loving, and gracious of masters? The more we grasp what we have in Christ, if we are true Christians, the more content we will be. "Let your conversation be without covetousness; and be content with such things as ye have: for he hath said, I will never leave thee, nor forsake thee" (Heb. 13:5).

The church as a body must also rest in this truth. It is true that we do not have apostles today and there were other things unique to that time before the Bible was complete. But Christ is still exalted; "for he must reign, till he hath put all enemies under his feet" (1 Cor. 15:25). The government is upon Christ's shoulders and He is head over all things to the church (that is, governing all things in her interests). Avoiding all manmade remedies, if the church is languishing, we must be faithful to our heavenly King and look for Him to turn the tide—the One who promised, "lo, I am with you alway, even unto the end of the world" (Matt. 28:20).

OCTOBER 2

God hath made that same Jesus, whom ye
have crucified, both Lord and Christ.

—ACTS 2:36

Are we in the last days? Yes, we certainly are, for the last days, in the biblical sense of the term, began with the New Testament age (see also Heb. 1:2, 1 John 2:18, 1 Pet. 1:20, 1 Cor. 10:11). This explains why Peter applies the prophecy of Joel about the last days to what was happening all those centuries ago on the day of Pentecost (v. 17). This special outpouring of the Holy Spirit signaled that the church in the New Testament is generally to have "fuller communications of the free Spirit of God, than believers under the law did ordinarily partake of" (*Westminster Confession*, 20:1).

But the Savior who sent forth the Holy Spirit at Pentecost and added three thousand souls to the church was "that same Jesus" who was crucified. He is now "declared to be the Son of God with power" (Rom. 1:4). All power in heaven and earth is His. The Triune Jehovah has committed the demonstration of His covenant faithfulness and absolute authority to the Second Person of the Godhead who had become a man in order to fulfill all righteousness and bear the just wrath of God as the Substitute for all His people. He is now exalted as the God-man Redeemer. He brings many sinners into subjection by the gospel of saving grace. At the end, He will subdue all others in judgment.

There are lessons for us here. We learn what a sympathetic High Priest we have. As God, He knows all. In His human nature, He was tempted in all points like as we are, yet without sin, and is able to succor them that are tempted (Heb. 4:15, 2:18).

We learn how we need to see our sin in order to see our need of Christ, the Savior of sinners. Peter is extremely direct—"whom ye crucified!" It was this that the Holy Spirit used to cause them to say, "What shall we do?" (v. 37). Conviction of sin is necessary if sinners are to see their need of Christ. Only when we see our sin can we possibly see our need of Him who said to sinners while He was on earth (and still sends the same message from heaven in the Scriptures and through His ministers), "Come unto me, all ye that labour and are heavy laden, and I will give you rest" (Matt. 11:28).

In the name of Jesus Christ of Nazareth rise up and walk.
—ACTS 3:6

The miracles in Scripture do not appear at random as meaningless displays of God's power. They are called "miracles" or "powers" because they display the power of God, and "wonders" because of the reaction they cause among men. But they are also called "signs" because they have meaning and significance. Sometimes that meaning is very specific, as when the Lord Jesus fed the five thousand, showing Himself to be the Bread of Life, or gave sight to the blind as being the Light of the World. More generally, however, the miracles were signs that God was speaking through His inspired spokesmen. The miraculous gifts exercised by apostles and conveyed to others through the apostles were signs of the apostles (2 Cor. 12:12, Heb. 2:3–4). The Old Testament prophets spoke in the name of Jehovah and performed signs (Deut. 34:10–12, 1 Kings 18:36, Ps. 74:9). The Lord Jesus, as God manifest in the flesh, spoke and healed in His own name: "Verily, verily, I say unto you." But here, Peter performs this miracle in the name of Jesus Christ.

This use of the name of Jesus Christ of Nazareth is full of meaning. It was "the historical Jesus" who grew up in Nazareth, and yet He is also the God-man Mediator who sits at God's right hand with all power in heaven and earth. He who came as the servant of Jehovah is Himself Jehovah. He is the Lord of glory!

Notice how Peter announced in advance that something was going to take place that only God could do—"such as I have give I thee…rise up and walk." This showed that he was a recipient of direct revelation from God. Many of the biblical miracles involved this inspired pre-knowledge as samples of infallible knowledge.

Christ gave this man more than silver and gold through Peter. But these miraculous reversals of some effects of God's curse on fallen man in sickness and death point to Christ as the one who can save from sin itself and give everlasting salvation. Peter, therefore, tells the crowd, "Repent ye therefore, and be converted" (v. 19). We do not have apostles today, but we have the whole Bible. In our Bibles we have the truth of God and the record of miracles that accompanied the revelation of God's Word (John 20:30–31). Are we making good use of what we have been given?

If we this day be examined of the good
deed done to the impotent man....

—ACTS 4:9

The priests were "grieved" (v. 2) that Peter and John taught the people the message of the risen Christ. Rulers should be a terror to the evildoers, but here they arrested the preachers and examined them about a good deed! They did not, indeed, could not, dispute the miracle (v. 16), but neither would they submit to the truth of God. They threatened and commanded the apostles to preach no more (vv. 17–18).

This account is full of instruction. For one thing, we learn the utter depravity of the human heart. The problem with these men was not lack of clarity or evidence. How easily we fall into the mistake of thinking that if we only present the gospel in a sufficiently clear and well-argued manner, surely men and women will believe it—but no! A sovereign work of the Holy Spirit in the heart is needed before any sinner will be willing to trust in Christ. Our Lord Jesus said, "Except a man be born again, he cannot see the kingdom of God" (John 3:3).

We also learn the power of the exalted Christ to build His church. The preachers were bound, but the Word of God was not bound, and the number of believing men was now five thousand (v. 4). How forlorn Peter and John had seemed when the Lord Jesus was crucified, but now they have been strengthened by the Spirit of Christ and their enemies marveled and "took knowledge of them that they had been with Jesus" (v. 13). They declared openly the fact that the Jewish leaders had crucified the Christ of God (v. 10). Christ is still at God's right hand and He can still give such boldness to His servants as He did, for example, during the Reformation when John Calvin withstood the enemies of the gospel in Geneva when they came to church with swords!

Today, it is often particularly the exclusiveness of the biblical gospel that is deemed unacceptable in Western countries; our failure to simply say, "Well, this works for me, but if something else suits you, that's okay." Believing readers, this we can never do. Whether ministers in public proclamation or the individual Christian in his stand for Christ in the world, we need the power of the exalted Christ by His Holy Spirit to be able to say, "Neither is there salvation in any other" (v. 12).

...against the Lord and against his Christ.
—ACTS 4:26

God answers prayer "by terrible things in righteousness" (Ps. 65:5). It was so here; the place was shaken and they were filled with the Holy Ghost (v. 31) and the boldness sought was given. This request for boldness (v. 29) for the ministers of the Word tells us something about true prayer. However legitimate it would have been to pray for safety, what they sought above all else was the continuance of the clear and forthright testimony to the truth. Our prayers must aim at God's glory, not like the purely selfish so-called prayers that the ungodly may offer.

They also used Scripture in prayer. We are told, "Take with you words" (Hos. 14:2) when we come to the Lord, and what better words to take than His own? There is a danger, when leading in corporate prayer, of proudly demonstrating one's knowledge of Scripture. Nevertheless, this should not discourage the right use of Scripture in prayer that honors the Lord by showing that we believe His Word and its threats and promises, and which also helps us to think biblically and rightly of God.

Psalm 2:1–2 is here applied to Herod and Pilate, not merely in their private conduct, but in their use of their position as civil rulers. This tells us that the later verses of the Psalm indicate not only what rulers should do in their personal lives, but also in their use of public office. They are to serve the Lord and to kiss the Son (Ps. 2:10–12). When Samuel anointed David as king, he kissed him in recognition of his authority (1 Sam. 10:1). Those who had kissed Baal were those who had bowed the knee to him (1 Kings 19:18). To kiss the Lord Jesus, in the context of the Psalm, is to acknowledge Christ's royal authority as "the prince of the kings of the earth" (Rev. 1:5) by openly ruling according to His Word. This is what all political rulers are duty bound to do.

In fact, no human activity, including our family life and daily work, should be done independently of the Word of God. Every thought should be brought captive to the obedience of Christ (2 Cor. 10:5). It must begin, however, in our hearts as individuals. Has your heart been captivated by the grace of Christ? Have you been made willing to rest upon the crucified Savior for acceptance with God? Has this happy submission to the Redeemer begun in you through the gospel?

And great fear came upon all the church.
—ACTS 5:11

The truth of Christ was to be heralded in Jerusalem, Judea, Samaria, and beyond (Acts 1:8), and Christ was now fulfilling His promise to build His church. Initially, the continuing church was emerging from the corrupt Israelite Old Testament church shell, but soon the Gentile wild olive branches would be grafted into the church (Rom. 11:17–24). Nevertheless, even the flourishing church after Pentecost was not free of "hypocrites, who are mixed in the Church with the good, yet are not of the Church, though externally in it" (*Belgic Confession*, 29). But the Lord always sees and can bring the truth to light in this world if He pleases, even as He surely will in the world to come.

Ananias and Sapphira were not forced to give all the proceeds of the land-sale to the church (v. 4). There was no communist regime operating in the apostolic church. Their sin lay in the pretence and falsehood. They wanted people to think well of them and were not acting out of love to the Lord. They were serving the creature—their own pride and the esteem of others—rather than the Creator. The Lord knew and judged even within the visible church. Ultimately, God will perfectly sift the professing church and the ungodly shall not stand in the congregation of the righteous. Even those pretenders who go unnoticed by others in the church will be exposed. The man without the wedding garment could not deceive the king (Matt. 22:11). Have you more than an outward form of Christianity that deceives even the minister and elders? The Lord knows.

In this case, the Lord judged by means of the apostles. Christ's miracles while He was on earth were virtually all of a positive, healing kind, pointing to His having come to save sinners. The disciples hadn't grasped this when they desired to repeat the miracle of judgment God did by Elijah (Luke 9:54–56). After Christ's resurrection, most of the miracles through the apostles were also positive since they were to preach the message of salvation. This is one of a few exceptions. The pre-announcement of the Lord's revelation of what He was about to do is similar to that of the miracle in chapter 3, but the event foretold was negative. This reminds us that, though we live in a time of gospel-preaching, the Lord is coming to judgment.

Rejoicing that they were counted worthy
to suffer shame for his name.

—ACTS 5:41

In Genesis 3:15, we read of two seeds. The Redeemer and the redeemed are the seed of the woman and those who serve the devil are the seed of the serpent. Christ triumphs over Satan and makes His own people more than conquerors. The devil sought to obliterate both the church and the promise of the Savior, given within it in the Old Testament, and hated Christ all through His earthly life and ministry. He continues to oppose the seed of the woman and to "make war with the remnant of her seed, which keep the commandments of God, and have the testimony of Jesus Christ" (Rev. 12:17). The victory of God's people is sure (Rom. 16:20).

In this passage in Acts, we have many of the features of the conflict highlighted. The indignation of the high priest and Sadducees (v. 17) at the healing of the sick and afflicted, the challenge to their prestigious and cozy grip on power and influence, their continued preoccupation with self-interest in the face of the miraculous deliverance of the apostles from prison (v. 24), and their continued unreasonable opposition scarcely held in check by Gamaliel's counsel (v. 40)—these things bear all the hallmarks of the enmity of the unrenewed heart to the truth of God. All pretence of reasonableness soon evaporates when the truth of God begins to strike home. "They were cut to the heart" (v. 33).

In stark contrast stands the boldness of the apostles. They defied earthly rulers when they were commanded by them to disobey God (v. 29). Peter took up the high priest's comment about bringing Christ's blood upon them and openly affirmed their guilt—"whom ye slew and hanged on a tree" (v. 30). After their beating and release, the apostles carried on with their ministry (v. 42). One fears that in too many of our church circles, such men would be labeled "extreme" and "unwise." There is, of course, an unbiblical rashness to be avoided, but that is quite different from an inordinate desire for a quiet life and a respectable image.

In devotion to Christ, in careful following of His Word, and in biblically governed zeal for His glory and royal prerogatives, let us be extremists! Can we really be too biblical? And if trouble comes as a result, let us seek such a high view of our Master in heaven that we, too, will rejoice at being counted worthy to suffer shame for His name!

Men of honest report, full of the Holy Ghost and wisdom.
—ACTS 6:3

Christ was adding to the church, judging within the church, and giving boldness to the ministers of His Word. He was also caring for the government of His church.

The office of elder is not specifically introduced in Acts, but merely appears. It needed no special introduction, since it was already known in the church of the Old Testament. Israel had elders for centuries and they were still present in the synagogues and Sanhedrin. The office of deacon, however, was new. The word "deacon" (*diakonos*) is not used here as elsewhere (Phil. 1:1, 1 Tim. 3:8), but the word "ministration" (v. 1) is a translation of the Greek word *diakonia*, and the verb form (*diakono*) is rendered "serve" in verse 2. Also, the word "tables" (v. 2) is *trapeza*—the same word rendered "bank" in Luke 19:23 and used of moneychangers' tables in Matthew 21:12 and John 2:15. This is definitely giving us the origin of the office of deacon, and they were to be men, not women (the word translated "men" in v. 3 is the word meaning male as opposed to female, not another word that speaks of mankind as opposed to animals, etc.). It is also clear that they were to look after the material affairs of the church.

They were not, however, merely to be efficient accountants. They were to be godly men—men who would look after church finance with zeal for Christ's glory and compassion toward others. One of these men, Philip, went on to be an evangelist (Acts 21:8) and was mightily used of God. Nevertheless, at this stage, he was content to be a deacon in the church. Godly people will be content with the role to which the Lord calls them, whether prominent before men or not. "I had rather be a doorkeeper in the house of my God, than to dwell in the tents of wickedness" (Ps. 84:10).

The offices Christ has appointed in the church show His care for His church, and we should not be impatient with biblical church order. Such impatience shows disbelief of the Lord's wisdom and love in appointing a form of church government in His Word. The Christian who unnecessarily "floats" from church to church without committing himself to any church that is biblical in doctrine, worship, and government, far from being spiritually minded, proudly imagines that he does not need what Christ has appointed. Let it not be true of us.

The patriarchs, moved with envy, sold Joseph
into Egypt: but God was with him.

—ACTS 7:9

The charge against Stephen was that he had insisted that there was to be divinely authorized change: "that this Jesus of Nazareth shall destroy this place, and shall change the customs which Moses delivered us" (Acts 6:14). Stephen's defense, far from being an incoherent ramble as some liberals claim, is a superb summary and application of Old Testament church history—we say "church history" advisedly, for such it was as we can see later on when Israel is called "the church in the wilderness" (v. 38).

We consider two things that Stephen brings out for the moment. First of all, he shows that God had never irrevocably tied Himself to one place. God had appeared to Abraham in Mesopotamia. He promised that Abraham's seed would inherit the land of Canaan, but only after four hundred years in a strange land; yet God was with Joseph in that land of Egypt and brought the house of Jacob there. Moses lived in Egypt and Midian before the great work of the Exodus. Israel was forty years in the wilderness and later was captive in Babylon. Even their place in the Promised Land was not automatic. "They could not enter in because of unbelief" (Heb. 3:19).

Secondly, Stephen shows that as God unfolded His revelation, there were changes in the form of worship that He authorized. When God gave His law at Sinai the tabernacle was set up, to be replaced by the temple in Solomon's time. But this, too, could only be symbolic and temporary (vv. 48–50).

In this case, the unwillingness to change was due to rejection of Christ and the final phase and climax of God's revelation in His coming into the world. All along, their "worship," even in those things that were outwardly scriptural, was being performed merely because of tradition and as part of their imaginary self-righteousness. When they were confronted with the Savior, of whom the Law and the prophets spoke, they despised Him.

If you are a churchgoer, why do you go and why do you do what you do when there? If we are true believers, who are redeemed by Christ's blood, surely we will go not just because we have always done so, but because we love Him who first loved us and desire consciously to worship Him exactly as He has appointed for His glory and our good—"to behold the beauty of the LORD" (Ps. 27:4).

Lord Jesus, receive my spirit.
—ACTS 7:59

James Guthrie, the Scottish martyr hanged for the gospel's sake in 1661, was known as "Sickerfoot" (Sure of Foot). He was once asked by a friend, "Will ye nae jouk (duck) a wee bit?" To this Guthrie replied, "There is nae jouking in the cause of Christ!" He had the Spirit of Christ in him as had Stephen centuries earlier.

Stephen, as we have seen, has shown that as God's revelation to the Old Testament church progressed, there were changes in the place and form of worship appointed by God. He also demonstrates, however, that the Old Testament history is one of repeated rejection of the truth of God. Joseph had been rejected by his brethren and Moses by the people. Idolatry was a recurring feature among the people who were to be holy to the Lord. Against this background, Stephen confronts the council with the fact that they are following in the footsteps not of the heroes of the faith, but the unbelieving covenant-breakers among their forefathers. They had the sign of the covenant (circumcision), but not the reality. They were still in their sins and had unrepentant hearts that would not receive the truth (vv. 51–53). His boldness is truly astonishing!

The fury of the enemy was unleashed. Stephen saw Christ at the right hand of God. It was not the will of the sovereign Savior to rescue Stephen from his enemies—though He could send legions of angels to do so if He pleased. Rather, He sustained His servant through the suffering to death and glory. Stephen did not ask to be delivered, but to be received into glory. The glory of Christ was enough to make him ready to leave this world behind. We cling inordinately to this present life because we have seen so little of His beauty. Oh, that it were more true of us what Samuel Rutherford has said: "Since He looked upon me, my heart is not mine own; He hath run away to Heaven with it."

If we are believers, our faithful Savior is able to be our comfort in life and in death. "For whether we live, we live unto the Lord; and whether we die, we die unto the Lord: whether we live therefore, or die, we are the Lord's" (Rom. 14:8).

Devout men…made great lamentation over him.
—ACTS 8:2

No doubt these devout men felt not only great personal sorrow, but also a great sense of loss to the church. Stephen had been so fearless in the cause of truth and so powerful in reasoning from the Scriptures! But the Lord is dependent on no man. We must see the wisdom of God in bringing so much good out of this evil! When godly men die, the Lord does not. When Jonathan Edwards, so greatly used of God in eighteenth-century New England, was on his deathbed and those around him (thinking him unconscious) began to lament the great loss to the church of God, he rallied to give one last sentence: "Trust in God, and ye need not fear."

"Saul was consenting to his death" (v. 1). Who would have thought this young man was one of God's elect? How foolish we are to try to guess! Spread the Word of God even among those who, to us, appear very unpromising candidates—there is a sovereign God in heaven! "In the morning sow thy seed, and in the evening withhold not thine hand: for thou knowest not whether shall prosper, either this or that, or whether they both shall be alike good" (Eccl. 11:6). The future apostle to the Gentiles was among the persecutors.

This was not all. Despite the "havoc" (v. 3) Saul caused, the Word of God was not bound. Believers went everywhere "preaching the word" (v. 4)—not the term normally used for public heralding by ministers, but simply "evangelizing." They spoke of what they knew. Philip, however, is said to have preached or heralded forth the Word to the Samaritans. The Lord blessed both the public preaching of His ministers and the general testimony of His people as a whole. Christ's church was not extinguished by Saul of Tarsus.

Samaria! How could the Word prosper in such a place? But had not the Lord Jesus said that His disciples would be witnesses in "Jerusalem, and in all Judea, and in Samaria, and unto the uttermost parts of the earth" (Acts 1:8)? Next, we have the Ethiopian eunuch. A chapter that begins with lamentation ends with the church expanding. "O the depth of the riches both of the wisdom and knowledge of God!" (Rom. 11:33). Pray to the God who sits upon the throne for your neighbors and for the preaching of the gospel among all nations. "And let the whole earth be filled with his glory; Amen, and Amen" (Ps. 72:19).

Saul, Saul, why persecutest thou me?
—ACTS 9:4

The Lord Jesus takes it very personally when men afflict His people. This is true even of neglect. "Inasmuch as ye did it not unto one of the least of these, ye did it not unto me" (Matt. 25:45). How much more does He notice when men actually seek to harm them. How we ought to love other Christians when we consider Christ's love for them! "But when ye so sin against the brethren…ye sin against Christ" (1 Cor. 8:12). How we should delight in Christ reflected in them—"the saints that are in the earth…the excellent, in whom is all my delight" (Ps. 16:3). As surely as the world has a distinctive hatred for God's people, so ought believers to have a distinctive love for the rest of the household of faith.

But Saul of Tarsus would only afflict the church for the Lord's appointed length of time for their good. They suffered "a while" (1 Pet. 5:10). All our trials are measured by our all-wise God. Sometimes the Lord ends the more intense affliction of His people by judging His and their enemies, as when He judged Pharaoh and the Egyptians at the Red Sea or King Belshazzar of Babylon. It was otherwise here. He brought Saul out of darkness into His marvelous light—the light of the gospel. "Then had the churches rest throughout all Judea and Galilee and Samaria, and were edified" (v. 31).

Saul's conversion to Christ shows the power of God and the sovereignty of His grace. The change wrought in him by the Holy Spirit was the fruit of God's eternal, electing love in Christ. It shows us that God's choice of the heirs of salvation is certainly not earned or merited in any way. "Howbeit for this cause I obtained mercy, that in me first Jesus Christ might show forth all longsuffering, for a pattern to them which should hereafter believe on him to life everlasting" (1 Tim. 1:16). What an encouragement to sinners ready to despair that their sins are beyond the grace of God—it is not so! He saves great sinners. And struggling believers, remember that He began the work in us and He will carry it through. As John Owen has written, "A river continually fed by a living fountain may as soon end its streams before it come to the ocean, as a stop be put to the course and progress of grace before it issue in glory."

On the Gentiles also was poured out the gift of the Holy Ghost.
—ACTS 10:45

Christ had said He would baptize with the Holy Ghost (Acts 1:5). So the Holy Spirit was "poured out" on the day of Pentecost (Acts 2:17). Some of the Samaritans (who had practiced a religion that was a corrupt mixture of Old Testament and pagan ideas) had been converted to Christ, and the Holy Spirit had "fallen upon" them (Acts 8:16). And now that same gift of the Holy Ghost is poured out upon these Gentile believers. The Samaritan and this Gentile sequel to Pentecost were demonstrations of the fact that the blessings of the Holy Spirit, including that distinct once-for-all baptism of the Holy Spirit signaling that the New Testament age of the exalted Christ was the age of the Holy Spirit in abundance, belonged equally to all sections of the church: Jew, Samaritan, and Gentile.

Peter, realizing this, declares that these Gentile believers must be treated fully as part of the church of Christ by being baptized. For whatever reason, he had been only an adherent of the synagogue and of the Old Testament church but this must not continue; Cornelius must be fully a member of the church now in its continuing New Testament phase. The church is international!

God is "no respecter of persons" (v. 34) and the church will ultimately be "a great multitude, which no man could number, of all nations, and kindreds, and people, and tongues, [standing] before the throne and the Lamb, clothed with white robes, and palms in their hands" (Rev. 7:9). The God of heaven sent the vision to Cornelius and the vision to Peter to coincide and so bring us the message that "in every nation he that feareth him, and worketh righteousness, is accepted with him" (v. 35).

Whatever kind of sinner you are, the Lord receives all sinners who come to Him in His appointed way: through faith in Jesus Christ. Jonathan Edwards affirms: "If persons thus come to God for mercy, the greatness of their sins will be no impediment to pardon. Let their sins be ever so many, and great, and aggravated, it will not make God in the least degree backward to pardon them.... Pardon is as much offered and promised to the greatest sinners as any, if they will come aright to God for mercy." This is good news. "The LORD is nigh unto all that call upon him, to all that call upon him in truth" (Ps. 145:18).

Who, when he came, and had seen the grace of God, was glad.

—ACTS 11:23

Why was Barnabas glad when he saw God's grace to sinners in Antioch? "For he was a good man, and full of the Holy Ghost and of faith" (v. 24). The truly godly, who know that their own salvation is all of God's grace in Christ, rejoice when they see that grace shown to others. They love God and their neighbor and therefore rejoice in the glory of God's grace being displayed and in the happiness and eternal good of their neighbor.

Self-righteous Pharisees cannot rejoice in God's grace to others. The elder brother could not rejoice in the gracious reception of the prodigal (Luke 15:28–29). He did not see himself as in need of grace—kindness to the undeserving or ill-deserving—and resented it being shown to anyone else, as it obliterated the distinction of his own superiority. Barnabas was an outstanding example of what is true of all who are indwelt by the Spirit of God and who therefore have faith in our Lord Jesus Christ.

It is the mark of a true believer that, although sometimes such can be doctrinally confused, they will always want to ascribe the whole of their salvation to God. "My soul shall make her boast in the LORD" (Ps. 34:2). "But God forbid that I should glory, save in the cross of our Lord Jesus Christ" (Gal. 6:14). The renewed heart has a God-glorifying disposition within it. "Not unto us, O LORD, not unto us, but unto thy name give glory, for thy mercy, and for thy truth's sake" (Ps. 115:1).

By natural disposition, it is quite the reverse. The desire to be "as gods" (Gen. 3:5) is so strong that, without being born again of the Holy Spirit, we cling to the idea of at least independently contributing something to our own salvation. This is part of the appeal of false religion to the heart of sinful man: a wrong view of God and a correspondingly wrong view of salvation, one which still leaves the pride of man intact. The saved sinner, however, says gladly that salvation is of the Lord and he loves the way God saves through the crucified Redeemer and the glory of God displayed in it. "Let such as love thy salvation say continually, Let God be magnified" (Ps. 70:4).

The angel of the Lord smote him.
—ACTS 12:23

How unfathomable are the ways of God! Herod killed James, but the Lord preserved Peter and judged Herod. How powerful also is the grace of God in the souls of His people! Peter could sleep in prison the night before he was due to be brought forth, and he had to be rather roughly awakened (v. 7). "So he giveth his beloved sleep" (Ps. 127:2).

But what was it that brought this outstanding divine judgment upon Herod? He was certainly a very wicked man in a multitude of ways, but what is specifically mentioned is that, when he gave his oration, "he gave not God the glory" (v. 23). That which makes all sin so sinful is the failure to treat God as God.

Few have the opportunity for self-glorification that Herod had. We do it in a more mundane fashion. We do our own thing in so many ways. Instead of fulfilling our chief end, which is to glorify God and enjoy Him forever, we defy His right to tell us how to act, speak, and think. This begins with pretending God is not really as He says. If we faced up to God as being the holy, sin-hating, and sin-punishing God that He really is, we would be truly alarmed at what this means for us: we are guilty before God. But we smother such thoughts with false ideas about God to convince ourselves that all is well. Then, we set up our own standards of right and wrong. We assume the role of lawgiver, which properly belongs to God. We do not give Him the glory! Having set up a false god in our minds, we set up false standards to go with them. Christ condemns lustful thoughts (Matt. 5:27–28), for example, but we excuse it. We set the test and tell ourselves we have passed.

But perhaps God has changed you from what you are by nature. How can we tell? Have you been brought heartily to accept that God is as He says He is? And that His law is the only real standard of right and wrong and that we are guilty and hell-deserving? Have you been brought to wholehearted dependence upon Christ, the sin-bearing Substitute of sinners, for acceptance with God? Do you see that God is right to be as He is, to require what He requires, and to save the way He saves through Christ alone? Have you begun to "glory in the Lord" (1 Cor. 1:31)?

Lo, we turn to the Gentiles.

—ACTS 13:46

Apparent openness to the gospel can turn sour. The Jews at Antioch in Pisidia seemed ready to listen at first, but when their prestige and position were in danger of being eclipsed, their unregenerate hearts broke out into open opposition to the gospel (v. 45). Men can seem unperturbed by the gospel until some treasured sin seems under threat and then they show their true colors. The gospel was "to the Jew first" (Rom. 1:16). They had been the visible church of God in the Old Testament, but the situation was changing. "Therefore I say unto you, the kingdom of God shall be taken from you, and given to a nation bringing forth the fruits thereof" (Matt. 21:43).

Even their outward position was to be taken away from them. Certainly, they continued to "play church," clinging on to the redundant signs of circumcision and Passover and rejecting the divine replacements of baptism and the Lord's Supper. They adhered to the Sanhedrin, despising the apostles and elders of the continuing church of God.

But many of the Gentiles listened and believed. Why? "As many as were ordained to eternal life believed." (v. 48). The Word was sent to all—"to you is the word of this salvation sent" (v. 26). Only some, however, were chosen from eternity to be the heirs of salvation, and therefore believed. If we have believed, thank God for His grace! Apart from His electing love and effectual call, we would still be lovers of darkness.

But the evidence of this saving grace is not mere church attendance. The Jews attended the synagogue and had, hitherto, been part of the outward membership of the church of God. As the message of the risen Christ was preached among them, however, their true state became all too obvious. It is right to attend the "means of grace," especially the preaching of the Word, but we must not trust in those means. "Means must be neither trusted nor neglected" says John Trapp, but we must use them to see Christ the Savior as the true object of our faith and trust. William Secker echoes this advice, when he says, "Neither be idle in the means, nor make an idol of the means." Are you a churchgoer and no more, or a believer in the Lord Jesus Christ? Is He all your salvation and all your desire?

But the multitude of the city was divided.
—ACTS 14:4

"Doctrine divides" is the complaint of many. But the question should be whether particular doctrines are true according to the Scriptures. A gospel that is doctrine-free is without content and is no gospel at all. The conversion of the Romans to Christ is described as "obeying from the heart the form of doctrine which was delivered unto you" (Rom. 6:17). The gospel is doctrinal, but truth does divide. Since the fall of man into sin, mankind has been divided into two: those who are born again of the Spirit of God respond to the truth while others resent it. The first death recorded in Scripture when Cain killed Abel was not only a murder, but martyrdom for the truth's sake.

Noticeably, those who were most zealous against the truth were the unbelieving Jews who "stirred up the Gentiles, and made their minds evil affected against the brethren" (v. 2). The more pride invested in false religious self-righteousness, the more venomous the enmity to the truth.

It is said that "part held with the Jews, and part held with the apostles." The Jews were those leaders who rejected Christ and remained part of that body which was no longer to be the true church of God on earth. The apostles led the continuing church of the Lord. The unbelieving "natural branches" (Rom. 11:17–25) were being broken off while Gentile "wild branches" were being grafted into the continuing olive tree of the professing church of God made up, as always, of those who "profess the true religion, together with their children" (*Westminster Confession*, 25:2).

The transition from the Old Testament phase of the church to the New reached its completion with the destruction of Jerusalem in A.D. 70 foretold by Christ. Godly Jews who lived through the period of Christ's earthly life continued, along with their children, within the church as they abandoned the unbelieving Israelite Sanhedrin and eldership and followed the apostles and embraced the replacement sacraments of the New Testament.

Sometimes, however, the division between those who love the truth and those who do not remains below the surface within the outward form of the church. There are those whose consciences will not allow them to deny the truth in which they have been nurtured since they were born, but they don't love the truth as it is in Jesus. I hope that you are not one of these.

> *For it seemed good to the Holy Ghost, and to us....*
> —ACTS 15:28

On May 6, 1646, the Westminster Assembly of Divines, which produced the Westminster Confession of Faith and Catechisms, met for a "day of humiliation." One member preached, Dr. John Arrowsmith. In his sermon on Isaiah 9:6, he sought to guide the members as to their duty in the Assembly with these points recorded in the minutes: "1) Take heed of voting against light. 2) Take heed of voting without light; let every man be fully persuaded. 3) Take heed of refusing to bring thy judgment to light by thy vote." John Murray comments, "These words might well be inscribed on the portals of every ecclesiastical assembly. The history of the church would have been different if they had been jealously observed by the courts of Christ's church."

This attitude prevailed centuries earlier in the council of Jerusalem, whose proceedings are recorded in this chapter. The problem in the church at Antioch was a serious one. Behind the question of the terms of Gentile admission to the church was the fundamental doctrine of salvation by grace alone through faith alone in Christ alone. The apostles and elders did what all church officers should do. They listened to God's Word. God had given a revelation to Peter, recorded in chapter 10, and Peter refers to this in verses 7–11 of our chapter. James appeals to the Old Testament, quoting from Amos 9:11–12 and applying it to the reviving and expansion of the church of Christ, not to a literal raising up of the temple or rebuilding of the temple (vv. 13–18).

The decision made had the approval of the Holy Spirit and imposed only "necessary things." These were, first, avoidance of things sinful in themselves, to which the Gentiles were prone, such as fornication; and second, practices not essentially sinful but which, when used in a manner that stumbled the consciences of other brethren, became sinful as contrary to love to our neighbor. Such careful decision-making reflects submission to Christ's kingship over His own church and results in the strengthening of the churches as the sequel shows (Acts 16:4–5). Such pastoral care in the government of the flock of God should meet with the acceptance of all who love Christ and unite His true sheep in the things He Himself has appointed.

Whose heart the Lord opened.
—ACTS 16:14

What must I do to be saved?
—ACTS 16:30

The experiences of the elect of God in being brought to faith in the Lord Jesus Christ vary widely. John Bunyan, the author of *Pilgrim's Progress*, suffered prolonged and severe conviction of sin before coming to a settled assurance of forgiveness in Christ. John Newton, the slave-trader, on the other hand, had only a mild sense of sin prior to his conversion to Christ though much more awareness of sin came afterwards. It seems that Lydia also had a much gentler experience of conversion than the Philippian jailor. Sometimes Christians can struggle with assurance of salvation. One cause can be that their experience does not match up to that of some worthy of the past of whose experience they have read or heard. This makes them ask, "Am I converted at all?"

God's providence brought Lydia under the sound of the gospel. C. H. Spurgeon says, "I wot it never entered into Lydia's heart, when she left Thyatira with her purple bales, that she was going to find Jesus Christ over at Philippi; neither did Paul guess, when he saw, in a vision, a man of Macedonia, and heard him say, 'Come over into Macedonia, and help us,' that the first person he would have to help would not be a man of Macedonia at all, but a woman of Thyatira."

God's providence brought the gospel to the jailor also, and even shook him to the core. He was ready to kill himself when he thought the prisoners had fled. But when reassured that this concern was unfounded, a deeper question remained: "What must I do to be saved?" Temporal trouble does not always lead to this question. The keepers who were terrified by the angel at the tomb of Christ soon went back to their ways when the fear had passed (Matt. 28:4, 15). But the Holy Spirit was working mightily in this man in the midst of all these God-ordained circumstances.

But what of our earlier question? Though Christ is offered to all sinners, what conviction of sin is necessary before anyone ever truly comes to Christ? The answer is, "As much conviction as causes him to give up all hope except in Christ." We must say, "There is no hope except in the Savior" (see Isa. 57:10).

God... now commandeth all men every where to repent.
—ACTS 17:30

At Thessalonica, the Jews accused Paul and Silas of preaching "another king, one Jesus" (v. 7). Pilate had once heard of this kingship and shrugged his shoulders and walked away (John 18:37–38). He had used it to mock the Jews, "Behold your king" (John 19:14). He had insisted on including it in the superscription on the cross (John 19:19–22). But here, this matter of kingship still hasn't gone away. Once more, the Jews are forced to pose as defenders of the kingship of Caesar in order to oppose the kingship of Jesus Christ.

After going to Berea, Paul comes to Athens and preaches to the thinkers of Mars hill. Much is often made, perhaps too much, of the fact that he begins "where they are," with their altar to the unknown God. He very quickly moves to where they needed to be—hearing of the risen Savior who would judge the world. God commands these men, and all men, to repent—to turn from sin to the Lord Jesus Christ. There can be no trusting in Jesus Christ and dependence upon Him for acceptance with God without turning from the proud desire to be as gods and especially to be the god of our own salvation. No one can have Christ as his Savior without also bowing the knee to Him as Lord. Unregenerate men dream of happiness in the world to come, without turning from sin in the present. This cannot be. "Except ye repent, ye shall all likewise perish" (Luke 13:3). Repentance does not merit acceptance before God, but it is the invariable accompaniment of faith in Christ and acceptance on account of His merits. Christ governs all by His power in providence, but in His kingdom of grace, He brings sinners into willing subjection through the gospel.

The issue of Christ's kingship never will disappear. God will judge by Jesus Christ. The Father "hath given him authority to execute judgment also, because he is the Son of man" (John 5:27). As the Incarnate Mediator and King, all enemies shall be put under His feet. The redeemed willingly bow to Him, imperfectly in this world and fully in the next. The rest will be brought into subjection under His wrath. Every knee shall bow (Phil. 2:10). Blessed are all they that trust in Him!

For I have much people in this city.
—ACTS 18:10

We often imagine that we know the kind of circumstances in which God will work the conversion of sinners. This is one of many ways in which, in our pride, we overreach ourselves. The ministry of the apostle Paul in Corinth shows how foolish such guesswork is. Paul had not received a very encouraging response in Athens. He came to Corinth and faced the hostility of the Jews. He then began separate meetings right next door to the synagogue. Imagine if a minister did that today! One can almost hear the howls of condemnation: "How insensitive!" "How provocative and, indeed, unloving!" But the apostle evangelized head on. And the Lord appeared to him in a night vision. To do what? Tell him to go easy and soft peddle a bit for a while? No, he is to preach boldly. He would be kept safe because the Lord had many for whom He died in that place, having been chosen of God the Father in eternity and given to the Son to redeem, who were now about to be effectually drawn to Christ. Then, amidst circumstances that were anything but tranquil over the next eighteen months, sinners were converted to Christ in pagan Corinth and a church was established.

Later in the chapter, we read of those in Achaia (of which Corinth was the main city) who had "believed through grace" (v. 27). Believing is a human activity, but it is one that is only performed by the grace of God—when the Holy Spirit gives not only understanding but also a willing heart that desires Christ. As the late Rev. Jacob Tamminga put it, "It is the same Spirit who not only makes me to know my sin, but who shows me also the gospel, and who opens in the gospel the promises of God, who leads me to the High Priest who has brought the sacrifices and burnt offering.... It is the same Spirit who reveals the King, who breaks the bonds of sin and delivers us out of the chains of Satan. How then the heart learns to love the salvation of the Lord!"

The Lord who sent Paul to plant also sent Apollos to water in Corinth (1 Cor. 3:6). Apollos "helped them much" (v. 27). The Lord was building His church and providing the ministry of the Word for it. The believers had tasted that the Lord is good and desired more of His truth.

So mightily grew the word of God and prevailed.
—ACTS 19:20

When Paul came to Ephesus, he was the means of bringing some disciples into the full privileges of the church in its New Testament phase. They received New Testament baptism as instituted by Christ after His resurrection (Matt. 28:19–20), which differed from the Old Testament ordinance administered by John the Baptist. They also received that greater abundance of the Holy Spirit that was to be the norm of all God's people in the New Testament period (1 Cor. 12:13). For these disciples who straddled the transition from the Old to the New Testament age, however, it was a distinct experience.

The apostle was not only to be the means of helping forward the existing believers, but also of heralding the gospel to pagan multitudes. The effect was twofold—many conversions and raging opposition. The verse above describes the first of these effects. By the power of God, the Word of God increased in its influence over the hearts of men. It was not some mindless experience; the Word was preached, understood, believed, and acted upon. They trusted in the Christ of God preached to them, repented of their sins, and brought forth the fruits of repentance—some even publicly burnt their books of magical arts (vv. 18–19). This is what happens when the Lord causes His Word to prevail and sinners bow the knee to Christ in the gospel. Has that Word prevailed in us and does it continue to prevail in us? Are our hearts tender toward the Word of the Lord? We need the Holy Spirit to work in us to become believers and we need the continuing work of the Holy Spirit in us daily to more and more bring our hearts and lives into subjection to the Word as we "grow in grace, and in the knowledge of our Lord and Saviour Jesus Christ" (2 Pet. 3:18).

As the Word prevailed among many, so it also provoked fury among others. "The election hath obtained it, and the rest were blinded" (Rom. 11:7). The greed-fueled ferment for the goddess Diana was orchestrated by Demetrius and his colleagues. Covetousness justified by false religious zeal is a potent force. Add to the mix some local pride (vv. 27–28), and it is not surprising that such a prolonged frenzy ensued. But the Lord's work in building His church in this place could not be undone. The gates of hell could not prevail.

Take heed therefore unto yourselves, and to all the flock....
—ACTS 20:28

The people of God at Troas assembled on the first day of the week, not the seventh (vv. 5–6), because the creation ordinance of a weekly Sabbath made for man—as a blessing and for his good—was now to be observed on the day of the week that Christ arose from the dead and appeared several times to His disciples before visibly ascending to glory (1 Cor. 16:1–2; Rev. 1:10).

Paul was accompanied by seven men (v. 4) who were possibly representing the various Gentile churches who had contributed money to relieve the church at Jerusalem. The apostle was deeply concerned that this help should be both given and received to express the oneness of the whole body of Christ, both Jew and Gentile (2 Cor. 8:1–5, 9:1–15; Rom. 15:25–28).

As he proceeds toward Jerusalem, he calls the elders of the Ephesian church to meet him at Miletus. In verse 28, he calls them "overseers" (*episkopos*), the word translated "bishop" in 1 Timothy 3:1, Titus 1:7, and Philippians 1:1, since elders and bishops describe the same office.

Paul's concern for the unity of the church was coupled with an ardent desire that the church should be soundly established in true doctrine, as his address to these elders clearly shows. Without the truth of the gospel being maintained, any supposed unity is a mere façade. That for which men will shed tears can be a strong indicator of what matters most deeply to them. Paul had shed many tears of concern for the Ephesian church (v. 31). Do you ever shed tears other than for yourself and those close to you by natural ties? Is Zion's cause dear to you? Does the church's living testimony to the truth of God matter immensely to you?

Heresy could arise from within (v. 30)—would the elders put truth first and personal ties of relatives or friendship second? Would they be so spiritually healthy as to treat false doctrine as poison that would be deadly for the flock of God? They needed to be taking heed to themselves now, as well as the flock, to not be found wanting in any future crisis. Heresy makes headway when doctrinally orthodox men are spiritually stagnant and thus become tolerant of that which should cause them alarm and stir them to resolute action.

OCTOBER 24

What mean ye to weep and to break mine heart? For I am ready not to be bound only, but also to die at Jerusalem for the name of the Lord Jesus.

—ACTS 21:13

To leave this world through death, it is necessary that we be assured of our being in Christ and that we have such a sense of the excellence of Christ and of going to be with Him, that any sense of loss of present enjoyments is thoroughly outweighed by the anticipation of the joys of the world to come.

Those whom we love in this world can disappoint us or else be removed from us. If not, we will in due time be removed from them by death. If they and we ourselves are believers in the Lord Jesus, this separation will be only temporary, but nevertheless real and potentially very painful. The thought of never again being together in this life can cause great anguish, even for God's people. "Friends are a great mercy, but they are not a sure mercy," said Joseph Caryl.

The apostle Paul has been represented by enemies of the truth as an unfeeling autocrat. That this is nonsense is evident from the sorrow of the Ephesian elders in the previous chapter (Acts 20:36–38). They sorrowed at the thought of not seeing him again! Likewise, at Caesarea in the verse quoted above, his friends and fellow believers wept as they pleaded with him not to endanger his life by going to Jerusalem. Far from being unmoved by this, his heart was ready to break. But he loved Christ above all and desired the presence and fellowship of Christ above all. He had tasted and seen that the Lord is good. We need much of fellowship with Christ on earth. We cannot have too much of this true heavenly mindedness. Then the prospect of severing all earthly ties will be swallowed up by the prospect of perfecting that fellowship we have already known in its sweetness. The break with people and scenes so dear to us will lose its wrenching distress. We will be convinced that "to die is gain" (Phil. 1:21). "To know the love of Christ, which passeth knowledge, that ye might be filled with all the fullness of God" (Eph. 3:19).

324

It is not fit that he should live.
—ACTS 22:22

Efforts to avoid unnecessary offense will not save us from causing necessary offense. Paul used great skill in speaking to the Jews in Jerusalem. He spoke in Hebrew, and assured them he was a Jew and understood their position, having been trained even under the famous Gamaliel. He had thought himself on the right track and that those who professed Jesus of Nazareth "this way" (v. 4) were heretics deserving punishment. He stresses the role of Ananias, a respected Jew, whom he reports as speaking of "the God of our fathers" (vv. 12–14). In relating not only his conversion, but also his call to be an apostle of Christ, he stresses his own past guilt, even in the death of Stephen. The outcome is that they cry out for his blood as one not fit to be left alive on the face of the earth.

Let us not think that if only we get the "seeker sensitive" package worked out, no one will take offense. Christ went about doing good, but He was crucified and slain. The disciple is not above his master. We must be ready to bear the reproach of Christ. His gospel is offensive to fallen man. Indeed, because it is the truth and the message that most consistently contradicts the pride of man, it is the most offensive message there could be. Let us not be discouraged then, if offense is taken to our loyalty to Christ and testimony to His truth; it does not have to mean we did it all wrong.

Now Paul is set on course for a series of court appearances that would lead him, via much travel and a shipwreck, to Rome. Most of us struggle with delays. We want difficult things over and done with, so that we can get back to "normal." It was not to be like that for Paul. He was to exercise his ministry for Christ amidst all the uncertainties of being "the prisoner of the Lord." He preached, wrote epistles to churches, and prayed without ceasing while a prisoner. The care of all the churches was upon him still. We must not postpone some aspect of our service to Christ because our circumstances seem less settled than we would like. Ministers must preach the Word fully, often in circumstances that do not seem ideal. John Brown of Haddington on his deathbed entreated his son, "Labor, labor for Christ while ye have strength."

Certain of the Jews banded together, and bound themselves under a curse, saying that they would neither eat nor drink till they had killed Paul.

—ACTS 23:12

The presumption of these men was extreme. What they purposed was wicked. Their assumption of being able to carry it out, as if God had promised success to their wickedness, even within the length of time they could deprive themselves of food and drink, is astonishing. Did these religious men have God in all their thoughts? Had they planned to do good, they had no right to assume success, for "except the LORD build the house, they labour in vain that build it" (Ps. 127:1). But did they expect the smile of heaven upon their iniquity? How wrong can men be? Very wrong indeed, is the answer. Our depravity of nature causes us to think that God is like ourselves, especially when His judgment does not fall speedily. "I kept silence; thou thoughtest I was altogether such an one as thyself" (Ps. 50:21).

The Lord did not give them their heart's desire. Paul's nephew and the captain of the guard were the means of Paul's safe transfer to Caesarea. "They imagined a mischievous device, which they are not able to perform" (Ps. 21:11). God does sometimes give short-term "success" to the plans of the ungodly, but on this occasion he did not. Paul was immortal until his work on earth was completed.

Not only must we not expect God to bless our sinful plans, but we must also recognize that, even with the good purposes of His children, God, in His infinite wisdom, may see fit to thwart our plans. David purposed to build a house unto the name of the Lord and was told "thou didst well that it was in thine heart" (1 Kings 8:18). Nevertheless, the house was to be built by Solomon instead. The only future things we know are those which have been revealed by God who knows the future because He has foreordained it all. God has revealed as much as it is good for us to know, otherwise we know nothing with certainty. "For ye know not what shall be on the morrow.... For that ye ought to say, If the Lord will, we shall live, and do this, or that" (James 4:14–15).

Felix trembled.
—ACTS 24:25

Heresy or development? Is the New Testament church an unwarranted departure from Old Testament religion or the true continuation of it? The Jews called Christianity a heresy (v. 14), but Paul shows it to be a result of God's unfolding of His revelation by speaking "in these last days by his Son" (Heb. 1:2) and that far from denying the Scriptures, he believed "all things which are written in the law and in the prophets." Later on, Felix heard Paul again "concerning the faith in Christ" (v. 24), perhaps because Drusila, his Jewish wife, wanted to hear more about this strange sect.

Paul spoke of righteousness and temperance—of God's standards and of the restrained and right way of responding to our physical appetites and desires. He also spoke of judgment to come, when God will vindicate His own standards, by punishing forever all unforgiven violation of those standards in thought, word, and deed. All of this was calculated to show Felix his need of the Savior of sinners, Jesus Christ. He trembled, but did he change? He was concerned, but did he turn to the Lord? His conscience was troubled, but did he learn to hate sin and not just fear the consequences of it? He felt a sense of guilt, but did he seek the Savior of the guilty? No, he did not. His love of money was not changed as he still hoped for a bribe from Paul (v. 26). He kept the Jews quiet by keeping Paul under house-arrest. Then he passed on the "problem" to Festus, his successor in office. No doubt his sense of sin subsided, but his guilt before God only increased.

In the Bible, Pharaoh, King Saul, and Judas all said, "I have sinned," but they did not turn from their sins to the Lord. David, like the prodigal son in the parable, also said, "I have sinned" and sought the Lord's mercy. "I said, I will confess my transgressions unto the LORD; and thou forgavest the iniquity of my sin" (Ps. 32:5). What about you? Are you convicted of your sin? Have you gone to the Lord with the one thing that is truly your own—your sin? Never mind "a more convenient season" (v. 25); it is time to seek the Lord. "Today if ye will hear his voice, harden not your heart" (Ps. 95:7–8).

To the Jews have I done no wrong, as thou very well knowest.
—ACTS 25:10

Paul was left a prisoner by Felix for two years (Acts 24:27). It has been thought that Felix's departure was because he had been summoned to Rome to answer complaints from the Jews and this explains his desire to "sweeten" them before he went. Festus stood his ground against the Jews, refusing their request that Paul be brought to Jerusalem for trial, hoping that they could kill him on the way there. Paul is able to defend himself against all charges, whether relating to Jewish law, profaning the temple, or Roman law (v. 8). But now Festus wants to keep the Jews happy (admittedly, always a problem for the Roman governors set over them), and he suggests a Jerusalem trial (v. 9) that would inevitably be to Paul's severe disadvantage. Paul appeals to Caesar which, as a Roman citizen, he was allowed to do in regard to most offenses. Festus, after checking the position, agrees (v. 12).

Agrippa and his sister Bernice arrive, probably to greet Festus as the new procurator of a neighboring province (v. 13). Festus puts a good complexion on his handling of the situation by suggesting that he had recommended a Jerusalem trial because the whole Sanhedrin might provide the necessary expertise in Jewish law to resolve the matter (v. 20). Since Paul had appealed to Caesar, however, he must send him but is embarrassed by the fact that he doesn't actually know what the charge is that is laid upon Paul.

The amazing thing is that, despite all this nonsense and injustice, we find Paul not bursting with frustration, but availing himself of every opportunity to make known the gospel. He was by no means indifferent to wrongdoing, but believed the truth of God's providence, that God governs all things, including the actions of sinful men, for His own glory and the good of His people and towards His own glorious foreordained end. If we are Christians, too often we still respond to God's providence like unbelievers, full of resentment as if we know better than the all-wise God. Thomas Watson aptly exhorts: "Remember God sees it is that which is fit for you, or it would not come. Your clothes cannot be so fit for you as your crosses. God's providence may sometimes be secret, but it is always wise."

I would to God, that not only thou, but also all that hear me this day, were both almost, and altogether such as I am, except these bonds.

—ACTS 26:29

Agrippa's words, "Almost thou persuadest me to be a Christian" (v. 28) have been much preached upon. Were they said in sarcasm? Probably not. They were certainly uttered by a man with no desire to change. For him, this was an academic matter of debate among the Jews. He had knowledge of the Scriptures (v. 3) and acknowledged their truthfulness (v. 27). Such things alone, however, do not guarantee salvation.

Paul's response provides a deep insight into the twin truths of God's sovereignty and man's responsibility. The apostle says, "I would to God," recognizing by this instant prayer that God alone can change a sinner's heart so that he desires Christ (Rom. 10:1). At the same time, he expresses his hearty desire for the conversion of Agrippa and all that were present. This desire is expressive of that Christian compassion that is a fruit of the work of the Holy Spirit in the heart. In connection with his countrymen, he speaks of this love as something that has the complete approval of the Holy Spirit (Rom. 9:1–3). Our belief in God's sovereign election need not, and indeed should not, dampen evangelistic compassion.

This love for our neighbor, as commanded in the law of God, expressing itself in a desire for their conversion and prayer for them (Matt. 5:44), is not only God-given, but reflects the love and kindness of God in this world. God has not decreed to save all men, but He does show His kindness to all in bestowing many benefits upon them which stop short of salvation. One such is His sending the gospel to them, even though He has decreed that only the elect will be saved through hearing it. Our love is to be patterned after His: "Be ye therefore perfect, even as your Father which is in heaven is perfect" (Matt. 5:48). He does not command us to love contrary to His own love. God shows no such love to the damned in hell and neither, therefore, will the redeemed in heaven be troubled for them. We cannot understand this in advance, nor do we need to. But let us, then, emulate Paul's indiscriminate evangelistic love in the sure knowledge that out of the midst of mankind, the elect of God, given by the Son to the Father, will surely come to Him.

I believe God.

—ACTS 27:25

What is immediately before our eyes does not tell us the mind of God. If we desire to know what we should do, we must look at God's precepts in Scripture. If we want to know what God will bring to pass, we must look to God's promises and prophesies in Scripture. As an apostle, however, Paul received revelation from the Lord by means of an angel. The angel told Paul two things: that he must appear before Caesar, and that the lives of all on the ship would be spared (v. 24). "Accidental death" is not outside the government of God. He controls who lives and who dies in any shipwreck or in any other accident or tragedy. When such things come, we may be utterly bewildered as to why a particular life was brought to an end in an apparently arbitrary way. Nevertheless, it is a comfort to bereaved believers to know that the ultimate cause is not "chance" or "luck," but our faithful God and Father in heaven. In this case, however, Paul was promised otherwise.

But God's providence can, for a time, seem to be going against His promises. Thomas Watson says, "God is to be trusted when his providences seem to run contrary to his promises.... God promised Paul the lives of all that were with him in the ship; but the providence of God seemed to run quite contrary to his promise, for the winds blew, the ship split and broke in pieces. Thus God fulfilled his promise; upon the broken pieces of the ship they all came safe to shore. Trust God when providences seem to run quite contrary to promises." God, in His providence, even restrained the soldiers from killing the prisoners, including Paul (vv. 42–43). What is also noticeable is Paul's boldness of speech in acknowledging the Lord throughout. He even "gave thanks to God in the presence of them all" (v. 35). We need such boldness! Too often, we settle for lowest common denominator speech with the world and end up conversing like atheists.

Above all, we must, unlike Eve in the Garden of Eden, believe God in all that He has said concerning this life and that which is to come. In the end, what else is there? "For I know whom I have believed, and am persuaded that he is able to keep that which I have committed unto him against that day" (2 Tim. 1:12).

Preaching the kingdom of God....
—ACTS 28:31

God preserved Paul from the viper (v. 5) as well as the seas. He had said he must testify at Rome (Acts 23:11), and so it must be. On the final journey to the capital of the empire, some of the brethren from Rome came to meet and accompany him. We read these touching words: "whom when Paul saw, he thanked God, and took courage" (v. 15). There is a fellowship among the heirs of the kingdom that the world does not understand—that immediate sense of a bond when one meets the Lord's people in the midst of an unbelieving world. Paul did not stand aloof from the joys of Christian fellowship, nor was he unwilling to openly acknowledge it as a blessing from God and a means of strengthening to him. It is a wrong kind of independence of man that makes us otherwise—one that comes from pride, not great faith.

In his dealings with his countrymen in Rome, Paul is both tactful and honest about what had happened at Jerusalem. He proclaims the Lord Jesus as Israel's promised Messiah, and this meets with considerable opposition. He declares them to be like the people of Isaiah's day who were under judicial blindness, and proclaims that the Gentiles will receive that gospel which they now despise. He then spent two years preaching to all who came to hear. His message was the kingdom of God and the things concerning the Lord Jesus Christ. These are two descriptions of the same thing. Christ is the King over all in His power, but His kingdom of grace is His bringing sinners into hearty subjection to Himself through the gospel.

Christians today are citizens of that kingdom too, and bear witness to that same message. The church's ministers are to publicly proclaim it also. If Paul was faithful even as a prisoner waiting in pagan Rome to appear before a wicked emperor, shall we not do what is in our power in the twenty-first century to uphold the name and honor of the Lord of Glory in the midst of this evil generation? Will you not risk your reputation and popularity for His name's sake? Be ashamed to be ashamed of Him! "For I am not ashamed of the gospel of Christ: for it is the power of God unto salvation to every one that believeth; to the Jew first, and also to the Greek" (Rom. 1:16).

MILK  HONEY

from Romans

BARTEL ELSHOUT

To all that be in Rome, beloved of God, called to be saints.
—ROMANS 1:7

What a profound description we have here of true believers! In fact, this is a compact outline of how Paul structures most of his epistles, setting before us both the status and obligations of the believer.

Paul tells believers in Rome that they are "beloved of God." What an extraordinary statement! In the not too distant past, these believers in Rome were as pagan in their hearts and lifestyle as the population surrounding them. However, as a result of divine and sovereign intervention (Eph. 2:1–2), they now belonged to those in whose hearts the love of God had been shed abroad (Rom. 5:5). They were the beloved of God purely because of His sovereign good pleasure; He loved them with an everlasting love (Jer. 31:3) because it pleased Him to choose them in Christ, the eternally beloved Son of God.

Dear believer, you too are God's beloved one because of *the* Beloved One, Jesus Christ. He gave Himself as a ransom in your place so that you could become the recipient of the eternal love with which the Father loves His Son (John 17:23)—a love that is eternal, unwavering, and infinite! There is but one reason why this is so: it pleased God!

No wonder that Paul adds that, in light of such a privilege, we are called to be saints, or holy ones. What a clear illustration that God's sovereignty defines our responsibility! Clearly, believers are redeemed in order to be a holy people unto the Lord. Later in this epistle, Paul tells us that we have been predestinated to be conformed to the image of God's Son (Rom. 8:29), of whom the Scriptures so often testify that He is the Holy One of God. And indeed, holiness is ultimately Christlikeness.

However, Paul not only implies that God has set us apart to become like His Son, but also that we are called to be Christlike—to be holy ones. This is what the Christian ought to be prayerfully striving for: to honor the Christ for whose sake alone I am the beloved of God.

Dear reader, is it also your yearning to be a saint? For that will always be the mark of the beloved of God!

> *Despisest thou the riches of his goodness and forbearance and longsuffer-*
> *ing; not knowing that the goodness of God leadeth thee to repentance?*
> —ROMANS 2:4

After having given a graphic description of the depravity of the human heart as it revealed itself in the Gentile world, Paul proceeds to focus on his own people, the Jews. Paul knew that they would be inclined to condemn the Gentiles for their wickedness, viewing themselves as being morally superior. In this chapter, it is Paul's intent to prove to the Jews that they are equally guilty before God, ultimately arriving at the conclusion that "there is none righteous, no, not one" (Rom. 3:10).

In the context of our text, however, Paul wishes to demonstrate to the Jews that their wickedness is even greater in light of the extraordinary privi-leges and advantages given to them by God. Not only is the history of the people of Israel replete with examples of God's faithful care toward them, but the most distinct feature of that history is God's sovereign gift of His Word to them. Paul designates this as the chief advantage of the Jews: "Because that unto them were committed the oracles of God" (Rom. 3:2).

And yet, what is Paul's tragic assessment of the response of a people so highly privileged? They despised "the riches of his goodness and forbear-ance and longsuffering." Instead, the gift of God's self-revelation, His Word, should have led them to repentance.

Dear reader, are you like the Jews who Paul was addressing? Do you still consider yourself morally superior to the ungodly that surround you? Do you still not recognize that your heart is as depraved as theirs, and that you need to repent as much as they do? Furthermore, has not your life also been an ongoing manifestation of the goodness of God?

An honest assessment of our lives cannot but prove that God has been good indeed! However, the fact that God has surrounded you with His Word has been the greatest manifestation of this goodness. It is especially by means of His Word that God has been leading you to repentance. What has been your response? Has there been, by His grace, a change of mind and a change of direction in your life? Have you surrendered to a God who is so very gracious and who has no pleasure in your death, but rather, that you would turn to Him and live (Ezek. 33:11)? If you have not yet repented, may your reflection on His goodness in Christ lead you to do so today!

That he might be just, and the justifier
of him which believeth in Jesus.
—ROMANS 3:26

Dear believer, here is a fountain of extraordinary comfort for you! In this passage and its context, Paul articulates a truth we find throughout the Scriptures: the Judge of all the earth will declare a guilty sinner righteous when he believes in Jesus. What a paradox this appears to be. How can a God who is just—a God who will uphold and vindicate the integrity of His law—at the same time be a God who will justify a sinner who is utterly void of the righteousness He requires? How can He declare someone righteous whose righteousness is as a filthy rag?

The resolution of this apparent paradox is to be found in the precious name of Jesus, who was nailed to the accursed cross of Golgotha. He who knew no sin was made sin in order that we might be made the righteousness of God (2 Cor. 5:19). By His perfect obedience (both active and passive), Jesus merited the perfect righteousness which a just God requires from every son and daughter of Adam.

This perfect righteousness is freely imputed to the sinner who believes in the Son of God's eternal good pleasure, the Lord Jesus Christ; on the basis of that imputed righteousness, a just God can declare us righteous in perfect harmony with His justice. How marvelous is this gospel truth! What a matter of unspeakable joy it is to know that, upon believing in Jesus, weak and feeble though my faith may be, God will fully and irreversibly justify me—not because my faith merits this, but because faith takes hold of Christ and His finished work!

Dear believer, rejoice in the fact that this is your privilege! By virtue of the fact that you too have taken refuge to Christ as a guilty and undone sinner and have "touched the hem of His garment," God has fully justified you—a reality that cannot be cancelled out by your remaining sin. In fact, your worst day cannot detract from your justification, nor will your best day add to it. Your acceptance with God is rooted in the imputed righteousness of Jesus alone. Thanks be unto God for His unspeakable gift!

Do we then make void the law through faith? God forbid.
—ROMANS 3:31

Two errors have always threatened the precious doctrine of justification by faith alone: legalism and antinomianism. In these early chapters of Romans, Paul addresses antinomianism. In fact, his enemies misinterpreted his clear teaching that by the deeds of the law no man shall be justified (v. 20), and slanderously charged him with promoting licentiousness (v. 8).

In the words of our text, however, Paul wants to make it clear that nothing is further from the truth. The faith that yields the justification of the guilty sinner does not render the law of God null and void. The latter is indeed the erroneous conclusion of the Antinomian. His mistaken notion is that Christ has delivered us from the law and its obligations.

However, a correct understanding of the gospel of the cross leads us to the opposite conclusion. By His perfect obedience, even to the death of the cross, Christ has fully vindicated and honored the law, and by His atoning death He has delivered His people from the curse and penalty of the law—but not from the obligations of the law. His death yields the grace which transforms law-breakers into law-keepers. In other words, the cross not only yields the full justification of the guilty sinner, but also the sanctification of the polluted sinner.

An obedient life is therefore one of the most essential marks of saving faith. We who are justified without the deeds of the law endeavor, by the grace of God, to live a life that honors that law as an expression of love and gratitude toward the Savior who saved us. In fact, it is only by way of an obedient life that we honor the Savior who gave Himself as a ransom in our place—not to merit His favor, but in response to His favor.

Dear reader, do you live a life that demonstrates that you truly love the Savior, or does your life make void the law of God? If the fruit of consistent (albeit imperfect) godliness is lacking in our lives, we lack the evidence that our faith is the faith of the saints. Let us therefore give heed to the unmistakable intent of Christ's words: "If ye love me, keep my commandments" (John 14:15).

He staggered not at the promise of God through unbelief.
—ROMANS 4:20

Do you perhaps find yourself in circumstances in which you are staggering at God's promises—that is, in which you are doubtful of them? Are the wheels of God's providence turning in a direction that appears to contradict what God promises you in His Word? Are the words "Where is thy God?" (Ps. 42:3, 10) ringing in your ears?

You are certainly not alone! Even Abraham had times when he staggered at the promise of God that he would have a son. He staggered at God's promise when he took his family to Egypt during a time of famine in the land of Canaan. Abraham was unable to believe that God would care for him and his family even during such adverse circumstances. He staggered at the promise of God when he lied about the real identity of his wife, Sarah, failing to believe that God could protect the woman of whom the promised son was to be born. Even Abraham, the father of the faithful, was a man of like passions as we are.

In each of these cases, Abraham's actions were governed by unbelief rather than faith. Like Abraham, we often reason with our circumstances rather than with the Word of the God who cannot lie. We are inclined to judge God by what we see, feel, or sense of Him, rather than by what He has revealed of Himself in Christ, in whom all of His promises are "yea and amen" (2 Cor. 1:20). How we grieve God's Spirit!

Yet, at a crucial moment in his life, Abraham did not stagger at God's promise when God asked him to sacrifice Isaac, the son of promise. Against the background of his failures, we know that this can solely be attributed to the grace of God, enabling him to trust in the Word of God alone when the circumstances of the moment fully militated against the fulfillment of God's promise.

That is the lesson God also wants to teach us. We must trust the promising God who will often allow the promise to die, so to speak, so that we will learn to rely fully on Him alone—the God who has promised that He will never forsake the work of His hands, and that all things, without exception, must work together for the spiritual good of all those who love Him (Rom. 8:28–29).

*Who was delivered for our offences, and was
raised again for our justification.*
—ROMANS 4:25

Job asked the urgent question of many: "How should man be just with God?" (Job 9:2). How can I be declared just by God when I am utterly guilty before Him? That dilemma brings us to the wonderful solution unveiled to us in our text. God gave His precious Son to be a Substitute for utterly unrighteous and guilty sinners. He was delivered for our offenses; God held Him accountable for our transgression of the law and demanded full payment for our transgression of the law of Him as Substitute.

Dear believer, thanks be to God for such a Savior! On Calvary's cross, He was wounded for our transgressions and bruised for our iniquities; the chastisement of our peace was upon Him (Isa. 53:5). As a divine and perfectly innocent Mediator, He merited the perfect righteousness God requires in order to declare a man just. On the basis of His perfect sacrifice, God was therefore able to declare the "guilty" Mediator just and righteous in His sight. He justified Him!

However, Christ was not merely raised for His personal justification. Rather, as Mediator, He was raised for *our* justification. He arose so that, on the basis of His justification, God would be able to justify us and declare us righteous in His sight. All of this is only possible because Jesus was also raised for *our* justification. Only because the Father publicly justified Him can He now justify us when we believe in this risen Christ.

This brings us to the magnificent conclusion of Paul's argument: "Therefore being justified by faith, we have peace with God through our Lord Jesus Christ" (Rom. 5:1). Believer, do you embrace the full ramifications of this? Do you believe that God has also justified you upon trusting in Christ; that your sins have been fully pardoned; that you are fully reconciled to God; and that you are an heir of eternal life? Or are you still living below your privileges?

Rejoice, you who love the Lord Jesus Christ in sincerity! The Christ who was delivered for all your offenses has been raised by His Father for your justification—by a Father who is both just and "the justifier of him which believeth in Jesus" (Rom 3:26). *Soli Deo Gloria!*

We glory in tribulations.
—ROMANS 5:3

Tribulations are the inescapable reality of life in a fallen world. And yet, Paul is not referring here to the afflictions that are common to all men. Rather, he is referring to the afflictions that are the inescapable lot of all who belong to the spiritual household of God—to those who, by grace, say, "Being justified by faith, we have peace with God" (Rom. 5:1).

Many of us would readily admit that we know what tribulations are. Perhaps you find yourself presently in very difficult and painful circumstances. However, are you prepared to say with Paul that you "glory" in your tribulations—or, as the Greek could be translated, that you "rejoice" in them? Your question might quite possibly be, "How can Paul make such an assertion, when I find my trials grievous and difficult to cope with?"

Paul clarifies this. In Christ's school of affliction, he has learned lessons of inestimable value—lessons he could not have learned in any other way. This experienced saint of the Lord had learned that the crucible of affliction yielded for him the rich benefits of patience, experience, and hope (vv. 3–4).

First, he was learning that tribulations impart the virtue of patience—we learn to wait patiently on the Lord even when it appears that our world is falling apart around us. It is only when we are afflicted that we really learn to exercise this virtue.

Second, it is in the crucible of affliction that we also acquire genuine Christian experience. When afflictions and tribulations are our portion, we truly and experientially deal with Christ, His Word, and His promises. During the trials of the Christian life, our intellectual knowledge of God's Word becomes experiential. We learn that God, for Christ's sake, is indeed our Refuge and our Strength, and a very present help in trouble (Ps. 46:1).

Third, it is by way of tribulations that God exercises the virtue of hope in His children, teaching us to hope against hope that God will be true to His Word and that His way will prove to be perfect.

We may therefore conclude that believers profit spiritually from their tribulations, resulting in what every believer yearns for: growth in the grace and knowledge of our Lord and Savior Jesus Christ. Thus we may, and should, glory in our tribulations!

NOVEMBER 8

The love of God is shed abroad in our hearts by the Holy Ghost.
—ROMANS 5:5

Can you say with Peter, "Lord, thou knowest all things; thou knowest that I love thee" (John 21:17)? If so, this can be attributed only to one cause: the love of God has been shed abroad in your heart by the Holy Ghost. In other words, when we love God, it is only because God has first loved us and has filled our heart with the love of His own heart.

In our text, Paul tells us that this is the special work of the Holy Spirit. This at once gives us a clear indication what the intent of the Spirit is in shedding abroad this love of God in our hearts. As the Spirit of Christ, it is His explicit objective to glorify Christ (John 16:13–15), and thus He sheds abroad the love of God in our hearts to equip us to glorify Christ.

When He does so, it will accomplish precisely that, for the great object of the love of God is the Son of God, the Lord Jesus Christ. John tells us eight times in his gospel that the Father loves the Son (John 3:35, etc.). Consequently, it is this love for His Son that properly defines God's love. When the Spirit sheds abroad this love in our hearts, it will have the Son of God, the Lord Jesus Christ, as its object.

It then follows that we will love the Lord Jesus Christ in sincerity. That, and that alone, is the only scriptural evidence that the Spirit of God, who glorifies Christ, has been savingly at work in our hearts!

Is this true for you? Is it your confession that this Jesus is white and ruddy, the chiefest among ten thousand, and that He is altogether lovely (Song 5:10, 16)? If your answer is negative, you need to heed Paul's solemn declaration in 1 Corinthians 16:22, "If any man love not the Lord Jesus Christ, let him be Anathema" (accursed)!

If, however, you can call God as a witness that this is so, it confirms that the love of God has indeed been shed abroad in your heart—and this love for Jesus will manifest itself also in the fruits of your life (John 14:15).

But where sin abounded, grace did much more abound.
—ROMANS 5:20

"But where sin abounded...." How readily every true believer will concur that this is the story of our lives! How exceedingly painful it is when the Spirit sheds light upon this truth and causes us to see our life from God's perspective! Then we agree with Isaiah: "The whole head is sick, and the whole heart faint. From the sole of the foot even unto the head there is no soundness in it" (Isa. 1:5–6)!

However, this is not only experienced when the Holy Spirit initially opens our spiritual eyes. It will be the ongoing, and progressively painful, discovery in the life of God's children that sin does indeed abound. The saintly Paul cried out in holy despair, "For I know that in me (that is, in my flesh,) dwelleth no good thing.... O wretched man that I am! who shall deliver me from the body of this death?" (Rom. 7:18, 24).

And yet, over against that troubling and ongoing discovery stands the other half of our text. Over against the abundance of sin stands the super-abounding grace of God! In the preceding verses, Paul has shown how God provided the second Adam, the Lord Jesus Christ, as His saving provision for sons and daughters of the first Adam. In Him God has provided grace—His unmerited favor toward sinners—that infinitely exceeds the abundance of our sin.

In Jesus Christ and on the basis of His finished work, God can freely give us the exact opposite of what we deserve: the very essence of grace. In Him, God has found a way to blot out the abundance of our sins through the blood of His Son which cleanses from all sin. The greatness of that salvation dramatically exceeds the greatness of our sins.

To that blessed Savior the Spirit of God draws us again and again. He accomplishes this by increasingly teaching us that sin abounds in our lives so that Christ and Him crucified will be the only hope of our lives. As we gain this experiential insight into the abundance of sin in our lives, we will proportionally grow in our understanding that in Christ the grace of God is truly super-abounding. The more we begin to grasp this, the more we will cry out with holy adoration, "Thanks be unto God for His unspeakable gift!"

Our old man is crucified with him.
—ROMANS 6:6

The old man no longer occupies the throne of the believer's heart. By the abundant grace of God, we have become new creatures in Christ. Old things have passed away; all things have become new (2 Cor. 5:18).

However, this does not mean that the believer must no longer deal with his old nature. It is the disconcerting discovery of every believer that his old nature will seize upon every opportunity to regain its original position of dominion in the heart. As a result, the life of believers consists of an ongoing spiritual warfare, for "the flesh [the old nature] lusteth against the Spirit, and the Spirit against the flesh" (Gal. 5:17).

This warfare can be so intense that, like David, we are inclined to think that we will perish from it. And yet, the encouraging truth of our text is that it shall not be so, for our old man *is* crucified!

Paul expounds the full ramifications of Christ's crucifixion for believers. Not only does the cross guarantee our justification, but Christ has also secured our sanctification on their behalf. The cross guarantees that every believer will ultimately be fully conformed to the image of Christ.

However, during this life, conformity to Christ only becomes a reality in proportion to the dying of the old nature. Since our old nature is incorrigibly corrupt and depraved, there is but one solution: it must be crucified. Yet, our text states that our old man *is* crucified. What an encouraging and uplifting truth this is when all the skirmishes in our warfare against the old man can leave us so discouraged!

What Paul is saying here has profound implications, for he is telling us that, in Christ our Substitute, our old man has already been crucified. It is destined for utter destruction and will therefore never gain dominion in our souls. Its annihilation is fully guaranteed by the cross. Christ's victory on the cross demands the crucifixion of our flesh, and God will therefore so lead us to that end.

Therefore, dear believer, be encouraged! In Christ and Him crucified the victory is sure, and the new man shall prevail at last. "Thanks be to God, which giveth us the victory through our Lord Jesus Christ!" (1 Cor. 15:57).

For the wages of sin is death; but the gift of God is eternal life through Jesus Christ our Lord.

—ROMANS 6:23

How striking is the contrast between life and death in this passage! This contrast draws our attention to the brilliant gospel message that shines forth in our text. Likewise, we will only value this gospel when we have experienced the reality of sin and death. How could we ever rejoice in the fact that God grants eternal life to sinners through Jesus Christ, His only begotten Son, unless we understand that we are worthy of death?

This is indeed the sobering truth of our text. As sinners, we are worthy of death, worthy of everlasting separation from God, His favor, and His presence. This is what constitutes the wretchedness of our natural state. It powerfully confirms what we are: covenant-breakers. Death is the fitting penalty for our breach of God's covenant with us. God's just penalty upon divorcing ourselves from Him is eternal separation from Him.

What an astonishing truth, that God is pleased to give eternal life to sinners who deserve death! This passage clearly illustrates that, in the gospel, God offers us the exact opposite of what we deserve, namely, eternal life! To sinners who deserve to be eternally separated from Him, God freely offers union and communion with Himself.

This, of course, brings us to the heart of the gospel: that through Jesus Christ, God is able to bestow the gift of eternal life to sinners—specifically on the basis of His substitutionary sacrifice on the cross. As the Substitute for sinners, He received the wages for our sin. He experienced the full reality of death. And thanks be to God that, based on the accomplished work of this precious Mediator, He can now freely give eternal life to sinners worthy of eternal death.

Has the wonder of this unspeakable gift become an experiential reality for you? Have you embraced Jesus Christ by faith, and has He become the Lord of your life? If so, may our lives be living testimonies of our gratitude for God's utterly underserved gift of eternal life through Jesus Christ our Lord!

O wretched man that I am! who shall deliver me from the body of this death? I thank God through Jesus Christ our Lord.

—ROMANS 7:24–25

One of the striking evidences of spiritual life is the daily struggle with sin. As a result of the marvelous, regenerating work of the Holy Spirit, the believer has become a new creature in Christ. The nature of this renewing and trans-forming work of God's Spirit is such that the inclination of the new nature will always be toward holiness. However, to our great dismay, we discover that our old nature is by no means dead. On the contrary! Though it has been expelled from the center of the new heart, it will ceaselessly and relentlessly seek to regain the territory it has lost. As a result, a holy warfare rages within the heart of every true believer (Gal. 5:17).

Is this the struggle of your life? Do you grapple with the perplexing real-ity that you do what you hate, and that you fail to do what you desire to do? Does it grieve you that you so often conduct yourself contrary to what you profess to be? Do you know the holy despair that caused godly Paul to cry out, "O wretched man that I am"? This will always be the cry of those who fear God and love the Lord Jesus Christ in sincerity. This is the groan of one who is weary from battling his flesh and who delights in the law of God after the inward man (v. 22).

It is the true believer who therefore so longs to be delivered from the body of this death—from sin and all that is related to it. Is this the deep yearning of your soul? What comfort we will then find in the words which follow: "I thank God through Jesus Christ our Lord." What a comfort to know that this deliverance has been fully achieved by Christ, that sin will therefore never again have dominion in the life of the believer, and that there will come a day when complete deliverance from sin shall be an everlasting reality!

Therefore, if the groan of our text is the groan of your heart, keep courage, for through Jesus Christ our Lord the day of full deliverance is dawning—the day when you shall forever be delivered from "the body of this death." Come, Lord Jesus, come quickly!

Now if any man have not the Spirit of Christ, he is none of his.
—ROMANS 8:9

This is a solemn and searching statement. Though I may profess the name of Christ, belong to the church of Christ, and be involved in advancing the cause of Christ, if I do not yet have the Spirit of Christ, I am none of His. In other words, all my religion, impressive though it may appear in the eyes of men, is null and void in the eyes of God unless I am indwelt by the Spirit of Christ.

What an important truth this is! It confirms that when Christ saves us, He will also dwell in us by His Spirit. Christ will never do the one without the other. He is a complete Savior who not only delivers us from the guilt, pollution, curse, and dominion of sin, but who also renews us after His own image by the indwelling ministry of His Spirit.

If there is no scriptural and verifiable evidence that the Spirit of God dwells in us, it must be concluded that we do not belong to Him—that there is no vital, life-giving, and life-sustaining union with Christ. When that union exists, of which Christ speaks in John 15, the fruits of our lives will confirm it, for union to Christ will always produce likeness to Christ. The Spirit of Christ is ceaselessly at work in the heart and life of the believer to conform him to Christ, as it is His special work to glorify Christ (John 16:14).

How then may we know whether we have the Spirit of Christ? When that Spirit dwells in us, Christ will be our all and in all. The Spirit of Christ will strip us of all our own righteousness in order that Christ becomes irresistibly attractive to our soul. As a result of His work, Christ will become so precious and lovely, that we will say with Paul, "That I may know him, and the power of his resurrection" (Phil. 3:10).

However, the indwelling of Christ's Spirit will also produce a Christ-like disposition—a disposition articulated in Galatians 5:22–23 as being the fruit of the Spirit: "love, joy, peace, longsuffering, gentleness, goodness, faith, meekness, temperance."

Is there genuine evidence that you have the Spirit of Christ?

NOVEMBER 14

Ye have received the Spirit of adoption,
whereby we cry, Abba, Father.
—ROMANS 8:15

In this text, Paul continues to highlight the role of the Spirit in the experience of the believer—the Spirit by whom all of God's children are led (v. 14)—referring to Him as the Spirit of adoption. The Dutch translation literally reads, "the Spirit of being accepted as children." This means that it is the special work of the Spirit of Christ to assure believers that, on the basis of the accomplished work of Christ, God is their Father and they are His adopted children.

How beautifully this confirms that Christ died and rose again for this very purpose! He said to Mary Magdalene, "Go to my brethren, and say unto them, I ascend unto my Father, and your Father; and to my God, and your God" (John 20:17). If this is the glorious purpose of Christ's redemptive work, it follows that the Spirit of Christ, as the Spirit of adoption, will not rest until He leads the believer to the assured knowledge that God, for Christ's sake, is also his Father.

Considering that Paul refers to the Spirit as both the Spirit of God (the Father) and the Spirit of Christ, we may conclude that as the Spirit of the Father He leads us to the Son for reconciliation, and as the Spirit of the Son He leads us to the Father to enjoy the full benefits of this reconciliation. As the Spirit of adoption, He does the one as well as the other, for we will never have freedom to cry out, "Abba, Father," unless we are fully assured that God is our Father for Christ's sake. Be certain, however, that nothing sounds sweeter in the ears of the Father than when one of His precious children, led by the Spirit of adoption, recognizes Him for who He is—just as an earthly father is delighted when his infant child calls him "father" for the first time.

Therefore, dear believer, having received the Spirit of adoption, do not hesitate to cry out, "Abba, Father." This will be music in the ears of the Father who chose you in Christ, gave you to Him, redeemed you through Him, and has united you to Him by His Spirit. The Father of the Lord Jesus Christ, for His sake, is also your Father, and He loves you with the same love with which He loves His Son (John 17:23, 26).

And we know that all things work together for good to them that love God, to them who are the called according to his purpose. For whom he did foreknow, he also did predestinate to be conformed to the image of his Son.

—ROMANS 8:28–29

We will never know how many believers have been comforted by these words in times of great trial and affliction. And indeed, this promise is explicitly addressed to believers—to those that love God. What an all-encompassing mark of grace this is! When the love of God is shed abroad in the heart of a sinner, he cannot but love God in return, and will therefore also love His Word, His church, His people and ordinances, and, above all, His Son.

Does this describe you? If so, this proves that you too have been called according to God's sovereign purpose. You have eternally been foreknown by God with the knowledge of His eternal love. You love God today because God has loved you eternally.

However, not only has God loved you with an everlasting love, but He has also predestined you for a very special purpose: to be conformed to the image of His well-beloved Son. The Father, who preeminently loves His Son, has eternally chosen you in Him (Eph. 1:4) in order that you might reflect His image and glory. This is why you have been saved, and this is the "good" that God is pursuing in your life.

God will so order your life that everything will work together to bring about this good. He is so committed to His eternal purpose regarding you that He will leave no stone unturned to accomplish this. He will not hesitate to put you into the furnace of affliction so that all that is of the flesh would be burned away in order for Christ's image to become visible in your life. As the great Sculptor, God will use the chisel of affliction to carve away your flesh so that you may begin to resemble your precious Savior.

God will not rest until He has accomplished this in your life. His goal is not to make you comfortable, but rather to conform you to the image of His Son. In love, this prompts Him to afflict and try you so that the glory of Christ will become visible in your life. Therefore, be encouraged, dear believer: God is molding you so that you would reflect the image of His Son.

Whom he justified, them he also glorified.
—ROMANS 8:30

How beautifully reassuring these words are to everyone who loves the Lord Jesus Christ in sincerity! They confirm what is taught throughout the Scriptures, namely, that God will never forsake the works of His own hands.

These words are part of the beautiful golden chain of redemption: predestination, calling, justification, and glorification. This chain is a masterpiece of God's own making, connecting eternity past and eternity future, and it cannot possibly be broken. Thus the linkage between justification and glorification is unbreakable.

In order for us to draw comfort from this, we must know that we are justified, for then, and then alone, shall we be glorified. Earlier, Paul taught that we are justified by faith (Rom. 5:1). Therefore, we must ask ourselves whether we have already exercised the faith that yields such extraordinary blessings to sinners.

This faith is the simple act of trusting in the Lord Jesus Christ and His finished work for the salvation of my soul. It is the act whereby a guilty, polluted, and wretched sinner touches the hem of Jesus' garment. It is the act of one who hungers and thirsts after Jesus and His righteousness, and who can only find rest in what He has accomplished on the cross. God is pleased to reward such faith by justifying a sinner—not because of the quality of this faith, but rather, because this faith honors His Son and His work.

If, by the grace of God, we have embraced Christ by faith, God will have justified us, and when He does this, He will certainly glorify us. This justification is irreversible and therefore the future glorification of every believer is guaranteed. This means that all to whom Jesus Christ is precious (a mark of saving faith) are going to make it home!

Has Jesus become altogether lovely to you, and do you repeatedly take refuge in Him by faith? The day is coming when you will forever be translated into His presence, for God's work in your life cannot possibly abort. All who love the Lord Jesus Christ in sincerity will be glorified. Why? Because you have been justified. Why? Because you have been called. Why? Because you have been predestined. Why? Because you have been loved with an everlasting love. Why? That is something you will never be able to fathom! *Soli Deo Gloria!*

Who is he that condemneth? It is Christ that died, yea rather, that is risen again, who is even at the right hand of God, who also maketh intercession for us.
—ROMANS 8:34

How often must we not condemn ourselves! When considering how easily we yield to temptation, how bent we are toward backsliding, how lethargic our prayers can be, how cold our hearts can be toward Christ, and how often we grieve God's Spirit, we cannot but condemn ourselves time and again.

However, in doing so, we must not lose sight of the gospel—something we can be so inclined to do. Self-condemnation will turn into spiritual despondency; such despondency is often, if not always, the result of erroneously concluding that our relationship with God is contingent upon our performance after all. How inclined we still are to secretly trust in our own righteousness, and how disillusioned we can be when our sin confronts us afresh that in our flesh "dwelleth no good thing"!

What need we have, therefore, to be taught repeatedly that all our good frames and good works are as filthy rags and that our only hope must be in Christ and His accomplished work alone! This is precisely what Paul does in our text. Though he knows that he stands condemned in himself, he cries out with holy boldness, "Who is he that condemneth?" By faith, he knows that for the believer the answer to that question is "No one!"

What basis does the apostle have for such confidence? His confidence is founded upon the rock-solid foundation of the redemptive work of Christ—a foundation supported by the four pillars of His death, resurrection, ascension, and intercession. Because of that marvelous work, we will never be condemned. His death assures us that the penalty for sin has been paid in full; His resurrection assures us of the Father's full acceptance of this payment; His ascension assures us of our restoration into God's presence and favor; and His ongoing intercession assures us of unbroken fellowship with God. Nothing can undo what Christ has accomplished—not even our sin. Though a stream of foul transgressions so often prevails from day to day, yet we must look outside of ourselves to Christ and His finished work. Then we will begin to understand that there is no condemnation for the people of God, though they must often condemn themselves. Thanks be unto God for the unspeakable gift of His precious Son!

Whosoever believeth on him shall not be ashamed.
—ROMANS 9:33

To appreciate Paul's quotation from the Old Testament here, it will be helpful to consider the literal meaning of the original Hebrew. We could read here that whosoever believes on Christ shall not make haste, shall not be agitated, or shall not be fearful. In other words, one of the blessed fruits of believing on Christ is that we will be calm and at peace.

Hasn't our personal experience proved that this is so? Haven't we felt that peace which passes all understanding whenever we put our trust in Christ and His promises? Was this not the experience of the disciples on the Sea of Galilee when Jesus came to them, walking on the waves? When unbelief prevailed and they deemed themselves forsaken by their Master, they were very agitated and fearful. But when Christ spoke the precious words, "Fear not, it is I," their fear dissipated, even though at that moment the storm continued to rage. Once the disciples responded believingly to the words of Christ, they were no longer ashamed or afraid; though their circumstances had not yet changed, trusting in Christ and His words changed their disposition.

We must learn to put our trust in Christ and His Word no matter what circumstances we find ourselves in. Do we not have reason to be ashamed when we consider our behavior in difficult and perplexing circumstances? How agitated and fearful we can be! We focus on our circumstances rather than Christ and His never-failing promises. How we grieve Him when we judge Him by our circumstances rather than by His Word!

We need to learn to exercise such faith when we find ourselves in the most difficult circumstances. We need to learn to live by faith rather than by sight or feeling. If we put our trust in Christ at all times, we will be able to sing God's praises in the most perplexing situations, like Paul and Silas in the prison cell in Philippi. "He shall not be afraid of evil tidings: his heart is fixed, trusting in the LORD" (Ps. 112:7).

The word is nigh thee.
—ROMANS 10:8

What an extraordinary privilege it is to have the Word of God in our possession! This can only be attributed to the wonderful providence of our sovereign God. Such had been the privilege of the nation of Israel, for whom the Apostle Paul had such a burden (v. 1). God had sovereignly elected them to receive His self-revelation and His Word. To them He had unveiled His heart in the ministry of reconciliation, and it was to them that He had sent His prophets to call them to repentance and to serve Him. God brought His Word to them.

In the context of our text, Paul argues that that Word is still near to them, particularly in the Person of the Lord Jesus Christ, the Living Word of God (John 1:1). What a blessed and profound truth this is: through His Word, God Himself draws near to us! When we have God's precious Word in our possession, we know that God, in Christ, is near to us.

The precious words of our text are a beautiful indication as to why God sovereignly favors us with the gift of His Word. He draws near to us in order that we would thereby be encouraged to draw near to Him. In His Word, and especially in His Son, the Lord Jesus Christ, God opens His eternal heart of love to us. He communicates to us that His delights are with the children of men and that He has no pleasure in the death of sinners, but rather, that they would turn to Him and live. What an extraordinary blessing it is to have this Word near to us!

How do we respond to this profound gift? Do we draw near to the God who has come so close to us through His Word? Do our lives demonstrate that this Word is the most precious treasure we possess here on earth? Are we diligent, prayerful students of it so that we might know the Living Word, the Lord Jesus Christ, whom to know is life eternal (John 17:3)? Has that Word borne such fruit in our lives that we confess with our mouths the Lord Jesus, and believe in our hearts that God has raised Him from the dead (v. 10)? For only then shall we be saved!

I was found of them that sought me not.
—ROMANS 10:20

As Paul continues to unfold God's sovereign good pleasure in sending forth His Word into a fallen world of Jews and Gentiles, significant passages of the Old Testament come to his mind. With joy in his heart, he quotes Isaiah 52:7 and writes, "How beautiful are the feet of them that preach the gospel of peace, and bring glad tidings of good things!" (v. 15).

What a marvelous thing it was for him that God had directed his feet to bring the "glad tidings of good things" to the Gentiles also! He knew that this was a confirmation of his Old Testament, and thus he quotes and summarizes Isaiah 65:1 by saying, "I am found of them that sought me not." He knew that his proclamation of the gospel to the Gentiles was not the result of them seeking God, but rather, of God seeking them. Without God sending him to preach Christ to them, no Gentile would have ever found God, for there was not a Gentile that sought after God.

How true this is for mankind in general! In Romans 3:11–12, Paul quotes Psalm 14:2–3: "The LORD looked down from heaven upon the children of men, to see if there were any that did understand, and seek God. They are all gone aside." In other words, man left to himself will never seek after God, unless God first seeks after him and draws near to him with the gospel of salvation.

If, by the grace of God, you are a believer, you will readily agree that these words apply to you as well. You know that if God had not sought after you, you would never have sought after Him. It is only because God sovereignly and irresistibly intervened in your life that you sought after God for the salvation of your soul. Only because He drew you with the cords of His love, shed abroad His love in your heart, and made you willing in the day of His power, did you repent and believe on the Lord Jesus Christ. All boasting is forever excluded! You love God today because He first loved you. You love a Savior today who died for you while you were still an enemy (Rom. 5:10). What amazing, sovereign, and unmerited love! What debtors we therefore are to the sovereign good pleasure of a triune God. To Him alone be all the glory for our salvation, "For of him, and through him, and to him, are all things: to whom be glory for ever. Amen" (Rom. 11:36).

All day long I have stretched forth my hands unto a disobedient and
gainsaying people.
—ROMANS 10:21

Paul takes many passages from the Old Testament and merges them into one summary passage. Here he summarizes God's gracious dealings with Israel and Israel's sinful response.

How aptly these words describe the extraordinary longsuffering and patience the Lord exercised toward His covenant people! His dealings with Israel during its forty-year journey in the wilderness immediately come to mind. "Forty years long was I grieved with this generation, and said, It is a people that do err in their heart, and they have not known my ways" (Ps. 95:10).

Israel's record after they settled in Canaan was not much better. They continued to be a "disobedient and gainsaying people" who refused to give heed to God's Word and rebelled against His ways. The description Paul gives reminds us of the conduct of children who not only disobey their parents, but who are also guilty of gainsaying, that is, of talking back. Such was Israel's wretched response to a God who had done nothing but stretch forth His hands of mercy toward them.

However, not only Israel is guilty of such conduct! The words of our text are also applicable to everyone who has lived under the gospel all his life and yet continues in an unbelieving and unrepentant state. Are you perhaps such a person? Would you readily agree that you are still unconverted? If so, you need to understand that your being unconverted is but a manifestation of the fact that you are an unbeliever—someone who is disobedient to Christ's command to repent and believe the gospel (Mark 1:15). Perhaps you are a gainsayer, excusing your failure to repent and believe by accusing God's sovereignty for your inability.

What a wonder, therefore, that the Christ whom you so offend by your persistent unbelief still continues to stretch forth His hands of mercy to you—hands that were pierced on Calvary's cross! He is willing today to receive you, promising that He will not cast you out. Will you, in spite of such sincere overtures of mercy, continue to be a disobedient and gainsaying sinner?

> *O the depth of the riches both of the*
> *wisdom and knowledge of God!*
> —ROMANS 11:33

Paul is overwhelmed when he writes these words, reflecting on God's magnificent good pleasure displayed toward both Jews and Gentiles—the natural and the ingrafted branches of the olive tree. He stands in awe of how this good pleasure unfolds itself in history when Israel's rejection of Christ results in the salvation of the Gentiles. What amazes him even more is that the Gentiles, in turn, will be the means to bring salvation to the natural seed of Abraham, in whom all the families of the earth will be blessed.

It is as if Paul stands on the Mount Everest of divine revelation and is dazzled by what he sees. He realizes that God's magnificent ways are infinitely beyond the grasp of his finite mind. All he can do at this point is bow in holy adoration before the God who so loved a world of sinners, that whosoever (whether Jew or Gentile) believes in His beloved Son would not perish but have eternal life (John 3:16).

How profitable it is for us continually to stand in awe of this good pleasure as it continues to unfold itself in the midst of our fallen world! God's Word continues to reach the most unlikely corners of the world, resulting in the salvation of men and women who never sought after God. We ourselves are the beneficiaries of God's marvelous deeds in history. In ways that are beyond our comprehension, God has seen to it that after so many centuries, the gospel has reached our generation. He has preserved the chain of the generations so that we would be the recipients of the glorious gospel of salvation—a gospel that by the grace of God has become a power unto salvation in the lives of all who love the Lord Jesus Christ in sincerity.

When that wonder begins to sink in, we stand before a bottomless ocean of God's unfathomable love in Christ who is the embodiment of God's wisdom and knowledge. If I reflect on the fact that God has sovereignly made me a recipient of that love, I can only stammer, "O the depth of the riches both of the wisdom and knowledge of God!" Do you have such an appreciation for these words?

I beseech you therefore, brethren, by the mercies of God, that ye present your bodies a living sacrifice, holy, acceptable unto God, which is your reasonable service.
—ROMANS 12:1

Paul exhorts Christians to reflect on all that he has written thus far. His own reflection caused him to end the previous chapter with a magnificent doxology, exhorting us to give all glory to Him of whom, through whom, and unto whom, are all things (Rom. 11:36).

Overflowing with adoration for the triune God who has provided so great a salvation, Paul emphasizes that we, being the recipients of such a salvation, owe a debt of gratitude for such a favor being bestowed upon us. Our salvation is a demonstration of the mercy and utterly unmerited favor of God. In bestowing salvation upon us, God has given us the exact opposite of what we deserve. As sinners, we deserve hell and damnation, and yet it pleased God to bestow salvation on us and to make us heirs of eternal life! What an extraordinary and profound favor indeed!

Given the context of the previous chapters, we know that the foundation for this salvation is the perfect sacrifice of the Lord Jesus Christ. He presented His body as a living sacrifice unto God. Willingly He gave Himself to be the Lamb of God that takes away the sins of the world; willingly He allowed Himself to be slain on Calvary's cross so that His precious blood could lay the foundation on which a holy and righteous God could be merciful to sinners. What a comfort it is to know that His sacrifice was truly holy and acceptable to God—a fact confirmed by God Himself in rending the veil of the temple—and that therefore I, a sinner, am holy and acceptable in His sight!

The realization of this profound truth must motivate the believer to give his life as a living sacrifice unto God. That Christ has given Himself for me should motivate me to give myself wholly to Him—a life that is utterly devoted to Him, His glory, and His cause. For meriting so great a salvation for me, I owe my Savior a lifelong debt of gratitude. The more I reflect on His inexpressible love for me, the more I should be motivated to love Him in return.

Dear believer, are you presenting your life as a living sacrifice to the Christ who gave Himself as a ransom for you? This is your reasonable service!

If it be possible, as much as lieth in you,
live peaceably with all men.

—ROMANS 12:18

Are you living peaceably with all men? This is a question we must answer in light of this text, for it is immediately evident that a Christian is obligated to do everything is his power to live at peace with all men.

It is fitting that in a chapter in which Paul addresses the subject of living a sanctified life, he also addresses the issue of our interpersonal contact with others. He recognized that one of the ways the indwelling ministry of the Holy Spirit manifests itself in the believer is that he will actively pursue harmonious relationships with his neighbors.

This is indeed a mark of grace! The Apostle John makes this crystal clear when he writes, "We know that we have passed from death unto life, because we love the brethren. He that loveth not his brother abideth in death. Whosoever hateth his brother is a murderer: and ye know that no murderer hath eternal life abiding in him" (1 John 3:14–15).

By nature, we are inclined to love ourselves and hate our neighbor. The world is filled with discord; men do not live peaceably together. We are born as "peacebreakers" rather than peacemakers. All of that changes, however, when the Holy Spirit regenerates a man and transforms him to be a peacemaker. Christ, therefore, stresses that being a peacemaker is one of the essential evidences of being a child of the living God (Matt. 5:9). Since God is the great Peacemaker (sending His Son into the world), and Christ the Prince of Peace, it only follows that God's children will reflect the character of their heavenly Father and be peacemakers as well.

This means that a believer is not merely someone who loves peace, but who actively seeks to make peace, taking the initiative to live at peace with his neighbor. Paul reminds us of this in our text. As peacemakers, we are called to do everything in our power to live at peace with our neighbors—even if this may prove elusive at times. We must have a clear conscience before God that we have left no stone unturned to foster harmonious relationships. If strained relationships continue, we must be certain that it is not for our lack of effort.

Are you living peaceably with everyone, as much as lies in you?

The night is far spent, the day is at hand.
—ROMANS 13:12

By referring to the night, Paul is describing the spiritual condition of a fallen world that is enveloped by the darkness of sin and unbelief. What is even worse, it is a world in which men love darkness rather than light (John 3:19).

How righteously God could have left man in this state of spiritual darkness! And yet, it pleased Him not to do so. All the way back in Paradise, a ray of light pierced the darkness when God promised that the seed of the woman would triumph over the seed of the serpent, and thus that light would triumph over darkness.

How wonderfully this was confirmed when Christ came into the world—when the Sun of Righteousness arose with healing in His wings (Mal. 4:2)! Ever since that day, God has been directing the light of the gospel to the far corners of this earth, shining upon sinners dwelling in darkness. Most importantly, God has caused that light to shine into the dark recesses of sinners' hearts, causing them to believe on the Lord Jesus Christ for the salvation of their soul.

The world at large still dwells in darkness. Our text tells us, however, that this long season of darkness is coming to an end, "until the day break and the shadows flee away" (Song 2:17). That will be a day of full deliverance, a day of which John wrote, "Beloved, now are we the sons of God, and it doth not yet appear what we shall be: but we know that, when he shall appear, we shall be like him; for we shall see him as he is" (1 John 3:2).

This eternal day is dawning, for Paul writes in the preceding verse, "Now is our salvation nearer than when we believed." What a day that will be—when Christ will usher His people into the new Jerusalem, of which John wrote, "And the city had no need of the sun, neither of the moon, to shine in it: for the glory of God did lighten it, and the Lamb is the light thereof" (Rev. 21:23).

Therefore, dear believer, keep courage, for this day is at hand! Let this motivate us to walk as children of the light, giving heed to Paul's exhortation, "Put ye on the Lord Jesus Christ, and make not provision for the flesh, to fulfil the lusts thereof" (Rom. 13:14).

And, unbeliever, before an eternal night will envelop your soul, cry out to Him who is the Light of the World and who will save all who put their trust in Him.

> *But put ye on the Lord Jesus Christ, and make not provision for the flesh, to fulfil the lusts thereof.*
>
> —ROMANS 13:14

How real is the Christian's daily struggle with the lusts of the flesh (Gal. 5:17)! At times, indwelling corruption can flare up so suddenly and unexpectedly that it seems as if there is no grace in his heart after all. This painful reality caused Paul to cry out, "For what I would, that do I not; but what I hate, that do I…. O wretched man that I am! who shall deliver me from the body of this death?" (Rom. 7:15, 24).

However, though Paul knew of such moments of holy despair, he also knew by bitter experience that there were other times that he made provision for the flesh; that is, that he catered to his flesh rather than crucifying it. Which Christian must not confess with shame and sorrow that he also knows of such times?

Such bitter defeats taught Paul that he had to take steps not to bring himself into situations that were attractive to his sinful flesh. In our text, he wants to pass on what he had learned in that respect. He had learned experientially that he could prevail against the ceaseless agitation of the flesh only through Christ—only by putting on the Lord Jesus Christ by faith could he succeed in not making provision for the flesh.

What does it mean to "put on the Lord Jesus Christ"? One commentator defines it as follows: "To be clothed with a person is a Greek phrase, signifying to assume the interests of another—to enter into his views, to imitate him, and be wholly on his side." It means to stay as close to Christ as possible, to follow closely in His footsteps, to walk in fellowship with Him—to put it simply, to abide in Him. Only when we abide in Him and His Word, and thereby nourish our inner man, shall we succeed in making no provision for our flesh.

Have we not found it to be true that only near Jesus all is well? That is when we experience that He will make His strength perfect in our weakness. In order to live a life that glorifies Christ, we need to abide in Christ by faith, for it is only then that He will also abide in us (John 15:5). Therefore, put on the Lord Jesus Christ!

Whether we live therefore, or die, we are the Lord's.
—ROMANS 14:8

How extraordinarily comforting it is to be able to confess, "We are the Lord's!" Paul is confessing that, in life and death, he knows he belongs to the Lord Jesus Christ.

What a blessing it is to be able to say this! This is the "only comfort in life and death" which the Heidelberg Catechism defines as "that I with body and soul, both in life and death, am not my own, but belong unto my faithful Savior Jesus Christ." This is indeed the *only* comfort—a comfort that will sustain us in whatever circumstances we may find ourselves in.

Why did Paul find such comfort in the knowledge that he was the property of his Savior? He knew that Christ had purchased him on the cross with the price of His precious blood—a purchase that cannot possibly be reversed. This purchase had been fully endorsed by God the Father when He raised His well-beloved Son from the dead. Paul understood the full ramifications of that divine endorsement, knowing that there is, therefore, now no condemnation for them who are in Christ Jesus (Rom. 8:1). That knowledge caused him to confess with great joy that nothing—either in life or death—can separate God's children from the love of God which is in Christ Jesus (Rom. 8:35–39).

This blessed knowledge enables believers to rejoice, even in tribulation. The comfort of knowing that he was Christ's property enabled Paul to worship God in the prison cell of Philippi, to encourage his fellow men in the midst of a raging storm on the Mediterranean Sea, and to serve Christ cheerfully while under house arrest in Rome. That knowledge enabled him to face death as well, knowing that it would be but a translation into the presence of His beloved Savior.

Is this comfort yours? All other comforts in this life are vain illusions and will fail us in the hour of need. Do not rest until you know on biblical grounds that you too are the Lord's; only then will all be well while you live and when you die.

Dear believer, do not live below your privileges, but rejoice in the fact that you are the Lord's. Continue your pilgrim's journey by looking unto the Lord who has also purchased you, and who is the Author and Finisher of your faith—a Savior who will never forsake the work of His hands!

Whatsoever is not of faith is sin.
—ROMANS 14:23

Painting with a very broad brush, Paul is saying that all activity that is not a fruit of faith is sin. This is a sobering thought! This means that all human activity, though highly esteemed by men, comes short of God's perfect and non-negotiable standard—a standard we sinners cannot possibly meet. Consequently, all religious activity, however zealous and impressive it may appear, is repugnant in the sight of God if it does not proceed from faith.

The question that immediately arises is this: why is only what is of faith not sin in God's sight? The answer is that the nature of saving faith is that it puts all of its trust and confidence in its great Object, the Lord Jesus Christ. Someone who exercises this faith has learned that all his righteousnesses are as filthy rags in God's sight, and that even his very best and devout religious actions come short of God's standard of perfection.

It is a painful experience when God's Spirit strips us of all our own righteousness and causes us to understand the words of Christ, "that except your righteousness shall exceed the righteousness of the scribes and Pharisees, ye shall in no case enter into the kingdom of heaven" (Matt. 5:20). And yet, it is a profitable experience, for that is the only way we will learn to put our trust in Christ and His finished work alone—not only for our justification, but also for our sanctification.

In other words, the believer learns that only by fully trusting in Christ's active and passive obedience can he serve God in a manner that is pleasing to Him. Such obedience is called evangelical obedience, for it is the obedience of one whose entire confidence is in the accomplished work of Christ. There is nothing more pleasing to God than when we serve Him by trusting in Christ alone for the acceptance of our obedience. That is why any trusting in our own righteousness is so obnoxious in the sight of God, for it discounts the fact that only the flawless obedience of Christ is acceptable to Him.

God is pleased only with obedience that flows out of an active faith in Christ and Him crucified. Anything else is sin—no matter how impressive it may seem in the eyes of men. Have we already learned this vital lesson?

Approved in Christ.
—ROMANS 16:10

Paul concludes his epistle by conveying his personal greetings to many believers in Rome. You will notice that he often describes their identity in terms of who they are in Christ. This teaches us the valuable lesson that the only identity that truly matters is whether we are in Him. This personal union with Christ is the only identity which will be of any real value when we reach the end of life's journey. Only when we are in Christ will we not have lived in vain.

Paul describes Apelles as a man who is "approved in Christ." This sheds additional light on the rich benefits that flow from a personal union with the Lord Jesus Christ: those who are in Christ are also approved in Him, approved in the sight of God.

What a rich and comforting truth this is for every believer! What an overwhelming thought it is to know that I, a sinner, am approved in the sight of a God who is of purer eyes than to behold evil. This wonder becomes progressively greater in proportion to an increased knowledge of ourselves. The more we recognize "that in me (that is, in my flesh,) dwelleth no good thing" (Rom. 7:18), the more we will marvel at the magnificent gospel truth that we are "accepted in the beloved" (Eph. 1:6).

How glorious a truth it is that in Christ, God views us without spot and wrinkle, completely righteous, and perfectly holy—so much so that it is as if we had never committed any sin! So complete and all-encompassing is God's acceptance of His people in Christ!

It is therefore so grieving to the Holy Spirit when, because of unbelief, we lose sight of that perfect acceptance and approval of God and are still inclined to believe that God's approval of us is contingent upon our performance rather than the finished work of Christ. How important a lesson it is to learn that the God who is well pleased with His well-beloved Son is well pleased with all who are united to His Son by a true, saving faith! We need to pray that the Lord would continue to teach us to glory in nothing else save Jesus Christ and Him crucified, so that we might understand and rejoice in the glorious truth that we are "approved in Christ!"

NOVEMBER 30

The grace of our Lord Jesus Christ be with you. Amen.
—ROMANS 16:20

It is both beautiful and fitting that Paul should conclude his remarkable epistle to the Romans with these words. What an appropriate summary they are of all he has been teaching us regarding the doctrine of salvation!

Having concluded that all of humanity—Jews and Gentiles—is under sin and that none are righteous before God, there is only one message of hope: the glorious gospel message regarding the grace of our Lord Jesus Christ. Apart from that grace, there can only be condemnation for fallen and rebellious sinners. Thanks be to God, therefore, for the unspeakable gift of the grace of the Lord Jesus Christ!

In order truly to appreciate the wonder of this grace, let us again consider the wonderful meaning of this word. For Paul, the word "grace" was inseparably connected to the cross of the Lord Jesus Christ. It was on the cross that Christ merited grace for vile and hell-worthy sinners. It is because of the shed blood of the Savior that God can be gracious to sinners—that He can be favorably disposed toward them. The favor that God bestows upon sinners is based exclusively upon the merits of His Son, radically excluding all human merit.

Grace can be accurately defined as the unmerited favor of God. And yet, this definition does not tell us the whole story. It is better to say that the grace of God is the *forfeited* favor of God. Having provoked God to wrath by the transgression of His law, we are worthy of being eternally subjected to that wrath. Therefore, when God is gracious to us in Christ, He bestows upon us the exact opposite of what we deserve. Though we deserve His wrath, He embraces us in love; though we deserve condemnation, He justifies us; though we deserve rejection, He accepts and adopts us; though we deserve to be cast away into hell, He will grant us heaven.

No wonder John Newton wrote in holy amazement, "Amazing grace, how sweet the sound, that saved a wretch like me!" How marvelous is the grace of God in Christ that enables Him to be favorably disposed toward those who believe in this precious Christ! The grace which will endure forever is a grace we will need until our dying day. Paul knew this, which explains why he concludes his epistle with these words, "the grace of the Lord Jesus Christ be with you. Amen."

MILK & HONEY

from 1 & 2 Peter
Revelation

DAVID CAMPBELL

Elect according to the foreknowledge of God the Father, through sanctification of the Spirit, unto obedience and sprinkling of the blood of Jesus Christ: Grace unto you, and peace, be multiplied. —1 PETER 1:2

The dignity of God's children is unseen and inexplicable to the world. It cannot be explained in terms of temporary advantage or honor in society, they being "strangers and pilgrims" here. Peter addresses believers in his epistle in terms that carry, in modern thinking, considerable shame. Believers being scattered strangers invites the charge of irrelevance, isolationism, and a singularity that contemporary society, as much as the ancient, finds offensive. There is nothing dignified about being a Christian in today's world where wealth, pride, pleasure, and self predominate. Christians have their dignity from another quarter altogether—their election of God.

Election is commonly associated in the modern mind with those who esteem themselves peculiarly worthy of God's favor and are therefore His special instruments in society. This is not how Scripture defines election. All is of grace, and unworthiness is central to the believer's perception of his election. They know the pit from which they have been dug. Peter associates the election of God's people with their calling. They are "elect…unto obedience and sprinkling of the blood of Jesus Christ." The end of their election is that they would be godly, conformed to the rule of holiness through the merits of Jesus Christ alone. God has "from the beginning chosen you to salvation through sanctification of the Spirit and belief of the truth" (2 Thess. 2:13). This is their dignity as believers in the world: to be sanctified and faithful to Him who has called them by the gospel.

We see their dignity in the central part that God Himself has in their salvation. Nothing is left to man in the life of believers. The three Persons of the Trinity are each mentioned with respect to their acting in the salvation of God's children. The Father elects or chooses them sovereignly "before the foundation of the world" (Eph. 1:4). The Son, Jesus Christ, suffers and dies for them as a sacrifice for sin, sprinkling His blood on their persons for justification and reconciliation. The Holy Spirit, sent on the basis of Christ's sacrifice, regenerates and makes them alive to holiness. He lives in their hearts to enable them to live holy lives. Here is true human dignity, and it brings men into blessed peace and also to glorify God for His mercy. Every spiritual "stranger" however alone, can joyously delight in this "abundant peace."

DECEMBER 2

Blessed be the God and Father of our Lord Jesus Christ, which according to his abundant mercy hath begotten us again unto a lively hope by the resurrection of Jesus Christ from the dead, To an inheritance incorruptible, and undefiled, and that fadeth not away, reserved in heaven for you.

—1 PETER 1:3–4

Hope is a grace which sufferers are invited to enjoy. It is their duty, their calling, and their dignity; and it is blessedly their comfort. Hope is not a doubtful uncertainty with which we often get ourselves into great anxiety over temporal things; it is an expectation of promises being fulfilled by the One most able and most willing to fulfill them. It focuses on what is unseen by the eye and enjoys the "evidence of things not seen." It both promotes and thrives upon patience, which, when it has "its perfect work," makes the hopeful person "perfect and entire, wanting nothing" (James 1:4). Hope growing together with patience and experience "maketh not ashamed, because the love of God is shed abroad in our hearts by the Holy Ghost which is given unto us" (Rom. 5:5).

It is no wonder then that Peter marvels at the "abundant mercy" of the Father who has begotten us unto this lively hope. But the source of this new birth to living hope is the greatest revelation of His abundant mercy—Jesus Christ. God is the Father of our Lord Jesus Christ in the highest sense in Trinitarian glory. He is His God in the gospel of His incarnation, death, and resurrection. It is in Christ that believers are made partakers of the benefits of sons; the Father views them in Him. They are justified in Him and adopted into the family, partaking of an inheritance which they have in common with each other. Believers are begotten again as sons of God and Christ's image is formed in them. This is the source from which hope and every other benefit comes.

This lively hope that believers have by virtue of their union with the risen Lord Jesus also has a most glorious content. It is not an empty and vacant wish. It is full of reality, of certainties, of eternal substance. We are called to hope for a pure, incorruptible, and eternal inheritance. Holiness of heart is in our hope, for nothing enters heaven that will defile. A body that can sustain a "weight of glory" without corruption is in our hope. A perpetual enjoyment of the secure reward, with all its hidden wonders is in our hope. Oh, for a more lively enjoyment now of those things hoped for.

Let Israel hope in the Lord, for with Him mercies be.

For all flesh is as grass, and all the glory
of man as the flower of grass.
—1 PETER 1:24

The mortality of man is well expressed by the word "flesh." We are body and spirit, but our frailty and readiness to dissolution and decay is emphasized by this humbling title. That we are flesh and that all flesh is as grass is frequently repeated in Scripture.

Moses acknowledged of man in Psalm 90:6 that like grass "in the morning it flourisheth, and groweth up; in the evening it is cut down and withereth." In Psalm 103:15–16, it is recorded that "As for man, his days are as grass: as a flower of the field so he flourisheth. For the wind passeth over it, and it is gone; and the place thereof shall know it no more." It is for our instruction that we are so often reminded of it. May we not ask with David, "LORD, make me to know mine end, and the measure of my days, what it is; that I may know how frail I am" (Ps. 39:4)?

As it is a humbling thought, it ought to be an alarming thought also if we have not rightly considered eternity. Earnest attention must be given to the fact that our days are uncertain here and that we cling to life by a thread. That we are exposed to death numerous times daily is demonstrated over and over at the expense of others. This frail life is easily cut down. Fear of death is natural to man, and it is not entirely lost in those justified in Christ and renewed by grace. A trembling sensitivity to the "issues from death" is appropriate for all who have understood the significance of eternal realities.

Doubtless, the dignity of human nature and the achievements of science suggest a glory beyond that which adorns the vegetable world. Perhaps the heart of man rebels against the comparison that he is as grass. Even if his glory were to be given a more pleasant name—"all the glory of man is as the flower of the field"—the brevity and uncertainty of it remains a stark fact. The highest dignity and honor to which man can rise is but short-lived and fading.

Yet there is hope, too. The words are part of a contrast: "But the word of the Lord endureth forever." Here is stability and security for man. The promises of the gospel relied upon put dying men in possession of life everlasting. Here alone is a hope of future glory that will not wither or decay.

As newborn babes, desire the sincere milk of the word, that ye may grow thereby: if so be ye have tasted that the Lord is gracious.

—1 PETER 2:2–3

True believers have many lovely characteristics illustrated by Scripture pictures; that of newborn babes is among the most attractive. It is the calling of all believers to live "as newborn babes." Except they be converted and become as little children, they cannot see the kingdom. Becoming as little children is one of life's great lessons, and without radical Spirit work in the soul no man will take on this likeness. Old men with child-like faith and babe-like desires are the adornment of Christianity and an evidence of the power of grace to a proud world. Spiritual growth is, with respect to self, downward. God's children are more ready for heaven the closer they resemble the newborn babe in the exercises of dependence and loving desire.

There is a beautiful simplicity in the desires of newborn babes. The singleness of purpose in seeking the mother's milk is seen from the very moment of birth. Only sickness prevents the infant from sucking the breast on which it exclusively relies for life and strength. The relation of the newborn child of grace to the Word of God mirrors this most natural of human responses and is a defining feature of true Christianity in the soul. It is an indisputable evidence of spiritual life that our souls draw strength and life out of the Word of God. Desire for the Scriptures of truth and seeking in them for daily feeding is the lifelong activity of Christians, and by this they grow to full maturity. It is as surely a sign of serious spiritual malady or worse when the Bible is neglected and its pages seldom turned.

What gives a Christian such an appetite for the "sincere milk of the word"? Doubtless, its veracity and truthfulness is a great appeal. They know not the voice of strangers and their faith rests in a divine revelation to which the Holy Spirit inwardly bears witness. But the message of that revelation is a message of God's grace. It is the "glad tidings of great joy." Christ comes to give grace and that grace is not only revealed in but conveyed by the truth. The mouth of the newborn babe soon masters the art of drawing forth milk. So, too, does faith, the mouth of the soul, when once it has tasted that the Lord is gracious, draw more and more from the Word. Having first tasted this grace, there will be a desire for more of it.

By whose stripes ye were healed.
—1 PETER 2:24

The example of Christ in suffering wrongfully is a motive to fortitude under unjust reproaches and afflictions. Who can murmur at suffering for well-doing who rightly considers the patience and meekness of the Lamb of God? He "opened not his mouth" against His persecutors. Believers are to follow this example and, in suffering for well-doing, must learn to "take it patiently." Their beloved Master Himself exhorts, "Learn of me for I am meek and lowly in heart."

But the sufferings of Christ are much more to suffering believers than an example. Indeed, Christ will not profit them as an example at all if He is nothing more than an example. There is no true gospel motive to holiness in mere martyrdom, however excellent the cause and however patient the sufferer. The gospel content in Christ's sufferings is, therefore, all important if believers are to find strengthening virtue in the example of Christ's sufferings. It is this that Peter lays emphasis on when exhorting them to follow Christ's example.

The stripes of Christ are healing from the guilt of sin. By enduring the accursed death of the cross, He "his own self bare our sins." Every wound points to Him as the Sin-bearer and the burden is removed from His believing people because He took it. His stripes also heal from the corruption and defilement of sin. It is through His death that believers die to sin and, by virtue of His resurrection, rise to newness of life in union with Him. Being dead to sins, they live unto righteousness. This is a wonderful healing which His own power alone could effect. It is the virtue that comes out of Him when the sin-sick soul touches the hem of His garment.

Under sufferings for His sake, believers are healed from the bitterness of the curse. They are sanctified by sufferings. Christ has taken the sting out of sufferings and, by looking on Him whom they pierced by their sins, they are made willing to endure with patience whatever He appoints for their sanctification. They cannot forget what He has done for them in bringing them out of "the horrible pit and the miry clay" and their remembrance of His mercy to them is the supreme motive to them in following His example and walking in His steps.

*And who is he that will harm you, if ye
be followers of that which is good?*
—1 PETER 3:13

The definition of good has always been the subject of controversy and of many wasted words. Any student of Scripture and conscience must conclude with Micah, "He hath shown thee, O man, what is good" (Mic. 6:8). Here the debate has an end. "Good works are only such as God hath commanded in his holy word, and not such as, without the warrant thereof, are devised by men out of blind zeal, or upon any pretence of good intention" (*Westminster Confession of Faith*, 16:1). The apostle in this chapter sets out clearly what following good entails when he exhorts to the relational duties of wives, husbands, and spiritual brethren. To Timothy, Paul states that "the end of the commandment is charity out of a pure heart, and of a good conscience, and of faith unfeigned" (1 Tim. 1:5). This is goodness in the eyes of the Lord.

Goodness will never arise in the heart of one who is a stranger to Christ. Union with Him is the root of all spiritual goodness in man. That union is effected by the Holy Spirit who begins "the good work" and will "perform it until the day of Jesus Christ." What men think to be good and what is called "spiritual" by men is utterly devoid of goodness when the soul is not the dwelling place of the Spirit of Christ. Christ has secured the gift of the indwelling of the Holy Spirit for all His children, and His righteousness, presented before God for them, is the only ground upon which the Spirit is sent to them. The faith by which they trust in the merit of Christ is His gift and by faith alone they stand as righteous before God.

Following good will often involves believers in hardship. Such afflictions as believers were to expect in apostolic times, we may also be called to for following good. How necessary in such circumstances is the *pure heart*—undivided in devotion to Him who is the Fountain of all goodness. How indispensible also is the *good conscience*, "purged from dead works" by the application to us of Christ's righteousness. To be a follower of that which is good, *unfeigned faith* in a gracious Savior, in God who orders providence and the Holy Spirit's sufficient grace to help in time of need is vital. With such a defense, death itself can be faced by the righteous. On such the tender eye of Jehovah is ever set.

For Christ also hath once suffered for sins, the just for the unjust, that he might bring us to God, being put to death in the flesh, but quickened by the Spirit.
—1 PETER 3:18

Few words of such simplicity sum up so much as the expression, "the just for the unjust." Here is the gospel in five words. Here is the hope of believers and the ground upon which all their worship, obedience, service, praise, and prayer is offered to God. Without this, they are helpless, lost, ruined, and miserable. Here are words to satisfy conscience, administer peace, stir up the most profound sense of admiration, and generate eternal praise among numberless redeemed souls. The truth that these words contain dry many tears, relieve many sorrows, bind up many broken hearts, and make many deathbeds soft and gentle. That Peter intended believers in suffering to receive their consolation here cannot be doubted. What they received, believers today can and also do receive.

Reflect for a little on the title "the just." Christ is God. He is infinite, eternal, and unchangeable in His holiness, justice, goodness, and truth. As Lawmaker, He is Righteousness itself. Consider His mediatorial Person. The Son of God took into union with His divine person a holy humanity. As Mediator, He is God-man. The nature He took was not sinful flesh, but "the likeness of sinful flesh." His humanity had no defilement. No actual sins in thought, word, or deed did He ever commit. All the infinite merit of His divine nature and the sinlessness of His human nature are in all His mediatorial acts. He is, therefore, perfectly, unchangeably, and gloriously "the Just One" (Acts 7:52).

Consider the words "for the unjust." As Mediator, Christ takes the place of sinners, standing in point of law exactly where they stood. He is Surety for their debt, Scapegoat for their sin, Near-kinsman for their redemption from sin and misery. He acts instead of them in obeying the law. He suffers instead of them in dying the accursed death of the cross. He suffers the hell of His people. The flaming sword awakes against Him who is their Shepherd. He gives His life for the sheep.

The life He gave was perfect. Exactly as their sins were imputed to the Mediator, so His righteousness is imputed to them. No less are they righteous than He is righteous. They who are unjust are "justified freely by his grace through the redemption that is in Christ Jesus" (Rom. 3:24). Because imputation is permitted, God is just when He justifies the ungodly who believe in Jesus. Here is the source of peace, consolation, and comfort.

Which sometimes were disobedient, when once the longsuffering of God waited in the days of Noah, while the ark was a-preparing, wherein few, that is, eight souls were saved by water.
—1 PETER 3:20

Disobedience implies that a law exists. "Where no law is, there is no transgression" (Rom. 4:15). Natural conscience tells us that a law exists, but these transgressors had more than that; they had God's revelation. This was therefore a most solemn disobedience. It is spoken of the generation of Noah about whom Christ said, "they did eat, they drank, they married wives, they were given in marriage" (Luke 17:27). But they were disobedient. "God saw that the wickedness of man was great in the earth, and that every imagination of the thoughts of his heart was only evil continually" (Gen. 6:5). Noah was "a preacher of righteousness" doubtless testifying, as Lot did, against their unlawful deeds (2 Pet. 2:5). His life and his words were their Bible, and they disobeyed the Word of God to them.

Peter says that Christ preached to them by the Spirit. They are now in the prison of hell, but, through Noah, the Spirit was striving with them (Gen. 6:1). The threatened flood was to act as the law does now in the conscience—condemning sin. Thus God, in great forbearance, left Noah among them for one hundred and twenty years after the command to build the ark was given. God waited these years and endured with much longsuffering their wicked deeds and disobedience. With every nail and every board in the ark's construction, Noah reasoned with them of "righteousness, temperance, and judgment to come" (Acts 24:25). Of none do we read that they trembled.

But consider God's longsuffering in another way. The preparation of the ark spoke of salvation from the flood, deliverance from punishment, and the promise of life. Was it not then an invitation to receive mercy? Christ "went and preached" to them. Giving them time to repent, God said of them, "Yet his days shall be one hundred and twenty years." Here was a gracious appeal to them to repent. The Scottish preacher, Charles Calder Mackintosh, once said, "It is plain that if any of us shall perish forever, it is not through want of mercy in God, or through want of merit in Christ to save us, and it is not through want of the fullest, freest, and most gratuitous tender of both to every soul that hears the gospel that we perish, but it is through our own wilful and most criminal contempt of the mercy of God and the Saviour of a lost world."

But the end of all things is at hand: be ye therefore sober, and watch unto prayer.
—1 PETER 4:7

The three duties that are here commended—sobriety, watchfulness, and prayer—comprehend the Christian warfare. Sobriety towards all outward things, watchfulness over his heart, and a private life of prayer become every Christian.

Towards all outward things, sobriety should be a marked feature of the believer. He is called to higher pleasures than what this world offers and should refrain from the indulgent characteristic of those whose portion is only here below. In the necessary use of earthly things, he must be measured and proportioned, keeping his heart from excessive attachment to them. Drunkenness, reveling, and such like, being works of the flesh, are wholly inconsistent with the spiritual frame of mind to which renewed souls are called.

The frame of soul most conducive to sobriety and prayer is watchfulness. The disciples needed it in the garden when Satan desired to sift them as wheat. It consists in that vigilant, wary, and wakeful posture which will not be surprised by temptations. It includes a daily care of our heart and careful self-scrutiny, discovering the deceit of our own corruption. The Christian is to be on military guard duty and that makes him suspicious of himself. He mistrusts the hidden pleasures offered by the world. Yet he must be as careful to avoid self-righteous moroseness.

The source of strength for the whole Christian life is in God Himself. Prayer is, therefore, the secret weapon of believers in their spiritual warfare. Prayer is the end aimed at in sobriety and watchfulness. As prayer is helpful to sobriety and to watchfulness, so they in turn enable us better in the duty of prayer. With them, we have that heavenly frame necessary for communion with God and they encourage a proper perspective on those things we would ask from God. Prayer must arise from a hungry soul that thirsts after God, seeking to be satisfied with His comforts. When our hearts are filled with worldly cares and pleasures, we cannot thirst for God.

Eternity is our watchword. We too often forget how near we are to the eternal world and need to be reminded of it. Since this world must soon end for us, what business have we to be laying out so much of our desires and endeavors on earthly things which will soon vanish, rather than for heavenly enjoyments and securities? "Whom have I in heaven but thee? And there is none upon earth that I desire beside thee" (Ps. 73:25).

But the end of all things is at hand: be ye therefore sober.
—1 PETER 4:7

Mortifying lust is a lifetime labor for the Christian and can only be performed through faith in Christ crucified. Peter explains in verse 1 that, as Christ suffered for His people by bearing their sins, so they must suffer by ceasing from sin. They must crucify their lusts, nailing the hands of lust, nailing the feet of lust, and piercing the heart of lust. They must in this way mortify their members which are upon the earth. It will not be without pain. Christians are called to be different from what they once were when they lived according to their lusts and gave them free rein. Their whole perspective on sin has been changed and they treat their own hearts with far greater seriousness than before. Soberness of mind should define Christians.

In every age, believers have had to endure the taunts of the world from whom they have separated themselves. Their former companions in sin will always think it strange that the change has been so complete and lasting. It is certain that as believers find the world crucified to them, so the world also finds believers crucified to it. This is how it should be, and however falsely accused they may be for their "good conversation in Christ," they must not return to the mire after having been washed. They cannot abandon themselves as before to add drunkenness to thirst. They must live soberly, righteously, and godly in this present world. As well as a new perspective on sin, they have a new focus on eternity. They know that they live here in preparation for another world and they should live under the shadow of it with serious and sober minds.

While believers have a right in Christ to a good hope for eternity and while the slavish fear of judgment is answered by the grace of God in justification, yet they live in soberness as they contemplate the judgment seat of Christ. While the ungodly may live as though they will be in this life forever, the Christian must soberly judge this life in light of its end. Believers should look beyond that great Day of Judgment to an eternal blessedness. Yet they must wrestle with sin and mortify lust while they are in the world, considering that they will give account to God at last. Their only hope in doing so is to seek grace from Christ daily for the conquering of sin.

For the time is come that judgment must begin at the house of God: and if it first begin at us, what shall the end be of them that obey not the gospel of God?

—1 PETER 4:17

Daniel was told that "many shall be purified, and made white, and tried" (Dan. 12:10). In accordance with this prophecy, Christians have always viewed suffering times as purging times. The great Scottish Covenanter statesman, Archibald Campbell, Marquis of Argyle, who suffered martyrdom in 1661, warned his contemporaries that the times would be either suffering or sinning times. His death was a choice of suffering before sinning and in this way he was purified and made white. As he made his way to execution, the godly Marquis said to his friends, "Come away, gentlemen, he that goes first goes cleanliest." Knowing that compromise would sully a pure conscience, he refused to deny his allegiance to Christ and his crown rights. He died in hope of glory. Many like him in Scotland died for conscience sake and were preserved from sinning in suffering times. In times like these, Christ sat as a refiner and purifier of silver, but, according to His promise, He brought "the third part through the fire."

Multitudes in countries all over the world for two thousand years have preferred suffering to sinning and have proved Christ true to His Word. It is through much tribulation that they entered the Kingdom. Judgment or trial in the house of God separates the genuine Christian from the mere formalist and the hypocrite. It is not a strange or new thing for that trial to come, and the grace to abide and endure it is a gift of Christ to those who "commit the keeping of their souls to him in well-doing." There is no shame in reproach for Christ's sake and a great honor in suffering "according to the will of God."

The shame will rather belong to those who prefer sinning to suffering. There have been many such in times of open persecution and many in times of moral laxity and spiritual decay. If the righteous must enter the kingdom through the fire of trial and suffering, how perilous will be the end of those who think to enter some other way! What will their end be who do not obey the gospel? The willing obedience of faith to the call of the gospel is always followed by the obedience of holiness to the law of the King. Disobedience here will bring on the head of sinners the wrath of the King when He comes to judge the world. Believers may be chastened and tried here, but it is so that they will not be "condemned with the world" at last.

> *Wherefore the rather, brethren, give diligence*
> *to make your calling and election sure.*
> —2 PETER 1:10

The calling of believers is to "glory and virtue" (v. 3), and their duty to practice virtue is not lessened by the dependence they have on grace to produce it in them. They are to be giving all diligence in adding virtue to their faith. Faith was never alone in them, but as faith grows, so virtue, knowledge, temperance, and the other adornments of the Christian grow in proportion. This is what they are called to and it is to be the whole activity of their lives to attain to that heavenly calling. Dependent on grace they most certainly are, but this is no excuse for negligence or indifference. It is rather a stimulus to diligence.

There are great and blessed advantages in the exercise of this diligence. Peter intimates these as an encouragement. Diligence in good works secures the believer from barrenness. Similarly, the lack of diligence in good works will open the door to many evils and to grievous troubles for the Christian. He will be blinded, short-sighted, and forgetful. These are relative evils for true believers but very troublesome in whatever degree they are found. Their blindness makes them unable to see those heavenly things that God has prepared for those who love Him. Their short-sightedness means that they cannot penetrate beyond this world and the things which are temporal. Their forgetfulness is a loss of the sense of pardon and the blessed peace which results from it. A believer in this condition loses his assurance that he is loved of God and has to that degree lost his comfort.

So Peter, in his exhortation to give diligent attention to the end and purpose of his calling, has in mind the Christian man's comfort. That comfort of knowing our election may only be had in being sure of our calling. The doctrine of election is, therefore, useful for the comfort of obedient and sincere believers. The security which it gives to the believer is absolute and enduring. In the path of gospel obedience, he is confirmed in the hope of heaven and can be assured that he will "never fall" into apostasy. Losing sight of their election of God destroys their comfort, and true believers will need to strive for its recovery. Peter points them to the method by which that comfort can be recovered: "give diligence to make your calling and election sure." The order cannot be reversed. We only know our election by being sure of our calling.

The Lord knoweth how to deliver the godly out of temptations.
—2 PETER 2:9

This wonderful truth is recorded concerning Lot. We may otherwise have foolishly questioned his godliness and piety in an uncharitable and hasty way. We remember how he was drawn away from the fellowship of Abraham by the hostility of his herdsmen and the attractiveness of the plain of Jordan. Doubtless the beauty and the fruitfulness of the place, likened to Eden itself, induced him to compromise himself and his family as he settled down in such close proximity to the wicked cities of Sodom and Gomorrah. We consider his choice to have been unwise and we can conclude that the Lord also disapproved of it. While he ultimately maintained his integrity, he did so by vexing his soul from day to day and with terrible consequences for his wife and family. But he was delivered.

The deliverance of Lot from Sodom was a very notable example of God's grace towards him and also of God's recognition of Abraham's prayers on his behalf. Wonderful, too, was the intimation made to him by the angel that the divine purpose concerning the destruction of Sodom could not be executed until Lot was removed from the place. Again we find God longsuffering towards him when He permitted him to live for a time in Zoar and spared that city while he was there. The evidence is so clear that nothing can compromise the Lord's care and protection of His own people, however culpable they may be for falling into the mire. God will open up avenues and secure means for their escape from every kind of danger into which sin and temptation will lead them. Whether they fall into temptation by yielding to their own lusts, or whether they are sovereignly tried and tested by the Lord with troubles and afflictions, the Lord always orders and appoints means by which they will endure the fire or escape the snare of temptation.

In this way we are to learn by experience that trust in the Lord is our defense. By this faith, His people obtain the victory over temptation. Surprising and alarming as temptation may be, let us look for the way of escape as we meet with trials, for it will certainly be provided. Thus, we can rejoice at last that we were "kept by the power of God through faith unto salvation" (1 Pet. 1:5).

> *The Lord is not slack concerning his promise,*
> *as some men count slackness.*
>
> —2 PETER 3:9

In the life of the believer, there are two sources of temptation which bring him to question the promises of God: afflictions may test his faith and hope to nearly the breaking point, and the scornful taunts of the world concerning God's promises may, in seasons of doubt, further shake his faith and confidence. The emphatic and direct assertions of Scripture are designed to banish such temptations and thus to strengthen and confirm faith in the promises. Considering these in humble faith, the believer can rest and wait through the sorest trials and amid the bitterest scorn. He can hope with expectation for the fulfillment of God's promises.

The promise of Christ's second coming is given much prominence in the New Testament. Yet scornful unbelievers in Peter's day asked, "Where is the promise of His coming?" They deliberately overlooked the clear demonstration of God's judgment in the universal flood; in God's revealed will, there is a similar promise of future judgment by fire. However long ago it may have been since "the fathers fell asleep," and however set on doing evil the hearts of men may be because "judgment against an evil work is not executed speedily," the Lord's promises will all be honored. Among men, delay may be counted slackness, change of mind, inability to act, or even unfaithfulness. No such view can be entertained concerning God's promises. The fulfillment of God's purposes must be viewed in the light of His relation to the passage of time—"one day is with the Lord as a thousand years, and a thousand years as one day."

So the Lord is not slack concerning His promise. He will surely come and will not tarry. Believers, though they are troubled, must rest until the Lord Jesus is revealed from heaven with His mighty angels in flaming fire. Only then will all wrongs be put right. He will come "to be glorified in his saints and admired in all them that believe" (2 Thess. 1:10). They say now, "Even so, come, Lord Jesus," and they wait with loving, hopeful, expectant faith for His appearing. They look for that day with sobriety and godly fear while knowing that it is to be the day of their full and final redemption in body as well as soul. The scorning unbeliever is more to be pitied than to be a cause for fretting.

But grow in grace, and in the knowledge of
our Lord and Saviour Jesus Christ.
—2 PETER 3:18

Peter's second epistle is particularly full of direct and challenging warnings for believers. The ever present danger of being caught in the snares of the devil was something with which he was personally acquainted. By constant and solemn warning, he strengthens his brethren. Knowing himself what the sifting of Satan was, he desires that the sheep and lambs of Christ would be spared the wounds which their enemies would inflict on them.

His closing exhortation is, however, a most winning and positive encouragement. It is one of those directions which are found sprinkled throughout the Bible in abundance—a comprehensive summary of the whole life of the child of God. Here is the conclusion of the whole epistle in which his great aim is encapsulated in a few brief words of great simplicity and depth. The Holy Spirit would thus rivet the attention of the church on its fundamental and essential character and the way in which it would be formed. Here is its privilege and its duty in one: "grow in grace, and in the knowledge of our Lord and Savior Jesus Christ."

The common style of Scripture is to give exhortations a double emphasis. This exhortation is set out in such a way as to point to the end in view, and also the means by which it will be reached. Growth in grace here may well be taken as the atmosphere of God's gracious covenant in which the tender plant is nourished. Grace is the nursery bed, or the soil, in which believers are planted and in which they develop spiritual roots and fruits. The warm atmosphere of that grace is where they are placed and in which they must remain until transplanted into the Eden of the heavenly paradise of God. This atmosphere is the privilege of believers and it defines the character of the life of grace.

Yet here, too, is duty. How are believers to remain in this atmosphere? They live in the cold and harsh climate of an ungodly world; how are they to abide in the grace of God? How are they to keep themselves in the love of God? It is by a growing and increasing acquaintance with Christ as their personal Lord and Savior. The more they know Him spiritually (and they must use appointed means, as reading, hearing, and meditation), the surer will be their growth and the firmer will be their hold as God's plants in the grace of Christ.

Behold, he cometh with clouds; and every eye shall see him, and they also which pierced him.
—REVELATION 1:7

To New Testament believers, Christ is "the faithful witness, and the first begotten from the dead, and the prince of the kings of the earth." His testimony seals Old Testament types and prophecies and dispenses with all shadows. His revelation is sufficient and reliable. He is the risen Lord, ascended on high, and has "received gifts…for the rebellious" (Ps. 68:18). He is Lord by whom "kings reign and princes decree justice" (Prov. 8:15), and is "head over all things to the church" (Eph. 1:22). To believers, He is that glorious one who "loved us, and washed us from our sins in his own blood." His glory is founded on this marvelous work for which He will be the object of their eternal praise.

Not recognized by the world nor valued for His grace, Christ's return will be welcomed by His beloved people who look for Him. But *every* human eye shall see Him: "Kings of the earth, and all people; princes, and all judges of the earth: both young men, and maidens; old men and children" (Ps. 148:11–12). Though after skin worms destroy the body, in our flesh we shall see God (Job 19:26).

Many eyes will then be filled with fear. Those who would not have Him reign over them will flee from Him and wail because of Him. The dead shall be raised from their graves and gathered before Him, and He will be seen in His glory and in His Father's glory with all the holy angels. He will then sit upon His glorious throne. They who pierced Christ shall see Him. The soldiers and wicked rulers who crucified Him will then meet Him. Believers, for whose sins He was pierced and who by faith looked upon Him whom they pierced with bitter repentance, will also see Him. Their view of the pierced One shall be joyous beyond description.

His coming will be in "like manner as ye have seen him go into heaven" (Acts 1:11)—He will come with clouds. This picture demonstrates power, dignity, superiority, and heavenly glory. He "maketh the clouds his chariot, who walketh on the wings of the wind" (Ps. 104:3). We need not stand "gazing up into heaven" to anticipate His return. We can look for Him with faith, hope, love, patience, and longing as we attend to the duties of our calling. Reconciled by His blood, we are saved from wrath through Him and are made heirs of blessedness.

Nevertheless I have somewhat against thee,
because thou hast left thy first love.
—REVELATION 2:4

Orthodoxy and faithfulness are beautiful and fitting adornments of the church of Jesus Christ. He recognizes, honors, and commends both in His message to the Ephesians. Nothing less is required than resistance to evil, whether in the form of doctrinal error or corrupt practice. The Ephesians were "created in Christ Jesus unto good works," and their labor and patience for His name is, through the Apostle John, highly praised by Christ Himself. Hating what Christ hates is an evidence of love to Him as King, and that love is not ignored or forgotten by Him.

Yet something is amiss when orthodoxy and even consistency in outward practice and church order is all that a Christian church is known for in the world. So much more is looked for by Christ than these commendable attributes. The charge of dead orthodoxy, so often leveled at sincere Christians earnestly contending for the faith, is only valid when their contending is not earnest enough or when that earnestness is not a response to the constraint of Christ's love to them. Legal motives directing orthodoxy not only tend to an eventual decline in orthodoxy, but they are also most offensive and grievous to the Savior, for whose sake alone Christians are to make their stand against evil in the world.

Not a few who begin with great outward zeal for the Savior fall into error or make shipwreck on some worldly lust. Many others, having been embraced by a loving Savior who passed them in "a time of love" and who continue faithful to their post in His service outwardly, often bemoan the coldness of their affections. Doubtless, the repentance urged by Christ will arise in the heart when they "look upon me whom they have pierced," and reflect afresh on the deep obligation they are under to a bruised Savior. Like Legion, they are called in their service to Christ to tell what great things the Lord has done for them, who has had compassion on them.

Nothing is so certainly effectual under the Spirit to recover our first love than those renewed discoveries of the dying love of Christ to us. No contending for the faith, under the Spirit's blessing, will have a more telling effect on the ungodly than that which comes from a heart aflame with love to a crucified and risen Savior.

Be thou faithful unto death, and I will give thee a crown of life.
—REVELATION 2:10

Christ's messages to this church in Smyrna and to the church in Philadelphia contain no rebuke or correction—only encouragement and admonition to constancy. Christ has the "tongue of the learned" and knows how to speak a word in season to the weary. Smyrna was already tried by poverty and would be further tried by persecution. Her constancy in the one, for she is commended for her spiritual riches, encouraged her to remain faithful under the other also. Christ tells her she is rich toward God to strengthen faith in the fire of persecution.

Many dear saints of God have throughout history been cast into prison for Christ's sake. Today, there are many who languish in prison or under cruel tyranny for Him also. While martyrs of past ages have left records of God's gracious visits at such times, it is not always, and perhaps not ordinarily, the experience of the saints under tribulation. Suffering and fear are as commonly the daily portion of imprisoned believers as Christ's love visits and what Samuel Rutherford called "Immanuel's sweet face." Christ knows that sorrow and recognizes that fear, that loneliness and bitter grief of being parted from friends and dear ones. He is touched with the feeling of their infirmities and addresses it with the utmost tenderness.

Consolation for Christ's prisoners certainly includes the fact of His knowledge and sympathy. He is also "able to succour them that are tempted." He provides strong reasons for every "fear not" that He offers. He sets a certain and prescribed limit on the time that the devil can trouble His saints and then holds back his chain. He intimates the assurance that all troubles here shall have their end eventually for those who "overcome by the blood of the Lamb and the word of their testimony." Most conspicuously of all, His comforts are the promise of the reward. Maybe He will not give emancipation from cruel deaths and bonds, but He will give emancipation in death to those who die for Him. To the tried Christian, the crown of life is a crown of joy and consolation. It brings Christ Himself and life in His presence. Often it is only those who suffer for Him here that find the joy in contemplating the crown of life.

To him that overcometh will I give to eat of the hidden manna.
—REVELATION 2:17

Pergamos already had a martyr for Christ in Antipas, but the church had proved faithful in spite of the horror of death threatening its constancy. Clearly, the world was peculiarly active in its opposition to the gospel in Pergamos, for Christ says that Satan dwelt there. Doubtless this will show itself in many ways today also. Satan dwells where men give free license to their lusts and serve him without restraint or hindrance. Like Balaam in olden times, Satan has succeeded in a strategy of deception when open violence has been unsuccessful. The church in Pergamos had been ensnared by uncleanness and false worship. There were those who held that same "doctrine of Balaam"—the Nicolaitans—and for their sakes Christ rebukes the church.

It is as true today that license being given to worldly practices and pleasures among Christians will eventually lead to corruption in God's worship. The sin of the church was to tolerate such laxity and innovation. In our own lives, we can be sure that our worship of God is corrupted if we are entertaining known lusts and sins. At best, it will be mere formalism and hypocrisy. At such times, Christ has "something against us" and requires that we put away the accursed thing and "cleanse our hands and purify our hearts."

Yet there was a majority in Pergamos who remained faithful and who had no taste for the worldly pleasures intruded on the Christian congregations there. Like Israel, they fed on manna in the wilderness. The Christian's manna in their journey to the heavenly Canaan is Christ Himself and particularly His atoning work—His broken body and shed blood. "The bread that I will give is my flesh which I will give for the life of the world." Faith feeds on the doctrine of Christ's Person, office, and work. Weak and strong faith both have their portion. He who gathers least has no lack and he who gathers most has nothing over. God promises the hidden manna to those who overcome. This is the same Christ in never-failing enjoyment, reserved in the heavenly tabernacle for them.

In heaven, believers will feed on Christ without distraction and without the intrusions of Balaam's doctrine. They will be filled with the contemplation of Christ in all His excellencies as their Redeemer and Lord. In praising, Him they will become like Him in holiness and enjoy the fullness of joy to all eternity.

The last to be more than the first.
—REVELATION 2:19

Like one who has planted a vine, Christ is always observing His church for signs of progress in grace. His commendation of Thyatira for charity, service, patience, and works is not complete without notice being taken that she had grown in these graces—the last was more than the first. Certainly, they had notable failings in discipline like Pergamos, but here is high praise. Such a commendation is intended by Christ for the comfort and further progress of His church. He desires to put no other burden on her than what she had already. He is kind and gentle in His recognition of what in reality must only be small growth in comparison with the perfection to be attained. He spoke softly to those who knew not "the depths of Satan" while thundering against those who were in these depths by sin. As ever, He comforts, encourages, and admonishes to constancy.

What progress have we made in grace since first we believed? This is a necessary question for Christians. The duty of self-examination is doubtless much neglected and often misrepresented as undue introspection. If it is engaged in superficially or in a legalistic manner, it will dishearten and vex our souls or it will feed pride and complacency. If it is honestly kept up as a regular exercise with the necessary dependence on the Spirit and with a constant eye to a gracious Master, it is designed for our comfort and growth. Christ's words are intended to be helpful to further growth. This commendation of Thyatira should encourage us to further and more thorough self-examination.

What growth should we look for? What evidence of growth in grace can we take comfort from? How is that comfort properly enjoyed so as not to arrest the very progress made? If we are growing in grace, we will be growing in proportion. Notice how the fruit of the Spirit is often given in its variety. Certainly, believers may excel in one grace, but not without some proportion in the whole Christian life. Growth in grace will comfort us when accompanied by love to our neighbor, when self-love is being crucified and when we have a desire to know and love Christ more. That comfort will quicken to further progress when Christ is seen as the only cause of all grace in us, and when He is expressly relied upon and looked to for its supply and for its every expression.

Thou hast a few names even in Sardis which have not defiled their garments; and they shall walk with me in white: for they are worthy.
—REVELATION 3:4

It is a most difficult duty to walk contrary to the popular opinion within the church of Christ. To live in a way that condemns other professing Christians is frequently judged to be censorious. Much grace is needed to avoid hypocrisy and evil-speaking when our conscience will not permit us to follow the accepted departures within the church. It was like this for some believers in Sardis. The expression "even in Sardis" is a withering rebuke to a declining church. The majority had defiled their garments and were tragically unaware of any corruption. Indeed, they had a reputation for liveliness, which doubtless bred pride. To Christ, a name was nothing, because He knew them to be dead. The few in Sardis who lived circumspectly and walked humbly with Him were very probably the object of scorn and ridicule. Such persecution from professing brethren is often the most difficult to bear.

Spiritual life in believers is often defined in the Bible in negative terms. The Ten Commandments are for the most part expressed in the negative. Paul commonly exhorts believers to avoid evil and to separate themselves from disorder and uncleanness. It is true that the positive duties of Christians are implied in every negative command and it is also true that holiness of life must have "good works" in a way that demonstrates the reality of faith. Yet, in a world of increasing immorality and in a professing church that walks with the world, the Christian is especially called to a separate life. To do so inoffensively and graciously is perhaps the greatest challenge.

The reward promised to a holy life is that they will walk with Christ in white. Believers have a white robe when they are justified. The white that is in this promise refers to their sanctification. The more tender in conscience a Christian is, the more afraid he is of the potential for sin in his own heart. They long for perfect holiness and they rejoice in the hope of heaven as a place where they will never sin. This promise is therefore most appealing to true believers. They know that Christ's generous estimation of their life here—that they have not defiled their garments—is a gracious "passing by transgression" and that they require much of His sanctifying grace. Heaven is a place of happiness to them because there they will see Christ as He is, and in seeing Him, they will be like Him. Nothing can compare to that.

Behold, I have set before thee an open door, and no man can shut it: for thou hast a little strength, and hast kept my word, and hast not denied my name.
— REVELATION 3:8

Philadelphia means "brotherly love" and this seems to have been a feature of this church because there were no divisions in doctrine or practice requiring Christ's rebuke. Unity and uniformity are marks of Christ's church. Christ represents Himself to this church as the one in possession of the key of David, which signified the government of the church (Isa. 22:22). By preaching and by discipline, the church has the ministerial power of the keys. Even a church with a little strength has this honor entrusted to it. Christ rewards faithfulness when He reviews and examines His church. What she does ministerially, Christ does as Lord and Governor in heaven. It is He who opens and shuts. No satanic or human power can reverse what He determines within the church.

An open door is needed in every field of labor that the church is called to. Too often, impatience, reliance on human wisdom, and unsanctified haste try to open doors where Christ has not given His key. All such efforts, however sincerely pursued, are doomed to disappointment. Evangelistic effort, missionary vision, and private witnessing for Christ must depend on and look to Christ Himself for an open door. Without this, success cannot be expected. Preachers must fervently pray for an open door of utterance and of "the demonstration of the Spirit and of power." Only when Christ opens the heart will any sinner attend to the things that are spoken.

Our reliance on Christ to open doors does not, however, encourage inactivity and neglect of duty. So often believers are called to go forward in faith and do not see the open door until faith obeys the leading of the Spirit in the Word. Prayer must be mixed with every duty and faithfulness to our duty should give us reason to look for an open door in the appointed time. Whether our calling is to preach or to witness for Christ in a less public manner in our home or place of work, Christ opens doors which no man can shut when His weak and dependent people wait on Him in believing prayer. There will be times when disappointment and doubt will overwhelm even the most faithful servant of Christ as he sees little fruit for his labor. There will be times of despondency for Christ's faithful witnesses in the hostile world, too. But the joy of an open door will more than compensate for our patient waiting.

Behold, I stand at the door and knock: if any man hear my voice and open the door, I will come in to him, and will sup with him, and he with me.
— REVELATION 3:20

Every church in Asia received a knock at the door when Christ said, "I know thy works." For some it is to commend faithfulness, for others to press to more care. To Laodicea and to multitudes of Christians and Christian churches today, it is to alarm and awaken from an unholy lukewarmness and self-satisfied neglect. Is it not so with our souls at times that Christ's knock finds us in sleepy ease and horrible indifference? It was thus with the church in Solomon's Song when she had put off her coat and was loathe to put it on again, and when she had washed her feet and found it irksome to defile them. This self-righteous and sadly self-ignorant spirit is no better than Laodicean lukewarmness. It neither renounces Christ entirely nor loves and serves Him ardently. In culpable blindness, it thinks all is well.

For Christ to stand at the door and knock at such a heart is a great wonder. He calls us to "behold" it, as though with amazement. Christ not only knocks, He calls—and His voice is one of great grace. "Grace is poured into His lips." He speaks as a seller of rich goods and commends these to the careless occupants. He gives counsel to buy at His market fine gold, white raiment, and eye-salve that can only represent spiritual benefits and graces to adorn and beautify her ugly, naked form. At what Samuel Rutherford called "The Poor Man's Market," Christ bids any man to buy grace and salvation without money and without price. Only be content to be in debt to free grace and the sure mercies of a Covenant God in Christ will be eternally yours.

So Christ's alarming knock with His alluring call is intended to arouse us to open to Him. Our hard hearts are often closed and our lazy souls are often slow to respond. But one taste of His grace and one faith's view of His plentiful provision must surely stir us to say like Laban, "Come in, thou blessed of the LORD; wherefore standest thou without?" It is a greater wonder still that Christ will come in and dine in our hearts, and that He will find it a pleasure to do so. Christ dines with us when He sees and is satisfied with what His grace has produced in our hearts. We dine with Him when our hearts are exercised in godly sorrow, loving faith, and humble obedience.

*Therefore are they before the throne of God, and serve him day and night
in his temple: and he that sitteth on the throne shall dwell among them.*
—REVELATION 7:15

Believers reach heaven on the ground of Christ's blood alone. It is the blood
of the Lamb that brings them "out of great tribulation," and in it they wash
their robes and make them white. Only this gives them their right and title
to be before the throne of God. Neither sufferings for Christ's sake, faithfulness to Christ's calling, nor the holiness wrought in them by the Spirit can
merit heaven for them. The blood of the Lamb alone does that.

The heaven of believers is a place of worship and service. There is no
concluding praise or parting blessing in the service of worship before God's
throne. They shall go out no more. Day and night, in a day without an evening, they sing God's praise unabated, unwearied, and unhindered. The weak
body that soon tires of praise will hunger, thirst, or faint no more forever. In
being conformed to the "glorious body" of Christ, it is a suitable dwelling
place for the perfected soul whose meat and drink is to worship and praise
the God of his salvation.

The heaven of believers is a place of near communion with God also.
The communion known and enjoyed on earth was transitory and punctuated
with sorrows. In heaven, it will be more intimate, enduring, and delightful to
soul and body. Having run the race set before them, they now arrive at the
goal without the weights or the sins which did then "so easily beset them."
Perfected and conformed to the image of the Son, they are now fit for the
unceasing discoveries of the Father's love. The length, breadth, depth, and
height of that love will now fully engage their redeemed faculties and their
knowledge of God will be unceasingly enlarged. No communion on earth
can compare to this knowledge. God shall then dwell among them, satisfying
their souls from the living fountains of water in His gracious Being. No tear
shall mar the vision of God in Christ which their glorified souls will then
admire. The weariness of the way to heaven will be more than compensated
for by the rest and joy of that presence before the throne and that feeding by
the Lamb who is in the midst of the throne. They have no less days to sing
God's praise than when they first began.

*They shall be brought with gladness great, and mirth of every side,
Into the palace of the King, and there they shall abide.*
(Psalm 45:15 Metrical)

And in their mouth was found no guile: for they are without fault before the throne of God.
                                              —REVELATION 14:5

Only He who shed His blood as the Lamb merits heaven for believers, but all before the throne are "without fault" on account of sanctifying grace. The blood of Christ cleanses from guilt and from pollution. The justification of believers secures heaven for them; their sanctification renders their being there most openly fitting and suitable. None enter who defile, and "without holiness no man shall see the Lord." Those whom God calls and justifies, He also sanctifies and glorifies. It should ever be the purpose of preaching to "lead on to perfection" those who have first trusted in Christ. The inseparable connection between justification and sanctification is well expressed in the words of Psalm 23: "He leadeth me in the paths of righteousness for his name's sake."

The faults of believers in this world are usually in some way connected with the mouth. The tongue, though a little member, is a world of iniquity, an unruly evil, and full of deadly poison. Blessing and cursing too often proceed from the same mouth. Deceit, hypocrisy, pride, and so many other heart sins find expression by means of this organ. No man can tame it. Much activity of soul in the life of grace must be directed to the bridling of the tongue if our religion is not to be proved vain at last. Sins of omission and sins of commission in word as well as in action will condemn multitudes to the "house of silence" in a lost eternity. It is not without reason that the solemn and dreadful descriptions of the place of woe record its inhabitants as "gnashing their teeth" and "gnawing their tongues for pain."

So he who desires life and who would see good must refrain his tongue from evil and his lips that they speak no guile (Ps. 34:12–14). The snaring of deceitful lips and the tongues that use deceit have no place in the presence of the God of truth. The works of darkness must, therefore, be cast off and the armor of light put on if we will be where perfect truth and light inspire perfect praise. The tongue that is to be used in God's praise cannot be a forked tongue. They who sing the song of Moses and the Lamb must be "Israelites indeed in whom is no guile." Sanctifying grace produces sincerity and truth in God's worship and, before His throne, His praise is to be from an honest and good heart. Honesty adorns God's worship below and will beautify it above also.

Great and marvellous are thy works, Lord God Almighty; just and
true are thy ways, thou King of saints.
                                                    —REVELATION 15:3

This song of Moses is occasioned by a deliverance like that of Israel from
Egyptian bondage. It is a deliverance of the saints of God from their great
enemies through the blood of the Lamb; therefore, it is the song of the
Lamb pre-eminently. It is the Lamb's victory that occasions it; it is with His
help that it is sung, and He is the great subject of it.

The names and titles of Christ in Scripture are so many revelations of
His nature and saving character towards His people. Here He is "King of
saints." Moses, and later Samuel also, told Israel that God was their King
and that they did not require an earthly king like other nations. God told
Moses that He would make Israel a "kingdom of priests," and, in the New
Testament, Peter describes them as "a royal priesthood, an holy nation and a
peculiar people" (1 Pet. 2:9). The relation that the Lord has towards them as
King of saints is reflected in these illustrious names given to them.

As King of saints, the Lord sanctifies His people. He only is holy with
that holiness which can be communicated to the creature. In the application
of the redemption purchased by Christ, the Holy Spirit, whom the Father
sends in Christ's name, sanctifies believers. He dwells in them and conforms
them to the image of the Son. This is a great and marvelous work of the Lord
God Almighty both in its beginnings and in its progress. The deliverance
from Egypt and the Red Sea, which occasioned the first Song of Moses,
reflects the regenerating work of the Spirit accomplished by the Spirit of
Christ. The deliverance of Israel from the wilderness, which occasioned the
second Song of Moses on the borders of the land of Canaan, reflects the
completion of the sanctifying process which fits believers for heaven.

As King of saints, the Lord also rules and defends them, restraining
and conquering all His and their enemies. The work of salvation is a work
of retribution upon the enemies of God. This too is a great and marvelous
work and one which will be manifestly "just and true." The victory over the
enemies of saints which occasions the Song of Moses and of the Lamb is a
proof of the great love wherewith He loved them in shedding His precious
blood for them.

*And I saw a great white throne, and him that sat on it.... And I saw
the dead, small and great, stand before God.*

—REVELATION 20:11, 12

The Scottish philosopher David Hume once acknowledged that there was
no statement in the English language so profound as this. Here the destiny
of man is brought into sharp and awful focus. The finality of the divine procedure in dealing with man is plainly revealed—there shall be a great Day
of Judgment.

The throne is the place of tribunal and trial before which all shall appear.
No citation will be ignored and no summons despised. The glorious hosts of
angels will, by their mighty power, gather every member of Adam's family.
Rank or status will not provide immunity from prosecution, nor will poverty
or fear excuse attendance. It is a "great white throne" and the procedure of
the court will be according to that description: righteous and pure.

He who sits on the throne is the Son of Man whom God has ordained
to be the Judge of the dead and the living. He will sit on "the throne of
His glory" and before Him will be gathered all nations. He is that Lord to
whom David's Lord said, "Sit on my right hand until I make thine enemies
thy footstool." He will be glorious in His power, wisdom, and honor on this
day. He loves righteousness and hates iniquity, and His judgment will be
according to truth.

The standard by which all will be judged is found in the books which
shall be opened. Out of the Bible, men's lives will be weighed in the balance. The books of personal, family, national, and international history will be
opened. All will be revealed; no error will appear, and no fact will be omitted.
All wrongs, injustice, deceit, malice, envy, evil-speaking, and evil thoughts
will be fully exposed by the all-seeing Judge. The testimony of every man's
conscience will affirm the truth of what is written in these books.

Words cannot describe the "terror of the Lord" when He rises to pro-
nounce His judgment. All that can be said is that those condemned by the
Judge will seek to flee from His face and there will not be found any place
for them. The dreadful sentence, "Depart from me ye cursed," will be heard
from the throne. This is the day in which the "wrath of the Lamb" will be
revealed. How will we stand on that day?

And another book was opened, which is the book of life.
— REVELATION 20:12

God is the author of all life, and of Christ it is said that "in him was life; and the life was the light of men" (John 1:4). It is most fitting and natural, therefore, that God would also sovereignly dispose of all life and that Christ who made all things would determine at last the end and destiny of all living. That this is so indeed is the clear testimony of Scripture. Man must bow with humility before the sovereign will of his Creator and Lord. The freedom of God to do with His creatures as seems good to Him lies behind all the events of providence. It is humbling to human pride, but is also a great security to those whom He has chosen to life to know that their eternal security is founded on His eternal purpose of love.

While the doctrine of predestination contains infinite mysteries which it would be wrong for us to try to explore or fathom, we can nevertheless be sure that the Judge of all the earth will do what is right. God only acts according to His nature and He cannot be unjust in His acts. His great tribunal at last will be ordered according to the terms of His justice. Men will be judged righteously. No complaint of injustice will be heard while the dead are judged according to their works. Yet, the truth remains that the judgment rests on the free and sovereign will of God in writing the names of certain sinners in the Lamb's book of life and omitting other names. All we can say is, "O the depth of the riches both of the wisdom and knowledge of God! How unsearchable are his judgments, and his ways past finding out" (Rom. 11:33).

We need wisdom to leave the matter there, as our Westminster divines did: "By the decree of God, for the manifestation of his glory, some men and angels are predestinated unto everlasting life, and others foreordained to everlasting death.... The doctrine of this high mystery of predestination is to be handled with special prudence and care, that men attending the will of God revealed in his word, and yielding obedience thereunto, may, from the certainty of their effectual vocation, be assured of their eternal election. So shall this doctrine afford matter of praise, reverence, and admiration of God, and of humility, diligence, and abundant consolation, to all that sincerely obey the Gospel" (*Westminster Confession of Faith*, III, 3, 8).

And there was no more sea.
—REVELATION 21:1

The sea is a symbol of separation, of distance, and of isolation. Even in Scripture's imagery, the "islands of the sea" are far away—removed from society by the sea. In these last chapters of John's Revelation, some expositors have found described the glory of the church on earth in its final state of spiritual progress and adornment. However the passage may be correctly interpreted, we do have an illustration of the glory of heaven here. Heaven is the absence of all separation from Christ and from the fellowship of the church, His bride. For the traveler heavenward, it is the home and the haven of rest which they desired to see. For believers, heaven is a place where there is "no more sea."

For those who live on islands, traveling home by sea can be a very emotional experience. The drawing power of home with all its isolation makes whatever perils and dangers the sea has to offer during the voyage worth enduring. The believer has this experience, more or less, as he views heaven as his home. As he nears that happy land beyond the horizon of this earthly life, he feels the drawing which helps him face trouble. Many times the waves roar, deep calling to deep in his experience. Loss and sickness, cold and weary nights of fear, contrary winds in providence, the heavy seas of trouble—these he encounters in his voyage. But he presses forward to the other side in hope. He has launched out into the deep at Christ's command and call, and he must ever check his course by the compass of Christ's Word. Holding the rudder firmly, he directs his little boat into the winds.

As he makes for the further shore, he looks up for consolation. Samuel Rutherford, amidst the tossing and struggle of his life, had that comfort and assurance which believers who long for the haven also have:

> *I have wrestled on toward Heaven 'gainst storm, and wind, and tide:*
> *Now, like a weary traveller, that leaneth on his guide,*
> *Amid the shades of evening, while sinks life's ling'ring sand,*
> *I hail the glory dawning from Immanuel's land.*

How blessed to live with this hope! How it shortens the times of loneliness; how it brightens the days of storm clouds; how it even makes contrary winds and raging billows profitable to our voyage!

And there shall be no night there.

—REVELATION 22:5

The heaven of the church of God defies the descriptions of men. Our earthly mind is greatly limited in conceiving of the place prepared and reserved in heaven for God's children. The Holy Spirit is therefore pleased to accommodate us by revealing the glory of heaven in earthly pictures. Further, by telling us what it is not, we gain light on what it is. In this way, we are drawn to desire it and contemplate its excellence according to our capacities. So we are told that the curse is removed; death and sin and pain are abolished and nothing that defiles will enter. The city has no need of the sun or the moon to shine in it. The days of mourning are ended.

But we are encouraged to rise above mere earthly aspirations. The absence of night and of darkness from heaven reveals it to be a place where the glory of God's presence is known. His presence is the light of His people and the "health of their countenance." There are dark nights for the soul in times when He withdraws His sensible presence from them. Then they long for the light to shine and they mourn like Job, "Oh that I were as in months past...when his candle shined upon my head, and when by his light I walked through darkness" (Job 29:2–3). Believers also look for light in dark times. In days when iniquity and ungodliness grieve away the Spirit of God from striving with men; when darkness covers the earth and gross darkness the people, then believers yearn for gospel light and power to rise with healing.

The glory of the church is her likeness to Christ. She looks forth as the morning, clear as the sun and fair as the moon. She reflects His glory even as she comes through the wilderness. Her path shines more and more until the perfect day. Then her sun shall no more go down and God shall be her everlasting light and the days of her mourning shall be ended. The memory of dark nights and of the "cloudy and dark day" will never diminish the joy and glory of heaven. Rather, it will make all the more joyful the eternal morning and the summer sunshine in the presence of Him who "brought them out of darkness and the shadow of death and brake their bands in sunder."

Surely I come quickly. Amen. Even so, come, Lord Jesus.
—REVELATION 22:20

This is Christ's parting promise to His church. He speaks of His return with emphasis when He says "surely" and "Amen." Here, too, is the believing response of His people to His promised return. Simple in its acceptance, humble in its profession, the church receives His message with reverence. There is much concerning the return of Christ that remains hidden behind a veil, and while we are encouraged to read and understand this book, it is unlikely that every mystery it contains will be uncovered until its prophecies are fulfilled. This final intimation, this last revelation, is, however, clear and plain: "Surely I come quickly."

Christ will come quickly in comparison to His first coming. The world was promised a redeemer in "the fullness of time" and waited with longing for that appearance. When He came, He grew up before men as a tender plant. It was as an infant wrapped in swaddling clothes that the King of Zion arrived. It was only after His departure that His glory was acknowledged and uncovered. But His Second Coming will be in the immediate and full splendor of His kingly power and the world shall see together the glory of the great God and our Savior Jesus Christ.

Christ's return will also be quick as a surprise to a world sunk in sloth and sin. Many will look up into the heavens with sudden fear as the clouds part to make way for His triumphant chariot and His glorious hosts of angels. The unpreparedness of men for His arrival is given frequent mention by Christ in His own parables. Those unwilling that He should reign over them will weep and wail because of Him. Having thought that the promise of His coming was forgotten or was reneged on, they will discover in a moment their error.

For believers, the great day of Christ's return produces awe and reverence as well as the welcome desire that is expressed here. Their welcoming Him as coming quickly fully accords with their patiently waiting for all His purposes to be fulfilled. While events of the church's history may yet roll out for many years to come, each generation can still respond with this welcome. The ingathering of the nations to the church will precede His arrival, but the church can still respond today in faith and hope and love. They look for Him. They welcome Him as those prepared. They await the Bridegroom with the oil of grace in their souls and their lamps burning. Are you among them?

Joel R. Beeke is president of Puritan Reformed Theological Seminary and minister in the Heritage Reformed Congregations.

Gerald M. Bilkes is professor at Puritan Reformed Theological Seminary and ordained in the Free Reformed Churches of North America.

Dirk J. Budding is minister in the Reformed Church of America (Providence congregation in Grand Rapids).

David Campbell is minister in the Free Presbyterian Church of Scotland.

Hugh Cartwright is minister in the Free Presbyterian Church of Scotland.

Bartel Elshout is minister in the Heritage Reformed Congregations.

David H. Kranendonk is minister in the Free Reformed Churches of North America.

Jerrold H. Lewis is minister in the Free Reformed Churches of North America.

Roy Mohon is minister in the Presbyterian Reformed Church.

David P. Murray is professor at Puritan Reformed Theological Seminary and has ministerial credentials in the Free Church of Scotland (Continuing).

Maurice Roberts is minister in the Free Church of Scotland (Continuing).

David Silversides is minister in the Reformed Presbyterian Church of Ireland.